America's Most Charming Towns & Villages

Open Road *is* Travel!

- "Profiles of 200 picturesque places travel agents don't know much about." – *US News & World Report*
- "A masterpiece of small-town boosterism..."– *Los Angeles Times*
- "A basic primer to the country's better small towns. Most are worth seeing."– *Fort Worth Star Telegram*
- "Virtually all the spots chosen are off the mainstream, from trout fishing to wine tasting..."– *Newsday*
- Also recommended by *Coast to Coast, Endless Vacation, Out West*, and many others!

Open Road Publishing

We offer travel guides to American and foreign locales. Our books tell it like it is, often with an opinionated edge, and our experienced authors always give you all the information you need to have the trip of a lifetime. Write for your free catalog of all our titles.

Open Road Publishing
P.O. Box 284, Cold Spring Harbor, NY 11724
E-mail: Jopenroad@aol.com

5th Edition

About the Author

Larry T. Brown taught psychology at Oklahoma State University from 1961 to 1990. He has authored and co-authored numerous research publications, several teaching manuals, and a psychology textbook. His interests include travel, conservation, and American cultural history. He makes his home in Albuquerque, New Mexico.

Front cover photo©Ian L. Barker, Atlanta, Georgia (camerai@hotmail.com). Back cover photo©Anthony Platt/EarthWater Stock Photography, Virginia Beach, Virgina.

The author has made every effort to be as accurate as possible, but neither he nor the publisher assumes responsibility for the services provided by any business listed in this guide; for any errors or omissions; or any loss, damage, or disruptions in your travels for any reason.

TEN PERCENT of the author's proceeds from this book are donated to The American Farmland Trust, working to stop the loss of productive farmland and to promote farming practices that lead to a healthy environment.

Contents

MAPS

Acknowledgments

I am grateful to the hundreds of chambers of commerce, visitor bureaus, and historic inns and restaurants for their help in updating this edition.

I am grateful also to my publishers, Jonathan Stein and Avery Cardoza, for their always sound advice.

Special thanks continue, too, to my late wife, Ausma, for her patience, encouragement, and objectivity during our many miles of travel and my many hours before the monitor.

As ever, an enormous debt of gratitude is due those who continue to preserve, renovate, rebuild, protect, and carefully manage the growth of America's rich legacy of beautiful small towns.

America's Most Charming Towns & Villages

OVERVIEW

A member of the chamber of commerce of one of the towns in this book recently asked me—with a slight hint of impatience—why I'm so interested in historic sites. I can understand why she asked the question. Just glance across the paragraphs of the town descriptions.

I plead guilty. I find the pre-war (referring to WW II) Main Street and courthouse square more inviting and attractive than the post-war strip mall. I also prefer the turn-of-the-20th-century residential street to the cul-de-sac of today's subdivision, although this bias is moderated by the popularity of traditional architecture in new construction. As for multi-family dwellings, I'll take the 1920s apartment house any day to the glass-tombstone condo or office complex.

I'm not alone in my bias, of course. B&B brochures boast of high ceilings and fireplaces and Victorian verandahs. TV commercials take place against pre-war downtown streets rather than post-war commercial sprawl. In a blatant act of hypocrisy, car commercials show 2-lane roads and open countryside and avoid 4-, 6-, and 8-lane highways and the clutter that follows them.

The same longing for the past can be seen in our dwellings. Here in New Mexico even mobile homes are sometimes modeled after 19th-century adobe cottages, and traditional Spanish and centuries-old Pueblo Revival styling dominate new residential construction. New homes in the East and South remain more or less faithful to various Colonial styles. Apartments in Manhattan hasten to insert "pre-war" in their ads.

Just why the past often seems rosier than the present can only be a matter of conjecture. Somewhere a social variable probably lurks—anyone over 50 can remember when neighborhoods and family get-togethers seemed friendlier. Let's face it, porch swings and rocking chairs support relaxed conversation more than do rooms built around TV sets. And main streets and corner stores promote friendship more so than do strip malls and businesses scattered along the highway.

It's also true that time brings with it an emotion variously described as nostalgia or sentimentality or yearning. (And in the case of the inanimate, value—even a battered pewter plate can fetch a good price if it's 250 years old.) The good old days! They really weren't all that good, of course. Just think medical science. But still, the past was associated with our youth—and the youths and lives of our parents and grandparents and those who preceded them. The past is a known, the future an unknown.

Whatever the reasons, history and charm are closely allied. Not perfectly, because contemporary commercial and residential development can be, and sometimes is, truly charming. But the alliance is strong enough to merit a strong respect for history in any discussion of charming towns.

PRICE CODES

Unless otherwise noted, the coded prices for **lodgings** refer to rates for a double room (double occupancy):

$, most rooms $80 or less
$$, most rooms $81 to $120
$$$, most rooms $121 to $160
$$$$, most rooms $161 or more

Room rates are determined by season, day of week, location, amenities, size, and other factors and often vary widely even within the same establishment. This may be especially true for historic inns. For that reason, the codes in this book are used only to describe general price ranges. As a rule, rates for the majority of rooms lie close to the lower end of the range and rates for suites and cottages fall toward the upper end.

"Continental" breakfasts usually consist of fruit and/or juice, pastry, and hot beverage. "Expanded Continental" breakfasts consist of a wider variety of selections (pastries, cereals, etc.) than Continental breakfasts, but generally do not include egg, meat, and/or cheese dishes.

Unless otherwise noted, the **restaurant** code designates the prices of evening meals, excluding alcoholic beverages, tips, or taxes:

$, most meals $10 or less
$$, most meals in $1l to $20 range
$$$, most meals in $21 to $30 range
$$$$, most meals $31 or more

It is usually safe to assume that lunch prices average about 60% to 70% of dinner prices. As many travelers quickly discover, the lunch menu often features meals that are only slightly smaller than but comparable in variety and quality to those on the dinner menu.

The listings for "historic" lodging and dining are not meant to be an exhaustive or "best-of" compilation. Part of the fun of visiting these destinations is beating the travel writer to the discovery of that very special back-street inn or café.

TRAVEL SUGGESTIONS

This guide is intended only as an introduction to a town or village's general character and principal points of interest. More detailed information, including admission fees and schedules and calendars of special events, is available from chambers of commerce, visitors bureaus, and (oftentimes) innkeepers.

The majority of the listed communities publish brochures for self-guided tours. This is sometimes noted, but not always.

Almost all national parks, national monuments, state parks, state historic sites, major museums, and large churches are open year-round. Many other sites and attractions, however, restrict visiting hours or close altogether during the winter months. *Always* inquire in advance when planning a visit after Labor Day and before Memorial Day.

Many of the communities can be very crowded during summer (and sometimes autumn) weekends. It may therefore be wise to schedule visits during weekdays or the off-season. This is especially true for Lenox/Stockbridge (MA), Cape May (NJ), Southampton (NY), Williamsburg (VA), and other popular towns near large metropolitan areas. Off-season travelers should bear in mind also that virtually every community but the tiniest sponsors some kind of "Victorian" Christmas celebration.

When planning itineraries and scheduling travel time, remember that most American towns of 10,000 or more population have developed lengthy commercial strips that can significantly slow travel. If a bypass is available, use it; if not, whenever possible try to remain on interstates or other limited-access highways, or on two-lane roads that pass only through very small towns.

SIX ITINERARIES

I've designed these six driving tours to give you a few ideas for some fun, beautiful trips to America's charming travel treasures and gems. Most of the towns below are detailed in later chapters; check the Table of Contents or index for full listings. Let me know how these trips work for you. Happy trails!

1. The Berkshires & Southern Vermont
• *Point of Departure and Return: Danbury, Connecticut*
• *Four Days, 535 Miles*

Hugging famous US 7, the first half of this tour passes through or near some of America's loveliest and most fabled towns and villages. The second half follows less known roads that wind through Vermont's **Green Mountains**, Massachusetts' **Berkshire Hills**, and rural Connecticut's rolling parkland. One of the tour's major gems – **Litchfield, Connecticut** – is reserved for the last day.

This is side-trip country, so take every opportunity to try the back roads, especially those leading off US 7. Side trips in Vermont to **Dorset** and to Robert Todd Lincoln's *Hildene* near Manchester are musts. Some other recommendations include lunch at the **Red Lion Inn** in **Stockbridge**, Massachusetts (reservations), a leisurely stroll about the campus of **Middlebury College** in Vermont, and a walking tour of Litchfield's Georgian homes.

Day 1 – *105 miles*

From intersection of I 84 with US 7 east of Danbury, drive north on US 7 to **Bull's Bridge** (covered bridge).

Continue north on US 7 to **Kent** (see listing).

Continue north on US 7 (visiting Kent Falls State Park en route) to **West Cornwall** (covered bridge).

Continue north on US 7 to intersection with CT 112. Drive west on CT 112 (via Lime Rock) to intersection with CT 41. Drive north on CT 41 to **Salisbury**.

Drive northeast on US 44 to intersection with US 7 (at Canaan). Drive north on US 7 to **Sheffield**, Massachusetts (covered bridge).

Continue north on US 7 to **Great Barrington**. Take side trip through **South Egremont** and other nearby Berkshire villages.

Continue north on US 7 to **Stockbridge** (see listing). Take side trip to **West Stockbridge**.

Continue north on US 7 and then 7A to **Lenox** (see listing).

Day 2 – *145 miles*

Continue north on US 7 (via Pittsfield) to **Williamstown** (Williams College, Sterling & Francine Clark Art Institute).

Continue north on US 7 to Bennington, Vermont, then north on US 7 or 7A to **Manchester Village/Manchester Center** (see listing). Visit nearby **Dorset** (see listing).

Continue north on US 7 (via Rutland) to **Middlebury** (see listing).

Day 3 – *130 miles*

Drive east on VT 125 (via Middlebury Gap) to intersection with VT 100 (at Hancock). Wind south on VT 100 to intersection with US 4. Drive east on US 4 to **Woodstock** (see listing).

Return via US 4 and VT 10A to intersection with VT 100. Travel south on VT 100 to **Weston** (Guild of Old Time Crafts & Industries, Vermont Country Store).

Continue south on VT 100 to intersection with VT 11 (at Londonderry). Travel west on VT 11 to Manchester/Dorset (see above).

Day 4 – *155 miles*
Return south on US 7 or 7A (via Bennington) to Williamstown, Massachusetts. Drive east on MA 2 to intersection with MA 8. Wind south on MA/CT 8 through Berkshire Hills to Torrington, Connecticut. Drive southwest on US 202 to **Litchfield** (see listing).
Drive southwest on US 202 (via New Milford) to Danbury (starting point).

2. Northern California
• *Point of Departure and Return: San Francisco*
• *3 days, 420 miles*
• *optional Ferndale excursion: 5 days, 750 miles*

A Spanish-American plaza, a traditional American square, a piece of New England, a slice of Victoriana, all form a collage that pays tribute to California's rich cultural diversity. Mediterranean vineyards, Pacific palisades, redwood groves, secluded beaches; these in turn pay tribute to the state's considerable scenic diversity.

The first part of this tour focuses on California's famed wine country, so take full advantage of the many winery tours, tasting rooms, and vineyard picnic sites. Then, your knowledge of California wines warmly extended, head westward along one of the country's most beautiful highways, CA 128, toward the beaches and cliffs of the blue Pacific beyond.

Tour additions might include the **Ferndale** excursion, described below, or **Half Moon Bay** south of San Francisco. If you've got two or three days more to spare, consider crossing the Central Valley for a night in **Grass Valley** or **Nevada City** in the foothills of the Sierra Nevadas. Or a tour of **Lake Tahoe** and little **Genoa**, Nevada, on the other side.

Day 1 – *100 miles*
Drive north from San Francisco on US 101 to intersection with CA 37. Drive east on CA 37 to intersection with CA 121. Drive north on CA 121 to intersection with CA 12. Continue north on CA 12 to **Sonoma** (see listing).
Return south on CA 12 to intersection with CA 121. Drive east on CA 12/121 to intersection with CA 29. Travel north on CA 29 through Napa Valley (vineyards, wineries) to **St. Helena** (wineries, Bale Grist Mill State Historic Park, Silverado Museum).
Continue north on CA 29 to **Calistoga** (springs, vineyards, Old Faithful Geyser of California, Petrified Forest, Sharpsteen Museum).

Day 2 – *140 miles*
Drive west on Calistoga Road to intersection with Mark West Springs

Road. Turn right on Mark West Springs Road and continue to intersection with US 101 north of Santa Rosa. Drive north on US 101 to **Healdsburg** (plaza, winery tasting rooms).

Continue north on US 101 to intersection with CA 128 (at Cloverdale). Making sure you have a tank full of gas, drive northwest on beautiful CA 128 to intersection with CA 1 on Pacific Coast. Drive north on CA 1 along coast to **Mendocino** (see listing).

Continue north on CA 1 to **Fort Bragg** (see listing).

Day 3 – *180 miles*

Returning south on CA 1, drive along coast to **Gualala**. (arts center, Point Arena Lighthouse).

Continue south on CA 1 along coast to intersection with US 101. Drive south on US 101 to San Francisco (starting point).

Optional Excursion to Ferndale – *two days, 330 miles*

• **Day 1** – From Healdsburg (see Day 2 above), drive north on US 101 (visiting redwood groves & *Avenue of the Giants* en route) to Fernbridge/Ferndale exit south of Eureka. Travel west to Victorian **Ferndale** (see listing).

• **Day 2** – Inquire locally concerning loop road via Lost Coast and Petrolia back to US 101. Depending on weather, time of year, nature of vehicle, and hardiness of travelers, the better option may be to return directly to US 101. Drive south on US 101 to intersection with CA 1. Drive south on CA 1 to Fort Bragg (see Day 2 of above itinerary).

3. The Lower Mississippi River

• *Non-looping tour along Mississippi River from Vicksburg, Mississippi to Baton Rouge, Louisiana.*

• *3 days, 255 miles*

The white-pillared mansions and the sleepy little towns of the romantic old South still exist in places. This tour explores one of the grandest and best preserved of these places, the stretch of cotton-rich land that winds along the **Mississippi River** south of Vicksburg, Mississippi.

The Deep South can be enjoyed any month of the year, but it is in late March and early April that the antebellum romance seems to reach full blossom. This is when many towns – **Natchez**, **St. Francisville**, and **Vicksburg** among them – open their doors during "pilgrimages." It's a busy time, and reservations should be made as early as possible. (October and Christmas can also be busy times down here.)

If this tour sharpens your desire to see more of the Old South, Alabama's **Black Belt**, another plantation area rich in pre-Civil War memories, is just two or three hours east of Jackson. Although little known, in and around

Demopolis, **Forkland**, **Eutaw** (see listing), and farther east, **Lowndesboro**, lies another superb collection of antebellum mansions.

Day 1 – *45 miles, from Vicksburg*
From Jackson, Mississippi drive west (or from Shreveport, La., drive E) on I 20 to exit 4B in **Vicksburg**. Drive north into city (antebellum mansions, Old Court House Museum, Toys & Soldiers Museum, Vicksburg National Military Park).
Drive south on US 61 to **Port Gibson** (see listing). Take side trip to **Grand Gulf State Park** on the Mississippi River. Also, inquire locally for information on (and advisability of) side trip to ghost town of Rodney. Spend balance of day relaxing on verandah and grounds of plantation home B&B in Port Gibson or Lorman areas.

Day 2 – *130 miles*
Continue south on US 61, or alternatively, the **Natchez Trace Pkwy.**, to **Natchez** (tours of antebellum homes and churches).
Continue south on US 61 to **Woodville** (see listing). Take side trip on Pinckneyville Rd. to Pond Store and Clark Creek Nature Area.
Continue south on US 61 to **St. Francisville** (see listing), Louisiana.

Day 3 – *80 miles*
Cross Mississippi River by ferry and drive south on LA 10 to **New Roads** in "French Louisiana." Return to St. Francisville.
Drive east on LA 10 to **Jackson** (see listing).
Continue east on LA 10 to **Clinton** (antebellum buildings).
Return west on LA 10 to intersection with LA 68 (just east of Jackson). Drive south on LA 68 to intersection with US 61. Continue south on US 61 to Baton Rouge.

4. Southern Colorado & Northern New Mexico
• *Point of Departure and Return: Denver*
• *6 days, 1,150 miles*
Colorado and New Mexico are doubly blessed. Each can boast some of the country's most beautiful scenery, and each can lay claim to an especially colorful collection of charming little towns. The itinerary first leads through several of Colorado's best-preserved old mining towns, each miniaturized against a breathtaking mountain backdrop. Along the way are the **San Juan Mountains** of southwestern Colorado, possibly the most beautiful mountain range in the U.S.
The second part of the itinerary includes legendary **Santa Fe** and **Taos** as well as several tiny Spanish-American villages hidden on the back roads. Here in northern New Mexico lies the birthplace of the "Santa Fe look," that special

cultural blend known around the world for its unique architecture, painting, furniture, jewelry, clothing, and cuisine. The scenery is also impressive, as the drive through the **Sangre de Cristo Mountains** east of Taos will soon make clear.

While in Colorado, take a Jeep tour for an exciting excursion into a back country dotted with old mining camps and ghost towns. And while in New Mexico, try both the red and the green chilis to decide which you prefer with your enchiladas (and have the chili served on the side).

Day 1 – *170 miles*

From Denver drive west on I-70 to **Georgetown** (see listing).

Continue west on US 70 to intersection with CO 91. Drive south on CO 91 to **Leadville** (old mining town, Victorian buildings, Healy House, museums, train tour).

Drive south on US 24 via **Buena Vista** to intersection with US 285 (at Johnson Village). Drive south on US 285 to intersection with CO 291. Continue south on CO 291 to **Salida** (see listing).

Day 2 – *185 miles*

Drive west on US 50 to **Gunnison** (Pioneer Museum).

Continue west on US 50 along Blue Mesa Reservoir to Montrose. Drive south on US 550 to **Ouray** (see listing).

Continue south on US 550 (the *Million Dollar Hwy.*) to **Silverton** (see listing).

Day 3 – 150 miles

Drive south on US 50 via spectacular Molas Divide to intersection with US 160 at Durango. Drive west on US 160 to Mesa Verde National Park.

Return on US 160 to Durango.

Day 4 – *225 miles*

Drive east on US 160 to Pagosa Springs. Drive south on US 84 via **Abiquiu**, New Mexico to **Santa Fe** (Plaza, Palace of the Governors, Mission of San Miguel of Santa Fe, museums, Canyon Road for galleries and charm).

Day 5 – *100 miles*

Drive north on US 84 to intersection with NM 502. Drive west on NM 502 to **San Ildefonso Pueblo** (pottery).

Return east on NM 503 to intersection with US 84 and continue east (now NM 503) to intersection with NM 520. Drive north on NM 520 to **Chimayo** (El Santuario de Nuestro Senor de Esquipulas).

Drive east on NM 76 via Spanish-American villages of **Truchas** and **Las Trampas** (church) to intersection with NM 75. Drive west on NM 75 via **Dixon** to intersection with NM 68. Drive north on NM 68 to **Taos** (see listing).

Day 6 – 320 miles
> Drive east on US 64 through Sangre de Cristo Mountains to **Cimarron** (old outlaw town).
>
> Continue east on US 64, paralleling **Santa Fe National Historic Trail**, to intersection with I-25. Drive north on I-25 for return to Denver (starting point).

5. Southern Indiana & Kentucky's Bluegrass Country
• *Point of Departure and Return: Indianapolis*
• *6 days, 800 miles*
> Indiana and Kentucky have long been associated with the nostalgia of the long ago and far away. Just listen to the words of their state songs: *On the Banks of the Wabash, Far Away* and *My Old Kentucky Home*. Along the byways of this nostalgic itinerary lie more than a dozen towns and villages in parts of these states that especially suggest the long ago and far away: the rolling woodland of southern Indiana and the incomparable **Bluegrass Country** of Kentucky.

> Two of the towns were founded as Utopian communities, Indiana's delightful little **New Harmony**, which in fact sits right on the Banks of the Wabash, and Kentucky's pastoral **Pleasant Hill**, with its quaint Shaker simplicity. Two of the towns are widely respected for their art and crafts, **Berea**, Kentucky, and **Nashville**, Indiana. Several of the towns in Kentucky's Bluegrass have historic inns that could stand proudly alongside their Virginia cousins. Indiana's **Madison** is probably the loveliest town on the **Ohio River**. And just in case the present be forgotten, **Columbus**, Indiana, scatters buildings of superb late 20th-century design about a town with a late 19th-century Main Street.

> You'll want to spend *at least* half of your last day, Day 6, in Madison. But should you still have several hours to spare, consider winding northeast by back roads from Madison up to the little canal town of **Metamora** (see listing) and then returning to Indianapolis by US 52.

Day 1 – *100 miles*
> From Indianapolis drive south on I-65 to **Columbus** (contemporary buildings designed by world-famous architects).
>
> Drive west on IN 46 to **Nashville** (see listing). Tour Brown County State Park, **Bean Blossom** (covered bridge), **Story**, and other Brown County sites (listed under Nashville).

Day 2 – *175 miles*
> Continue west on IN 46 to **Bloomington** (Indiana University campus).
> Drive south on IN 37 to intersection with IN 60 (at Mitchell). Drive east on US 60 to Spring Mill State Park and **Spring Mill Village**.

Return via IN 60 to IN 37. Drive south on IN 37 to intersection with US 150 (at Paoli). Drive west on US 150 to intersection with IN 56. Drive south on IN 56 to **French Lick/West Baden Springs** (see listing).

Continue south on IN 56 to intersection with US 231. Drive south on US 231 to intersection with I 64. Drive west on I 64 to intersection with IN 68 (exit 12). Drive southwest on IN 68 to **New Harmony** (see listing).

Day 3 – *200 miles*

Drive east on IN 66 (via Evansville and along the Ohio River) to intersection with IN 462 (at Sulphur). Drive east on IN 462 to **Corydon** (see listing).

Drive north on IN 135 to I 64. Drive east on I 64 to intersection with I 65 (in Louisville, Kentucky). Drive south on I-65 to intersection with KY 245 (exit 112). Drive east on KY 245, stopping at the gardens of the **Bernheim Forest**, to **Bardstown** (see listing).

Day 4 – *110 miles*

Drive south on US 150 to intersection with US 68 (at Perryville). Drive north on US 68 to **Harrodsburg** (see listing).

Continue north on US 68 to **Pleasant Hill** (see listing).

Drive south on KY 33 to **Danville** (Constitution Square State Historic Site, McDowell House).

Drive east on KY 52 via **Lancaster** to intersection with KY 21. Drive south on KY 21 to **Berea** (see listing).

Day 5 – *165 miles*

Drive north on I-75 (stopping en route at White Hall State Historic Site, exit 95) to intersection with US 27/68 (in Lexington). Drive east on US 27/68, past horse farms, to **Paris**.

Drive west on US 460 via **Georgetown** to **Frankfort** (State Capitol, Frankfort Cemetery, Liberty Hall Historic Site, Old Governor's Mansion, Old State Capitol/Kentucky History Museum).

Drive north on US 421 (crossing Ohio River) to **Madison**, Indiana (see listing).

Day 6 – *50 miles*

Drive north on IN 7 to intersection with I-65 (at Columbus). Return north on I-65 to Indianapolis (starting point).

6. The Carolinas & Georgia Upcountry

• *Point of Departure and Return: Asheville, North Carolina*
• *4 days, 395 miles*

This itinerary is not to be hurried. To hurry through the **Upcountry** would be to miss the very soul of the countryside and its people. For generations a place of summer retreat from Southern coastal climes, and more recently a four-season place of retirement from Eastern cities, the Upcountry is for leisurely strolling, forest hiking, river rafting, fishing, golfing. Even in the car, enjoyment of the winding roads, scenic overlooks, streams, and waterfalls demands time. Moreover, the people in this corner of the world are especially friendly, and their hospitality does not allow for haste – or worry.

The tour begins with the sophisticated resort towns of Upcountry North Carolina and then turns south toward historical little towns in Upcountry Georgia and South Carolina. Along the way lies delightful little **Dahlonega**, Georgia and the Bavarian village of **Helen**, also in Georgia. Not to be missed in the North Carolina towns are the performing arts. Check with the chambers of commerce in advance for schedules and information. Also, be on the lookout throughout the tour for local crafts – the people of the **Blue Ridge Mountains** have a long tradition of quality craftsmanship.

For a non-looping tour, wind westward across the mountains of northern Georgia from **Dahlonega** or **Helen** (Day 3) to the little mountain resort of **Mentone**, Alabama.

Day 1 – *107 miles*

From **Asheville** (Biltmore Estate, Biltmore Homespun Shops, Thomas Wolfe Memorial) drive south on I-26 to **Hendersonville** (exit 18; see listing).

Drive west on US 64 via **Brevard** (waterfalls) and **Cashiers** (mountain resort) to **Highlands** (see listing).

Day 2 – *88 miles*

Wind north on US 64 through mountains to Franklin. Drive west on US 64 to intersection with NC 175. Drive south on NC 175 (becoming GA 75) to **Hiawasee**, Georgia (mountain resort, Georgia's highest peak).

Drive west on US 76 to intersection with US 19 (at Blairsville). Turn south on US 19 to **Dahlonega** (see listing).

Day 3 – *100 miles*

Drive east on GA 52 to intersection with GA 115. Continue east on GA 115 to intersection with US 129 (at Cleveland). Drive north on US 129 about 1 mile to intersection with GA 75. Continue north on GA 75 to **Helen** (see listing).

Drive east on GA 17 to Toccoa. Continue east on US 123 to Westminster, SC. Turn north on SC 183 to old German town of **Walhalla**.

Drive south on SC 28 to US 123/76. Drive east on US 123/76 to **Clemson** (Clemson University, Fort Hill plantation house, Hanover House).

Drive south on SC 28B to **Pendleton** (see listing).

Day 4 – *100 miles*

Drive south on US 76 to I-85. Drive east on I-85 to US 25 (in Greenville).

Travel north on US 25 to I-26 (in North Carolina). Turn south on I-26 to **Saluda** (next exit, exit 28).
Return north on I-26 to Asheville (starting point).

GREAT VINTAGE TRAIN RIDES
• Black River & Western Railroad (between Flemington & Ringoes, NJ) – Flemington, NJ
• California Western Railroad *Skunk* trains (between Ft. Bragg & Willits, CA) – Fort Bragg, CA
• Durango & Silverton Narrow Gauge Railroad Company (between Durango & Silverton, CO) –Silverton, CO
• Eureka Springs & North Arkansas Railway (Ozark Mountains) – Eureka Springs, AR
• French Lick, West Baden, & Southern Railroad (Hoosier National Forest) – French Lick, IN
Georgetown Loop (between Georgetown & Silver Plume, CO) – Georgetown, CO
• Minnesota Zephyr (St. Croix River Valley) – Stillwater, MN
• New Hope & Ivyland Rail Road (Pennsylvania countryside) – New Hope, PA
• Scenic Ozark Railway (Ozark Mountains) – Van Buren, AR
• Valley Railroad Company (between Essex & Chester, CT) – Essex/Chester, CT
• West Shore Railroad (Pennsylvania countryside) – Lewisburg, PA

BEST ETHNIC TOWNS
• Alsatian – Castroville, TX
• Bavarian – Leavenworth, WA & Helen, GA
• Danish – Solvang, CA
• Dutch – Pella, IA
• French – Ste. Genevieve, MO
• German – Hermann, MO & the Amana Colonies, IA
• Hispanic – Mesilla, NM & San Juan Bautista, CA
• Moravian – Lititz, PA
• Norwegian – Petersburg, AK
• Swedish – Lindsborg, KS & Bishop Hill, IL
• Swiss – New Glarus, WI

TOP 10 TOWNS OF THE OLD SOUTH
• Beaufort, SC
• Bardstown, KY
• Eufaula, AL
• Eureka Springs, AR
• Holly Springs, MS

- Jonesborough, TN
- Lexington, VA
- Madison, GA
- St. Francisville, LA
- Williamsburg, VA

TOP 10 TOWNS OF THE WILD WEST
- Abilene, KS
- Deadwood, SD
- Fort Benton, MT
- Fort Davis, TX
- Lincoln, NM
- Medora, ND
- Saratoga, WY
- Silverton, CO
- Tombstone, AZ
- Wallace, ID

WONDERFUL COLONIAL VILLAGES
- Beaufort, NC
- Camden, SC
- Chestertown, MD
- Edgartown, MA
- Essex, CT
- Exeter, NH
- Odessa, DE
- Old Lyme, CT
- Rockport, MA
- St. Mary's City, MD
- Wickford, RI

CLASSIC COVERED BRIDGES
- Bean Blossom Bridge (1880), near Nashville, IN
- Brown County State Park Bridge (1838, double-barreled), near Nashville, IN
- Bull's Bridge, near Kent, CT
- Emily's Bridge, near Stowe, VT
- Goddard Covered Bridge (1820), near Maysville/Washington, KY
- Green Sergeants Bridge, near Stockton, NJ
- Pulp Mill Bridge (1806, double-barreled), near Middlebury, VT
- Red Mill Bridge (1970, from original plans), near Rural, WI
- Sheffield Bridge (1837, rebuilt 1995), near Great Barrington, MA
- Sunday River Bridge (1870), near Bethel, ME
- White Caps Bridge, near Stowe, VT

INTERESTING OLD MILLS

- Fly Creek Cider Mill (1856), Cooperstown, NY
- Ledford Mill (1884), Lynchburg, TN
- Meek Grist Mill (1878), Bonaparte (Van Buren County), IA
- The Old Mill (1746), Nantucket Town, MA
- Old Stone Mill (1836), Clinton, NJ
- Prallsville mills (18th & 19th century), Delaware & Raritan Canal State Park, Stockton, NJ
- Red Mill (ca 1763), Clinton, NJ
- Red Mill (1855), near Rural, WI
- Waterloo Village mills (18th & 19th century), Waterloo Village, NJ
- White's Mill, Abingdon, VA
- Zeitinger's Mill (1859), Maeystown, IL

Chapter 1

ALABAMA

EUFAULA
Population 13,320

With antebellum houses azaleas, dogwoods, and a history of wealth centering on cotton, **Eufaula** (you FALL uh) is unmistakably the Deep South. Located on the **Chattahoochee River**, the town was once an ideal riverboat port for planters from across a broad swath of Alabama, Georgia, and Florida. And as was so often true in the South during the 1840s and 1850s, the planters and merchants converted their wealth into magnificent homes, churches, and other buildings.

Spared by the Yankees (the Confederacy had surrendered by the time Union troops reached the town), many of the antebellum structures still stand. In the post-war years many other beautiful structures went up, and these too have been preserved. The result is that Eufaula, with over 700 historic buildings, boasts Alabama's finest 19th-century small-town commercial district as well as its grandest collection of domestic Italianate architecture. Many of the historic houses are in the Seth Lore-Irwinton Historic District and many of the historic commercial buildings are on Broad Street.

The oldest commercial structure in town - and also the oldest frame structure – is **The Tavern**, originally an 1830s inn, later a Confederate hospital, and now a private residence listed on the National Register of Historic Places.

The best-known home is the **Shorter Mansion** (open to the public). Built in 1884 and enlarged and rebuilt in 1906, it is one of Alabama's finest neoclassical mansions. Another fine mansion, **Fendall Hall** (1860), is topped by a square cupola so characteristic of the Italianate style. Waterford chandeliers, hand-stenciled walls, and murals grace the interior (open to the public).

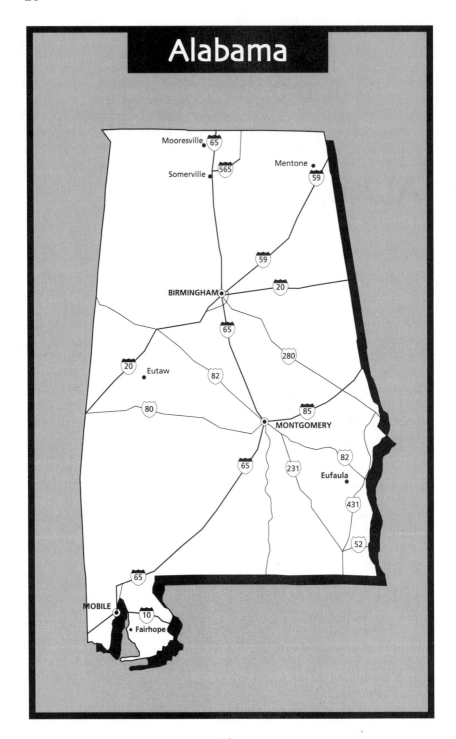

The **Holleman-Foy Home** (1907) and its columned rotunda entrance provide a magnificent example of turn-of-the-century Neoclassical Eclectic architecture. The house has been in the same family since 1909. Other important Eufaula houses include the Greek Revival **Hart-Milton House** (1843) and **Kendall Manor,** a stately Italianate mansion.

Brochures for walking and driving tours of the many homes in the historic district are available at the Visitors Bureau (CoC). Most of the homes are private, but during Eufaula's Pilgrimage in April many of the owners open the doors and allow visitors to explore the rooms and family heirlooms within. The pilgrimage also features open-air art exhibits, tea gardens, concerts, and a major antique show.

> The twice-weekly local newspaper carries the phrase, "Symbol of the Old South, Cradle of the New."

Special Features

Bordered by 640 miles of shoreline, **Lake Eufaula** is sometimes called *The Bass Capital of the World*. The 25-year-old reservoir is surrounded by many weedy sloughs and stump rows and is dotted with 48 fish attractors. Two full-service marinas and many public-use areas serve fishermen as well as other water sportsmen.

Further Information

Eufaula/Barbour County Chamber of Commerce, Visitors Bureau, *P.O. Box 697, Eufaula, AL 36072 (800) 524-7529, www.eufaula-barbourchamber.com.*

Directions

From Montgomery, US 82 southeast through Union Springs to Eufaula.

EUTAW
Population 2, 281

Eutaw is the seat of Greene County, a county known for its meandering rivers and white-pillared plantation houses. Located on the black, fertile soil of west Alabama, Greene County was (and to some extent still is) cotton country. Both the county and Eutaw fully participated in the romantic "Golden Era" of the plantation south, the period between 1840 and 1860.

In large part because of the defense provided by the bridgeless rivers surrounding the town, Union troops showed little interest in harming Eutaw, and much of the old town therefore survives. In the center of town is a charming public square, and on the square sits a lovely little Greek Revival **courthouse** (1839\68). On the streets about the square are 53 antebellum structures and dozens of homes from the Victorian period. Rural, and distant from anything that isn't, the place smacks of another era. The town even boasts a country store with a high ceiling that still delivers groceries and cuts off pieces of cheese from a large round (called "hoop" cheese).

A few of Eutaw's buildings are open to the public. In cases of doubt, simply ask – you'll find that Eutaw is an especially friendly town.

The meticulously restored **Kirkwood Mansion** (1860) is one of the most striking of Eutaw's antebellum homes. The four-story mansion is lined on two sides with massive columns and has wrought-iron railings, four tall chimneys, and a reconstructed cupola. The **Captain Edwin Reese House** (1858), with four two-story fluted Ionic columns, and the Greek Revival **Coleman-Banks House** (ca 1847) are two other lovely houses. On the grounds of the latter are the original smokehouse and kitchen/wash-house. The charming **Vaughn-Morrow House** (1841) has been restored as the headquarters of the county historical society.

One of the most interesting of the non-residential structures is the 1851 Greek Revival **First Presbyterian Church**. The church's slave gallery is still in place, as are the original whale-oil pulpit lamps.

Special Features

Ionic-columned **Thornhill** (1832) and what is possibly Alabama's most beautiful mansion, **Rosemount** (1825-32), are located in the tiny community of Forkland, 13 miles south of Eutaw on US 43.

The Greek Revival **Ebenezer Presbyterian Church** (1859) in Clinton, 6 miles north on AL 14, has been recently restored.

• Eutaw only came into being because, in 1838, Greene County needed a new government seat.
• As with many Southern counties, the timber industry is today more important to Greene County than cotton.

Further Information

Green County Historical Society, *310 Main St., P.O. Box 746, Eutaw, AL 35462; Eutaw Chamber of Commerce, P.O. Box 31, (205) 372-9769 or 372-9002.*

Directions
From Birmingham, I-20 southwest to exit 40, AL 14 south to Eutaw.

FAIRHOPE
Population 22,055

Part bayside resort, part exclusive suburb, part artists' colony, part subtropical paradise, **Fairhope** is a beautiful place. The "Village of Fairhope," situated on the eastern shore of Mobile Bay, has beaches, boats, and broad sea views. The waterfront gives way very quickly, however, to gorgeous homes, moss-draped oaks, lush gardens of azaleas, roses, camellias, magnolias, and every other flower or plant that the gardener or artist might dream of. And not far away, still within the garden setting, is a delightful downtown area with canopied galleries, boutiques, and tempting specialty shops. There seems to be a feeling—one given substance by Fairhope's calendar—that an arts and crafts show isn't far off, in time or place.

Fairhope was founded in 1894 by a group of Iowans who were followers of American social reformer Henry George. It was George who proposed the idea of a single tax, one drawn exclusively from increases in the value of land; putting George's ideas into practice, Fairhope's settlers held the land in common ownership and enjoyed it individually through long-term leases. (For reasons that aren't completely clear, towns founded by 19th-century utopian societies seem to find their way into this book. Fairhope is no exception.)

One of the best places to begin a visit here is the **Fairhope Municipal Pier**, which houses a restaurant as well as fishing and marina facilities. Strolling the pier in the evening or early morning can be a truly memorable experience. At the foot of the pier is a stately **fountain**, and adjacent to the fountain an exceptionally lush waterside **park**. There is also a public **beach**. The area is best toured with the kind of timetable that allows for plenty of strolling, sea viewing, and just plain relaxing.

The **Eastern Shore Art Center**, a few blocks away, features monthly exhibitions of oils, watercolors, weavings, pottery, and other media. Concerts, films, and lectures are also offered.

Fairhope hosts a busy schedule of annual events ranging from Mardi Gras and Christmas parades to environmental activities to a 3-day arts and crafts festival in March. Between events visitors can enjoy sport fishing, jet skiing, and boating. Golfers will find the finest public course on Mobile Bay's Eastern Shore. And, of course, lovers of seafood will find flounder, crab, and shrimp fresh from the bay.

Special Features

Fairhope is within short-excursion distance of a number of attractions: historic **Fort Gaines** and **Fort Morgan** at the entrance to Mobile Bay, the beaches of **Gulf Shores**, the inimitable **Bellingrath Gardens** across the bay, **Historic Blakeley State Park** (site of the last major battle of the Civil War), and the many sights of **Mobile** and **Pensacola**.

> The Greek Orthodox Malbis Memorial Church (1965) in nearby Malbis is a copy of a Byzantine church in Athens (guided tours).

▶ HISTORIC HOTEL ◀

GRAND HOTEL MARRIOTT RESORT, GOLF CLUB & SPA, One Grand Blvd. (Scenic US 98), Point Clear, AL 36564, (251) 928-9201, (800) 544-9933, fax (251) 928-1149, www.marriottgrand.com. 1847/1939 bay-front resort hotel (served as Confederate hospital—Civil War cemetery on grounds), 400 rooms, 35 suites, private baths, TV & phones, several restaurants & lounges, new European health spa, 36 holes of golf, clubhouse, 8 tennis courts, 2 outdoor & 1 indoor swimming pools, beach, jet skis, bicycles, marina, sailboats, charter yachts, fishing, horseback riding, nature trails, jogging paths, children's playground & game room (also activity programs), lawn sports, afternoon tea, shops, hair salon, special packages, MAP. $$$ to $$$$

Further Information

Eastern Shore Chamber of Commerce, P.O. Drawer 310, Daphne, AL 36526-0310 (334) 920-6387, fax (334) 928-6389, www.eschamber.com.

Directions

From Mobile, I-10 east across Mobile Bay to US 98, south to ALT 98 (US Scenic 98), south to Fairhope.

MENTONE
Population 474

Wilderness, rippling streams, and spectacular mountain views may not be among the images conjured up by the mention of Alabama, yet these are the very kinds of things that describe the mountain-top village of **Mentone** in lovely northeastern Alabama. They are also the kinds of things that make Mentone so many places in one: in the warmer months, an artist colony, a golf resort, a dude ranch, a nature lover's paradise; in the winter, the Southeast's southernmost ski resort. During all times of the year, shops along the town square and elsewhere offer a variety of unique mountain arts and crafts. A good example is *Gourdies* – dolls made from gourds.

The cooler temperatures and clear mountain air attracted visitors here throughout the 19th century, but it wasn't until the construction of the **Mentone Springs Hotel** in the 1880s that the village began to enjoy widespread popularity as a vacation retreat. The hotel was an active resort from the late 19th century to the early 1930s. Recently renovated and opened as a bed and breakfast, the *Grand Ol' Lady* stands as a living reminder of another era.

St. Joseph's-on-the-Mountain Episcopal Church began as a log cabin in 1870 and with the help of donated furnishings and decorations ended up a lovely church. The stained-glass windows, more than a century old, were hand-painted and fired in France.

Special Features

One of the best ways to take in the area's scenery is to drive south seven miles to **DeSoto State Park**. The top sites here are **Little River Canyon**, which is one of the deepest gorges east of the Mississippi River, and the majestic 110-foot **DeSoto Falls**.

- Mentone averages about 10 degrees (F) cooler than the surrounding valley.
- Fort Payne, 13 miles south, is both the "Sock Capital of the World" and the home of Alabama, "The Country Group of the Last Decade."

Further Information

DeKalb County Tourist Association, *P.O. Box 681165, Fort Payne, AL 35968 (888) 805-4740, (256) 845-3957, fax (256) 845-3946, www.tourdekalb.com (ZIP for Mentone is 35984).*

Directions

From Chattanooga (40 miles), I-59 south to exit 231, south on AL 117 to Mentone.

MOORESVILLE
Population about 60

Mooresville was incorporated in 1818, making it the oldest incorporated community in Alabama. Both Andrew Johnson and James A. Garfield spent time here years before their presidential days. Small then and small now, the village doesn't go much farther than three or four blocks in any direction. Almost all of its buildings are on the National Register, and all but one or two are lived or worked in. Though out of the past, picturesque little Mooresville is a living village.

Bypassed by the interstate, the village is kind of tucked away, unknown even to people in nearby towns. On most maps of the state it looks as though the village has disappeared into some kind of urban sprawl connecting Decatur and Huntsville. In actual fact, the community is surrounded by cotton fields. Large towns are not far away, and many of the townspeople commute to them, but Mooresville still retains its rural charm—and setting. It is peaceful here.

Spanning as they do more than 150 years, Mooresville's buildings vary in style, size, and construction. Some are brick, some are white or pastel frame. All are shaded by beautiful old oaks, magnolias, and other trees. The town's most famous building is probably the **Mooresville Post Office**, which has been in continuous use since 1844. The wooden cubby holes receiving mail today are the same that received mail in Civil War times.

Two churches are of special historic interest. One, the circa 1838 red brick **community church**, still has one of the original chandeliers and the slave balcony (though boarded up after the Civil War). The pulpit of the second, the 1854 white-frame **Church of Christ**, was where General Garfield, then a teacher, read from the Bible.

Among the other buildings of special note is the 1820s stagecoach tavern, recently restored, and a house dating from around 1825 that owes its survival to the Union general, Garfield, who ordered that it not be vandalized.

Special Features
The **Old State Bank** in neighboring Decatur is the oldest bank in the state (1833). Recently restored, the bank was one of only four buildings in Decatur still standing at the end of the Civil War. Decatur is also home to two well-preserved Victorian residential areas.

Mooresville borders the **Wheeler National Wildlife Refuge**, the largest wildlife refuge in Alabama. The refuge includes a wildlife interpretive center and an observation platform from which migratory waterfowl may be viewed.

Only ancient cedars lining the front walk remain of the Female Institute (1830). The institute, which had 55 "lady pupils," was destroyed by Union soldiers.

Further Information
North Alabama Tourism Association, *P.O. Box 1075, Mooresville, AL 35649-1075, (866) 667-8425, www.northalabama.org*

Directions
From Huntsville, I-565 west to Mooresville exit (just before intersection with I-65)

SOMERVILLE
Population 208

Known as *Morgan County's Grand Old Gal*, **Somerville** is one of those rare little towns where the flavor of the Old South—the real Old South—still lingers. Of course, some of the new has invaded the town. The **Town Hall** is new, for example, and there are telephones (at least in some of the buildings) and electricity. But as an old-fashioned stroll around the square should make clear, very little has happened here since the 19th century.

Settled around 1818, Somerville was a 19th-century cotton town. It served as the county seat until 1891, when despite an uproar and even threats of violence, county government was moved to Decatur. Then total quiet took over. In recent years the town has become a home for people working in Decatur and Huntsville, and this, combined with the beginnings of tourism, has stirred up some activity. But not much.

Somerville's most imposing building, and one straight out of the Old South, is the partially renovated **Old Morgan County Courthouse** (1837). The two-story Federal-style brick structure, listed on the National Register, is Alabama's oldest courthouse. The bell in the belfry is still rung to welcome in each new year. (An appointment is advised for visitors wishing to tour the interior—check at the Town Hall.)

Sprinkled about town are a number of old homes, all private residences. Architecturally the most interesting is the **Rice House** (ca 1835), a Federal-style Tidewater-type cottage. On the National Register, the one-and-a-half-story house has original woodwork and mantels. The house is unique in that the brick was laid in Flemish bond around the entire building rather than just in front.

Other interesting houses include the restored **Gilchrist-Williams House** (probably mid 19th-century), the late 19th-century **Lyle House**, and the antebellum **Mikell House**, with original Federal woodwork. The 1880 **Binford-Peck House** was home to the town's telephone switchboard during the 1930s. A visit to the lovely old **Somerville Cemetery** can provide a good introduction to local history.

Note: I wish to thank historian David W. Whitehorn, author of *Historic Somerville* for providing some of the information for this selection. A copy of *Historic Somerville* may be obtained by writing the Somerville Public Library, P.O. Box 178, Somerville, AL 35670.

Special Features

Huntsville is home to the **US Space and Rocket Center** (hands-on exhibits, Spacedome Theater, bus tours of NASA's Marshall Space Flight Center). Among the city's many other attractions is the **Twickenham Historic District**, containing one of Alabama's largest and finest collections of antebellum homes.

> To avoid what could have been an unpleasant confrontation over moving the county seat (in 1891), people from Decatur quietly removed the county records from Somerville by night.

Further Information

Town Hall, *Somerville, AL 35670 (256) 778-8282.*

Directions

From Birmingham, I-65 north to exit 328, Al 36 east to AL 67, AL 67 north to Somerville.

Other Charming Alabama Towns
Demopolis
Lowndesboro
Marion

Chapter 2

ALASKA

PETERSBURG
Population 3,356

From the docks of **Petersburg's** harbor you can see snow-capped mountains, their upper reaches partly obscured by clouds, their lower reaches dark with forests. They rise steeply from the fjords. This is southeast Alaska's Inside Passage, not Norway, but it could be either.

Petersburg, or *Little Norway*, was settled by Norwegians (1897), and the heritage is still very important. The Chamber of Commerce sponsors an annual **Little Norway Festival** (see below), rosemaling decorates old Scandinavian-style frame buildings, and fishing and logging continue to dominate daily lives, just as in the Old Country (although tourism is making an entry).

One of the most picturesque of the older buildings is the **Sons of Norway Hall** (1912), a National Historic Site, constructed on pilings over a slough. Next to the hall is **Fishermans Memorial Park** (1998) and the *Valhalla*, a Viking ship built in 1976 to participate in the U.S. Bicentennial Parade of Ships in New York Harbor.

The **Clausen Memorial Museum** has a number of unusual attractions, like the giant lens from the Cape Decision Lighthouse, a 126.5-lb. King Salmon, and *Fisk* (Norwegian for "fish"), a lovely fountain sculpture.

Although small, Petersburg is a major fishing port—9th in the country in fact – and visitors enjoy exploring the docks of the three colorful harbors. The most popular catches are salmon (summer), halibut and herring (spring), crab (winter), and shrimp (all year).

Petersburg offers a variety of boat charters and rentals for fishing, sightseeing, whale watching, and wildlife observing. Air charters are also available for sightseeing. The area is a major migratory stopover and spring

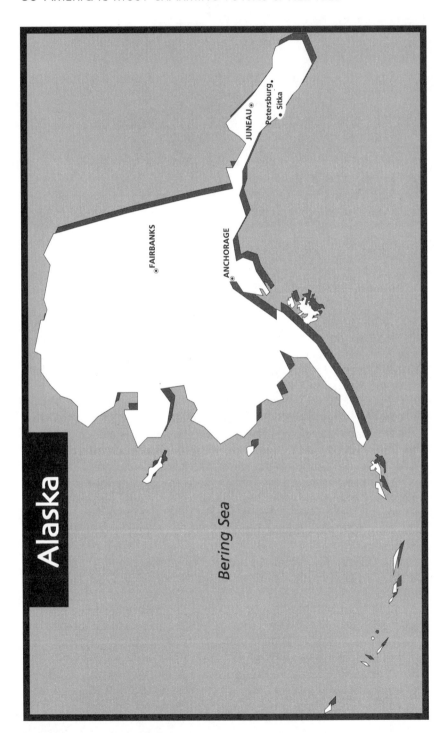

bird-watchers report fantastic sightings – especially of bald eagles at the **Stikine River Flats**. This is the Alaska Panhandle, Alaska's *banana belt*, and so the weather is much milder and far more supportive of outdoor activities than in more northerly parts of the state.

Special Features

People in Norwegian, Viking, and Valkyrie costumes dance, feast, compete, and have a good time at the **Little Norway Festival**, held on the third full weekend in May (Norwegian Independence Day). This is the time to sample from an authentic Smorgasbord.

Several Petersburg companies offer boat tours of beautiful **LeConte Glacier**, the world's southernmost active tidal glacier. The glacier can also be toured by air.

Spectacular scenery and navigational challenges make the ferry trip through the **Wrangell Narrows** especially interesting.

- A 2,000-year-old native fish trap archaeological site may be visited near Sandy Beach.
- Petersburg is the Alaska center for humpback whale research. Approximately 500 humpback whales enter Frederick Sound, adjacent to Petersburg, each summer.
- Alaskan King Crabs can have a "wingspan" of up to eight feet.

Further Information

Petersburg Visitors Information Center, *P.O. Box 649, Petersburg AK 99833, (907) 772-4636, www.petersburg.org.*

Directions

Petersburg is on an island, so you'll have to make arrangements to get here by boat or plane. Alaska Airlines offers jet service to Petersburg from Seattle and Anchorage, and Alaska One offers scheduled service between Petersburg and other Alaskan cities.

A spectacularly beautiful trip to Petersburg aboard a large ship (and ferry) is available through Alaska Marine Highway, Bellingham, Washington. Shallow waters prevent large cruise ships from putting to port here.

SITKA
Population 9,000

Lucky—and wonderful—indeed is the town that can boast of spectacular scenery, a long and rich history, and a bountifulness of wildlife that would be the envy of any zoo or animal park. **Sitka** has all of these. From Russian and Alaska Native dances to an onion-domed cathedral and stately totem poles, the town is full of reminders of the region's centuries-old Tlingit (KLINK et) and 19th-century Russian colonial cultures. In addition, Sitka is embraced by the Pacific Ocean on one side and gorgeous snowcapped mountains and forests of spruces and hemlocks on the others. And people travel thousands of miles to fish Sitka's waters for salmon and halibut and to view the area's many bald eagles, seabirds, and marine mammals, including humpback whales.

The Russians landed in the Sitka region in 1799 and, following a short period of courageous but ultimately futile opposition from the Tlingits, established Sitka as the capital of Russian America. The town, called New Archangel by the Russians, became the base for the immensely profitable fur-trading Russian-American Company and, at least for a fortunate few, a place of relative luxury, the "Paris of the Pacific." Then, for several reasons, including the perceived likelihood that in time the colony would certainly fall to the British or Americans, the tsar decided to withdraw and in 1867 sold Alaska to the United States.

The domes of **St. Michael's Cathedral** (1844-48, rebuilt 1966) set a mood that is more Byzantine than Yankee or Western European. Within the National Historic Landmark are art treasures and memorabilia of the Russian Orthodox Church, among them a superb collection of icons (open to public). A second Russian building, the restored **Russian Bishop's House** (1842), is the largest Russian log structure in North America. Also a National Historic Landmark, the building contains original furnishings and other mementos of the Russian period (reservations advised).

Reminders of Russian America continue with yet another National Historic Landmark, **Castle Hill** (Baranov Castle State Historic Site). Several buildings once existed here; surviving are the stone walls and cannons from the most famous, "Baranov's Castle" (1837), which burned in 1894. The castle was the site of the transfer of Alaska to the United States in 1867.

The 107-acre **Sitka National Historical Park** marks the site of a battle between the Tlingits and Russians in 1804. Within the visitors center is the **Southeast Alaska Indian Cultural Center**, where guests may watch and talk to native carvers and other native artists. A fine collection of totem poles lines the park's wooded pathways.

Two museums commemorate Sitka's and Alaska's colorful pasts. The many exhibits of the **Isabel Miller Museum** chronicle the histories of the Tlingits and Russian-Americans, as well as the region's logging, mining, and fishing industries. The excellent collections of the **Sheldon Jackson Museum** (building erected in 1895) focus on the cultural achievements of Alaska's many native peoples.

Sitka has two churches of special note in addition to St. Michael's Cathedral. The first, **Sitka Lutheran Church**, contains objects from the Finnish Lutheran Church (1843) that originally occupied the site. The second, **St. Peter's by the Sea Episcopal Church**, held its first service in 1899. Behind the church is the bishop's residence, or **"See House"** (1905).

Most of Sitka's in-town sights can be toured in the course of a short walk. Visitors wishing to take in the coastal and other scenery will find a nice selection of tours: narrated land tours, walking tours of forest trails, boat tours, air tours, and a variety of wildlife cruises. Sightseeing is just one of a number of activities available to the visitor. The fishing is fabulous, of course, and so are the hiking and biking. What is less well-known is that **Sitka Sound** offers some of the best kayaking in the world (rentals and instruction available). The incentives for another favorite activity, shopping, come in the form of stunning examples of Tlingit beadwork, basketry, and painting. As is true for the Indians of the Pacific Northwest in general, the woodcarving is magnificent.

Special Features

Whale Park, some 6 miles south of downtown, features a boardwalk from which to view wildlife, including whales. Whales are prominent in the early fall and winter, and again in March, making the park a great placing for viewing.

During the summer months birdwatchers can view puffins, petrels, and other seabirds on **St. Lazaria Island**, a federal wildlife refuge. The refuge is accessible by boat.

Providing yet another example of the costs associated with the failure to conserve, a decline in the fur trade due to the over-hunting of sea otters and seals was one of the principal factors leading to Russia's decision to sell Alaska to the United States.

Further Information

Sitka Convention & Visitors Bureau, *P.O. Box 1226, Sitka, AK 99835 (907) 747-5940, fax (907) 747-3739, www.sitka.org.*

Directions

Sitka cannot be reached by road and, as with nearby Petersburg (see selection), visitors must rely on boat or air transportation.

The Alaska Marine Highway offers ferry/passenger service from Prince Rupert, BC (18 hours) and Bellingham, WA (3 days). Cruise ships also put into Sitka. The protected waters of the Inside Passage make travel by private yacht yet another option.

Alaska Airlines provide daily direct service from Seattle and Anchorage and connecting service from Juneau. Car rentals and taxi service are locally available.

Other Charming Alaska Towns
Skagway
Talkeetna
Valdez

Chapter 3

ARIZONA

BISBEE

Population 6,090

Perhaps the two most memorable things about **Bisbee** are the **Lavender Pit Open Mine** and the **historic district**. The former is roughly one mile, or more, in diameter and 950 feet deep. The size is breathtaking, if not downright frightening. In contrast, the shops, art galleries, antique stores, and coffee houses of the historic district invite. As do the turn-of-the-century homes perched on the hillside. The close proximity of an open pit and a charming, prosperous town is of course no coincidence, for as the people of Yorkshire, England are fond of saying, "Where there's muck, there's money."

Bisbee and the surrounding **Mule Mountains** produced enormous quantities of gold, copper, silver, and other minerals during the late 19th and early 20th centuries. The town, founded in 1880, grew to become one of the largest—and most colorful—places between the Mississippi and the West Coast. When large-scale mining operations closed in the 1970s, the populated declined but by no means disappeared. Like other surviving old-West mining towns, Bisbee developed an artist colony and, thanks to one of the best climates in the country (see below), also became an important retirement community.

Most visitors will want to begin their visit by exploring the shops, galleries, and cafes of the beautifully preserved historic district. It doesn't take much imagination to understand why so many film companies have chosen these winding, century-old streets for their settings. Squint your eyes and you can almost see a provincial Italian town, or turn-of-the-century New York City.

Arizona

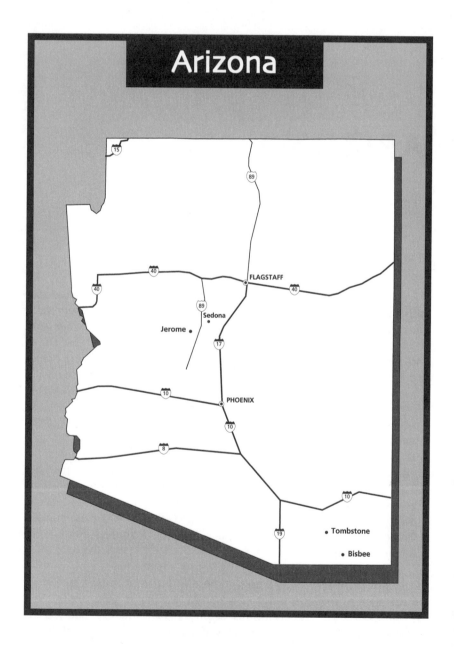

In one neck of the district is once-notorious **Brewery Gulch**, a quarter known in earlier days for its many saloons and brothels. (Although smaller, nearby Tombstone had a similar reputation—see listing.)

The historic district has three museums, each focusing on a different aspect of Bisbee's past: The **Bisbee Mining & Historical Museum**, an affiliate of the Smithsonian; the **Bisbee Restoration Museum**; and the **Muheim Museum Heritage House**. The latter, built between 1898 and 1915, has period furnishings and commands a panoramic view of the town and mountains.

The arts are obviously important to Bisbee. In addition to the many galleries and craft shops, there are street dances, concerts, and productions of the Bisbee Repertory Theatre. The more casual visitor will find cafes with poetry readings and historic saloons featuring live music.

That there were once numerous miners' boarding houses means that there are now numerous charming bed and breakfasts. Indeed, Bisbee boasts the largest concentration of historic B&Bs and inns in Arizona.

Touring options include walking tours, Bisbee Trolly tours, and Lavender jeep tours. A self-guided walking tour, complete with map, may be obtained at the visitor center. The **Queen Mine Tour** offers visitors an underground trip into a now-inactive copper mine.

Special Features

Over 800 varieties of high desert plant life are on exhibit at the **Arizona Cactus & Succulent Research**. The center offers guided tours, classes on landscaping, and an extensive library.

The Mexican border town of **Naco** is just a few miles south.

Bisbee boasts over 294 sunny days a year. Winters are mild and summer evenings cool.

▶ HISTORIC DINING ◀

CAFÉ ROKA, 35 Main St., P.O. Box 1251, (520) 432-5153, www.caferoka.com. In restored 1907 Art Deco bldg.; New American cuisine (with California, Italian, & New Vegetarian elements); Gulf Shrimp Tossed with Lobster Ravioli, Roasted Half Duck among specialties. $$ to $$$ (traditional 4-course dinner).

Further Information

Bisbee Chamber of Commerce & Visitor Center, 31 Subway St., P.O. Box BA, Bisbee, AZ 85603, (866) 224-7233, (520) 432-5421, www.bisbeearizona.com.

Directions

From Tucson, I-10 east to Benson, AZ 80 south to Bisbee.

JEROME
Population 460

Founded in 1876 and incorporated in 1899, **Jerome** was by the 1920s a bustling copper-mining city of 15,000 people. In 1953 the mines closed, and by the late 1950s Jerome had become the world's largest ghost town—population maybe 100. Then in the 1960s and 1970s the town's winding hillside streets were rediscovered by artists and others of the rebellious generation in search of a simpler life. Today Jerome is a National Historic Landmark dotted with galleries, specialty shops, restaurants, bed and breakfasts, museums. The population is up to about 460.

Sundry buildings have been renovated to house Jerome's new businesses and handful of residents, but some structures remain abandoned. The place is in other words still part ghost town, and that inescapable perception can evoke a sense of nostalgia, a feeling even of downright unworldliness—especially when placed against the starkness of the desert-mountain setting. Striving to keep the visitor ever in the present, however, are working artists' studios, a fine collection of art galleries and artisans' shops, a selection of food establishments, and of course, a couple of genuine old-time saloons.

Two museums remind of a town that during its 70 years of active life yielded over a billion dollars worth of copper and other ores (and that still hides beneath its surface over 100 miles of tunnels and mine shafts). Central to **Jerome State Historic Park** is the **Douglas Mansion** (1916), originally the home of mining developer "Rawhide Jimmy " Douglas and now a museum focusing on the area's history. Among the exhibits of the second museum, the **Jerome Historical Society Mine Museum**, are local ores and examples of early mining equipment.

Special Features

Many of Jerome's homes and public buildings may be visited the third weekend in May during the **Annual Jerome Home Tour** (also called *Paseo de Casas*), the oldest such tour in Arizona.

Ruins of Indian pueblos occupied from the 12th to the 14th centuries may be toured at nearby **Tuzigoot National Monument**. Located at **Montezuma Castle National Monument**, a little farther away, is a well-preserved five-story cliff dwelling (circa 1050 to 1450).

The "Sliding Jail" slid 225 feet downhill and across the highway as a result of shock waves from dynamiting in the open-pit mines.

▶ HISTORIC HOTEL ◀

JEROME GRAND HOTEL, *P.O. Box H, 200 Hill St., (928) 634-8200, (888) 817-6788, e-mail: hotel@wildapache.net, www.jeromegrandhotel.net.* Hotel renovated from 1926 Spanish Mission structure, National Historic Landmark, 21 rooms & 1 suite, private baths, TV & phones, Cont. breakfasts, 1920s-style lounge & restaurant, period furnishings, 1926 Otis elevator, gift shop, massage by appt., at top of Jerome with panoramic views. $$ to $$$

Further Information

Jerome Chamber of Commerce, *P.O. Box K, Jerome, AZ 86331 (928) 634-2900.*

Directions

From Phoenix, I-17 north to AZ 260, northwest to AZ 89A (at Cottonwood), west to Jerome.

SEDONA
Population 10,500

It's hard to imagine that any town lying at the mouth of **Oak Creek Canyon** in central Arizona could avoid a listing in this book. The towering red rocks, fiery in the sun, dramatic in any season, make the area one of the most photographed in the country. Arizonans claim that "God created the Grand Canyon but He lives in Sedona." But even without the surroundings, **Sedona** has much to offer the visitor: first-class art galleries, boutiques, upscale restaurants, luxury resorts.

Sedona boasts almost 80 galleries exhibiting creations by some of the most talented artists and craftspeople in the country. The picturesque Mexican-style **Tlaquepaque**, an arts and crafts village, is especially recommended for lovers of charm. Even people who hate to shop will enjoy a stroll through the village's quaint courtyards.

For an especially beautiful view of the red-rock formations, drive up to the **Chapel of the Holy Cross** (1956). The chapel is built on a nearly 250-ft-high spur that juts from a 1,000-ft-high rock wall.

Dramatic country like this is hardly of recent discovery: Native American settlers were attracted to the area hundreds of years ago. The remains of prehistoric cultures—cliff dwellings, villages, petroglyphs and pictographs – abound in the Sedona region.

The touring options form an appetizing menu: In addition to the usual driving and hiking tours, there are airplane, helicopter, even hot-air balloon tours for seeing the scenery. The back country, and the ancient Indian ruins in particular, can be explored by guided jeep or horseback tours. Jeeps can also be rented for self-guided touring.

Special Features

Some of the most photographed scenery in the world can be seen at **Red Rock Crossing/Crescent Moon Ranch**, a few miles west of town.

Eight miles southwest of town is **Red Rock State Park**, an environmental park where hikers, bikers, and others can experience first-hand the contrast between the coolness of tree-lined **Oak Creek** and the barrenness of the red cliffs and spires.

To the north, **Oak Creek Canyon**, a gorge with streams and waterfalls between sheer rock walls, provides one of the most scenic drives in the country.

A natural water slide at **Slide Rock State Park** tempts everyone, adult as well as kid, to jump in and go with the current. There are also natural swimming pools and opportunities for trout fishing.

• With over three million visitors, Sedona rivals the Grand Canyon in popularity.

• The Red Rock Country in Sedona was recently rated the "Most Beautiful Place in America" by a national magazine.

• A veritable back lot for Hollywood, many celebrities have worked and/or lived in Sedona. Among them – John Wayne, Elvis Presley, Lucille Ball, Orson Welles, Walt Disney.

Further Information

Sedona-Oak Creek Canyon Chamber of Commerce, *P.O. Box 478, Sedona, AZ 86339 (800) 288-7336, (928) 204-1123, www.VisitSedona.com.*

Directions

From Flagstaff (28 miles), Hwy. 89A south to Sedona; from Phoenix (120 miles), I-17 north to Exit 298, AZ 179 north to Sedona.

TOMBSTONE
Population 1,220

It's not easy putting into words the kind of spell that Tombstone casts. For a short time in history the Old West took center stage here. It was quite a show. And then it was all over, and then. . .nothing. The place didn't grow much, but "The Town Too Tough To Die" didn't rot away, either. Tourism eventually came and things were freshened up a bit, but not much more than was needed to preserve and restore what was. Some have likened Tombstone to a museum. To me it's rather more like an old attic, but an attic whose dusty inhabitants still sparkle with a little of their old color.

It all began in 1879 with the discovery of silver. A year later Tombstone was the fastest growing city between St. Louis and San Francisco. The quick wealth, brassy saloons, and countless gunfights—including the legendary shoot-out at the O.K. Corral—helped give substance to a chapter in American history that more often than not is fashioned by the novelist and screenwriter. The cast of characters included Wyatt Earp, Doc Holliday, and Bat Masterson. By the end of the 1880s, however, uncontrollable underground water and falling silver prices brought it all to an end.

The **Bird Cage Theatre**, in operation 24 hours a day from 1881 to 1889, provides the ideal starting place for a tour. After service as one of the wickedest spots in the country, the theater was boarded up and left that way until 1934, when it was opened as a historic landmark. It is preserved in its original state as a National Monument, more of an "attic" than a museum, with even the chairs in the poker room standing exactly where they were when the place was sealed.

The theater was named for the 14 crib compartments, suspended from the ceiling (and still in place), where prostitutes provided their services. The theater's massive grand piano and coin-operated juke box, as well as the original Boothill hearse trimmed in 24K gold and sterling silver, are among the exhibits.

Not far from the theater are the restored **Crystal Palace** (1879), the fabled saloon; the offices of The Tombstone Epitaph (founded 1880), with original equipment and presses; and the **O.K. Corral**, site of the infamous gun battle between the Earps and Clantons. The **Tombstone Historama**, adjacent to the corral, offers a unique audio-visual presentation of Tombstone's roaring history, narrated by Vincent Price.

Several buildings merit a special visit or walk-by. One of these is the **Tombstone Courthouse State Historic Park** (1882), whose exhibits provide a good glimpse of the area's early history. Others include the town's original **firehouse** (1880s), **city hall** (1882), and **St. Pauls Episcopal Church** (1882), now the oldest Protestant church building in Arizona.

And then there is of course **Boothill Graveyard** (used from 1879 to 1884), where authenticated grave sites mark the final resting places of a number of Tombstone's early residents, including many gunslingers. A visit here is almost obligatory, part of a pilgrimage to the Old West.

Tombstone's several streets are home to a variety of restaurants and saloons. There are also galleries and shops, including several specializing in Western wear and Indian jewelry. Theatrical groups present re-enactments of Western-style shoot-outs—inquire at the tourism office (see below) for details.

Tombstone is just the right size to be explored on foot. For added color, and maybe comfort, there are also horse-drawn tours and stagecoach rides.

> The refrain, "She's only a bird in a gilded cage," was inspired by the crib compartments at the Bird Cage Theatre.

Further Information

Tombstone Office of Tourism, *P.O. Box 917, Tombstone, AZ 85638 (800) 457-3423.*

Directions

From Tucson, I-10 east to Exit 313 (Benson), AZ 80 south to Tombstone.

Other Charming Arizona Towns
Ajo
Carefree
Pine/Strawberry
Tubac
Wickenburg

Chapter 4

ARKANSAS

EUREKA SPRINGS
Population 1900

Eureka Springs is a beautifully unique blend of the Victorian and the Ozarks. The colorful array of Victorian buildings earned the entire downtown shopping district and residential area a listing on the National Register of Historic Places. But there are also narrow, winding mountain streets and lovely limestone walls built from native stone. Streets are sometimes hundreds of feet higher, or lower, than adjacent streets. And when streets cross, they never do so at right angles. You're in the **Ozarks**.

Belief in the healing powers of its spring waters was Eureka Springs's forebear. The town grew as thousands of health seekers journeyed, first by stagecoach and later by train, to the bathhouses of the growing resort. Today the town's native limestone buildings, gingerbread houses, shaded trails, springs and gazebos preserve the Victorian atmosphere.

Eureka Springs is to be explored by some combination of trolley and foot, probably in that order. There are no fewer than six trolley routes, each designated by a color displayed on a sign in the front window, and they serve most of the town's places of lodging. Information on the trolley routes and a copy of the Scenic Walking Tours booklet can be obtained at the Chamber of Commerce.

Three Victorian homes are open to the public: the **Queen Anne Mansion** (1891), with exceptional interior oak and cherry woodwork; the lovely **Rosalie** (1880s), with period furnishings and accessories; and the **Gables**, known for its superb collection of Victoriana.

Just west of town (on US 62W) are two especially inspiring attractions, the exquisitely beautiful **Thorncrown Chapel**, an architectural masterpiece, and

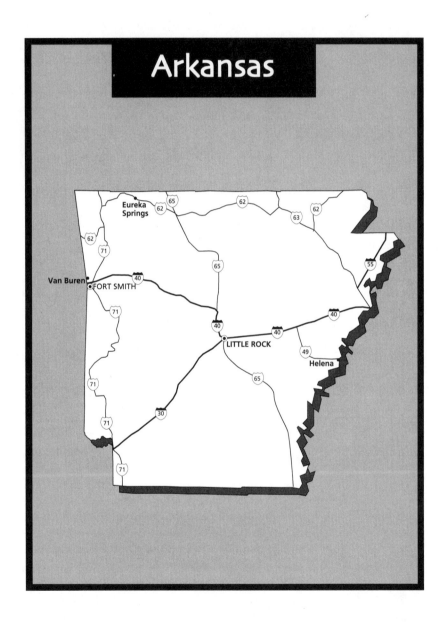

Arkansas

the **Blue Spring Heritage Center**. Blue Spring pours 38 millions gallons of water each day into a trout-stocked lagoon. Also featured are a historic bluff shelter and 33 acres of informal grounds that display a variety of hardwood trees and native plants.

Special Features

The **Eureka Springs and North Arkansas Railway** offers a lunch train, dinner train, and excursion train (departing hourly). A more leisurely tour of the mountains is available by cruise boat on scenic **Beaver Lake**.

- Eureka Springs is home to the regionally famous Great Passion Play, a spectacular outdoor drama depicting the life, death, and resurrection of Christ.
- Known as an artists' colony as early as the 1930s and 1940s, Eureka Springs is now one of the most respected fine arts centers of the mid-South.

▶ HISTORIC HOTEL ◀

CRESCENT HOTEL, *75 Prospect St., (800) 342-9766, fax (479) 253-5296, e-mail: reservations@crescent-hotel.com, www.crescent-hotel.com.* "Queen of the Ozarks" with Victorian guest rooms, National Landmark, 60 rooms, 12 suites, private baths, TV, phones, dining room, antiques, small pets, outdoor swimming pool, carriage rides, 4 acres of beautifully landscaped gardens with walking paths. $$$ to $$$$

Further Information

Eureka Springs Chamber of Commerce, *P.O. Box 551, Eureka Springs, AR 72632 (479) 253-8737, www.eurekaspringschamber.com .*

Directions

From Springfield (MO), US 65 south to US 62, west to Eureka Springs; from Little Rock, I-40 north to US 65 (at Conway), north to US 62, west to Eureka Springs.

HELENA
Population 7,491

Situated on a rise overlooking the Mississippi, **Helena** was described by Mark Twain as occupying "one of the prettiest situations on the river."

Although much of Arkansas belongs geographically and culturally to the mid-South, Helena is unmistakably part of the Deep South. The second oldest city in Arkansas (founded in 1820), its history is that of steamboats, cotton, and the Mississippi Delta. Helena was the home of seven Confederate generals. It is today home to one of the Delta's major cultural events, the **Annual King Biscuit Blues Festival** (second weekend of October, Thursday - Sunday).

The **Cherry Street Historic District** is a well-preserved business district of the late 19th and early 20th centuries. The district's appearance and ambiance are those of a traditional river town. A top site is the new **Delta Cultural Center**, an important regional museum (costing $8.5 million) that chronicles the history of the Delta and its people. The center is housed in the 1903 **Helena Train Depot**.

Helena has a handsome collection of antebellum, Victorian, and Edwardian homes. Many are listed on the National Register of Historic Places (some offer tours by appointment – check with *Main Street Helena*, 338-9144). Three important antebellum homes are **Estevan Hall**, a magnificent home preserved by the descendants of the original owners; the 1860 red brick **Moore-Hornor Home**, with 18-foot ceilings and parlor doors that still bear shell marks from the Battle of Helena (see below); and the spacious 1858 Greek Revival **Tappan-Pillow Mansion**, with the original two-room brick kitchen out back.

Among the most elegant of the postbellum houses are the Italianate **Hornor-Gladin House** (1880), with original fireplaces and mantels; the grand Georgian-Revival **West-Webb House** (1900), with parquet floors and quarter-sawn oak woodwork; and the **Pillow-Thompson House** (1896), considered one of the finest examples of Queen Anne architecture in the south.

The restored **Old Almer Store**, constructed in 1872 of cypress, was once a market for dairy products and, later, a neighborhood grocery. Entered on the National Register, the store now serves as an area-wide arts and crafts cooperative.

High on Crowley's Ridge, the **Confederate Cemetery** offers a panoramic view of the Mississippi River. Another view of the water may be enjoyed from the boardwalk of **Riverfront Park**.

• The Battle of Helena was fought in 1863 as a Confederate attempt to relieve pressure on Vicksburg downriver. The Confederate troops suffered heavy casualties.
• The riverboats "Delta Queen" and "Mississippi Queen" often put into Helena for tours of Cherry Street.
• The bridge at Helena is the only Mississippi River bridge between West Memphis (to the north) and Lake Village (to the south).

Special Features

Both the **St. Francis National Forest** and the **White River National Wildlife Refuge** offer superb opportunities for fishing and wildlife observation.

Further Information

Phillips County Chamber of Commerce, *P.O. Box 447, 111 Hickory Hill, Helena, AR 72342 (870) 338-8327, fax (870) 338-6445.*

Directions

From Little Rock, I-40 east to exit 216 (Brinkley), US 49 southeast to Helena.

VAN BUREN
Population 17,460

Largely bypassed by much larger Fort Smith across the Arkansas River, **Van Buren** retains much of the quaint ole river town atmosphere. **Main Street**, which looks pretty much like it did 100 years ago, has appeared in several films and in the TV mini-series *The Blue and the Gray*. The street has seen everything from wagon trains to Union and Confederate troops to stagecoaches headed west. And wagons hauling freight to and from the many steamboats on the Arkansas. More than 70 buildings in the Main Street area are on the National Register of Historic Places.

Crawford County Courthouse, built in 1841 and rebuilt in 1877, is the oldest active county courthouse west of the Mississippi. The Seth Thomas clock in the tower has been tolling the hour for nearly 120 years.

The elegant 1890s **King Opera House**, recently restored, offers a diverse and colorful performance schedule. Jenny Lind and William Jennings Bryant appeared here.

Van Buren's shops, respected throughout western Arkansas and eastern Oklahoma, display dolls, stained glass, jewelry, cutlery, quilts, pottery, and other items handmade by local artists. The emphasis is on the handcrafted and the Victorian. Antiques and the fine arts are also represented.

Special Features

On selected days, April through November, the **Ozark Scenic Railway** offers 3-hour excursions to the mountain village of **Winslow**. Passengers relax in early 1900s cars with restored inlaid mahogany interiors as they travel over trestles and through a tunnel built in 1882. The train embarks from the **Old**

Frisco Depot, now restored and home to the Chamber of Commerce as well as to a collection of Bob "Bazooka" Burns memorabilia.

The towering bluffs along the Arkansas River can be seen from the decks of the 138-passenger *Frontier Belle*. The main deck is enclosed for comfort in all weather.

Across the river, the **Fort Smith National Historic Site**, **Belle Grove Historic District**, and the **Old Fort Museum** are especially worth a visit.

• Fort Smith was established in 1817 to help keep peace among the region's Indians.
• On the back of the river wall in the Mike Meyer Riverfront Park is a mural history of Van Buren painted by Van Buren High School art students.

Further Information
The Van Buren Chamber of Commerce, *P.O. Box 652, Van Buren, AR 72957 (800) 332-5889, (501) 474-2761.*

Directions
From Little Rock, I-40 west to exit 5 (Van Buren/Fort Smith exit).

Other Charming Arkansas Towns
Hardy
Mountain View
Scott
Washington

Chapter 5

CALIFORNIA

AVALON
Population 3,500

Overlooking a gorgeous harbor, and ocean beyond, **Avalon** could be on the French or Italian Riviera. There are few communities in Southern California with its charm. There are even fewer with its beauty – the blue harbor, coastal hillsides, beaches, crystal-clear water, and clear skies (except when the wind's blowing from Los Angeles).

Situated on lovely **Catalina Island** some 26 miles off the Southern California coast, Avalon has been a popular pleasure resort since the 1890s. The village is small, no more than about one square mile in area, and so its winding streets can be explored by foot. Although the foot may offer the best way to absorb the late 19th-century charm, there are others: tram tours, bus tours, golf cart and bicycle rentals.

The 1929 Art Deco **Casino Building**, located on one side of the harbor, includes the **Avalon Theatre** and **Casino Ballroom**. The Avalon Theatre, known for its excellent acoustics and murals by John Gabriel Beckman, has a full-scale pipe organ whose largest pipe measures 16 feet and shortest a mere 1/4 inch. The circular Casino Ballroom, the largest of its type in the world, was a symbol of the Big Band Era of the 1930s, 40s, and 50s. Today the casino is the site of music festivals, dances, holiday celebrations, and other special events. (Daily walking tours available.)

Avalon's underwater scenery is spectacular: The octopus, barracuda, spiny lobsters, kelp forests, even wrecks make snorkeling and scuba diving very popular. There are glass-bottom boat and semi-sub tours, night as well as day, for underwater sightseers who wish to remain dry.

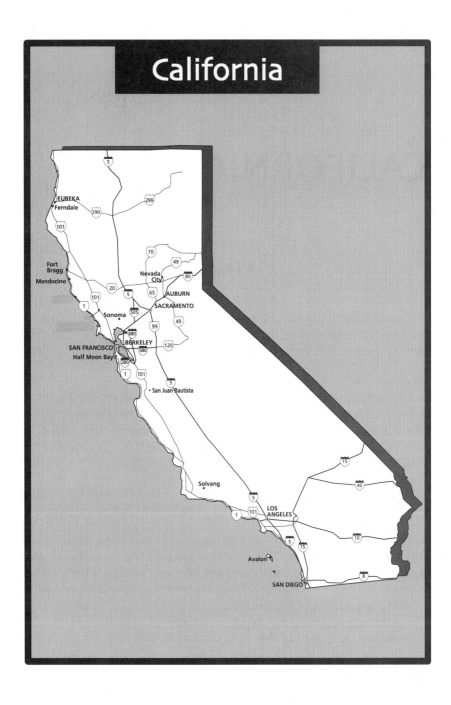

Special Features

The Seal Rocks down the coast can be visited by tour boat (migratory sea lions rather than seals sun on the rocks).

• Pigeons were used to carry messages between Catalina and the mainland from the 1850s to as late as 1899.
• Avalon was the first city in California empowered by the state legislature to control the number, size, speed, and noise of vehicles operating within the city limits.
• About 88% of the island is owned by the Santa Catalina Island Conservancy, a nonprofit group whose mission is to restore and preserve the land in a natural state.

Further Information

Catalina Island Visitors Bureau & Chamber of Commerce, *P.O. Box 217, Avalon, CA 90704 (310) 510-1520, www.catalina.com.*

Directions

Boats depart for Catalina Island from Long Beach, San Pedro, Dana Point, and Newport Beach. Year-round helicopter service is available from Long Beach and San Pedro. Check with the Visitor Bureau for scheduling. Travel time to the island is one to one and a half hours by sea and 15 minutes by helicopter.

FERNDALE
Population 1,331

The **"Victorian Village of Ferndale"** is tucked between the Eel River and northern California's "Lost Coast." Although geographically one of California's most western towns, Ferndale is architecturally one of the state's most eastern. **Main Street** (on the National Register) as well as the side streets are bordered by carefully restored, brightly painted Victorian buildings. Even the Victorian-style public restrooms are beautifully painted. Flower boxes and nicely kept gardens add to the color, and the palm trees, camellias, roses, rhododendrons, and other lush plants impart a unique, almost enchanting beauty that sets the town apart from most other Victorian communities.

Situated in a rich dairying region, Ferndale became the agricultural center of northern California during the final decades of the 19th century. The area's wealth helped build ornate Victorian homes, nicknamed *Butterfat Palaces*. The town changed very little after the late 1800s. In the 1960s the picturesque buildings were discovered by artists and craftspeople and Ferndale's revitalization was underway. Today the thriving Main Street is lined with specialty shops, an old-fashioned mercantile, antique stores, and studios/galleries.

The principal architecture of the historic homes is Eastlake and Stick, although Gothic Revival and other Victorian styles are never far away. Some of the commercial structures are late Victorian, some early Modernistic (1920-1936). Much of the picturesque town can be taken in on a two-hour self-guided walking tour (especially with the assistance of the souvenir edition *Ferndale Enterprise*) or horse-drawn carriage tour. An excellent stop on the tour, if not in fact its starting point, is the **Ferndale Museum**. Among the museum's displays are Victorian room settings, a working forge, seismograph (earthquakes are not unknown here), and early agricultural equipment.

Ferndale's spirit is evident in its often-offbeat attractions. The newly restored **Ferndale Art & Cultural Center** features a **Kinetic Sculpture Museum**, and the pioneer **Ferndale Cemetery** is popular for its expansive views of the ocean and Eel River valley. The **Ferndale Repertory Theatre** stages performances year-round.

Special Features

Ferndale consistently ranks in the top 20 of Audubon bird counts, with 355 varieties of birds spotted in the area. Good locations for bird watching, and nature watching in general, are the **Eel River State Wildlife Area**, the **Humboldt Bay National Wildlife Refuge**, and Ferndale's own **Russ Park**, a lovely 105-acre wilderness preserve. One of the best ways to see the giant redwoods is to drive along the **Avenue of the Giants**, a winding stretch of old US 101 southeast of Ferndale.

Ferndale is the gateway to California's "**Lost Coast**." Take the Wildcat Road to Petrolia and loop through the redwoods back to US 101 for a quick view of pristine shorelines (three-hour drive), or camp and hike in the **King Range** for a longer visit.

• The verdant countryside of Northern California's Eel River Valley looked like home to the immigrating Danes of the 19th century.
• Ferndale won a Prettiest Painted Place Award in 1997, and in 2002 the National Trust for Historic Preservation named Ferndale one of America's Dozen Distinctive Destinations for the town's success in protecting its unique character and sense of place.

Further Information

Ferndale Chamber of Commerce, P.O. Box 325, Ferndale, CA 95536
(707) 786-4477, www.victorianferndale.org/chamber.

Directions

From San Francisco, US 101 north to Fernbridge/Ferndale exit (south of Eureka), west to Ferndale.

FORT BRAGG
Population 7,100

Fort Bragg is an old coastal lumber mill town that is gradually turning into a tourist center. It is a town with many faces.

There is first of all Fort Bragg the American hometown. The facades of early 1900s buildings along downtown streets are painted in Victorian four-color schemes and decorated with canvas awnings. Bungalows of the Craftsman and other traditional California styles dot several adjacent neighborhoods.

Then there is Fort Bragg the coastal resort, with inns, fine restaurants, and other amenities for visitors wishing to enjoy the rugged Pacific scenery. Magnificent headlands, coves, natural arches, redwood forests, beaches, and tidepools are just minutes away.

Fort Bragg is also a fishing village. Down in **Noyo Harbor** is a commercial fishing fleet along with everything needed to service it. There are also facilities for recreational craft. Seafood restaurants, fishing charters, and boat excursions cater to the tourist, and add to the color.

An art center is beginning to look as though it may be Fort Bragg's newest identity. Several good galleries have grown up, including the **Northcoast Artists Cooperative**. The **Fort Bragg Center for the Arts** sponsors exhibitions of photographs, weavings, collage art, sculpture, and other media.

Fort Bragg's logging history is recalled in three museums. The **Guest House Museum**, a handsome three-story 1892 home, displays photos and other artifacts of the lumber industry. The **Fort Bragg Depot** houses logging and railroad artifacts, and the landmark, all-redwood **Union Lumber Company Store** is home to an impressive collection of historical photographs.

Special Features

The famous California Western Railroad *Skunk* trains run 40 miles from Fort Bragg to the inland town of **Willits**. Once a logging railroad, the "Skunk" delivers mail and groceries to remote areas. The line's half-day and full-day round trips through the redwoods are one of Fort Bragg's top attractions.

Sometimes the "trains" operate as motorcars on rails, at other times passenger cars are pulled by diesel or historic steam locomotives.

MacKerricher State Park north of town has miles of beautiful beaches.

- Visitors to Glass Beach, once the town dump, can find interesting, often attractive ocean-cleansed glass and pottery shards.
- The 1906 Earthquake devastated Fort Bragg as well as San Francisco. However, San Francisco's demand for lumber to rebuild brought prosperity to Fort Bragg.

▶ HISTORIC LODGINGS ◀

THE GREY WHALE INN, 615 N. Main St., (707) 964-0640, (800) 382-7244, fax (707) 964-4408, e-mail: stay@greywhaleinn.com, www.greywhaleinn.com. 1915 redwood bldg. (town hospital until 1971), 14 rooms, private baths, TV & phones, full breakfasts, fireplaces, tea/coffee, local artwork, recreation area with pool table, gardens, ocean view. $$$ to $$$$

OLD COAST HOTEL, BAR & GRILL. 101 N. Franklin St., (707) 961-4488, (800) 468-3550, fax (707) 961-4480, e-mail: oldcoast@mcn.org. 1892 hotel, 16 rooms, private baths, TV, Cont. breakfasts, restaurant, some fireplaces, sundeck & fountain patio garden, ocean or garden views. $$ to $$$$ (depending on season)

Further Information

Fort Bragg-Mendocino Coast Chamber of Commerce, P.O. Box 1141, Fort Bragg, CA 95437 (707) 961-6300, (800) 726-2780, www.mendocinocoast.com.

Directions

From San Francisco, US 101 north to CA 20 (at Willits), CA 20 west to Fort Bragg.

HALF MOON BAY
Population 8,886

Boasting miles of beautiful beaches and rugged bluffs, and separated from San Francisco by a half hour's drive and from the Silicon Valley by a coastal mountain range, it's only to be expected that **Half Moon Bay** should be a popular Bay Area retreat. The town is also the floriculture center of the

San Mateo Coast: Fields of flowers can be seen from the road, and fresh cut flowers are a given in area homes, inns, and restaurants.

Many of the homes and commercial structures in Half Moon Bay's historic district, once known as Spanishtown, date to the 19th century. Restored storefronts provide an interesting backdrop for art and craft galleries, restaurants, and quaint gift shops. Group walking tours may be arranged through the Spanishtown Historical Society (726-7200).

The **James Johnston House**, outside of town, is a saltbox structure (ca 1857) whose design was copied from the builder's Ohio home. Now on the National Register, plans call for the house and grounds to open after restoration is completed.

Located just north of town, **Pillar Point Harbor** is a bustling haven for pleasure craft and a commercial fishing fleet. The colorful harbor offers full marina services.

Widely known for its natural coastal beauty and abundant flora and fauna, Half Moon Bay provides a rich menu of recreational and sightseeing options. To list a few: whale-watching tours (January/April), air-taxi rides, horseback riding along the cliffs, salmon and rock fishing (charters available), sailing, beachcombing. Cyclists will find a 12-mile coastal bicycle trail and golfers two courses that overlook the Pacific. Half Moon Bay also has an interesting variety of night clubs.

Special Features

A nature lover's paradise, the Half Moon Bay area offers the visitor a choice among a variety of field trips. Some suggestions:

For birdwatching – **Pescadero Marsh National Preserve**. (Twenty percent of all known North American species can be seen here.)

For hiking/biking among giant trees and wildflowers – **Purissima Creek Redwoods**.

For touring elephant-seal breeding grounds (December/March) – **Ano Nuevo State Reserve** (reservations).

For tide pooling – **Fitzgerald Marine Reserve**.

Visitors may pick their own berries, pumpkins, and kiwi at farms along the coastline.

▶ HISTORIC HOTEL ◀

SAN BENITO HOUSE, *356 Main St., (650) 726-3425, www.sanbenitohouse.com.* 1905 hotel with European feel, 12 rooms, private baths with claw-foot tubs, full breakfasts, dining room, antiques, contemporary paintings, sauna, English-style garden. $$ to $$$

Further Information
Half Moon Bay Coastside Chamber of Commerce & Visitors Bureau, *520 Kelly Ave., Half Moon Bay, CA 94019 (650) 726-8380, e-mail: info@halfmoonbaychamber.org, www.halfmoonbaychamber.org.*

Directions
From San Francisco, CA 1 south to Half Moon Bay.

MENDOCINO
Population 1008

When leaving CA 1 to enter **Mendocino**, take the northern approach (Lansing Street). Before you will appear a charming New England-like village looking down upon the blue Pacific. It's a beautiful sight. You'd have to travel nearly 3,000 miles - to the Maine Coast - to find anything like it.

Many of the loggers and mill workers attracted to Mendocino by the redwoods came from New England, hence the Cape Cod or Down East ambiance of the village they built. After the mill operations ceased in the 1930s, the town went into a sort of hibernation and remained there until artists and others rediscovered its charm. Today there is a commitment by the people to preserve that charm: The Mendocino Historical Review Board, whose function it is to preserve Mendocino's traditional appearance, takes its job very seriously – just talk to anyone who has tried to build or remodel a house here.

Main Street is a wonderful juxtaposition of shops and businesses on one side and **headlands** (called palisades in Southern California) and ocean on the other. On the street is the **Mendocino Presbyterian Church** (1868), the oldest Presbyterian church in continuous operation in the state. The historic **Ford House** (1854), also on the street, is now a museum and visitor center for **Mendocino Headlands State Park** (see below).

The 1861 **Kelley House**, built of rough-sawn redwood boards, was erected by an early Mendocino entrepreneur. The house, gardens, and spring-fed duck pond are now a museum.

Along Main and the several inland streets are some first-class art galleries and an unusually broad variety of unique shops. The **Mendocino Art Center** is the arts headquarters, with galleries, an art shop, library, gardens, classes, and a theater.

Special Features
Mendocino is surrounded by **Mendocino Headlands State Park**. Get a

map of the park at Ford House and take in the sights, sounds, and smell of the ocean from a walk on the headlands. Guided tours are sometimes available.

Aquatic opportunities include deep-sea fishing, snorkeling at Little River Beach, canoeing on Big River, and whale watching (out of nearby Noyo Harbor - winter months).

> • Scenes for the "Maine" village of Cabot Cove in the TV series "Murder, She Wrote" were in fact filmed in Mendocino.
> • Mendocino's first known settler was the sole survivor of an 1850 shipwreck.

▶ HISTORIC HOTEL ◀

MENDOCINO HOTEL & GARDEN SUITES, *45080 Main St., (800) 548-0513, e-mail: reservations@mendocinohotel.com, www.mendocinohotel.com.* Hotel est. 1878 (member National Trust Historic Hotels of America), 45 rooms, 6 suites, many private baths, phones & some TV, dining rooms, antiques, fireplaces, comforters, lounges, gardens. $$ to $$$$

Further Information

The Fort Bragg-Mendocino Coast Chamber of Commerce, *P.O. Box 1141, Fort Bragg, CA 95437 (707) 961-6300, www.mendocinocoast.com (Zip for Mendocino is 95460).*

Directions

From San Francisco, CA 1 north to Mendocino; or US 101 north to CA 128 (at Cloverdale), CA 128 west to CA 1, CA 1 north to Mendocino.

NEVADA CITY
Population 2855

Mix two parts Victoriana with one part Old West mining town. Make sure the Victoriana is colorfully painted and has plenty of balconies. Add winding streets, high-reaching trees, and natural-gas lights. Then place in the pine forests of the Sierra foothills. What you will have is an unusually pretty town with a truly distinctive charm.

Nevada City began in 1849 with a store selling miners' supplies. One year later the town had a government, post office, and population of some 10,000! Since that year the population has swung up and down, mostly down. Today, what began as a Gold Rush mining town is a kind of living museum with a kind of reputation that attracts artists, musicians, writers – and visitors. Strict building codes and underground wiring throughout are guaranteed to help preserve that reputation.

Nevada City's downtown, full of interesting shops, is listed on the National Register of Historic Places. Of special interest is the **National Hotel** (1854-57), California's oldest continuously-operating hotel. Herbert Hoover, Lola Montez, Jane Wyman, Martha Raye, and Tim Conway are among the many notables who have entered its doors. The square grand piano in the lobby once journeyed around Cape Horn, and the ornate back bar was originally the dining room buffet in the Spreckels mansion in San Francisco. Horse-drawn carriage tours can be taken from the hotel.

The Victorian bell tower and gingerbread trim of **Firehouse No. 1** were added after the building's construction in 1861. Its contemporary, **Firehouse No. 2** (1861), continues in use. The **Nevada Theatre** (1865) is the state's oldest building constructed as a theater. Musicians, actors, and others still perform here.

The many restored homes, some of them historic, merit a drive or walk through the neighborhoods surrounding the downtown. Evening strolls along the gas-lighted streets downtown are popular here.

Special Features

Grass Valley, similar to Nevada City in charm and history, is just four miles away, in the next valley.

Nevada City is known for its fall colors, perhaps the most beautiful in California. The best time to enjoy it all is mid-October through Thanksgiving.

• In the general election of 1856 only Sacramento and San Francisco cast more ballots than Nevada City.
• During the 1960s and 70s hippies and back-to-the-landers began opening shops and other small businesses in the decaying downtown. Such efforts contributed much toward putting the town back on the map.

▶ HISTORIC HOTEL ◀

NATIONAL HOTEL, *211 Broad St., (530) 265-4551, (530) 265-2445.* California's oldest continuously-operating hotel (1854-57), National Register, 42 rooms, 9 suites, some private baths, TV, Victorian dining room, antiques, ornate back bar, swimming pool, 115-ft veranda overlooking Nevada City. $ to $$$

Further Information
Nevada City Chamber of Commerce, *132 Main St., Nevada City, CA 95959 (530) 265-2692, www.nevadacitychamber.com.*

Directions
From Sacramento, I-80 north to Auburn, CA 49 north to Nevada City.

SAN JUAN BAUTISTA
Population 1,570

If you're looking for a little piece of Old California, you won't do much better than **San Juan Bautista**. Graced by a classic Spanish plaza, romantic old mission, and narrow streets flanked by quaint Mexican, Early Californian, and Victorian dwellings, San Juan Bautista is the kind of place that somehow managed to flirt with, but never really embrace, the 20th century. It's the kind of town where food is served in picturesque courtyards rather than fast-food drive-ups, and where shoppers browse in unique street-side shops rather than look-alike strip malls. Obviously impressed by San Juan Bautista's character and charm, Hollywood has chosen the town as a setting for a number of movies.

In 1797 Spanish Franciscan friars chose this as the site of their 15th California mission, and soon thereafter Mission San Juan Bautista (after St. John the Baptist) became the core of a thriving Mexican pueblo and early California city. At one time the population was served by no fewer than four newspapers, and four times that many saloons. Suffering the same fate as many towns in this book, however, San Juan Bautista was bypassed by the railroad, and this meant that to a large extent it was to be bypassed by the 20th century as well.

Mission San Juan Bautista (1797-1812), the largest and one of the best preserved of the 21 California missions (see also **Solvang** and **Sonoma**), comprises a colorful 40-foot-tall chapel along with a museum and gift shop. On the grounds are a garden and Indian/Early California cemetery. The mission continues as an active Roman Catholic church (open).

Adjacent to the mission on the plaza is **San Juan Bautista State Historical Park**, composed of four very brightly colored structures: the **Plaza Hotel**, an 1858 inn restored to its Victorian finest; the **Plaza Hall**, an 1860s building with a varied history, including unrealized service as a government hall; the 1860s **Plaza Stable**, now a museum featuring a remarkable collection of horse-drawn carriages and wagons; and the balconied 1830s **Castro-Breen Adobe**, a lovely old structure that functioned variously as a residence and as the headquarters of the Mexican government.

A strongly recommended way to tour San Juan Bautista's many other historic structures is by means of a walking-tour brochure distributed by the Chamber of Commerce. Making up the 41 historic sites are homes, mercantiles, cantinas, and other buildings from the mid and late 19th century. Most are of Spanish Colonial, Greek Revival, or Victorian ancestry. Some house private residences, others are open to the public as boutiques, art galleries, and restaurants. The range of craft and specialty items is remarkable for a town of this size.

Adding to San Juan Bautista's uniqueness are performances by the renowned **El Teatro Campesino**. The theater stages original productions year-round in its playhouse.

Special Features

Fremont Peak State Park, situated at the end of a winding nine-mile road south of San Juan Bautista, is the place to visit for spectacular sunsets and panoramic views of San Benito County, the Salinas Valley, and the Pacific Ocean. The park is home to the Fremont Peak Observatory, which boasts a 30-inch reflecting telescope (open on selected dates).

Also south of town is **Pinnacles National Monument**, site of remnants of an ancient volcano. Included among the attractions are miles of hiking trails, caves (bring your own flashlights!), and excellent rock-climbing opportunities. The monument is home to rare birds of prey as well as to displays of poppies, lupines, and other spring wildflowers.

▶ HISTORIC HOTEL ◀

POSADA DE SAN JUAN HOTEL/INN, *P.O. Box 820, (831) 623-4030, fax (831) 623-2378.* Early 1900s Spanish Colonial-style inn, 33 rooms, private baths, TV & phones, antiques, fireplaces, balconies. $$ to $$$$

Further Information

San Juan Bautista Chamber of Commerce, *1 Polk St., Box 1037, San Juan Bautista, CA 95045 (831) 623-2454, fax (831) 623-0674, www.san-juan-bautista.ca.us.*

Directions

From the Bay Area, US 101 south to CA 156, south and east 2 miles to San Juan Bautista.

SOLVANG
Population 5,300

Separated from the Pacific by a coastal mountain range to the south, but open to climate-moderating ocean breezes from the west, lovely **Santa Ynez Valley** is sunny, temperate, and smog-free. The gently rolling valley is home to vineyards, horse ranches, apple orchards and, as unlikely as it may seem, the *Danish Capital of America*, **Solvang**.

Solvang (*sunny field* in Danish) was founded in 1911 by Danes from the Midwest seeking to establish a West-Coast Danish colony and folk school. Over the years the town began to look more and more Danish as the townspeople, perhaps encouraged by visits from Danish royalty, turned increasingly to Danish-style architecture.

Today the buildings sport exteriors of timber-framed white stucco, sloping green-copper or wood-shingle roofs, and lots of gables and dormers and towers. Up on top are hand-carved storks, down below are cobblestone sidewalks, outdoor cafes, and shops with leaded-glass windows. There are four windmills; one still turns. Visiting Danes say that the town looks more like Denmark than Denmark.

Specific Danish sites include the **Little Mermaid**, a half-scale copy of the original in Copenhagen harbor, and the **Bethania Lutheran Church**, a typical rural Danish church with hand-carved pulpit and a scale model of a Danish sailing ship hanging from the ceiling. The half-timbered **Elverhoj Museum**, once a residence, presents the story of Solvang with old photographs, crafts, period rooms, and other exhibits. The **Hans Christian Andersen Museum** honors the life and work of the father and master of the modern fairy tale.

Solvang's most historic site is not Danish. The adobe **Mission Santa Ines**, established in 1804 as the 19th of the 21 missions built in California by Spanish Franciscan priests, has been beautifully restored (visitors welcome). The chapel, in continuous use since 1817, is decorated with murals by Indian artists as well as by masterpieces of Moorish art and sculpture. The **Mission Museum** displays a number of treasures, among them 16th-century church vestments. On the grounds are the cemetery and semi-formal gardens.

Solvang boasts no fewer than 200 shops! Danish offerings include pastries (of course), music boxes, porcelain figurines, knitted sweaters, folk art, handmade lace, and Danish costumes. The shops are also noted for their selections of paintings and antiques.

Tours of Solvang may be taken on the Honen, a replica of a turn-of-the-century Copenhagen streetcar pulled by a pair of Belgian draft horses. Gliders and bicycles offer two of the best ways to tour the valley: The air currents are ideal for the former, and the many delightful country roads are designed for the latter.

Critically acclaimed musicals, dramas, and comedies are staged in Solvang's outdoor **Festival Theater** from summer through early fall by the **Pacific Conservatory of the Performing Arts Theaterfest**. Four spectacular area courses offer a variety of golfing challenges.

Special Features

Over 20 **Santa Barbara County wineries** are open to visitors, most without appointment. Many provide picnic tables. A wine touring map may be picked up at the visitors center.

Lake Cachuma, 15 minutes southeast, is home to a host of wildlife, including 275 species of birds. Eagle boat cruises (winter), nature cruises (summer), and boat rentals are available.

The Pacific Ocean may be enjoyed at **Gaviota State Park** and **Refugio** and **El Capitan** state beaches.

> Santa Barbara County now boasts over 50 wineries. All classic grape varieties can be grown in the county because of the many microclimates.

Further Information

Solvang Conference & Visitor's Bureau, *P.O. Box 70, Solvang, CA 93464 (800) 468-6765, www.solvangusa.com (Zip for Solvang is 93463.)*

Directions

From Los Angeles, US 101 west to Buellton, CA 246 east to Solvang.

SONOMA
Population 8,738

Old adobe buildings look on as children in **Sonoma's** enormous **plaza** play or point at ducks in the pond. Fountains splash and people enjoy their lunches or simply relax under the pines, palms, and redwoods. Flowers and sunshine are in every direction. There is Mexican blood in Sonoma's ancestry.

Mission San Francisco Solano de Sonoma was founded in 1823, when California was still a province of Mexico. The mission was the last and most northerly of California's 21 Franciscan missions. A few years after the mission was built, Mexican General Mariano Vallejo, headquartered here, laid out the 8-acre plaza (1834). The plaza was to become the center of Sonoma.

Still the center of Sonoma, the plaza today is bordered by historic buildings, quaint old hotels (see listing below), art galleries, and a host of inviting specialty shops. The best known of the buildings dating from Mexican times is the adobe **San Francisco Solano Mission church**, built by General Vallejo in 1840 to replace an earlier structure. The attached padres' quarters go back to about 1825 and are Sonoma's oldest structure. The 1836 **Sonoma Barracks** and 1850s **Toscano Hotel** (originally a general store and library) join the mission church in making up the **Sonoma State Historic Park**.

Among the historic houses on or near the plaza are the 1840s **Salvador Vallejo Home**, the 1836 adobe *Casa Grande*, and the 1847 **Nash-Patton Adobe**. A house of special interest away from the plaza is **Lachryma Montis**, the two-story Gothic Revival house built in 1851 by the now-American General Vallejo as his permanent home. The house, designated a state historical monument, was prefabricated and shipped around the Horn. Check with the Sonoma Valley Visitors Bureau on the plaza for touring information on these and many other historic buildings.

The visitors bureau also offers information on winery tours. Tours of the **Sebastiani Winery**, located just a few blocks off the plaza, are among the most popular. Sonoma's association with wine is nearly as old as the town itself. Cuttings of the Mission grape, used to make wines for the Mass, were brought to Sonoma as early as 1825 by Franciscan missionaries. The real birth of the wine industry, however, dates to 1857 when a Hungarian nobleman introduced cuttings of old-world varietals to the area and established **Buena Vista Winery**. Lining the beautiful Tuscany-like **Sonoma Valley** are now 36 or so wineries and some 13,000 acres of vineyards. Most of the tasting rooms along the 17-mile-long valley are open year round, and tastings are free in about 99% of them.

The Sonoma Valley is the site of an all-too-common struggle between rural charm and urban sprawl. Although the sprawl seems to have an advantage in parts, the vineyards, a national treasure, continue to predominate.

Special Features

Jack London built his hillside ranch, which he called his *Beauty Ranch*, near Glen Ellen north of Sonoma. What is now **Jack London State Historic Park** comprises about 800 acres of trees and spectacular scenery. On the grounds are The **House of Happy Walls** built in 1919 by London's widow, Charmian, and the remaining walls of **Wolf House**, a stone mansion that mysteriously burned a few days before the Londons were due to move in. London memorabilia are on display in The House of Happy Walls.

The **Sonoma Valley** is made-to-order for picnics. Pick up some local cheese, French bread, and other items from the specialty food shops around the plaza and journey out to the vineyards to purchase a bottle of wine. Many of the wineries have set aside picturesque areas for picnics.

> Sonoma Valley wines are by custom served only in distinctive blue-stemmed wine glasses.

▶ HISTORIC HOTEL ◀

FAIRMONT SONOMA MISSION INN & SPA, *P.O. Box 1447, (707) 938-9000, fax (707) 938-8327, e-mail: loriann.mcclintock@fairmont.com, www.fairmont.com/sonoma.* 1927 mission-style hotel, 228 rooms & suites, private baths, TV & phones, restaurant, 40,000-square-foot state-of-art spa featuring European bathing ritual, all pools with natural mineral waters, extensive grounds. $$$$

Further Information

Sonoma Valley Visitors Bureau, *453 First St. East, Sonoma, CA 95476 (707) 996-1090, www.sonomavalley.com.*

Directions

From San Francisco, US 101 north to CA 37, CA 37 northeast to CA 121, CA 121 north to CA 12, CA 12 north to Sonoma.

Other Charming California Towns
Calistoga
Cambria
Gualala
Healdsburg
Lone Pine
Quincy
St. Helena

Chapter 6

COLORADO

GEORGETOWN
Population 950

With over 200 original Victorian buildings, narrow streets, a narrow-gauge railroad, and Rocky Mountain scenery, **Georgetown** is the quintessential Old West mining town. So much so in fact that it has served as a setting in films and television commercials. The town has a second, less obvious distinction as well: Its location just 45 miles west of Denver and within 45 minutes of some of the top sights and ski areas in Colorado makes it ideal as a base for getting to know this beautiful state.

Georgetown began in 1859 as a gold prospectors' camp, but it was silver that turned the town into a busy commercial and service center. Unlike many mining communities of the era, the town was not destroyed by fire (see **Silverton**). Following the pattern common to so many well-preserved19th century towns, prosperity reached a peak and then plunged, sending the town into decades of near oblivion—and safekeeping. The peak year was 1877, when the valley's population reached 5,000, and the year of bad fortune 1893, when the country went on a gold standard. True to pattern, the sleeping little town was rediscovered in the latter half of the 20th century, its valley declared a National Historic Landmark District, and restoration efforts begun.

Notable among Georgetown's historic buildings is the **Hamill House Museum**, a Gothic Revival home built in 1879 by the town's best-known silver baron. The house retains its original hand-painted wallpaper and imported marble fireplaces. Also of note is the **Hotel de Paris Museum** (1875), the restoration of an elegantly decorated hotel that was once renowned for its lavish accommodations and table. Among its many luxuries was steam heat, virtually unknown at the time.

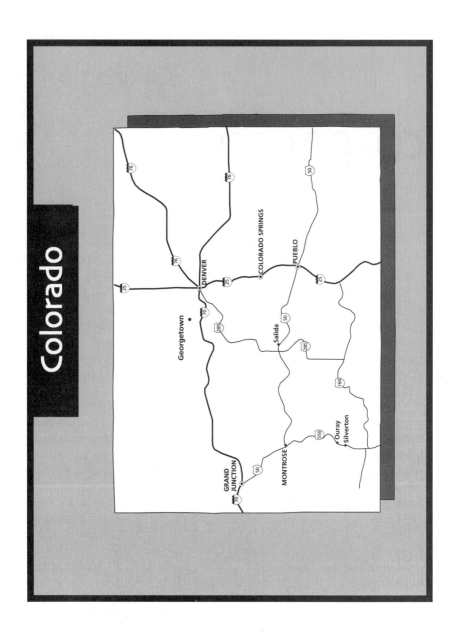

Colorado

The Georgetown Hydroelectric Station, constructed in 1900, is the second oldest hydroelectric plant in the state. Now an **Energy Museum**, much of the original equipment is still in use. Among the many other historic buildings are the **First Presbyterian** (1874) and **Grace Episcopal** (1869) **churches,** the **Old Jail** (1860s), and the **Alpine Hose No. 2** (1874).

The reconstructed **Georgetown Loop** offers a six-mile round trip between Georgetown and Silver Plume aboard a 1920 narrow-gauge steam train. Along the way is the spectacular 95-foot-high **Devil's Gate Viaduct**. A walking tour of the **Lebanon Silver Mine**, which can be reached only by the train, is optional. (Check with the Old Georgetown Station for schedules, reservations, etc.)

Georgetown can be toured by foot, but perhaps the most interesting (and informative) way to see the town is by means of a narrated tour by horse-drawn trolley. Private carriage tours are also available.

The area's eye-dazzling scenery can be enjoyed by driving from Georgetown to Grant over the **Guanella Pass Scenic Byway,** or less comfortably but more spectacularly by maneuvering a 4-wheel-drive over the very narrow and rocky **Saxon Mountain Road**. Then of course there are snowshoeing and cross-country skiing for seeing the landscape in the winter. Bikers should check locally for information on guided half-day downhill mountain-bike tours, complete with uphill transportation, bike, lunch, and more.

Special Features

Christmas Market, the first two weekends in December, is a time of crafts, special foods, and other holiday attractions. The evening reflections of the Christmas lights off the snow-packed streets add to the special enchantment of the season.

Just 14 miles west of town is **Loveland**, Georgetown's own ski area, with slopes for all levels.

A herd of Rocky Mountain Bighorn Sheep (Colorado's state animal) can sometimes be seen from the Watchable Wildlife Viewing Station near Georgetown Lake (year-round viewing). The station is the only one of its kind in Colorado.

Further Information

Georgetown Community Center, *P.O. Box 444, Georgetown, CO 80444 (800) 472-8230;* also, **Historic Georgetown, Inc.**, *P.O. Box 667 (303) 569-2840, www.historicgeorgetown.org.*

Directions

From Denver, I-70 west to Georgetown (exit 228).

OURAY
Population 800

Travelers sometimes allot a couple of hours to **Ouray** before speeding on to their next destination. They often come back, but this time for a week, or more. True, Ouray (pronounced you RAY, but YOU ray will get the job done) is a quaint old Victorian mining town with no traffic lights, malls, freeways, or fast-food restaurants.

But Ouray is more than that, as visitors soon discover. Ouray is also a popular spa; the *Jeep Capital of the World*, with over 500 miles of off-road Jeep trails; a developing winter resort with excellent ice climbing and skating; and the proud owner of some of the most spectacular scenery on the planet. Lying 7,800 ft. up in the sky, and surrounded by mountains that soar yet another 5,000, the town's favorite descriptor is "heavenly."

All of Ouray is a National Historic District. The buildings, most of them restored, go back to the last two decades of the 19th century and the first decade of the 20th. Although quiet and charming today, Ouray was once wild and wide open: Not a few of the structures that now house respectable bed & breakfasts, restaurants, and residences were once saloons, brothels, and cribs.

The **Ouray County Museum** is the best place to start a tour of the town. The museum, once a miners' hospital (1887), contains 27 room-sized exhibits of everything from a cellblock out of the old **Ouray Jail** to a child's bedroom to an outstanding mineral collection.

Sweet, hot mineral water (105 degrees F) flowing from **Box Canyon** pours into the **Ouray Hot Springs Pool**. The pool is divided into several sections of differing temperatures. The hottest is a soaking section, the coolest a diving and lap lane section. The pool complex includes a fitness center and park and is very popular in the winter, especially with sore-muscled cross-country skiers and ice climbers. Waters from other mineral springs heat buildings and fill hotel hot tubs and vaporcaves.

Nationally known guest artists are featured in **Suzanne's Broadway to Branson Stage Show**, while the **Z-Bar Chuckwagon Western Show & Cowboy Supper** offer a variety of family entertainment.

Special Features

The surrounding country is laced with old mule trails, stagecoach trails, and mining roads that have found new life as 4-wheel-drive roads. Along these roads are old mines and boarding houses, ghost towns, alpine flowers, waterfalls, and other treasures. The best way to do these roads is by guided tour, at least on the first time out. If you think you'd be comfortable driving along the top of a 3,000-foot canyon, go for a rental.

A mine train carries visitors 3,500 horizontal feet into Gold Hill for a guided tour of the **Bachelor Mine** (silver was discovered here in 1884 by three bachelors). The silver and gold mine is about two miles from Ouray.

Canyon Creek plunges 285 feet through a rock to form spectacular Box **Canyon Falls**, on the outskirts of town. Trails, stairs, and bridges lead to views of both the top and bottom of the falls.

• Scenes from "True Grit" and "How the West Was Won" were filmed in the Ouray area.

• Ouray Ice Park, the world's first ice-climbing park, offers climbers one-half mile of ice-covered canyon walls.

▶ HISTORIC HOTEL ◀

ST. ELMO HOTEL, *426 Main St., P.O. Box 667, (970) 325-4951, e-mail: innkeeper@stelmohotel.com, www.stelmohotel.com.* Restored 1898 hotel on National Register, 8 rooms, 1 suite, private baths, full buffet breakfasts, restaurant (reservations recommended), antiques, afternoon social hour, sunny breakfast room. $$ to $$$

Further Information

Ouray Chamber Resort Association, *P.O. Box 145, Ouray, CO 81427 (800) 228-1876, www.ouraycolorado.com.*

Directions

From Denver, I-70 west to exit 37 (before Grand Junction), CO 141 south to US 50, US 50 south to US 550 (at Montrose), US 550 south to Ouray.

SALIDA

Population 5,500 (Elevation 7036 ft)

Salida (sa LYE da) is easy to picture – simply conjure up an image of what a Colorado town ought to look like: Turn-of-the-century streets nestled in a valley surrounded by snow-capped mountains, crystal-clear streams, wild-flower-covered slopes, and bright yellow aspens against Colorado blue skies. It is with good reason that Salida has been nicknamed the *Heart of the Rockies*.

Established in 1880, Salida has an agricultural, mining, and railroad history – and the largest historic district in Colorado. The colorful and unusually healthy downtown doesn't look like it has changed much from the first half of the 20th century. Flanking the side streets is an interesting collection of turn-of-the-century brick apartment dwellings.

One of the most active of the historic sites is the **Salida Hot Springs Pool**, the largest indoor hot springs pool in Colorado. As popular today as 50 years ago, the odorless mineral waters are used for everything from swimming and water games to arthritis classes. There are three pools in addition to private hot baths.

With its many fine galleries and artists' studios, Salida is respected as one of the best small art towns in Colorado. Each summer the downtown streets turn into a vast and very colorful gallery during the annual **Art Walk** (end of June).

Sometimes called the **Banana Belt** because of its surprisingly mild climate, Salida is a year-round sportsman's paradise. Rafting, kayaking, hiking, backpacking, golfing, horseback riding, and four-wheeling are all popular. The **Monarch Ski Area** is just minutes away. For mountain bikers there are leisurely rides, rides in the mid-ability range, and rides like the Monarch Crest Trail, considered one of the best in the world.

The **Arkansas River**, which flows through Salida, offers guided family float trips, high-adventure white-water trips, and everything in between, including fishing excursions. Trips vary from quarter-day to several-day and offer splendid opportunities to view wildlife and majestic scenery. Large brown, rainbow, cutthroat, and brook trout are plentiful in the Arkansas and in countless streams, lakes, and beaver ponds.

Special Features

The high country and several ghost towns can be visited by half-day to all-day car tours. A four-wheel drive isn't necessary. Check with the Chamber of Commerce for routings.

Buena Vista, another 19th-century Colorado town with a quaint downtown area, is 25 miles north of Salida.

- One of the most beautiful of the town's seasonal attractions occurs each year right after Thanksgiving when some 22,000 colored lights are strung in the shape of an enormous Christmas tree on the side of Tenderfoot Mountain.
- The Salida area is sometimes called the "14ers Region" because of the number of peaks over 14,000 feet in the Sawatch Range to the west.
- Over 40 percent of the trout used to stock Colorado's waters come from nearby Mt. Shavano Fish Hatchery.

Further Information

Heart of the Rockies Chamber of Commerce, *406 W. Rainbow Blvd., Salida, CO 81201 (877) 772-5432, (719) 539-2068, fax (719) 539-7844, www.salidachamber.org.*

Directions

From Denver, I-25 south to exit 102 (Pueblo), US 50 west to Salida; or US 285 south to US 50, US 50 east four miles to Salida.

SILVERTON
Population 450

Nestled in a narrow valley in the county with the highest mean elevation of any county in the United States, **Silverton's** "low" altitude is a mere 9,318 feet. At this altitude you may need a blanket on a summer evening, but on a sunny day in winter you can sport in the snow with a tee-shirt instead of a jacket or sweater. The surrounding countryside is 100% scenery – there's not so much as one acre of agriculture in the entire county.

Victorian Silverton, now a National Historic Landmark, is one of the best-preserved but least-discovered of Colorado's romantic old mining camps. Having never experienced a major fire (unlike most mining towns), Silverton retains most of its original homes and commercial buildings. The **San Juan County Historical Society Museum** (1902), once the county jail, provides a good short introduction to the town and ideal starting point for a walking tour (maps available at Chamber of Commerce). The **San Juan County Courthouse** (1907), next to the museum, is one of the most beautiful in Colorado. Another impressive public building, the native stone **Town Hall** (1909), has been faithfully restored to its original self.

"Notorious" **Blair Street** once housed 40 saloons and brothels, integral parts of every proper mining and railroad town. The street has provided settings for several Western movies.

The **Old Hundred Gold Mine Tour** proves that there are experiences that can be both educational and exciting. The one-hour tour, set up by local miners, consists of a narrow-gauge train ride into an authentic gold mine deep in a mountain. An experienced miner serves as the guide.

Although tiny, Silverton is home to no fewer than 15 or so studios and galleries of local artists and craftspeople. There are several options for the evening. Enjoying the saloons, a time-honored recreation in any mining town, is one. Another is attending a production of *A Theatre Group* in the **Miners' Union Theatre**. A variety of plays are staged each year.

Special Features

One of the best ways to enjoy the area's spectacular scenery is to board a coal-fired, steam-operated train of the **Durango & Silverton Narrow Gauge Railroad Company** for a trip to Durango. The train, serving Silverton since 1882, offers breathtaking views. During some months it is possible to take a railroad-operated bus to Durango and return to Silverton by train the same day. Another option is to make the Durango-Silverton-Durango loop and stop over for one or more nights in Silverton.

Daily tours are offered at the **Mayflower Gold Mill** two miles northeast of Silverton. The mill produced gold and silver from 1929 to 1991.

• Some of the nation's best 4-wheel-drive roads are in the Silverton area. Check with the Chamber of Commerce for a detailed Jeep map and for information on Jeep rentals and tours.
• Some of the clearest and cleanest air in the U.S. is just south of Silverton on top of Molas Pass. Here you can hike or bike the Colorado Trail.

▶ HISTORIC HOTEL ◀

THE GRAND IMPERIAL HOTEL, *1219 Greene St., (970) 387-5527, fax (970) 387-5529, e-mail: grandimperial@frontier.net, www.grandimperialhotel.com.* 1882 hotel with mountain views, 38 rooms, 2 suites, private baths, TV, restaurant, antiques, 100-year-old saloon, magnificent back bars. $ to $$$$ (summer)

Further Information

Silverton Area Chamber of Commerce, *P. O. Box 565, Silverton, CO 81433 (970) 387-5654, (800) 752-4494.*

Directions

From Denver, I-70 west to exit 37 (before Grand Junction), CO 141 south to US 50, south to US 550 (at Montrose), south to Silverton (about 8 hours); from Albuquerque (NM), I 25 north to NM 44 (at Bernalillo), north to NM 544 (at Bloomfield), north to US 550 (at Aztec), north to Silverton (about 5 1/2 hours).

Other Charming Colorado Towns

Crested Butte	Lake City
Cripple Creek	Leadville
Estes Park	Pagosa Springs
	Redstone

Chapter 7

CONNECTICUT

ESSEX/CHESTER
Population 5,930/3,500

The villages of **Essex** and **Chester** are the kinds of places you go when you wish to experience that New England of Christmas cards, picture calendars, and romantic old movies. Here you can start the day by jogging or biking along a wooded country road past little clusters of white clapboard houses. You can then spend part of the day sightseeing along the beautiful **Connecticut River**, and the rest browsing in galleries, boutiques, and sophisticated shops. In the evening you can relax by the fire in a gorgeous old inn after seeing a good play and dining in a world-class restaurant. It doesn't come much better.

The **Connecticut River Museum** in Essex offers a thoroughly enjoyable introduction to the region. Housed in an 1878 dockhouse, the museum's permanent and seasonal exhibits recall the long and colorful history of the Connecticut River and its beautiful valley.

Quaint shops in both villages offer a wide selection of fine and decorative artwork. For arts and crafts from another time, there's the Colonial **Pratt House** (1732/1734) in Essex. Connecticut redware and American furnishings of the 17th, 18th, and 19th centuries are among the collections of this house museum.

The natural beauty of the **Connecticut River Valley** combines with the picturesque beauty of villages like Essex and Chester to make this region an especially attractive one. There are several good ways to take in the beauty. The **Valley Railroad Company** in Essex offers excursions in vintage 1920s' steam trains along the Connecticut River to Chester and back. At **Deep River**, there's the option of getting off for a riverboat cruise up river past **Gillette Castle State Park** and the **Goodspeed Opera House**.

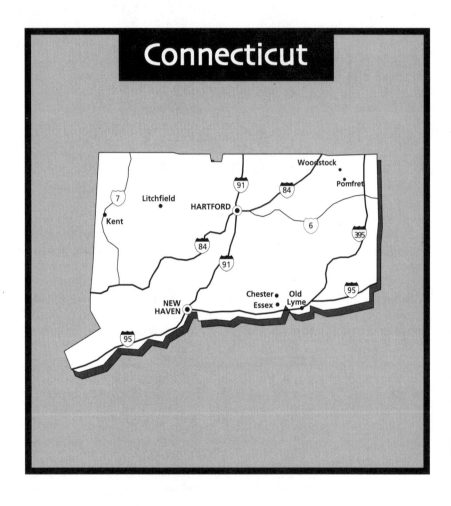

Chester Airport offers 25-minute scenic flights over the lower Connecticut River Valley. For more traditional (and shorter and cheaper) sightseeing, there's the trip across the river on the **Chester-Hadlyme Ferry**, one of the oldest continuously operating ferries in the nation.

The theater has long been important in Connecticut, and Essex and Chester maintain the tradition. Among the best-known productions are those of the **Ivoryton Playhouse** in the Ivoryton section of Essex (summer repertory) and the **Goodspeed-at-Chester/Norma Terris Theatre** (new musicals-in-progress) in the village of Chester.

• The last 38 miles on the Connecticut River have been designated one of the "Last Great Places" by The Nature Conservancy.

• Although there is still some commerce and light industry in the region, Essex—like so many places in Connecticut – is better known today as an upscale residential community.

▶ HISTORIC INN ◀

GRISWOLD INN, *36 Main St. (Essex, 06426), (860) 767-1776, fax (860) 767-0481, e-mail: griswoldinn@snet.net, www.griswoldinn.com.* Complex composed of 7 historic bldgs. in village setting, main inn the first 3-story wooden structure in Conn. (1776), 31 rooms (incl. suites), private baths, phones, expanded Cont. breakfasts, several charming dining rooms, antiques, pets with permission, acclaimed barroom, library of historic firearms, collection of marine art, entertainment, front porch on main inn. $$$ to $$$$ (seasonal)

Further Information

Connecticut River Valley & Shoreline Visitors Council, *393 Main St., Middletown, CT 06457 (860) 347-0028, (800) 486-3346, www.cttourism.org.*

Directions

From New Haven, I-95 east to exit 69, Rte. 9 north to Essex.

KENT
Population 2,900

The three parallel lines on the map signify that **Kent** is nestled in some special countryside. One of the lines is scenic U.S. 7 winding its way through the **Litchfield Hills**. A second is the **Housatonic River**, flowing alongside the highway. The third, a little to the west, is the **Appalachian Trail**, synonymous with breathtaking scenery. In addition to its lovely countryside, Kent has many beautiful mementos of some three centuries of history. The village also offers some fabulous shopping.

The sites of Kent are neatly ordered along the three parallel lines. Approaching from the south, the visitor first passes **Bull's Bridge** (1842, with ancestry to 1760), one of the only two covered bridges in Connecticut open to automobiles. The bridge and the falls beneath it are very frequently viewed through camera lenses.

Kent Center, a little more up the road, is the place for antiques, museum-quality art galleries, and both traditional and contemporary American crafts. It is also the place for some of the finest and most unusual clothing shops around.

Two miles north of Kent Center is the **Sloane-Stanley Museum**, which features works of art by noted author and artist, Eric Sloane. There is also a re-creation of Sloane's studio, an extensive collection of Early American woodworking tools and implements, and the remains of the **Kent Iron Furnace**, in operation from 1826 to 1892.

Yet a little farther north is the **Flanders Historic District**, a cluster of houses that were once part of the center of Kent. Especially noteworthy here is the **Seven Hearths Museum**, the 1754 home of the great portrait painter, George Lawrence Nelson. The home, now a museum, displays an impressive collection of Nelson's artwork and lithographs.

Special Features

Kent Falls State Park, north on U.S. 7, is known for its dramatic 200-foot cascade, the largest in the state.

With its iron ore and many smelting furnaces, this part of Connecticut was able to supply the Continental Armies in the War for Independence with hundreds of cannon.

▶ HISTORIC INN ◀

THE HOPKINS INN, *22 Hopkins Rd. (New Preston 06777), (860) 868-7295, fax (860) 868-7464, www.thehopkinsinn.com.* 1847 Federal inn overlooking Lake Waramaug, 11 rooms, 2 suites, private baths, respected dining room, country antiques, private beach, next to winery. $

Further Information

The Litchfield Hills Travel Council, *P.O. Box 968, Litchfield, CT 06759-0968 (860) 567-4506, fax (860) 567-5214, www.litchfieldhills.com (ZIP for Kent is 06757.)*.

Directions

From New York City, I-684 north to I-84, east to exit 7, north on US 7 to Kent.

LITCHFIELD
Population 1378

Litchfield is one of the finest examples of mid- and late-18th-century architecture in the U.S. It is also one of the most beautiful Colonial villages in New England. The village has been favorably compared with Williamsburg, Virginia.

The difference is that Williamsburg is a reconstruction and Litchfield is the real thing. The lovely **Litchfield Green** was laid out in the 1770s and hasn't changed much since. On the green are exactly what ought to be there: quaint shops, cozy restaurants, art galleries, and a **Congregational Church** (1829) that — of course — happens to be one of the most photographed in New England.

Grand maple-lined streets, gracious old homes, and "gentrification" in general carry the park-like Colonial charm beyond the green. Along CT 63 north and south of the green lie a living museum of gorgeous Colonial and Federal Georgian homes. To name just three: the house once owned by **Benjamin Tallmadge** (ca 1760), an aide to George Washington; **Sheldon's Tavern** (1760), where George Washington really did sleep; and the birthsite of **Harriett Beecher Stowe** (1775), author of *Uncle Tom's Cabin*.

Also on CT 63 (South) is the Neoclassical **Litchfield Historical Society Museum** with seven galleries featuring an especially fine selection of early Americana. The museum traces the history of Litchfield from Indian country to the village as it is today.

Just a little south of the museum is the **Tapping Reeve House and Law School**, the country's first law school (1774). Graduates included Vice Presidents Aaron Burr and John C. Calhoun, three Supreme Court justices, and well over a hundred cabinet members, governors, and members of Congress. The house, with finely furnished period rooms, and school are open to the public.

Special Features

Just west of Litchfield Center is Connecticut's largest natural lake, **Bantam Lake**. Bordering a major part of the shoreline is **White Memorial Foundation and Conservation Center**, Connecticut's largest nature sanctuary (4,000 acres) and nature museum.

White Flower Farm, approximately two miles from the village, is a nationally recognized nursery. Five acres of display gardens may be explored—the tuberous begonias make a visit here in July and August imperative.

Situated atop a 1,230-ft knoll just east of the village, **Topsmead State Forest** offers several miles of excellent hiking and cross-country ski trails. An English-Tudor-style "cottage" (1924), the park's principal attraction, is open during the summer months.

• Litchfield's beautiful homes and tree-lined streets belie its early history as a manufacturing center.

• Lourdes in Litchfield Shrine is modeled after Lourdes Grotto in France. The peaceful, non-commercial 35-acre shrine is a dedicated place of pilgrimage (open daily).

▶ HISTORIC INN ◀

TOLLGATE HILL INN & RESTAURANT, *Rte. 202 & Tollgate Rd., P.O. Box 1339, (860) 567-4545, fax (860) 567-8397, www.litchfieldct.com/dng/ tollgate.html.* Restored 1745 tavern on National Register, 10 rooms, 4 suites (with queen canopy beds), private baths, TV & phones, Cont. breakfasts, award-winning restaurant, antiques, pets with permission, fireplaces, outdoor decks. $$$ to $$$$

Further Information

Litchfield Hills Travel Council, *P.O. Box 968, Litchfield, CT 06759 (860) 567-4506, fax (860) 567-5214, www.litchfieldhills.com*

Directions

From Hartford, I-84 to Farmington, CT 4 west to CT 118, CT 118 west to US 202, US 202 into Litchfield.

OLD LYME
Population less than 1,000 in village

It sometimes happens that the best of an era becomes concentrated in one small spot on the map. When that happens, the beauty of the spot can become almost overwhelming. A common human reaction seems to be to grab a brush or a camera, as though caging the beauty were the only way to control it. And so it's been with **Old Lyme**.

Through the 18th century and well into the 19th, some of the most fortunate beneficiaries of the region's maritime commerce, including sea captains, built grand homes along **Lyme Street**. A few of the earliest houses were pre-Georgian; later ones displayed Georgian, Greek Revival, Italianate, and various mixtures of styles. The houses were, and are, separated by stone walls and vast, beautifully groomed grounds. Those on one side of the street back onto the **Lieutenant River**, and so views of water and salt marshes enter the scene.

It was only a matter of time before the landscape would begin attracting serious artists. And so it did, in 1899. From that year until 1937 Old Lyme was home to one of the country's first art colonies, and the center of American Impressionism. At the heart of the activity was Florence Griswold, daughter of a sea captain and heiress to one of Lyme Street's lovely mansions. Griswold didn't have the money to maintain the home, and so turned to inn keeping. The house-turned-inn became home to the art colony, and Florence Griswold became the colony's friend and advocate.

Sitting proudly on eleven landscaped acres, the 1817 Georgian mansion is now the **Florence Griswold Museum** and a National Historic Landmark. Painted on the doors and wooden dining-room panels of the house are various works of "Miss Florence's" boarders. Each has its story. A museum of history as well as art, the house features several period room settings. The addition of the recently donated **Hartford Steam Boiler Collection** makes the "Gris" one of the premier art museums of New England. The new collection is housed in the riverfront **Krieble Gallery**, a work of art in its own right and one that echoes the lighthouses, tobacco barns, coast, and river that are so iconic in Connecticut. Not far from the museum is the **Chadwick Studio**, an authentic turn-of-the-century artist's studio.

Art is also exhibited at other addresses on Lyme Street. Housed in a Federal-style home (1817, on National Register), the **Lyme Academy of Fine Arts** exhibits paintings, sculptures, and other works by students, faculty, and others. The gallery of the **Lyme Art Association** offers year-round shows of works by association members.

Even with its art aside, beautiful Old Lyme is worth some serious exploring. A National Historic District, the village is a living museum of gracious old mansions. It is also a center for fine antiques.

Special Features

Down the coast in the southeastern corner of the state is another quintessential New England seaside village, **Stonington Borough**. The borough is home to the last commercial fishing fleet in Connecticut. Of special note here are the **Old Lighthouse Museum** and the many fine examples of 18th- and 19th-century architecture. The main street is flanked by boutiques, antique shops, and several fine restaurants.

Sound View Beach is a public beach with parking and other facilities. Local residents tend to avoid the place during the warmer months.

▶ HISTORIC INN ◀

OLD LYME INN, *85 Lyme St., (860) 434-2600, (800) 434-5352, fax (860) 434-5352, olinn@aol.com, www.oldlymeinn.com.* 1850s mansion, 12 rooms, 2 suites, private baths, TV & phones, "country continental" breakfasts, highly rated dining room, antiques, pets with permission. $$$ to $$$$

Further Information

Southeastern Connecticut Tourism District, *P.O. Box 89, New London, CT 06320 (800) 863-6569*; or **Florence Griswold Museum**, *96 Lyme St., Old Lyme, CT 06371 (860) 434-5542.*

Directions

From New Haven, I-95 east to exit 70.

POMFRET/WOODSTOCK
Populations 3,220 & 6,180

Pomfret and **Woodstock** are neighboring towns up in "Connecticut's Quiet Corner." This (the northeastern) corner of the state is called "quiet" because there are no major cities or geological formations or resorts to attract major crowds of visitors. There are countless things to see and do, however, and they're the kinds of things that can be selected and combined daily—or hourly—to please any whim of mood or weather. One day might be right for the antique and craft shops, a flea market or two, and maybe a little golf. Another day might include a country fair, a trip along CT State Route 169 (a National Scenic Byway), an hour or so of apple picking. Some other options:

fishing, shopping at roadside stands, reading by the fireside, exploring quaint country roads by foot, bike, or ski.

Pomfret and Woodstock are *towns* in the New England sense, which means they are geographical-political entities that include rural areas as well as clusters of villages. Both have similar histories—largely agricultural in the 1700s, a mix of agriculture and industry in the 1800s, summer colonies for New York City's wealthy in the late 1800s and early 1900s (earning the area the nickname "the other Newport"). In recent times the towns, especially Woodstock, have attracted several small businesses, but the overall character remains rural, albeit more residential-rural than agricultural-rural.

The oldest and one of the most charming of the towns' villages is **Woodstock Hill** (settled in 1686). The oldest stone in the village's cemetery is dated 1687; many of the houses go back to the late 1700s. The pointed arches and stained-glass windows of the village's most famous house, **Bowen House** ("Roseland Cottage," 1846), speak unmistakably of the Gothic Revival period. The house's furnishings date from the mid-19th century, as does the handsome boxwood parterre garden. Guests attending Independence Day parties here included four presidents and writer Oliver Wendell Holmes. (open to public)

The **Brayton Grist Mill** and **Marcy Blacksmith Museum** in Pomfret's **Mashamoquet Brook State Park** provide an interesting view of the towns' 19th-century industrial heritage. The three-generation Marcy Blacksmith Collection, housed on the fourth floor of the mill, includes tools used for horse-shoeing, wheelwrighting, and other aspects of iron manufacture and repair.

Pure New England towns like Pomfret and Woodstock can be counted on to have several interesting old churches, and maybe a private boarding school or two. Historic churches here include Woodstock's **Baptist Church** (1840) and Pomfret's **Congregational Church** (1832) and **Christ Church** (Episcopal, 1882); the latter has several windows of Tiffany design. Some of Pomfret's prettiest buildings belong to the private **Pomfret School** (founded 1894) and **Rectory School** (founded 1921).

Special Features

Nearby **Putnam** is known as the "Antique Capital of the Northeast."

The wolf den in Pomfret's Mashamoquet Brook State Park is said to be where Revolutionary War hero General Israel Putnam slayed the last she-wolf in northeastern Connecticut.

Further Information

Northeast Connecticut Visitors District, *13 Canterbury Road, Suite 3 (MAP), P.O. Box 145, Brooklyn, CT 06234-0145 (888) 628-1228, (860) 779-6383, fax (860) 779-6390, www.ctquietcorner.org.*

Directions

From Hartford, I-84 east to exit 69, CT 74 east to US 44, east to Pomfret; also from Hartford, I-84 east to exit 73, CT 190 east to CT 197, east to North Woodstock; from Providence (RI), RI 101 or US 44 west to CT 169.

Other Charming Connecticut Towns
Madison
Salisbury
Stonington Borough
West Cornwall
Woodbury

Chapter 8

DELAWARE

NEW CASTLE
Population 4,837

Located on the **Delaware River** just south of Wilmington, **New Castle** is one of our country's finest but least known Colonial treasures. In the historic part of town are not only buildings but whole streets, some even cobbled, that look very much like they did 200 years ago. Although a town today, New Castle was once a prosperous Colonial city. Which is what makes New Castle's historic district so very precious – it isn't a reconstructed village, it's a preserved 18th-century American city!

When an 18th-century American city enters the 21st century largely intact, something in history took a wrong turn. And so it did. During the 1600s New Castle shifted back and forth between Swedish, Dutch, and English control. In the 1700s the town became the capital of the colony and, later, state of Delaware. It also became the largest city in Delaware, and one known for its wealth and refinement.

Following the Revolution, the town prospered as a transportation and trade center. Then, it happened: Around 1840, long-distance rail lines were laid through Wilmington, not New Castle. The town/city remained virtually forgotten until rediscovery in the early 1920s.

New Castle's *Heritage Trail* comprises 26 historic sites, some of them entire streets or rows of houses. The buildings, usually brick, were built throughout the 18th and into the early 19th centuries. They show several architectural styles, including Dutch, Georgian, and Federal. Most of the houses are private residences.

The **Court House** was the Colonial capitol between 1732 (date of construction) and 1777, when Dover became Delaware's capital. Standing on

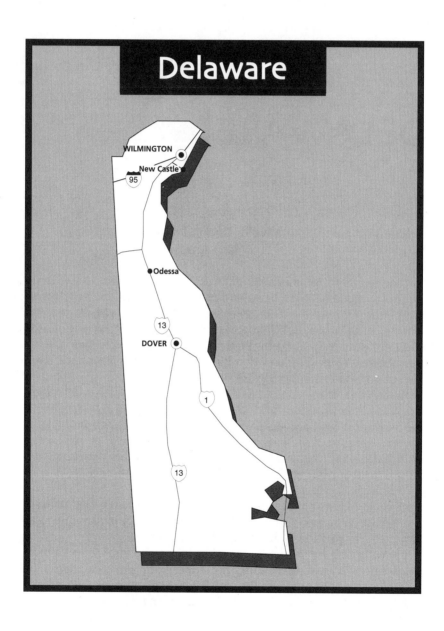

the edge of the **Green** (1655), the building is now a Delaware State Museum Site. The prisoners' dock, witness stand, and judge's bench can be seen in the restored courtroom (group tours may be arranged).

Immanuel Episcopal Church (1703; tower, 1822) was the first parish of the Church of England in Delaware. The church was rebuilt, using the original walls, after a fire in 1980. Signers of the Declaration of Independence, governors, and other historic figures are buried in the cemetery.

There are three house museums, all with period furnishings. The first, the **Dutch House** (1700), is a rare and relatively undisturbed example of a house common in Colonial times. Standing in contrast, the elegant **Amstel House** (1738) was the home of Governor Van Dyke. George Washington attended a wedding here in 1784. The third house is the Federal-style **George Read II House** (1801). With its 22 rooms and 14,000 square feet, it was once the largest house in the state. The formal garden, installed in 1847, is the oldest surviving garden in Delaware.

Special Features

Many historic homes and gardens are open to the public on *A Day in Old New Castle*, held the third Saturday in May.

Several lovely, historic mansions and gardens in or near Wilmington, several miles to the north, are open to the public. One of the most celebrated is **Winterthur**, where American decorative arts from 1640 to 1860 are displayed in two buildings on a nearly 1,000-acre estate. In one, a gallery, is an introductory exhibition; in the second, the mansion of Henry Francis du Pont, are 175 period room settings (guided tours). Complementing the house museum are 60 acres of carefully restored gardens. The garden landscape is noted for its color combinations, naturalistic planning, and finely orchestrated sequence of blooms. **Rockwood** (1851), another 19th-century estate, provides a superb example of Rural Gothic architecture and Gardenesque landscape design.

> • Famous visitors to old New Castle included William Penn, George Washington, Thomas Jefferson, the Marquis de Lafayette, Harriet Tubman, Jenny Lind, and Enrico Caruso.
> • The interior and basement of the hexagonal Old Library Museum (1892) are illuminated in part by skylights and light-sinks.

▶ HISTORIC TAVERN ◀

JESSOP'S TAVERN, *114 Delaware St., (302) 322-6111*. Tavern & Colonial restaurant in circa 1724 building serving "Dutch cheeses, English pub fare,

Swedish sauces, & old American dishes"; William & Mary Rib of Beef, Chicken Fricassee, Colonial Pot Pie among specialties. $$ to $$$

Further Information

New Castle Visitors Bureau, *P.O. Box 465, New Castle, DE 19720 (800) 758-1550;* or **George Read II House**, *42 The Strand, New Castle, DE 19720 (302) 322-8411;* or **Historical Society of Delaware**, *505 Market St., Wilmington, DE 19801 (302) 655-7161.*

Directions

From Wilmington, DE 9 south to Historic Old New Castle.

ODESSA

Population about 300

Rural **Odessa**, known until 1855 as **Cantwell's Bridge**, prospered during the 18th and 19th centuries from grain shipping and, later, the peach trade. The sources of prosperity didn't last, however, and the town's growth came to an end. Many handsome buildings from the 18th and 19th centuries survived, in large part because Odessa's commercial life had always proceeded in cooperation rather than competition with existing buildings. Today the buildings, some exquisitely restored, line the town's tree-shaded brick sidewalks.

Four of the town's most historic buildings are owned by the Winterthur Museum and Gardens. The first, the **Corbit-Sharp House** (1772/1774), is the finest example of mid-Georgian architecture in the state. Landscaped with sweeping lawns and formal gardens, the house is beautifully furnished in the style of the late 18th century.

The second structure, the stately **Wilson-Warner House** (1769), typifies a simpler form of Georgian architecture commonly found in Delaware. Itemized lists of the house's contents from 1829 have aided the Winterthur Museum in selecting and arranging the furnishings. In the rear of the house are beehive ovens and a muskrat-skinning shack. One of Delaware's oldest houses, the early 18th-century long-and-frame **Collins-Sharp House** was formed by joining two small houses. The fourth Winterthur-owned structure, the **Brick Hotel**, looks today much as it did back in 1822. Considered a step-up from the usual tavern, the hotel offered merchants, ship captains, and visitors to Cantwell's Bridge fine dining, gaming, and accommodations.

Several lovely private homes in Odessa open their doors as part of the annual *Christmas in Odessa*, first weekend in December. One of them, the circa 1780 **January House**, commands a spectacular view of the

Appoquinimink Creek and surrounding marshland. Another, the **Charles T. Polk House** (1852), is a mansion exemplifying the late Federal style.

Special Features
DE 9, which passes just to the east of town, is (deservedly) a designated scenic drive.

To the southeast of Odessa on DE 9 is the 15,122-acre **Bombay Hook National Wildlife Refuge**, a haven for waterfowl. Within the refuge are auto tour routes, walking paths, and observation trails and towers. The **Allee House**, a circa 1753 brick plantation house, is also part of the refuge (open to the public).

> In 1855, the town optimistically renamed itself Odessa after the great Russian grain-shipping port.

Further Information
Winterthur, *Rte. 52, Winterthur, DE 19735 (302) 888-4600.*

Directions
From Wilmington, US 13 south to Odessa.

Other Charming Delaware Towns
Arden
Bethel
Delaware City
Lewes

Chapter 9

FLORIDA

APALACHICOLA
Population 2,796

If the U.S. were to be divided according to its various brands of charm, the **Florida panhandle** would receive a separate listing. For it is here that the South begins to take on a hint of the tropics, and the mix can be lovely, even haunting. A very good example is **Apalachicola**, where antebellum homes and other buildings out of history share a water-surrounded town with fishing and shrimping vessels from the Gulf of Mexico.

Located at the mouth of the **Apalachicola River**, the port was one of the busiest on the gulf in the 19th century. Before the Civil War, steamboats carried cotton, timber, and other products up and down the river between here and Georgia and elsewhere. In more recent times the economy has shifted to seafood; the surrounding waters now produce most of Florida's oysters and a major part of the shellfish.

Nestled as it is on Florida's *Forgotten Coast*, Apalachicola is a quiet town with one flashing traffic light and no shopping mall within 60 miles. There are over 200 homes and commercial structures (including a sponge exchange) listed on the National Register. The moss-draped historic district and the fishing and shrimping boats have been joined by art galleries, an old-fashioned soda fountain, and families busy restoring the old houses.

There are also two small but interesting museums. The **John Gorrie State Museum** features a replica of the world's first ice machine, invented by Gorrie. The **St. Vincent National Wildlife Refuge Visitors Center** has exhibits and information on coastal wildlife and is located in town because the refuge itself occupies a barrier island accessible only by private boat.

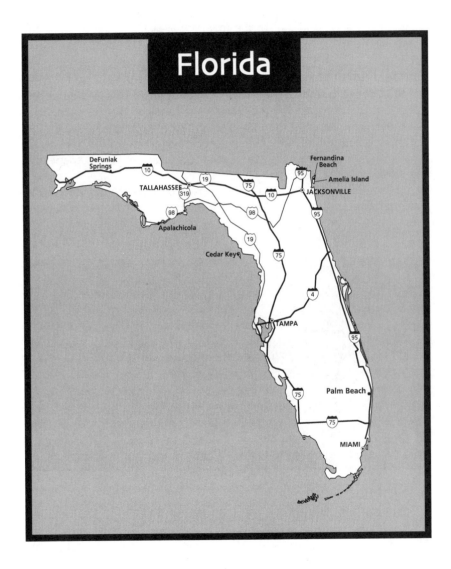

Apalachicola is obviously the place for those who love oysters, shrimp, scallops, and/or fresh fish. The seafood industry is honored the first weekend in November with the celebration of the **Florida Seafood Festival**. Among the festival's highlights are demonstrations of oyster tonging, an oyster-shucking contest, the blessing of the fleet, and arts and crafts exhibits.

Maps for a walking tour of the town are available at the chamber of commerce.

Special Features

St. George Island State Park, located 10 miles east and south of Apalachicola, is considered one of Florida's most beautiful state parks. The island park has nine miles of undeveloped beaches and dunes. Along the island's beaches, salt marshes, and forests of slash pines and live oaks dwell osprey, raccoons, ghost crabs, diamondback terrapin, and many species of shorebirds.

Encompassing over 246,000 acres in Apalachicola Bay, the **Apalachicola National Estuarine Research Reserve** is the second largest estuarine research system in the nation. The reserve's educational center includes an aviary, giant fish tanks, and exhibits on the flora and fauna of the area.

• The structure for lovely Trinity Episcopal Church (1837) was prefabricated in New York of white pine and floated in sections by schooner down the Atlantic Coast and around the Florida Keys for assembly in Apalachicola. (Trinity is the second oldest church in Florida with regularly scheduled services.) Similarly, the wood for the 1838 Thomas Ormond home, now the Ormond House State Park, was cut to measure in New York and also shipped around the keys.

• Private boaters headed for the St. Vincent National Wildlife Refuge should be prepared for the shallow waters and mosquitoes and other discomforts of this coastal wilderness.

▶ HISTORIC HOTEL ◀

THE GIBSON INN, *51 Ave. C ("at the bridge")*, *(850) 653-2191*, *e-mail: info@gibsoninn.com, www.gibsoninn.com*. Restored 1907 hotel on National Register, 30 rooms, private baths, TV & phones, Cont. breakfasts, restaurant & bar, antiques, some pets, ambiance, large wrap-around porch. $$ to $$$

Further Information
Apalachicola Bay Chamber of Commerce, *99 Market Street, Apalachicola, FL 32320 (850) 653-9419, e-mail: info@apalachicolabay.org, www.apalachicolabay.org.*

Directions
From Tallahassee, US 319/98 south to Apalachicola.

CEDAR KEY
Population 790

Three miles out in the **Gulf of Mexico** there is a little island community with just one main street, one grocery store, and no stoplights. The houses of tabby and wood, with porches and balconies, are home to families who have lived here for generations and who continue to maintain the island's traditions and memories. **Cedar Key's** atmosphere is something that has become very, very rare — something called Old Florida.

The island's 200-year history is highlighted in both the **Cedar Key State Museum** and the **Cedar Key Historical Society Museum**. Inquire at the historical society for information on a walking tour of the historic district. But take your time—hurrying doesn't agree with Cedar Key's culture, nor climate.

Very appropriately, this part of Florida's coast is called the *Nature Coast*. Cedar Key and the other tiny keys around it are a naturalist's paradise, with hundreds of species of birds and animals. Strolling along the shorelines and marshes is a favorite way to pass the time. Ospreys build their nests, Great Blue Herons and egrets wade the waters, pelicans dive and fish, dolphins play.

Cedar Key is understandably popular with seafood lovers. This is the place to sample, or gorge on if you like, smoked mullet, grouper, clams, shrimp, stone crab claws, blue crabs, soft shell crabs, oysters—all fresh from the Gulf.

Special Features
A pastime designed for lovers of charm is renting a **boat** or **kayak** and exploring the many uninhabited keys in the surrounding waters. Beyond the abundant wildlife, there's an 1850s lighthouse and artifacts, exposed by the shifting sands, from ancient Indian communities.

In addition to its first-magnitude spring, **Manatee Springs State Park** (near Chiefland) has canoe rentals and an elevated boardwalk that leads the visitor through cypress swampland on the Suwanee River.

▶ **HISTORIC HOTEL** ◀
ISLAND HOTEL, *P.O. Box 460, (352) 543-5111, (800) 432-6949, e-mail:*

tony@islandhotel-cedarkey.com, www.islandhotel-cedarkey.com. 1859 Jacobean-style inn on National Register, 10 rooms, private baths, full breakfasts, restaurant, antiques, lounge bar, long balcony with rockers. $ to $$$

> • Naturalist John Muir walked 1000 miles in 1867 to reach his destination here. He wrote, "Today I reached the sea and many gems of tiny islets called keys."
> • There are probably more artists and writers per capita on Cedar Key than in any other Florida town.

Further Information
Cedar Key Area Chamber of Commerce, *P.O. Box 610, Cedar Key, FL 32625 (352) 543-5600, www.cedarkey.org*

Directions
From Tallahassee, US 27 east to US 19, US 19 east to FL 24 (at Otter Creek), west to Cedar Key Note: From Clearwater/St. Petersburg consider using US 41 & 98 (via Brooksville) to bypass the excessive strip development on US 19 south of Spring Hill.

DEFUNIAK SPRINGS
Population 5,120

One natural event and one human event combined to produce what may be the most unique one-mile hike in the country. The natural event was the formation of a spring-fed lake, 60 feet deep and about one mile in circumference, that is almost perfectly round. It was inevitable that such a beautiful little lake would make **DeFuniak** (dee FEW nee ack) **Springs** a rather special kind of town.

The human event was the establishment of the winter capital of **Chautauqua** on the shores of the lake. Chautauqua was an institution formed in upstate New York in the latter part of the 19th century to provide summer cultural, educational, and religious programs (see Chautauqua, New York). From 1885 until the early 1920s the institution migrated to DeFuniak Springs for a winter session. Some of the people who migrated with it built handsome houses around the lake and, in some cases, became permanent residents.

The path about the lake therefore offers vistas of crystal-clear water on one side and a series of grand late 19th- and early 20th-century homes on the other. The Chamber of Commerce distributes a map and description of the buildings for a self-guided tour. Motorists may take the tour by following **Circle Drive**. The most prominent of the buildings is the **Chautauqua Auditorium** (1885, expanded in 1909), which once housed an auditorium with 4,000 inclined seats, as well as halls and classrooms. The building was reduced in size and altered in appearance by a 1975 hurricane.

One of the smallest buildings on the lake is the **Walton-DeFuniak Library**, which claims to be the "oldest structure in Florida built as a library and still serving that purpose." Inside is a substantial collection of swords and other weaponry.

Houses make up the majority of the buildings and illustrate a wide array of turn-of-the-century architectural styles. One of the most noteworthy is **Dream Cottage** (ca 1888), a Gothic Stick chalet-style house built by Wallace Bruce, American ambassador to Scotland. Four bells hanging from the gable produce a range of tones when stirred by the wind.

Two other imposing houses are **Magnolia House** (1887), which boasts 50 windows and 12 magnolia trees, and the **Elliot Home** (1907), decorated with massive Doric columns, five soaring chimneys, and an octagonal tent-roofed tower. The latter house was used to entertain celebrities during the Chautauqua sessions.

Special Features

An annual modern-day **Chautauqua Festival** is held around the lake in April.

The beaches of the **Gulf of Mexico** are only a half hour's drive to the south.

Vortex Springs at nearby Ponce de Leon offers the largest diving facility in Florida.

On the lake is a circa 1840 magnolia tree with a spreading crown of 72 feet and a trunk with a circumference of 12 1/2 feet.

Further Information

Walton County Chamber of Commerce, *95 Circle Dr., DeFuniak Springs, FL 32435 (850) 892-3191, www.waltoncountychamber.com*

Directions

From Tallahassee, I-10 west to exit 14 (DeFuniak Springs exit)

FERNANDINA BEACH
Population 10,549

American Victoriana and an ocean beach make an unlikely couple, albeit an engaging one. When the setting is palmetto Florida, the coupling is even more unlikely, and engaging. Add to the scene draping Spanish moss and the scent of magnolias and you'll understand the lure of the old seaport of **Fernandina Beach** on **Amelia Island**.

There was a time back in the 19th century when it looked as though Fernandina Beach might become a major resort center. But then, in the parting years of the century, tycoon Henry M. Flagler's East Coast Railroad bypassed the village on its way south. The railroad – and more reliably warm winter temperatures – carried tourists farther south. Today Fernandina Beach, more Southern than Floridian, boasts some 450 structures built before 1927, and more than 50 blocks of the downtown area form a historic district listed on the National Register.

The **Palace Saloon** is Florida's oldest tavern (1878). The 40-foot hand-carved mahogany bar, the stuff of which great saloons are made, provides just one of several reasons why the visitor might want to step inside. General Ulysses S. Grant once stayed at the **Florida House Inn** (1857), another gem in the historic district, now authentically restored and still very much in business (see below). The inn, built to accommodate travelers of David Levy Yulee's "Cross-Florida Railroad," is the oldest tourist hotel in continuous operation in the state. (The railroad linked Fernandina Beach to Cedar Key [see listing] on the Gulf of Mexico.)

Centre Street, the hub of the district, has been returned to a turn-of-the-century shopping district with gas lanterns and brick walks. A number of homes in the district are separately listed on the National Register; several are bed and breakfast inns.

Special Features

Construction on the brick fort in nearby **Ft. Clinch State Park** began in 1847, and continued during the Union occupation in the latter part of the Civil War, but was never completed because of obsolescence. The soldiers' barracks, prison, guardhouse, and a wooden drawbridge are among the structures that can be visited. State park reenactors portray Union troops performing daily duties such as cooking and repairing rifles. Candlelight tours are conducted on some weekends. The park's unspoiled beaches afford a view of a Florida that has largely disappeared.

Amelia Island has 13 miles of dunes and white sand beaches. Beachside horseback riding, kayaking, and fresh and saltwater fishing are among the many activities that the island offers.

• Amelia Island is sometimes called the "Isle of Eight Flags" because it is the only land in the United States that has been under eight flags.
• Fernandina Beach, the birthplace of the modern shrimping industry, is home to the world's largest producer of hand-made shrimp nets.
• Amelia Island was chosen as the mystical land for the 1998 film "Pippi Longstocking."

▶ HISTORIC HOTEL ◀

FLORIDA HOUSE INN, *22 S. 3rd St., P.O. Box 688, (800) 258-3301, fax (904) 277-3831, e-mail: Innkeepers@floridahouseinn.com, www.Floridahouseinn.com.* Oldest continuously operated hotel in Florida (1857), National Register, 14 rooms & 1 suite, private baths (some whirlpools), TV & phones, full breakfasts, dining room with country cooking served boarding-house style, pub, antiques, some pets, many fireplaces, 2-story porches front & back, large brick courtyard with fountain. $ to $$$$

Further Information

Amelia Island Chamber of Commerce, *961687 Gateway Blvd., Fernandina Beach, FL 32034 (800) 226-3542, www.ameliaisland.org.*

Directions

From Jacksonville, I-95 north to exit 373, FL A1A east 15 miles to Amelia Island.

PALM BEACH
Population 9,814 (x 2 or 3 during winter months)

The palms and the beaches are here, necessary but not sufficient. Part of the story. The other part has to do with what happens when enormous amounts of human wealth are used to turn the palms and the beaches and their 14-mile by 1/2-mile-or-so strip of land into a paradise. Not just any paradise, but a subtropical one with gorgeous flower beds and lush foliage and pastel-colored buildings that look part Spanish, part Moroccan, part Riviera. And fountains, sophisticated shops, and fashionable people. The result is **Palm Beach**, for generations an international symbol for the privileged at play.

Before Henry Morrison Flagler came along this strip of land may have looked good to shipwrecked sailors, but probably few others. Then in 1894

Flagler, one of the two or three tycoons who turned Florida into a resort state, built a large luxury hotel and connected it by means of a special spur to the main line of his Florida East Coast Railway. Other resort hotels followed and Palm Beach acquired a reputation as a playground of millionaires. Later, in the 1920s, an important part of the present town's character was molded when opulent Mediterranean palaces designed for winter escapees appeared.

The most important "sight" in Palm Beach is probably Palm Beach itself, for much of the town's beauty lies in its magnificently landscaped hotels (including the famed **Breakers**), apartment complexes, and mansions, and many of these can be enjoyed—at least from a distance—by foot, car, or bicycle. Some of the grandest of the mansions face **Ocean Boulevard**. The resort's renowned shopping district—clad in charming Mediterranean style—lies along palm-lined **Worth Avenue**.

The single best-known site is the **Henry Morrison Flagler Museum** (1901), originally a home (*Whitehall*) built by Flagler for his wife Mary Lily, then a luxury hotel, and finally a museum restored to the house's original opulence. On view are the Flaglers' period rooms—the Louis XIV Music Room, for example—with many of their original furnishings. Exhibits include collections of family art and household treasures as well as artifacts of local and Florida history. On the grounds is the restored *Rambler*, Mr. Flagler's personal railroad car (1886).

Palm Beach has had a long love affair with the arts, maybe especially the performing arts, but certainly also the fine arts. **Society of the Four Arts** (Four Arts Plaza) includes an art museum, library, and lovely gardens, all open to the public. The **Hibel Museum of Art**, dedicated to the work of Edna Hibel, is located in the flowered and fountained Regency-style **Royal Poinciana Plaza** (1957).

Broadway and off-Broadway productions are hosted by the beautiful **Royal Poinciana Playhouse**, also in the plaza. In West Palm Beach a diversity of theatrical and musical performances, some 300 of them annually, are presented on the stages of the main concert hall, playhouse, and amphitheater of the world-class **Raymond F. Kravis Center for the Performing Arts** (1992).

Palm Beach may be a playground for the rich, but the not-so-rich may play here, too. There are public beaches, municipal tennis courts, and of course, offshore sports fishing. As for golfing, Palm Beach County boasts some 160 courses! The wonderful bike trails along Northlake Way are especially recommended for those seeking to blend a little sightseeing with their exercise. (And those seeking to balance their exercise with a little nourishment are advised to check out the array of premier eateries on Worth and Australian avenues.)

Special Features

Other towns in **Palm Beach County**, just across the bridge, include **West Palm Beach**, **Lake Worth**, **Delray Beach**, and **Boca Raton**. Stop by the county's Convention and Visitors Bureau (see below) for more information.

• The land occupied by Palm Beach County is the closest in southern Florida to the climate-mellowing Gulf Stream.
• The story goes that in 1878 the "Providencia" wrecked with a large cargo of coconuts and that the palms grown from the coconuts joined the beaches in prompting the choice of the young resort's name.

Palm Beach is virtually synonymous with posh resort hotels featuring tropical gardens, pools, tennis courts, fitness centers, formal and informal dining rooms, lounges, live entertainment, etc. Some are listed on the National Register of Historic Places. Daily rates for a double in the winter months can run into hundreds of dollars; during the warmer months, however, rates may fall to less than $150, sometimes less than $100. In addition to the Chesterfield (below), a list of the grand hotels would include the **Brazilian Court**, **Breakers**, **Four Seasons Resort Palm Beach**, **Palm Beach Hilton**, **Palm Beach Hotel**, and **Ritz-Carlton, Palm Beach**.

▶ HISTORIC HOTEL ◀

CHESTERFIELD HOTEL, *363 Cocoanut Row, (561) 659-5800, (800) 243-7871.* Beautifully restored 1926 hotel, 55 individually decorated rooms, private baths, TV & phones, restaurant, Leopard Lounge (popular with celebrities), library, cigar room, swimming pool with lush tropical vegetation, legendary following. $$$ to $$$$ (seasonal)

Further Information

Palm Beach Chamber of Commerce, *45 Cocoanut Row, Palm Beach, FL 33480*; also, **Palm Beach County Convention and Visitors Bureau**, *1555 Palm Beach Lakes Blvd., Suite 800, West Palm Beach, FL 33401 (561) 233-3000, (800) 554-PALM, fax (561) 471-3990, www.palmbeachfl.com.*

Directions

From Fort Lauderdale and Miami, north on I-95 or Florida's Turnpike to FL 704 (Okeechobee Blvd.), east to Palm Beach.

Other Charming Florida Towns

Cabbage Key/Useppa Island	Seaside
Micanopy	Starke
Mt. Dora	St. Augustine

Chapter 10

GEORGIA

DAHLONEGA
Population 3,700

Nestled in the foothills of the beautiful **Blue Ridge Mountains**, pictur-esque **Dahlonega** is probably the only town in the country where you can pan for gold in the morning, shop for Appalachian crafts in the afternoon, dine on fried chicken served country-style in the evening, and canoe the next morning on a mountain stream.

Twenty years before gold was discovered in California, the Cherokee Nation in northern Georgia saw the first major gold rush in the United States. The smell of gold attracted thousands to the area in 1828, and prospectors continued coming for the next 20 years. Dahlonega (accent on second syllable) did well: Over $6 million in gold was coined by the U.S. Branch Mint in Dahlonega between 1838 and 1861.

Gold is still very much a part of the Dahlonega scene. The **Gold Museum**, once the **Lumpkin County Courthouse** (1836), is the oldest public building in north Georgia (it is also one of the state's most visited historic sites.) Here are displayed gold coins minted at Dahlonega as well as locally discovered gold nuggets, one over 5 ounces.

Dahlonega's delightful little true-shaded **square** could be used to define the term" charming. True to form, dozens of 19th-century houses and shops listed on the National Register of Historic Sites dot the square and surrounding streets. Local crafts and gold jewelry are among the items of special regional interest offered in the many colorful shops. (See the welcome center for walking and auto tours.)

Consolidated Gold Mines, the largest gold mining operation east of the Mississippi (closed in the 1930s), offers tours which include a trip down a 250-

Georgia

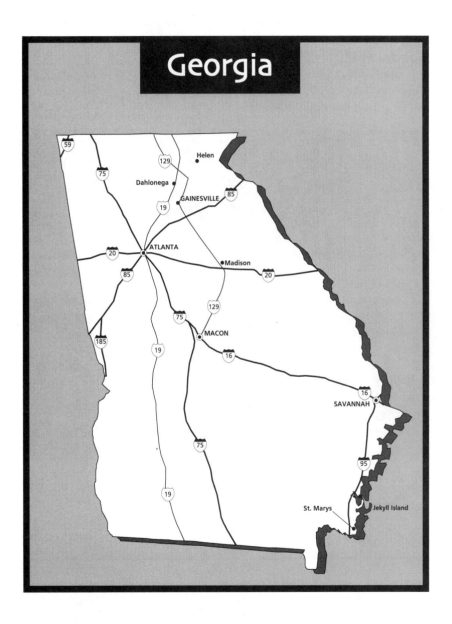

foot hole (called the *Glory Hole*). Here and at several other places in the area visitors preferring the do-it-yourself (and keep-what-you-find) route are welcome to pan for gold. Prospecting equipment is available in shops in town and at the panning sites. Trying to "find color" is Dahlonega's most popular visitor pastime.

Special Features

With 47% of Lumpkin County in the national forest, and **Appalachian Trail** and **Desoto Falls Scenic Area** just a few miles away, hiking, camping, fishing, and canoeing opportunities abound.

- The Smith House (1884) is a 70-year-old restaurant, an old-fashioned mountain inn, and beloved town landmark.
- A prospecting party from nearby Auraria founded the first settlement at the present site of Denver, Colorado and named it after their hometown (Aurora is now a major Denver suburb).

▶ HISTORIC INN ◀

THE SMITH HOUSE, *84 S. Chestatee St., (800) 852-9577, (706) 867-7000, fax (706) 864-7564, e-mail: info@smithhouse.com, www.smithhouse.com.* 1884 home converted to inn in 1922, 16 rooms & 2 villas, private baths, TV & phones, expanded Cont. breakfasts, dining room serving Southern-style cooking family-style, some antiques, wide verandah, pool, general store, on vein of gold. $ to $$$$

Further Information

Dahlonega-Lumpkin County Chamber of Commerce, *13 South Park St., Dahlonega, GA 30533 (800) 231-5543, (706) 864-3711.*

Directions

From Atlanta, US 19 / GA 400N north to Dahlonega.

HELEN
Population 300

The 'Alpine Village of Helen' is a picture-book Bavarian village nestled among the mountains, forests, lakes, and waterfalls of northeast Georgia. Viewed from afar, the village is a cluster of old-world towers, rust-colored roofs, and gabled Bavarian facades.

Closer up, the place becomes a colorful mosaic of cobblestone alleys, balconies, outdoor cafes, and cascading flower baskets. Some of the townspeople dress in Bavarian attire. The little Georgia town obviously has a story to tell.

Helen's story has a much larger Cinderella component than do the stories of most towns. Originally a gold-mining town (part of Georgia's "Great Gold Rush"), then until the 1920s a sawmill town, Helen entered the post-war era without much of a future. In the late 1960s several local businessmen decided that the bleak little place could stand some improvement. They turned to John Kollock, a local artist, and within a week were presented with a set of watercolor sketches of an Alpine Helen. Liking what they saw, a decision was made to proceed.

The transformation quickly became a community affair. Business people renovated their shops, the city put up quaint street lights and planters, and the townsfolk planted trees and flowers. New businesses put up new buildings. Power lines went underground. The work is still in progress.

More than 200 specialty and import shops now line Helen's streets and alleys. There is also a delightful collection of pubs and lodgings. The restaurant menus are about as loyal to their German and Austrian counterparts as menus on this side of the Atlantic are likely to get. For those not wishing to tour the town on foot, there are horse-drawn buggies and a village trolley.

Because the **Chattahoochee River** runs right through town, Helen is able to provide a morning of shopping to one part of the family while offering tubing, canoeing, gold mining, or trout fishing to another. Golfing is also an option. Hiking, backpacking, and horseback riding are just a few of the other activities pursued in the area. The **Appalachian Trail** passes north of town.

Special Features

Unicoi State Park, just north of Helen, provides a scenic setting for canoeing, fishing, and also has public beaches and a dining room.

Beginning just outside of town, the **Richard B. Russell Scenic Highway** (GA 348) winds through a particularly beautiful section of Georgia's **Blue Ridge Mountains**.

• Helen's 6-to-8-week Oktoberfest attracts as many as 150,000 visitors.
• Artist John Kollock's Alpine images were inspired by a stay in Bavaria with the army.

Further Information

Alpine Helen/White County Convention & Visitors Bureau, *P.O. Box 730, Helen, GA 30545 (706) 878-2181, (800) 858-8027, fax (706) 878-4032, www.helenga.org.*

Directions

From Atlanta, I-85 northeast to exit 45, I-985 / GA 365 north to GA 384, GA 384 to GA 75, GA 75 north to Helen.

JEKYLL ISLAND
Population 1,000

A sea of green surrounds your car as you drive to **Jekyll Island**. No strip malls or suburban sprawl, just lush marshland (called the marshes of Glynn) as far as the eye can focus. But getting to Jekyll Island only hints at what lies ahead, for at the end of the causeway awaits an island community that must surely rank among the most idyllic in the country.

Lying just six miles out to sea, Jekyll Island attracted any number of early visitors: the Guale Indians, Spanish missionaries, pirates, British explorers, plantation owners. The island's modern history began in 1886, when a group of American millionaires purchased the island and established the Jekyll Island Club. With a membership roster restricted to 100, and including such names as Rockefeller, Pulitzer, Morgan, Gould, Vanderbilt, Goodyear, and Macy, the club became one of the most exclusive in the world. Many of the members stayed at the Club House, but others built mansions modestly called "cottages" (see also Lenox and Stockbridge, Mass.).

The Depression and demands of W.W. II finally brought an end to the club in 1942. The State of Georgia bought the island in 1947, and in the following years the causeway was built and, in what became one of the largest restoration projects in the Southeast, preservation of the historic club buildings begun. In 1978 the 240-acre **Jekyll Island Club Historic District** was designated a National Historic Landmark.

Today there are two Jekyll Islands: the historic district and the Jekyll Island resort community. The historic district includes more than 30 buildings, many restored and others undergoing restoration. Of particular interest are the elegant **Jekyll Island Club Hotel** (see below), originally the Club House and every bit as grand as it was 100 years ago, and **Faith Chapel** (1904), a charming structure adorned by a Tiffany stained-glass window and, inside, hand-carved animal heads on the exposed beams. There are also the various "cottages" (ca 1884 to ca 1927); many now house period furnishings, art treasures, photograph collections, and other mementos of the Jekyll Island

Club era. Several of the structures may be visited via historic and architectural tours (information and tickets available at the Museum Visitors Center).

Jekyll Island's **resort community** is a collection of motor inns, resorts, restaurants, condominiums, private homes, and shops carefully placed among expanses of natural woodland to create an uncluttered, relaxed park-like setting. The recreational facilities are impressive: four golf courses, a 13-court tennis complex, inshore and offshore fishing (both salt- and fresh-water), cruises that specialize in everything from dolphins to sunsets, an 11-acre water park, 20 miles of bike and jogging trails, a fitness center. And above all, miles and miles of uncrowded beaches!

- The first transcontinental phone call was made from Jekyll Island on January 25, 1915.
- The country's last major cargo of slaves was unloaded on Jekyll Island in 1858.

▶ HISTORIC HOTEL ◀

THE JEKYLL ISLAND CLUB HOTEL, *371 Riverview Dr., (800) 535-9547, fax (912) 635-2818, e-mail: jekyllsales@jekyllclub.com, www.jekyllclub.com.* Turn-of-century hotel, National Historic Landmark, 157 rooms, 19 suites, 2 cottages, 1 condominium, private baths, TV & phones, grand dining room, antiques, 4-story grand staircase, chandeliers, antique mirrors, potted palms in Oriental vases, mahogany furnishings, cafe, English-style pub, grill, snack bar, boutiques, verandahs with wicker rockers, 1927 pool, croquet greensward, marina, golf, tennis. $$ to $$$$

Further Information

Jekyll Island Convention & Visitors Bureau, *P.O. Box 13186, Jekyll Island, GA 31527 (877) 453-5955, (912) 635-3636, www.jekyllisland.com*

Directions

From Savanna, I-95 south to exit 6, US 17 east to Jekyll Island causeway (GA 520); from Jacksonville, FL, I-95 north to exit 6, as above

MADISON
Population 3,800

Gone with the Wind was a work of fiction, but a Grand Old South did in fact exist in Georgia, at least for a fortunate few, and a number of scenes from

Georgia's Old South may still be seen. **Madison** is one of them. The town's National Historic District is an image from another era. Parts of it are virtually the same today as they were on the eve of the Civil War. Maybe they're even prettier.

The town lay smack in the middle of General Sherman's path, and yet survived. It seems that as the Yankees advanced, a delegation of men led by Senator Joshua Hill (an early foe of secession) pleaded with the general to spare the town. Sherman obliged – although the railroad station and some surrounding plantations were kindled – and the town was subsequently known as "the town Sherman refused to burn."

The welcome center, housed in the 1887 city hall and fire station, provides a brochure for a walking tour of the historic district. Among the over 40 structures on the tour are four whose doors are regularly open to the public: The oldest is the **Rogers House** (circa 1809-1810), which has been carefully restored to what it probably looked like in 1873. The house, a fine example of the Piedmont-Plain style of architecture, has mid-19th-century furnishings. The stately Greek Revival **Heritage Hall** (1833-35) is currently the home of the **Morgan County Historical Society**. Built by a doctor who served with the Confederacy, the house is distinguished by its window etchings, ghost bedroom, and exquisite period furnishings.

The **Madison-Morgan Cultural Center**, a restored 1895 Romanesque Revival school building, boasts an 1895 Schoolroom Museum, art galleries, Piedmont History Museum, and unique auditorium. The center sponsors a rich variety of cultural and educational programs. The **African-American Museum**, the fourth historic building open to the public, is housed in the recently restored **Horace Moore House** (ca 1895). The museum displays paintings, other works of art, and memorabilia honoring the area's Black heritage.

Many of the houses are shown during tours in May, October, and December. Private tours of some may also be arranged during other months. Whether or not their doors are open, the unusually well-restored and maintained homes in the historic district merit a walk- or drive-by.

Three antebellum churches also merit a visit: The **Advent Episcopal Church** (ca 1842) with its wrought-iron chandeliers and slave gallery, now used for the organ and choir; the **Madison Baptist Church** (1858), built by bricks hand-made by slaves on a local plantation; and the "Old English"-style **Presbyterian Church** (1842), noted for its Tiffany stained windows and a silver communion service, still in use, that was stolen during the Civil War and later returned by Federal orders. The churches are usually open daily.

Madison's preserved downtown is the kind designed to delight antique hunters, casual shoppers, and just plain lovers of charm. There are brick sidewalks, an old-fashioned soda fountain, and interesting shops. One of the largest antique stores is located in a restored 1880s hotel building.

Special Features

Madison's antebellum homes weren't the only ones to escape General Sherman's march to the sea. Other antebellum structures within easy driving distance from Madison may be found in **Eatonton**, **Social Circle**, and **Washington**.

With 19,000 acres, **Lake Oconee**, east of town, is Georgia's second largest lake. The lake's shores and waters offer numerous recreational opportunities.

> Madison was once described as the "wealthiest and most aristocratic town" on the stagecoach route between Charleston and New Orleans.

Further Information

Madison Convention & Visitors Bureau, *P.O. Box 826, Madison, GA 30650 (706) 342-4454, (800) 709-7406, fax (706) 342-4455.*

Directions

From Atlanta, I-20 east to exit 51, north on US 441.

ST. MARYS
Population 8,187

With lovely antebellum buildings, gentle breezes off the sea, and wide avenues shaded by ancient live oaks, **St. Marys** is a town of many memories and moods. As the gateway to **Cumberland Island National Seashore** (see below) and neighbor to a naval base, St. Marys has a present and future as well as a past. But it is quiet here, and very beautiful.

Turbulent is perhaps the best term to describe St. Marys's past. Settled in 1787, the town has known smuggling, a slave trade, the scourge of yellow fever, periods of economic depression, and ravaging by the British in the War of 1812 and the Yankees in the Civil War. But there have also been times of peace and – thanks to shipping, timber, shrimping and, more recently, a paper mill and submarine base – periods of prosperity.

A 20-block area in the older section of town has been placed on the National Register of Historic Places. The streets in this district are the same as on the original 1788 town map and bear the names of the town's founders.

Orange Hall, St. Marys's venerable landmark, is a circa 1830 Greek Revival Mansion built by the town's first Presbyterian minister. The house is listed on the National Register and now serves as a welcome center for the tourism council (open daily).

Among the historic district's antebellum buildings are several churches with interesting credentials. The **First Presbyterian Church** (1808) is the oldest Presbyterian church in continuous use in Georgia. **St. Marys Methodist Church** (1858), organized in 1799, is the Mother Church of Methodism in Florida (which begins just across the St. Marys River). And the **Old Catholic Church** is housed in the oldest masonry bank building still standing in Georgia (1837).

The **Toonerville Trolley** is probably the district's most unique possession. A passenger rail car on the St. Marys Railroad from 1928 until 1938, the trolley was made famous in the nationally syndicated comic strip *Wash Tubbs and Easy* in 1935. It is still operated on special occasions.

On display at the **St. Marys Submarine Museum** are a working periscope, models of torpedoes, submarine uniforms, and countless other submarine memorabilia. The museum is housed in an early 19th-century movie theater on the town's waterfront.

Soldiers of every American war, yellow fever victims, Acadians, and others are buried in **Oak Grove Cemetery**. The oldest marked gravesites are dated 1801.

Surrounded by water, St. Marys is an ideal spot for photographers, hikers, bikers, birders, fishermen, and boaters. A good place to see the flora and fauna is on a nature trail at **Crooked River State Park**. Visitors are welcome on the greens of nearby **Osprey Cove Golf Course**.

Special Features

Boats depart daily from St. Marys for **Cumberland Island National Seashore**, located on the southernmost of Georgia's sea islands. Here there are 16 miles of undisturbed white-sand beach bordered by dunes that rise as high as 40 feet. Herds of horses graze openly on the island, and loggerhead turtles come ashore to lay their eggs. No vehicles are available, so walking and swimming (no lifeguards) are the only ways of moving about.

On some Sundays the boat to Cumberland Island puts in at **Plum Orchard Dock**. Plum Orchard is a magnificent Georgian Revival mansion constructed by Lucy Carnegie for her son and his wife in 1898.

- The Washington Pump, still around, was the only source of fresh water during the tidal wave of 1880.
- Many sites in the historic district are marked in Braille for sight-impaired visitors.

▶ HISTORIC HOTELS ◀

RIVERVIEW HOTEL, *105 Osborne St., (912) 882-3242, e-mail: gaila@eagnet.com.* 1916 hotel owned by same family since early 1920s, private baths, TV, Cont. breakfasts, Seagle's Waterfront Café, period furnishings, pets with permission, picnic lunches, verandah with rocking chairs, overlooking St. Marys River and historic downtown. $

THE SPENCER HOUSE INN, *200 Osborne St., (912) 882-1872, www.spencerhouseinn.com.* Renovated 1872 hotel with original moldings/ floors, 14 rooms, private baths, TV & phones, full breakfasts, elegant furnishings, elevator, 2 verandahs overlooking historic downtown. $$ to $$$

Further Information

St. Marys Tourism Council, *P.O. Box 1291, St. Marys, GA 31558 (912) 882-6200, (800) 868-8687, fax (912) 882-5506, e-mail: info@stmaryswelcome.com, www.stmaryswelcome.com.*

Directions

From Jacksonville (FL), I-95 north to exit 2, GA 40 east to St. Marys.

Other Charming Georgia Towns
Cleveland
Eatonton
Hiawasee
Newnan
Pine Mt./Warm Springs
St. Simons Island
Social Circle
Washington

Chapter 11

HAWAII

HALEIWA, OAHU
Population 2,442

Haleiwa's brand of charm is one of the most delightfully unusual in the country. The old wooden buildings along the main road, or **Kam.** (for **Kamehameha**) **Highway**, look very much like those you might find in an old Western town. Yet many of the shops sell clothing and supplies for distinctly non-Old-West surfers, snorkelers, and other ocean sports fans. In the restaurants, surf enthusiasts mingle with art enthusiasts attracted by Haleiwa's first-rate galleries. Down the road lies a picturesque little harbor offering charters for deep-sea fishing, snorkel excursions (summer), and whale-watch sails (winter). And then come miles of coastline boasting some of the most beautiful beaches in the world!

Oahu's **North Shore**, on which Haleiwa rests, is the world's surfing capital. Most of the year the waters are quiet, ideal for all kinds of water activities. But from October through March the waters become very active (and dangerous)—and a paradise for professional surfers. As an example, the average height of the winter waves at **Sunset Beach** is 15 feet. Monster waves measuring 35 and 40 feet are not unknown. Surfers from around the world come to meet the challenge, and surfing spectators follow for the excitement and beauty.

Haleiwa (hah lay EE vah) is of course also active during the winter months, in concert with the swells and those who ride and watch them. But during the rest of the year the town, like the water, is quiet. This is a part of Oahu that is still largely rural. The area is in fact called "the country." There are still pineapple fields here. Proud of its plantation/rural heritage, Haleiwa actively strives to preserve it. The facades of historic wood buildings are protected, and

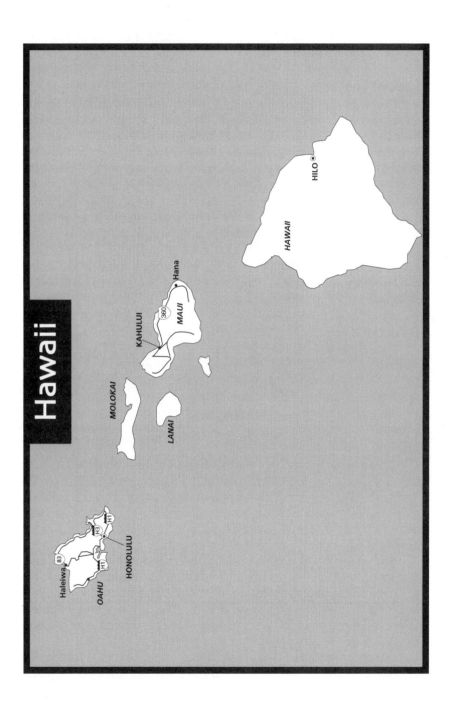

the historic appearance of Kamehameha Highway is maintained by imposing strict design codes on new construction. The result is a lovely little rural town on Hawaii's most urbanized island.

Special Features

Down the coast just a few miles is one of Hawaii's most beautiful and historic properties, **Waimea Falls Park**. The 1,800-acre park is home to native birds and animals and to thousands of tropical plants displayed in more than 30 gardens. The lush, exotic grounds and the 45-foot waterfall may be toured by foot and/or by open-air tram. Among the park's many attractions are cliff divers and demonstrations of traditional Hawaiian games. It is also a popular location for garden weddings.

At the **Dole Plantation** near **Wahiawa**, a garden featuring a variety of pineapple plants is open to the public.

Further Information

North Shore News, *P. O. Box 1117, Haleiwa, Oahu, HI 96712 (808) 637-3138, www.northshorenews.com.*

Directions

From Honolulu, I-H1 west to HI 99, HI 99 north to HI 83, HI 83 north to Haleiwa.

HANA, MAUI
Population about 1,200

Once a bustling sugar town, historic **Hana** is today a country-quiet village famed for its untouched natural beauty and relaxed lifestyle. Far from the intense development elsewhere on Maui, this is a peaceful tropical paradise, the enchanting Hawaii of picture postcard and movie. This is the Hawaii where swimmers may choose between a tropical pool or one of several ocean beaches – a black one, a red one, and a silver one.

Consistent with its gorgeous setting, Hana has little commercial development. And what little there is can be interesting. For example, the bank has a sign announcing that the doors are open from 3:00 to 4:30 p.m. daily, except on Fridays, when closing time is extended to 6:00. And **Hasegawa's General Store**, in business since 1910, stocks horseshoe nails, barbed wire, and bolo knives side by side with potato chips and pickled turnips.

One of the most interesting of Hana's historic structures is the **Wananalua Church** (circa 1840), built of lava rock. The area is rich with archaeological remnants from the early Hawaiian culture; most are unmarked, however, so inquire locally for information.

Driving to Hana is itself an eye-dazzling adventure. The narrow coastal road (HI 360) twists along cliffs, over streams and waterfalls, and through lush tropical foliage. People who have counted them report that the road has over 600 curves and 55 or so one-lane bridges. Allow about 3 hours each way.

Note: I wish to thank Carl Lindquist, long-time Hana resident and author of *On the Hana Coast*, for his contributions to this piece. (*On the Hana Coast* may be obtained by writing P. O. Box 507, Hana, Hawaii 96713.)

Special Features

Eleven miles down the coast from Hana is **'Ohe'o Gulch**, renowned for its series of lovely stream-carved pools and tropical rain forest setting. Trails lead to several waterfalls. The gulch is a section of **Haleakala National Park**.

Cabins and camping are available at nearby **Wai'anapanapa State Park** (permit required). The park features a cave and scenic hiking trails along the shore. Camping is also available at **Kipahulu Federal Park** (part of Haleakala National Park).

> One of the most popular tourist items in Hana is a t-shirt proclaiming that its wearer has "Survived the Road to Hana."

▶ HISTORIC HOTEL ◀

HOTEL HANA-MAUI *(Hana, Maui 96713), (808) 248-8211, (800) 321-4262, fax (808) 248-7202, e-mail: information@hotelhanamaui.com, www.hotelhanamaui.com.* Small hotel & cottages of old sugar plantation, 18 rooms, 7 suites, 40 cottages, 1 house, private baths, phones, dining room, Hawaiian art & antiques, fruit baskets, meal-inclusive packages, gardens & grounds, pool, wellness center, Jeep excursions, horseback riding. $$$$

Further Information

Maui Visitors Bureau, *1727 Wili Pa Loop, P.O. Box 580, Wailuku, HI 96793 (800) 525-6284, (808) 244-3530, www.visitmaui.com (ZIP for Hana is 96713.)*

Directions

From Kahului, HI 360 east to Hana. Hana is also served by **Pacific Wings**.

Other Charming Hawaiian Towns

Hanalei, Kauai
Kailua Kona, Hawaii
Kilauea, Kauai
Lahaina, Maui

Chapter 12

IDAHO

STANLEY
Population 92

Only 92 souls and sundry aspens, pines, and firs live along **Stanley's** few streets. The streets are gravel, even the main street, and there are no sidewalks. Many of the homes are old cabins. Yet the town, elevation 6,260 feet, is surrounded by some of the most glorious scenery on the continent.

Situated on the Salmon River in the northern part of the spectacular **Sawtooth National Recreation Area**, Stanley is nestled among pristine mountain ranges, dense forests, and over 1,100 lakes. Three **National Forest Scenic Byways** – the **Sawtooth**, the **Ponderosa Pine**, and the **Salmon River** – converge on the town. Stanley was obviously designed for the nature lover, the outdoor sportsperson, the photographer, and the artist.

The **Stanley Museum** displays artifacts and photographs from the early days of the Sawtooth Valley and the Stanley Basin. The **Custer Museum**, 30 minutes north of town, features a ghost town and mining-history museum. Interesting old tombstones can be found in **Boot Hill Cemetery**, near the museum.

Virtually every land sport – and many of the water ones, too — known to the Western world can be pursued in these parts. Outfitters and guides abound. For snowmobilers there is the groomed *Highway to Heaven* trail from Boise or Lowman to Stanley. For hut skiers there are stationary circular tents with bunks, cooking equipment, and wood stoves. For wilderness floaters there is the **Middle Fork** of the beautiful **Salmon River** (three- to six-day trips by raft, oar boat, and paddle boat can be arranged in Stanley).

And for people in a hurry there are scenic air tours.

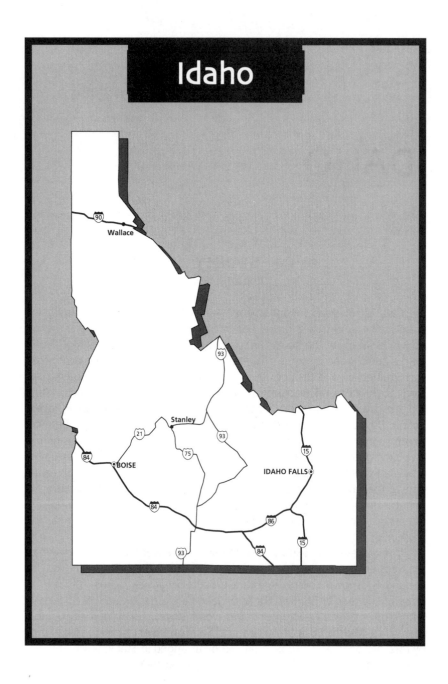

Special Features

The **Sawtooth National Recreation** area is an eye-dazzling wilderness tamed only by the occasional guest ranch, resort, and horse trail. This is the kind of country that deserves to be seen from the back of a horse, and outfitters and guides are available to help you do just that.

> Stanley really consists of two towns, incorporated upper Stanley and unincorporated lower Stanley. The two are about one mile apart and have different histories.

Further Information

Stanley-Sawtooth Chamber of Commerce, *P.O. Box 8, Stanley, ID 83278 (208) 774-3411, (800) 878-7950, www.Stanleycc.org.*

Directions

From Boise, ID 21 east and north to Stanley; from Twin Falls, ID 75 north to Stanley.

WALLACE
Population 1010

Many of the descendants of late 19th-century mining towns are today among the West's most charming places. And so it is with **Wallace**, now listed on the National Historic Register and featuring turn-of-the-century buildings, unique shops, art galleries, museums, a new visitor center and **Mine Heritage Exhibition**, even a melodrama.

Wallace's history is nicely wrapped up in its nickname, *The Silver Capital of the World*. At the turn of the century Wallace was the center of action in the **Silver Valley**, a scenic valley that happens (even to this day) to be one of the richest mining districts on the planet. As might be expected, most of Wallace's top attractions relate in one way or another to silver.

The displays and exhibits of the **Wallace District Mining Museum** portray without glamour life as it was in the old mines and mining camps. A 20-minute video presentation discusses the history and technology of mining. Included in the exhibits are old photographs, a collection of paintings by James R. Buckham (born and raised in Wallace), and the world's largest "silver" dollar, weighing in at 150 pounds.

The bricks used to build the **Northern Pacific Depot**, now a railroad museum, served as ballast in sailing ships coming over from China. The restored building houses photographs and artifacts from the mining district's early days.

The escorted tour of the **Sierra Silver Mine** proceeds through an underground tunnel that stretches for five blocks. Along the way is a 149-foot shaft now filled with water. A guide explains and demonstrates mining procedures, equipment, and safety precautions. A trolley carries visitors to and from the mine's entrance.

The **Oasis Bordello Museum** gives visitors a look at the bawdier side of old Wild West mining communities.

On a different note, art exhibits and classes are offered at the **Wallace District Arts Council**. Bullet marks resulting from an old shootout can be seen in the wooden floors of the building (1908) housing the center. The **Sixth Street Melodrama Theatre** hosts live performances year 'round.

Detailed descriptions of Wallace's many well-preserved turn-of-the-century buildings are provided in a booklet distributed by the CoC. The information is nicely arranged for a self-guided walking tour. Some of Wallace's attractions are seasonal, but many are not. Skiers, snowmobilers, and other off-season visitors will discover that Wallace's charm can be enjoyed year-round.

Special Feature

The Wallace CoC distributes instructions for a scenic and historical loop that includes a "living ghost town," gold rush camps, ancient towering cedars, and the spot where Wyatt Earp owned and operated a saloon.

- Wallace was established in 1884 by prospector William R. Wallace, cousin to novelist, general, and statesman Lew Wallace. The town was first called Placer Village and renamed in 1985.
- Idahoans are proud to boast that the Silver Valley is the only place in the world that has produced a "billion" ounces of silver in less than a century.
- Wallace has starred in two productions of the silver screen, "Heaven's Gate" and "Dante's Peak."

▶ HISTORIC HOTEL ◀

JAMESON B&B, *304 6th St., (208) 556-6000, fax (208) 753-0981, e-mail: rshaffer@nidlink.com.* Restored 3-story 1892 hotel on National Register, 6 rooms, "limited" breakfasts, 1900 dining room, antiques, saloon with 12-ft Brunswick mirror back bar, sitting/reading area, setting for films. $$

Further Information

Historic Wallace Chamber of Commerce and Visitor Center, *P.O. Box 1167, #10 River St., Wallace, ID 83873 (208) 753-7151, www.historicwallace.org.*

Directions

From Spokane (WA), I-90 east to exits 61 and 62 (Wallace exits); from Missoula (MT), I-90 west to exits 62 and 61.

Other Charming Idaho Towns
Lava Hot Springs
McCall
Sandpoint

Chapter 13

ILLINOIS

BISHOP HILL
Population 135

Communal societies founded by groups of Europeans seeking religious freedom once dotted the fertile Midwestern countryside. The history of their settlement in America usually began with a year or so of hardship, continued with several years of prosperity, and then, for various reasons, ended in a period of abandonment and decay. In many cases the settlements' remnants were "discovered" a century later, a preservation society formed, and restoration begun. One of their legacies today is a group of unusually quaint towns and villages sprinkled across the rich American prairie. No fewer than five of them appear in this book: New Harmony, Ind.; the Amana Colonies in Iowa; Pleasant Hill, Ky.; Zoar Village, Ohio; and **Bishop Hill**, Ill.

Bishop Hill, called "Utopia on the Prairie," began in 1846 with a group of Swedish religious dissidents. After spending their first months hungry and living in dugouts, the colonists entered an era of amazing commercial and agricultural activity, and then, rather suddenly, disbanded (in 1861)—in this case because of charges of financial mismanagement, internal dissension, and events associated with the Civil War.

Following a period of inactivity, interest in preserving, restoring, and rebuilding the colony's buildings prompted the formation in 1962 of the Bishop Hill Heritage Association. Still undergoing restoration, Bishop Hill is today a quaint little town out on the Illinois prairie with status as a National Historic Landmark and State Historic Site.

The Illinois Historic Preservation Agency maintains three of the village buildings—the Colony Church, Colony Hotel, and Bishop Hill Museum—as well as the lovely village park (1853). The basement and first floor of the **Colony**

Illinois

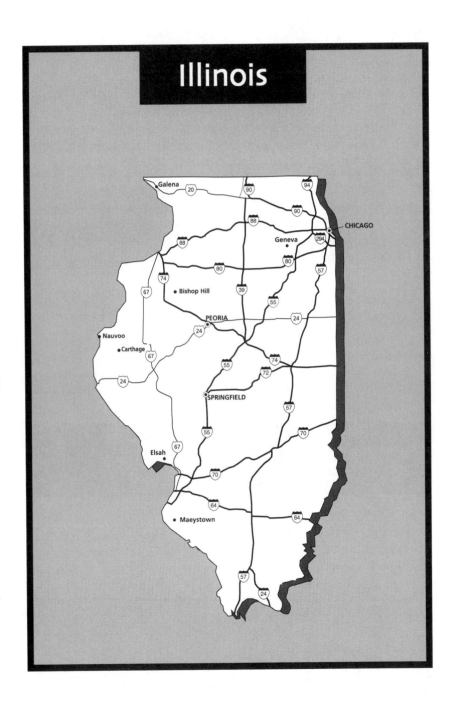

Church (1848; open to public), the settlement's first permanent building, were used as living quarters. The sanctuary, on the second floor, is noteworthy for its simplicity and handmade black walnut pews. The women's and men's pews are separated by a divider.

The restored **Colony Hotel** (1852; open to public) sports a square cupola and a third-floor ballroom. Named the Bjorklund Hotel after its second proprietor, the establishment was once communally owned.

Paintings by folk artist and early resident Olof Krans are on display in the **Bishop Hill Museum**. These as well as other exhibits give a glimpse of the Bishop Hill Colony.

In addition to the Colony Church and Colony Hotel, 10 or so of the colony's original buildings still stand. Of special note is the **Steeple Building** (1854), housing the exhibits of the **Bishop Hill Heritage Museum** (open to public).

Scattered about the village are a number of interesting shops stocked with antiques, collectibles, and gifts; as might be expected, many of the items are handcrafted and/or of Swedish import. The village also features craft demonstrations and an especially rich calendar of events (check with the heritage association—see below).

Special Features

The **Jenny Lind Chapel** is located in nearby **Andover**. The little Greek Revival chapel was endowed by the famous opera star.

A farm museum (tours available) is housed on the main floor of **Ryan's Round Barn** (1910), a beautifully preserved structure in **Johnson Sauk Trail State Park** a few miles east of Bishop Hill.

> Many of the colony's first settlers walked the 160 miles from Chicago to Bishop Hill.

▶ HISTORIC INN ◀

THE BISHOP HILL COLONY HOSPITAL B&B, *110 N. Olson St., P.O. Box 97, (309) 927-3506, fax (309) 927-3506, e-mail: colhosbb@winco.net, www.bishophilllodging.com.* Ca 1855 Greek Revival colony building, 4 rooms & 1 suite, private baths, TV, expanded Cont. breakfasts, period furnishings, some pets, common room with wood-burning stove, back porches for sunset views. $ to $$

Further Information

Bishop Hill Heritage Association, *P.O. Box 92, 103 N. Bishop Hill St., Bishop Hill, IL 61419-0092 (309) 927-3899, e-mail: bhha@winco.net.*

Directions

From Peoria, I-74 west to exit 71, IL 78 north to US 34, US 34 west through Galva plus about 2 mi, right (north) to Bishop Hill; from the Quad Cities (on Mississippi River), I-74 south to exit 32 (at Woodhull), IL 17 east to junction with US 34, left about 2 mi, left (north) to Bishop Hill.

CARTHAGE
Population 2,725

Settled in 1833, **Carthage** is a pretty little Midwestern town with an old courthouse on a square, a bustling downtown around the square, and tree-lined streets with homes representing over a century of architectural styles. The courthouse and 19th-century commercial buildings about the square have been designated an historic district. There are no discount stores or malls on Carthage's outskirts, so the downtown looks very much like the downtown of a traditional county seat.

The two-story limestone **Old Carthage Jail** is the site of the mob murder of Mormon prophet Joseph Smith and his brother Hyrum in 1844. Now a museum and visitor center, the jail has become a kind of Mormon shrine; thousands of people of the Mormon Church visit the site every year (although non-Mormons are by all means welcome).

The **Hancock County Court House** (1908), an unusually beautiful stone structure, is a favorite subject of photographers and painters. Inside is a large genealogical card index and collection of local artifacts.

Carthage is home to an interesting history and natural history museum, the **Alice Kibbe Museum**. The museum features collections of Native American, Mormon, Civil War, and late 19th century artifacts.

> You'll see fields of corn and soybeans around Carthage, but very few farm animals – farmers say they can no longer afford the feed and other supplies needed to keep livestock.

Special Features

Kids will enjoy the **World of Wonders Playground** (known locally as "WOW Park"), a 10,000-square-foot wooden playground with slides, mazes, even dragons and a pirate ship.

Several historic barns and charming old two-story farmhouses can be spotted in the countryside around Carthage. Many of the old farmhouses here and elsewhere in the Midwest have weathered away or been destroyed, but fortunately, some farm families have invested considerable time and money to preserve these "gems of the prairie."

The **Great River Road** along the Mississippi is a few miles west of town.

Further Information

Carthage Chamber of Commerce, *P.O. Box 247, Carthage, IL 62321 (217) 357-3024, www.carthage-il.com.*

Directions

From Peoria, US 24 southwest to US 136, US 136 west to Carthage.

ELSAH
Population 851

Once a steamboat stop on the Mississippi, unspoiled little **Elsah** is the kind of village where you go to pick apples and peaches, watch for bald eagles, or linger beside old flower gardens. It's an enchanting spot.

The first village in the country to be listed in its entirety on the National Register of Historic Places, Elsah seems to be charmingly stuck in the last century. Indeed, most of the old and (thanks to stringent codes) new buildings are of an architecture belonging to the 1850-1900 period.

The lovely campus of nearby **Principia College** is worth a special visit. The college has been placed on the National Register of Historic Places.

Guarded by bluffs, Elsah offers splendid views of the **Mississippi River Valley**. The riverside beauty can be enjoyed by renting a bike and cycling along the water on the newly paved **Vadalabene Bike Trail**. Horseback and boat rides are also popular. Catering more to the automobile, the 50-mile-long **Meeting of the Great River Scenic Byway** offers sweeping views of the river on one side and magnificent limestone cliffs on the other.

Special Features

Pere Marquette Park, about 5 miles west of Elsah, is the largest state park in Illinois (8,000 acres). The park overlooks the Illinois River and boasts an especially beautiful 1930s stone lodge.

Elsah's charm spills over onto **Grafton**, about 4 miles upriver, and **Alton**, about 10 miles downriver. Both towns are noted for their old homes and fabulous antiquing.

The new **Lewis and Clark Interpretive Center**, downriver in Hartford, focuses on the months Lewis and Clark spent in Illinois preparing for their expedition. The museum features replicas of an outdoor camp (interactive) and a 55-foot keelboat (with cutaway sections).

Eagle tours and group tours of underground railroad sites (Illinois was a free state, Missouri was not) depart from Alton. Check with the visitors bureau.

> Ferries cross the Illinois and Mississippi Rivers at five points upriver from Elsah. Motorists wishing to play "river rat" may make all crossings in one day.

Further Information

Greater Alton/Twin Rivers Convention & Visitors Bureau, *200 Piasa, Alton, IL 62002 (800) 258-6645, fax (618) 465-6151, www.visitalton.org* (ZIP for Elsah is 62028.)

Directions

From St. Louis (MO), US 67 north (across Mississippi River) to IL 100, IL 100 north to Elsah.

GALENA
Population 3,460

Surrounded by some of the most beautiful rolling countryside in Illinois, **Galena** is a little town of historic mansions, handsome brick commercial buildings, and churches with hand-carved altars and pulpits. The lure of this delightful place can be underscored by noting that Chicago CEOs have chosen to retire here and that several members of the renowned Chicago Symphony have selected this as their second home.

With economic roots in lead mining, smelting, and riverboating, Galena was once the largest Mississippi River port between St. Louis and St. Paul. But the railroad was to replace the riverboat, and this and other developments eventually plunged the town into a depression that lasted from the 1890s until the 1960s. The many grand old buildings were neither modernized nor torn down simply because no one had enough to money to do so. Artists from Chicago began restoring the town in the 1960s and, joined by other groups, changed Galena from a sleepy, decaying river town to one of the most charming and sophisticated spots in Illinois, the Midwest, and the United States.

Galena and **Jo Daviess County** claim 11 antique shops, 47 bed and breakfasts, 7 galleries, 5 private studios, and 100+ specialty shops. Ranking as one of the most popular destinations in the Midwest, visitors may find accommodations scarce on weekends. Reservations are advised—the visitors bureau monitors weekend and holiday lodging availabilities.

Eighty-five percent of Galena is listed on the National Register. Architectural styles include Federal, Italianate, Greek Revival, Queen Anne, Romanesque Revival, and Gothic Revival. The number of historic sites and other points of interest is greater than for many large cities. A good starting point for a tour of the town is the **Galena/Jo Daviess County History Museum**. Housed in an 1858 Italianate mansion, the museum features paintings, toys and dolls, household items, clothing, and a Civil War exhibit that includes Thomas Nast's original painting, *Peace in Union*.

One of Galena's most famous sites is the **Ulysses S. Grant Home State Historic Site**, the 1860 Italianate home that was presented to Grant in 1865 on his return from the Civil War. The restored home contains original furnishings and personal items of the Grant family.

The **Old Market House State Historic Site** is an 1845/1846 Greek Revival building that once served as the center of Galena's community life. Among its many functions today are a center for historical and architectural exhibits, an open-air farmer's market during the summer and fall, and a hospitality center during the Christmas season.

Among the historic homes open to the public are the **Dowling House** (1826) and the **Belvedere Mansion** (1857). The native limestone Dowling House, Galena's oldest house, contains primitive period furniture and a large collection of Galena pottery. The 22-room Italianate Belvedere Mansion has Victorian furnishings, items from Liberace's estate, and the famous green drapes from Tara in *Gone with the Wind*.

Also of interest are the limestone **Galena Post Office** (1857/1859), the oldest continuously operating post office in the United States; the Greek Revival **Galena Public Library** (1906), which has a reading room with a mosaic fireplace in the style of Frank Lloyd Wright; and the **Washburne House**, a Greek Revival home built in 1844 by a U.S. congressman. It was in the library of Washburne House that Grant received word of his election to the presidency (1868). The **Vinegar Hill Historic Lead Mine and Museum** offers a guided tour of an 1822 underground lead mine.

Recreational opportunities abound in the Galena area. A casino cruise ship plies the nearby **Mississippi River**. Mississippi riverboats also offer sightseeing excursions, including two-day round-trip cruises.

Summer sports include hiking, horseback riding, bicycling, and some of the best golfing in the country. With winter come skating, sledding, tobogganing, snow-shoeing, and some of the best downhill skiing in the Midwest. Horse-drawn sleigh rides are popular.

Cultural offerings range from chamber music to blues to performances by professional theatrical troupes.

Special Features

Check with the Visitor Information Center for help on planning a scenic drive. **Jo Daviess County** is full of winding country roads.

> Ulysses S. and Julia Dent Grant considered Galena their hometown even though the general actually lived in the town for no more than about two years.

▶ HISTORIC HOTEL ◀

DeSOTO HOUSE HOTEL, *230 S. Main St., (800) 343-6562, (815) 777-0090, fax (815) 777-9529, e-mail: desoto@galenalink.com, www.desotohouse.com.* Restored 1855 hotel on National Register, 55 rooms, 4 suites, private baths, TV & phones, variety of dining options, antiques, 4-story atrium, gift shop, packages, Abraham Lincoln & Mark Twain among many famous guests. $$ to $$$

Further Information

Galena/Jo Daviess County Convention & Visitors Bureau, *720 Park Ave., Galena, IL 61036 (800) 747-9377, fax (815) 777-3566, www.galena.org.*

Directions

From Chicago, I-90 (Northwest Tollway) to US 20 at Rockford, US 20 west to Galena; also from Chicago, I-88 to I-39, I-39 north to US 20 at Rockford, US 20 west to Galena.

GENEVA

Population 20,500

Flowing just beyond the reach of Chicago's western suburbs is the beautiful **Fox River**. Each of the towns along the river has a waterside park, and the parks' bike trails have been connected to offer bicyclists, roller bladers, hikers, and joggers 30 miles of uninterrupted scenery.

Geneva is one of the prettiest and most historic of the towns along the river. The town's considerable charm is in part due to the convergence of its historic beauty, its 150-year-old reputation as a shopping center, and its lovely and unique location. Founded in the 1830s, Geneva has two historic districts and more than 200 homes, churches, and other buildings on the National Register of Historic Places. Most of the homes and churches were built in the middle of the 19th century, with the decades of the 1840s, 1850s, and 1860s predominating.

Encouraged by Geneva's beautiful setting – and the tastes of area residents – it was inevitable that during the decades of the 20th century the shops and the historic homes would begin to find each other. And so they did. Geneva boasts over 100 antique shops, galleries, specialty shops, restaurants, and cafes, many nestled within the walls of beautiful old homes. The union of upscale shopping with the town's architectural treasures and romantic riverside setting has earned Geneva a respected reputation in Chicagoland, and beyond.

The interior of the **Kane County Courthouse** is laced with wrought-iron balconies from the first to the fourth floors and displays eight large murals by Edward Holslag. The murals provide a good view of the surrounding country-side as it appeared in 1910.

Among the local memorabilia showcased by the **Geneva History Center**, in **Wheeler Park**, are furniture made by area cabinetmakers from local walnut and period costumes and hats from the shops of town merchants.

Special Features

Bikes and roller blades can be rented riverside. The **Fox River bike trails** extend from Aurora to Elgin, and beyond, and connect with a vast network of bike paths on Chicago's western outskirts.

Geneva's lovely Island Park is ideal for picnicking.

▶ HISTORIC INN ◀

OSCAR SWAN COUNTRY INN, *1800 W. State St., (630) 232-0173, fax (630) 232-2706, www.oscarswan.com.* 1902 Colonial Revival estate on 8 acres, 6 rooms, 1 suite, private baths, TV & phones, full breakfasts (weekends), antiques, some pets, pre-arranged meals, art, pool, gardens, 2-story restored 1836 barn for variety of social functions. $$ to $$$

Further Information

Geneva Chamber of Commerce, *P.O. Box 481, Geneva, IL 60134 (630) 232-6060, (866) 443-6382, www.genevachamber.com.*

Directions

From Chicago, IL 38 west (approximately 35 miles).

MAEYSTOWN
Population 116

Cluster an old stone church, a little stone bridge, an inn, several stores, a few houses, and a handful of outbuildings in the Illinois Mississipi River bluffs, and you have the quaint little German village of **Maeystown**. The land was never graded to form level lots; instead, the buildings were set into the hillside. This means that to go upstairs you have the choice between climbing stairs or going outside and climbing a little hill to a door on the next floor. The effect is an integration of building and landscape; the overall result is a village straight out of a storybook.

The entire village of Maeystown, founded in 1852, is listed on the National Register. The village is so tiny that until very recently it wasn't even listed on several major road maps. Some of the more significant of the buildings include the original **stone church** (1865-67); the home (1860-65) of the town's founder, **Jacob Maeys**; and the old **stone mill** (1859), now the home of the **Maeystown Preservation Society Museum** and **Visitor Center**. The picturesque old one-lane **stone bridge** (1881) is still in use.

Tour the village on foot or let a horse-drawn carriage do it for you. Everyone greets everyone else on the village's half dozen streets, and conversation comes easy. A very pleasant morning or afternoon can be spent by getting to know those lingering in the restaurant, inn, or old-fashioned general store.

Special Features

The original powder magazine and reconstructed north wall and guard-house may be explored at **Fort de Chartres State Historic Site**, several miles south of town near the Mississippi. The original fort (1753) had 3-foot-thick stone walls and was built by the French to protect settlers in Prairie du Rocher.

The **Waterloo Winery**, eight miles north, offers cellar tours, wine tasting, and relaxation in an arbored wine garden.

> • Services at the original stone church were sometimes held in German until Christmas 1943.
> • Many of the original barns, smokehouses, summer kitchens, sheds, and outhouses are still standing behind the village's homes.

▶ HISTORIC HOTEL ◀

CORNER GEORGE INN BED & BREALFAST, *Main & Mill, (618) 458-6660, (800) 458-6020, e-mail: cornrgeo@htc.net, www.cornergeorgeinn.com.*

Restored 1884 hotel & 3 small 19th-century bldgs., National Register, 3 rooms & 3 suites, 1 cottage, private baths, full breakfasts, antiques, whirlpool suite, breakfast in ballroom. $ to $$$

Further Information

The Innkeepers, *Corner George Inn, Maeystown, IL 62256 (618) 458-6660.*

Directions

From St. Louis (MO), I-255 (across Mississippi River) to exit 6, IL 3 south through Columbia to Waterloo, IL 156 west toward Valmeyer, left on Lakeview Dr. to Maeystown.

NAUVOO
Population 1108

Located on a bluff overlooking the Mississippi, **Nauvoo** (nah VOO) is the idyllic early 19th-century American town with lovely shade trees and green parkland blended with stately old brick buildings. The atmosphere is small-town and peaceful. There is no commercialization, and in fact you're not likely to come across the town except by a lucky stumble. That is, unless you happen to know something about Mormon history.

Fleeing persecution elsewhere, the Mormons settled in Nauvoo in 1839. There, granted autonomy by the Illinois legislature, they prospered. During the 1840s, Nauvoo, which means *a beautiful place* in Hebrew, became the largest town in Illinois and one of the largest in the country. Troubles continued to plague the church, however, and following the murder of Mormon leader Joseph Smith, the Mormons left Illinois. Nauvoo was abandoned.

In 1849 a group from France known as the Icarians chose Nauvoo for an experiment in communal living. The Icarian colony in Nauvoo survived until 1860. After its break-up, some of the members remaining in Nauvoo joined with their German and Swiss neighbors to begin the cultivation of grapes and the making of fine wines. Although Prohibition put an end to the wine industry, at least for a while, the wine cellars were found ideal for the aging of cheese and in 1936 a blue-cheese industry was born. The town celebrates its grape harvest with a festival every Labor Day weekend.

The best way to explore Nauvoo is by driving tour aided by a map and cassette obtained from the **Nauvoo Chamber of Commerce Uptown Tourist Center** (across from Hotel Nauvoo). The two best-known sites, or clusters of sites, help define the historic district, once inhabited by Mormons. Both are taken from the pages of Mormon history:

On the south side of the historic district is the **Joseph Smith Historic Site** (associated with the Community of Christ). The center comprises the log **Homestead** (1803), **Mansion House** (1842), and **Red Brick Store** (1842), all family properties of Joseph Smith. The Red Brick Store displays merchandise typical of the early 1840s. Near the store is the **Smith family cemetery**, burial place of Joseph Smith and his wife and brother, Emma and Hyrum.

The **Historic Nauvoo Visitors Center** (associated with the Church of Jesus Christ of Latter-day Saints), on the north side of the district, maintains the **Monument to Women Gardens**. The center provides a good introduction to the district and offers guided tours of its many beautifully restored homes and shops.

Mormon Nauvoo's most important site, the **Nauvoo Temple of the Church of Jesus Christ of Latter-day Saints**, was destroyed by fire (1848) and tornado (1850). Reconstruction of the temple was completed over 150 years later (2002) and the stone exterior, a faithful copy of the original, once again takes its prominent place in Nauvoo's townscape. Unlike other Mormon sites, which are open to people of all faiths, the interior is closed to the public.

A goal of the **Icarian Living History Museum** is "to promote the preservation of French heritage in America." Among the items on display in the renovated 1846 house are artifacts of the Icarian period (1849-1860).

Special Features

Daily demonstrations of Nauvoo's old crafts are provided all over town, and because they are indoors, in all seasons. Woodworking, blacksmith, and cooper demonstrations are just a few that can be seen. All are performed by skilled artisans – the sheer intelligence and inventiveness of the craftsmanship are guaranteed to amaze.

- What with the bald eagles wintering in the area, the sleigh bells, and the traditional holiday decorations, many find December the best season to visit Nauvoo.
- Held on the first week of August, the outdoor musical "City of Joseph" employs song, dance, costumes, fireworks, and a computerized sound and lighting system to tell the story of Nauvoo's Mormon period.

Further Information

Nauvoo Tourism, *P.O. Box 41, Nauvoo, IL 62354 (217) 453-6648.*

Directions

From Peoria, US 24 southwest to US 136, US 136 west to IL 96, IL 96 north (along Mississippi River) to Nauvoo.

Other Charming Illinois Towns
Golconda
Mt. Carroll
Petersburg (New Salem)
Woodstock

Chapter 14

INDIANA

CORYDON
Population 2,661

Here and there among the hills and forests of southern Indiana are little towns whose streets look much as they did 50 years ago, or more. Too small to grow into cities, but too big to disappear, such towns somehow hang on, often with the help of tourist dollars attracted by a bit of Hoosier nostalgia. **Corydon** is a wonderful example of such a little town, and it has a lot of genuine Hoosier nostalgia to work with.

Corydon's downtown has an ambiance that beautifully complements the Hoosier heritage. Many of the businesses proudly display – and restore and preserve – ornamental iron store fronts from the 1890s. Included among the businesses are specialty shops, antique and art malls, restaurants, and a soda fountain. Corydon is especially known for its sculptured art glass objects.

On the square is the charming little **State Capitol Building**, Indiana's first state capitol (1816-1825). The 40-foot-square building, today a state historic site, is constructed of rough blue limestone and has first-floor walls that are 2 1/2 feet thick.

Not far away is the 1817 Federal-style brick **Governor Hendricks's Headquarters**. This two-story building, open to the public, was the home and headquarters of William Hendricks while he was governor of Indiana (1822-1825). Also near the square is a one-story brick building (1817) that was rented to the state for offices, making it the first state office building.

Another beautiful old building that is open to the public is the **Posey House**, a large brick house built in 1817. Other historic buildings include the restored two-story log **Branham Tavern** (1800), the 1807 log **Westfall**

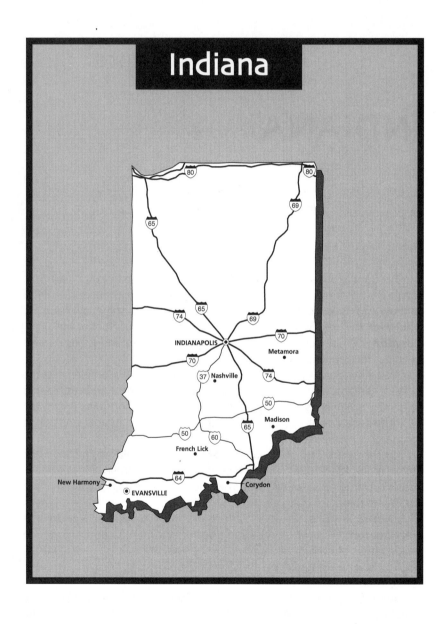

Indiana

House, and the Federal-style office of the weekly newspaper, the *Corydon Democrat*, originally built as a residence and drug store (1842).

Special Features

Scheduled trains operate 16-mile excursions on an 1883 scenic railroad. The excursions last about 1 1/2 hours.

In the rolling countryside not far from Corydon are some of the country's most beautiful caves. The best known, all open to the public, are **Wyandotte Cave**, **Little Wyandotte Cave**, **Marengo Cave**, and **Squire Boone Caverns**. Many farmers have wild caves that they allow visitors to explore.

Along the **Ohio River Scenic Route** lie cypress swamps, river overlooks, rock outcroppings, caves, forested hills, and pieces of history and prehistory. Formed by IN 156, 56, 62, and 66, the route passes through Corydon.

- The Battle of Corydon Memorial Park south of town was the site of one of the few Civil War battles fought on Northern soil.
- The Harrison County Fair is the oldest continuous fair in Indiana (dating from 1860). The fairgrounds are south of town.

▶ HISTORIC HOTEL ◀

KINTNER HOUSE INN B&B, *101 S. Capitol Ave., (812) 738-2020.* Restored 1873 hotel featured on Christmas cards, National Register, 15 rooms, private baths, TV & phones, full breakfasts, antiques, fireplaces, inviting large porch. $ to $$

Further Information

Harrison County Chamber of Commerce, *310 N. Elm St., Corydon, IN 47112 (888) 738-2137, (812) 738-2137.*

Directions

From Louisville (KY), I-64 west to exit 105, IN 135 south to Corydon.

FRENCH LICK/WEST BADEN SPRINGS
Population 2,087

Nestled among the scenic knobs of southern Indiana, **French Lick** and **West Baden Springs** are, were, and have always been among the Midwest's great resorts. Belief in the medicinal and generally beneficial effects of the area's mineral waters turned French Lick and the neighboring village of **West Baden Springs** into a fashionable spa as early as the middle of the 19th century. The wealthy and the not-so-wealthy came here to take the waters, promenade, and enjoy the restaurants and black-tie casinos. Some of the wealthy even came in their own railroad cars. An opera house was built. As the resort seasoned, major-league baseball teams came here to train. The grandest of the spa's hotels, the **West Baden Spring's Hotel** and the neighboring **French Lick Springs Resort**, were built in 1902.

French Lick and West Baden Springs's popularity continued until the years of the Depression. Thereafter the resorts had their ups and downs, but never died. In 1991 the French Lick Springs Resort underwent extensive restoration. The result is a hotel whose reputation as the largest, most complete all-season resort in the Midwest continues unchallenged. The hotel features an Olympic-sized outdoor pool, a glass-domed indoor pool, two 18-hole golf courses, 18 tennis courts, 30 miles of trails for horseback riding, and a health and fitness spa.

Now a National Historic Landmark, the West Baden Springs's Hotel was famous for its 6-story free-span atrium dome, the largest in the world until the construction of Houston's astrodome in 1966. The garden, mineral-springs pavilions, circular lobby, dining room, and gilded atrium have been restored under the watchful eye of the Historic Landmarks Foundation of Indiana. Special tours and regularly scheduled one-hour tours are available (812-936-4034 for information).

French Lick and West Baden Springs can fill out a pleasant day even for those not staying at the resort. **Maple Street** and a couple of adjacent streets in French Lick have an interesting assortment of gift and antique shops as well as the quaint appearance that people expect of southern Indiana. Several very pleasant hours can also be spent touring the West Baden Spring's Hotel and strolling the beautiful lobby, verandah, and vast landscaped grounds of the French Lick Springs Resort (on the grounds is the renowned **Pluto Spring** - see below).

Adjacent to the resort is the **Indiana Railway Museum**. A trip of less than two hours can be taken through 20 miles of the **Hoosier National Forest** on the **French Lick, West Baden and Southern Railroad**. Along the way is the 2,200-ft. **Burton Tunnel**, one of the longest railway tunnels in the state. The museum also displays several vintage locomotives and a number of old railroad cars.

The water from one of the artesian mineral springs, the Pluto Spring, was once bottled and widely distributed as "Pluto Water."

▶ HISTORIC HOTEL ◀

FRENCH LICK SPRINGS RESORT & SPA, *8670 W. State Rd. 56, (800) 457-4042, fax (812) 936-2430, www.frenchlick.com*. Historic 1902 resort hotel on 2,600 acres, 471 rooms, private baths, TV & phones, variety of restaurants & menus, front porch/verandah, golf, tennis, swimming pools, stables, health spa, bikes, children's activities, shops. $ to $$$$

Further Information

French Lick-West Baden Chamber of Commerce, *P.O. Box 347, French Lick, IN 47432 (812) 936-2405.*

Directions

From Indianapolis, IN 37 south to US 150 (at Paoli), west to Prospect, IN 56 south to French Lick/West Baden springs; from Louisville (KY), US 150 northwest to Prospect, as above.

MADISON
Population 13,000

Every visitor to Madison should reserve time for a stroll on the beautiful brick walk along the riverfront. On one side is the **Ohio River**, with the hazy hills of Kentucky beyond, and on the other are the wooded heights and limestone cliffs of Indiana overlooking and sheltering the finest concentration of early 19th-century architecture in the Midwest.

Madison's entire downtown, 133 blocks worth, is listed on the National Register of Historic Places. Most of the buildings on **Main Street** – one of the finest in the country – were in place at the time of the Civil War, yet the street is as alive as any main street ever was. Interwoven with the usual businesses, here and on adjacent streets, are some unusually fine antique, craft, and specialty shops. The charm of the district reaches a peak at N. Broadway and Main, where a Victorian fountain, called the **Broadway Fountain**, commands a little square. The fountain, originally cast in iron and recast in bronze in 1976, was presented in 1876 to the Philadelphia Centennial Exposition by France.

One of Madison's best-known citizens was financier James Lanier, who loaned financially troubled Indiana money during the Civil War so that the state could equip Union troops. Lanier built a Classic Revival mansion (1844) that has become Madison's most popular attraction. Now the **J. F. D. Lanier State Historic Site**, the splendid home has period furnishings and a south portico with a commanding view of the **Ohio River** that, by itself, would justify a trip to Madison. The lovely gardens, carefully restored, include fragrant 1850 peonies (thought to be original to the garden) and heirloom varieties of roses.

The Greek Revival **Shrewsbury House** (1849) is another lovely Madison landmark. Especially noteworthy inside are the plasterwork and three-story freestanding spiral staircase. The house and its period furnishings are open to public view.

The **Jeremiah Sullivan House** (1818), an outstanding example of Federal architecture, was probably Madison's first mansion (open). Also in the Federal style, the **Masonic Schofield House** (ca 1816) is believed to be the first two-story brick house/tavern in Madison (open).

The contents, including medical instruments, of **Dr. William D. Hutchings's Office** (1848) are exactly the same as they were at the time of Dr. Hutchings's death in 1903 (open). The **Schroeder Saddletree Factory Museum** includes woodworking machinery and steam engines used by generations of the same family (1878-1972) to manufacture wooden clothespins and frames for saddles.

Eleutherian College (est. 1848, completed 1855) was the first college in Indiana to offer college-level education to all regardless of gender or race. The college, now a National Historic Landmark, was affiliated with the Underground Railroad and Neil's Creek Anti-slavery Society.

Wineries in and around Madison offer wine tasting, tours, dining, picnics—and historic settings. A brochure with descriptions and a map is available at the visitors bureau.

Special Features

Several dramatic waterfalls, deep gorges, and bluffs overlooking the Ohio River can be found at nearby **Clifty Falls State Park**. Bowing a little to civilization, the park also offers an inn, Olympic-sized swimming pool, and more than 12 miles of moderate to rugged hiking trails.

Hanover College, founded in 1827, is seven miles west of town. The campus consists of thirty Georgian-style buildings located on a hilltop overlooking the Ohio River Valley.

IN 56E offers a picturesque tour of the countryside along the **Ohio River Scenic Byway**.

• The Fair Play Fire Company is Indiana's oldest existing volunteer fire department (1841).
• Settlers often put into Madison for provisions on their way to their new homes in the Northwest Territory, now the eastern part of the Midwest.

Further Information
Madison Area Convention & Visitors Bureau, *301 E. Main St., Madison, IN 47250 (812) 265-2956, (800) 559-2956, www.visitmadison.org.*

Directions
From Louisville (KY), I-65 north to exit 33, IN 256 east to Madison; from Cincinnati (OH), I-71 south to Carrollton (KY), KY 36 west to Milton (KY), cross bridge (US 421) to Madison; from Indianapolis, I-65 south to exit 33, IN 256 east to Madison.

METAMORA
Population about 200

Tiny **Metamora's** (first) golden days came in the 1840s and 1850s when the village prospered as a port on the 76-mile-long **Whitewater Canal** (1845). Floods, mismanagement, the coming of the railroad, and other factors ganged up on the canal, and the old waterway fell into disrepair. And so it remained until the 1940s, when the Indiana Department of Natural Resources acquired 14 miles of it and began restoration. Included in the restoration was a covered aqueduct, built in 1843, that carried the canal 16 feet over **Duck Creek**.

Today, the restored canal, aqueduct, and working grist mill make up the **Whitewater Canal State Historic Site**. A horse-drawn canal boat, the *Ben Franklin III*, takes on passengers and travels through the aqueduct, the only operational covered-bridge aqueduct in the United States (hourly departures May through October).

With well over 100 shops, the village has become so popular that it now counts Nashville (which see) as its main rival. Many of the shops are housed in quaint 19th-century houses and other buildings. The goods and wares include dolls, oak and cherry furniture, paintings, oak baskets, candles, wooden folk art, Amish cheese, wood signs, nutcrackers, quilts, tinware, and ceramics. Shoppers come from as far away as Cincinnati, Indianapolis, Dayton, and Louisville.

Special Features
In addition to rides on the canal boat, on weekends the village offers buggy rides and 1/2-hour train excursions on the Whitewater Valley Railroad. (Longer rail excursions are available from Connersville, to the north.)

> Indiana's canal system drove the state into bankruptcy. The experience badly hurt Indiana's reputation and led to legislation that even today prohibits the state from contracting debt.

Further Information

Merchants Association of Metamora, *P.O. Box 117, Metamora, IN 47030. Welcome Line: (765) 647-2109, www.metamora.com.*

Directions

From Indianapolis, US 52 east (via Rushville) to Metamora; from Cincinnati (OH), I-74 west to US 52, US 52 to Metamora.

NASHVILLE
Population 873

Unlike so many other charming villages, **Nashville** didn't arise from the wealth of lumbermen, cotton planters, bankers, or gold miners. Nashville's charm originated instead in the backwoods beauty of **Brown County**, a county with winding country roads, old covered bridges, log cabins, and homey stone buildings.

Standing in contrast with the flatness of so much of the Midwest, the rolling hills and peaceful valleys of Brown County began attracting artists over a hundred years ago. One of the earliest and most prominent of the artists was Theodore C. Steele, the Impressionistic artist of Hoosier Group fame. Steele's home, studio, gardens, and grounds now form the **T. C. Steele State Historic Site**, about eight miles southwest of town. Many of the artist's landscape paintings are on display in the house and studio (1907). Steele and fellow impressionist Adolph Schulz established Brown County as the "Art Colony of the Midwest."

Nashville's center of attraction is the **Brown County Courthouse Historic District** (1873-1937). The district includes a picture-book brick courthouse, the **Historical Society Museum Building**, the **Old Log Jail**, and several other log structures.

Along Nashville's picturesque streets are over 350 art galleries, craft shops, and antique stores. Entertainment ranging from country music to marionette shows to professional summer stock is offered by theaters in and about town.

Nashville is tiny, so park your car and walk. Carriage tours are available for those looking for a little romance.

Special Features
Within the borders of Brown County are **Brown County State Park** (the largest in the state), **Yellowwood State Forest**, and parts of the **Hoosier National Forest**. In and out of the woods are numerous roads and trails, making the county ideal for nature hikes, horseback rides, and bicycle tours.

> One study has ranked Brown County, along with neighboring Bloomington, among the ten most desirable places in the U.S. in which to retire.

▶ HISTORIC RESTAURANT ◀
HOBNOB CORNER, *17 W. Main St., P.O. Box 899, (812) 988-4114.* Locally respected restaurant in Nashville's oldest commercial bldg., Midwestern cooking—e.g., homemade soups, "exciting" salads, home-baked pastries. $ to $$

Further Information
Nashville/Brown County Convention & Visitors Bureau, *P.O. Box 840, Nashville, IN 47448 (800) 753-3255, fax (812) 988-1070, www.browncounty.com.*

Directions
From Indianapolis, I-65 south to exit 68, west on IN 46 to Nashville.

NEW HARMONY
Population 846

New Harmony was laid out and settled by Harmonists – Lutheran Separatists – in 1814. Ten years later the town was taken over by a second communal society, this one lasting only a couple of years. Both communities faded, and their utopian ideals were never realized, but each stressed intellectual and cultural achievement, and that legacy lives on. For today the quaint little town of New Harmony is alive with musical performances, workshops and conferences, summer theater productions, craft demonstrations, and art exhibitions. In addition, many of the tour sites (see below) offer permanent exhibits of art, history, and science.

The bridge between New Harmony's past and present is a unique one. Beginning in 1937 various preservation and restoration efforts were undertaken. In the late 1950s construction began on the first of several contemporary structures. In the years since, the town has been zoned and its infrastructure upgraded and modernized. New buildings, including a visitors' center, medical clinic, and townhouses, have gone up. Their architecture has often united modern elements with traditional ones, especially those of the Harmonist tradition. Many of the historic buildings have been restored and converted to museums. The resulting town is a delightful mix of the authentic old with the creative new, of unique shops and good restaurants with history museums and art galleries.

Every visitor should go first to the **Atheneum/Visitors' Center**, a striking contemporary structure designed by Richard Meier. The center offers an orientation film and exhibits, including a scale model of the town in 1824. All tours begin here. The tours range from a 45-minute orientation tour to an all-day, go-at-your-own-pace amble.

There are 15 tour sites in all, as well as several sites open to the public free of charge. Among the tour sites are **Community House #2**, a large dormitory built for single Harmonists and later the site of a Pestalozzian school; **Thrall's Opera House**, originally a Harmonist community house and later remodeled for theatrical performances; and the **Workingmen's Institute**, Indiana's oldest continuously open public library (1838). Another site, the **George Keppler House**, contains exhibits on the life and work of David Dale Owen, Indiana State Geologist and later Chief Geologist for the U.S. Government. The **Maximilian-Bodmer Collection** showcases original artwork from the 1832/1834 expedition of Prince Maximilian and artist Karl Bodmer to the Upper Missouri Territory.

The single-path **Cathedral Labyrinth and Sacred Garden** form one of the sites open to the public free of charge. The geometry of the labyrinth and garden is based on the sacred geometry of Chartres Cathedral in France. Other free sites include the **Roofless Church** (1960), an interdenominational church that won an award for its designer, Philip Johnson, and **Tillich Park**, the burial place of theologian Paul Johannes Tillich.

Special Features

Nearby **Harmonie State Park** features an Olympic-size pool, 110-ft water slide, and boat launch on the Wabash River. Wildlife, wildflower, and fall foliage viewers have six hiking trails to choose from.

• New Harmony was one of the country's most important training and research centers for geology between 1830 and 1860.
• Congressman Robert Dale Owen, a New Harmony resident, sponsored legislation to establish the Smithsonian Institution.

Further Information

Historic New Harmony, *P.O. Box 579, New Harmony, IN 47631(800) 231-2168, fax (812) 682-4313, www.newharmony.org*

Directions

From Evansville, IN 66 west to New Harmony; from I-64, exit 4 (Griffin), south 7 miles to IN 66, west to New Harmony

Other Charming Indiana Towns

Bethlehem
Dana
Fountain City
Oldenburg
Spring Mill Village

Chapter 15

IOWA

THE AMANA COLONIES
Population 1,700

Iowa's **Amana Colonies** form a little country of their own. The "country" is 26,000 acres large and has seven villages, each at least an hour's ox-cart drive from the next: **Amana**, **Middle Amana**, **East Amana**, **West Amana**, **South Amana**, **High Amana**, and **Homestead**. The villages are laid out in the manner of the "Dorf" of the 19th-century German states, with one long street and several branches, and are distinguished by picturesque gabled sandstone and brick buildings, also from the 19th century. Some buildings are fitted with trellises to support fruit-bearing (and shade-providing) vines. Rich farmlands and wooded hillsides, even a large lily pond (**Lily Lake**), assure that the charm isn't confined to the village limits.

The colonies were begun in 1855 by members of a German/Swiss/French religious group who had come to America seeking a place to worship in peace. The colonists developed a communal lifestyle in which everything—including work and meals—was shared. The villages were built by hand and most of what the colonists needed was made by hand—the formation of bricks and quarrying of stones, weaving of fabrics, construction of grandfather clocks, pressing of grapes for wine, printing and binding of books. In 1932 came "The Great Change," when the free enterprise system was fully adopted and isolation from the outside world ended. Today the Amana Colonies form a National Historic Landmark, one that can boast some 475 sites and structures.

Most of the villages lie along the "Amana Colonies Trail," a loop formed by IA 220 and US 6 and 151 (guide maps and other information are available at area visitors centers). Amana has the largest share of shops, restaurants, and other businesses; all villages, however, have their own special attractions.

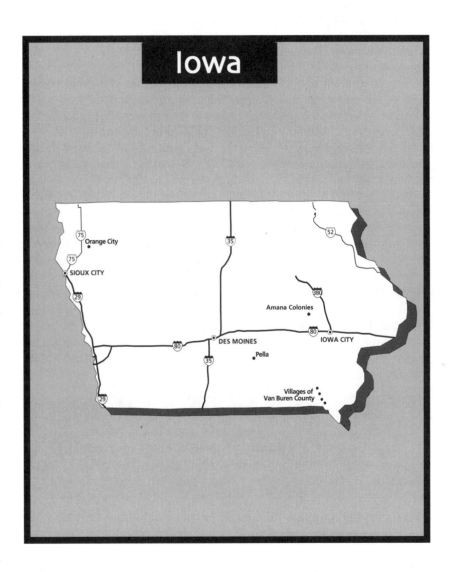

Iowa

Orange City

SIOUX CITY

Amana Colonies

DES MOINES

IOWA CITY

Pella

Villages of
Van Buren County

Four of the seven villages have one or more museums. Amana, for example, has the **Museum of Amana History**, with three buildings of exhibits and an award-winning video presentation. In South Amana there is the **Communal Agriculture Museum** and in Middle Amana the **Communal Kitchen and Coopershop**; both provide opportunities to learn more about the Amana Colonies' highly successful communal lifestyle. The **Community Church Museum** in Homestead introduces visitors to the colonists' religious practices and beliefs.

It goes without saying that a group of villages respected since the middle of the 19th century for their handcrafted products would possess an exceptional collection of shops. Among the best of the offerings are the hardwood furniture, clocks, woolens, and quilts. The colonies' breads, pastries, and smoked meats are renowned, as are the wines and beer. Antique lovers should be prepared for a long visit. And even the short-term visitor should experience at least one meal: Some restaurants descend from the original communal kitchens, and their simple but delicious food, often prepared from old Amana recipes, is served family-style.

For visitors seeking a change of pace there are a golf course, a nature trail, and a professional theater troupe (the **Old Creamery Theatre Company**). There is also a new recreational trial linking Amana and Middle Amana—depending on time and weather, biking and hiking may offer the very best way to take in this delightful bit of America's heartland.

Special Features

Kalona, an Amish and Mennonite community, is about 30 miles southeast of the Amana Colonies. Of special interest here is the collection of 19th-century buildings preserved in the **Kalona Historical Village**.

> Hearty soups, cucumbers in cream sauce, cooked or pickled red cabbage, fried potatoes, rouladen with dumplings, fried chicken, and rhubarb pie are among the items you can expect to find on local menus.

▶ HISTORIC INN ◀

DIE HEIMAT COUNTRY INN, *4430 V St. (Homestead, 52236), (319) 622-3937, www.dheimat.com.* Inn for travelers as early as 1858 & later a communal kitchen, 18 rooms, private baths, TV, full breakfasts, antiques, pets with permission, Amana furniture, quilts, large shaded yard with "Amana" glider swing & picnic table. $

Further Information

Amana Colonies Convention & Visitors Bureau, *39 38th Ave., Suite 100, Amana, IA 52203 (800) 579-2294, (319) 622-7622, fax (319) 622-6395, www.AmanaColonies.com.*

Directions

From Des Moines, I-80 east to exits 220 or 225, north to Amana Colonies.

ORANGE CITY
Population 5,582

Some of the shops of this delightful little town out on the prairies of northwestern Iowa stock Delft pottery, wooden shoes, Dutch dolls, and lace and needlework imported from the Netherlands. Other shops sell Dutch pastries, home-cured dried beef, homemade bologna and bratwurst, and imported Dutch cheese. Among the highlights of the three-day **Tulip Festival** on the third weekend in May are a **Volksparade**, **Klompen Dancers**, and a **Straatmarkt**. And colorful tulip beds. **Orange City's** founders were obviously Dutch.

Many of the businesses in downtown Orange City have added facades with architectural elements modeled after 17th- and 18th-century Dutch buildings. Every year the number of Dutch store fronts grows. The city has in fact sent a delegation of its citizens to the Netherlands to study that country's architecture.

There are of course replicas of Dutch **windmills**. Two of them have been built by Orange City businesses: One houses the welcome center and chamber office. The other, built by a paint company, is a working mill with authentically furnished living quarters (open to the public).

Although the town was settled by Dutch immigrants (in 1870), the Dutch architecture is relatively new. The town's more historic buildings are solidly American. The most imposing of these is the **Sioux County Courthouse** (1904), built in the Richardsonian Romanesque style and listed on the National Register. This grand building has so much to offer, including a 10-foot bronze statue of "Justice" on top of its tower, that a detailed brochure has been prepared for self-guided tours.

The **Century House** is a restored 1900 home decorated and furnished in the manner of the early 1900s (open for tours). Another restored structure, the **Little White Store** (1870s), was moved to its present location in 1880. Typical of its kind, the building has a false Western front and upstairs apartment (check locally for hours).

Zwemer Hall (1894), on the campus of **Northwestern College**, is listed on the National Register. The sandstone building is open to the public.

Special Features

Klompen dancers, a Straatmarkt, two Volksparades each day, and horse-drawn streetcar tours add color and excitement to Orange City's annual **Tulip Festival** (third weekend in May). The three-day festival attracts 150,000 visitors.

> Loyal to its Dutch heritage, Orange City has two Christmas traditions, Welcoming Sinterklaas and Piet into Holland (the first weekend in December) and the traditional religious holiday of Christmas. The beauty of the lighted religious symbols that decorate the downtown in December is responsible for the town's nickname, "The City of White Lights."

Further Information

Orange City Chamber of Commerce, *P.O. Box 36, Orange City, IA 51041 (712) 707-4510, www.orangecityiowa.com*

Directions

From Sioux City, US 75 north to IA 10 (just beyond Maurice), IA 10 east to Orange City.

PELLA
Population 9,685

What a delightful contrast! After driving past Iowa cornfields and rolling pastureland, you enter a town whose gardens, streets, even shop windows speak of Holland. Many of the buildings look like those you'd find in Amsterdam. Parks alive with flowers, fountains, and—of course—windmills seem to beckon at every turn. The town is neat, pretty, unusually clean, prosperous. Old World but also very progressive, **Pella** attributes its good fortune to "old-fashioned virtues like hard work, thrift, honesty and integrity."

The **Dutch Fronts** program, an example of "old-fashioned virtues," is responsible for much of the charm of Pella's buildings. The program encourages businesses to incorporate stepped gables and other elements of Low Country architecture in their construction and renovation. As a result, even McDonald's has a delightfully Dutch look.

One of the program's most enchanting accomplishments is the **Klokkenspel** (*Glockenspiels* in German), a musical clock that sets animated figures in motion. On one side the figures tell of Pella's history, on the other side they step out of the Tulip Time festival. A computer-driven 147-bell carillon provides the music. The Klokkenspel is one of only four animated clock towers in the United States.

The **Pella Historical Village** encompasses some 20 buildings linked by red-brick walkways and, in season, tulips. The **Pella Windmill Interpretive Center**, which forms one entrance to the village, comprises a full-size, functioning 1850 Dutch grain windmill and an authentically Dutch structure that houses the welcome and interpretive center. The windmill, constructed in the Netherlands and reconstructed in Pella, is the largest authentic Dutch windmill in the country. An elevator in the welcome center carries visitors to the mill's outdoor decking, or "stage," 40 feet above the street.

Complementing the mill is the **Molengracht**, or mill canal, and complementing the canal is a full-size **Dutch drawbridge**. Among the most interesting of the other sites in the historical village are the boyhood home of **Wyatt Earp**, the **Sterrenberg Library**, the **Scholte Church**, and the **Miniature Dutch Village**. Shops, a restaurant, condominiums, offices, a theater, and a European-style hotel (the Royal Amsterdam) complete the scene.

The picturesque **Scholte House** (1848), built by Pella's founder, features a fine collection of French and Italian antiques. The National Register house may be toured by appointment. The **Scholte Gardens**, behind the house, display over 25,000 tulips and annuals.

Flowering trees and literally hundreds of thousands of tulips and other flowers contribute to Pella's Old World flavor. (Much of this beauty is the result of a comprehensive planting project, another example of the town's energetic planning.) The tulips and everything associated with them are especially colorful during Pella's annual **Tulip Time**, second weekend in May.

Pella is small enough that its beauty and charm can be absorbed on foot. Park your car and enjoy a little bit of Holland!

Special Features

Lake Red Rock, Iowa's largest lake, is less than four miles from town. The winds make the lake especially popular with sailors, and the over 50,000 acres of diverse habitat attract a variety of nature lovers.

The new **Bos Landen Golf Club** features a 4-star 18-hole championship course. One of Iowa's premier public facilities, Box Landen (Dutch for "Lands of Woods") also boasts an athletic club, 5-acre lake, and 200-year-old hickories and oaks.

• Pella shops display Delftware, fine lace, and other imports from the Netherlands.
• Scrubbing the streets before the Tulip Time parade is a Pella tradition.
• The grinding stones inside the windmill weigh almost three tons.

▶ HISTORIC INN ◀

STRAWTOWN INN, *1111 Washington St., (641) 621-9500, e-mail: innkeeper@strawtown.com, www.strawtown.com. Mid-1800s buildings on National Register, 17 rooms, 17 suites, private baths, TV & phones, full "true Dutch" breakfasts, restaurant, antiques, sunroom with hot tub, country store. $ to $$*

Further Information

Pella Convention & Visitors Bureau, *518 Franklin St., Pella, IA 50219 (888) 746-3882, fax (641) 628-9697, www.Pella.org.*

Directions

From Des Moines, IA 163 southeast to Pella.

THE VILLAGES OF VAN BUREN COUNTY
Population from about 20 to 1,020

Here and there in the Midwest and South, usually far from the city, you can still find a little river town where steamboats once stopped, a place that should have died when the boats stopped coming and industry and trains refused to come. Sometimes the town has one or two old brick stores, but not enough to draw many visitors – or merit a listing in a travel book. If **Van Buren County**, tucked away in a remote part of southeastern Iowa, had one town like that, few would care. But Van Buren County has at least *four* such towns, forming a collection that more than merits a visit.

The four riverboat towns of Van Buren County lie along the banks of the winding **Des Moines River**. Each is within biking distance of the next. Each has its own personality.

Bentonsport (1839), a National Historic District and the tiniest of the towns, has a number of buildings dating from the 1840s-1860s. Adding to the charm of the riverside setting are a one-lane iron bridge (1882), open now only to pedestrians and bikes, and a planting of old garden roses within the picturesque ruins of an ancient mill. The town is the only one of the four to boast crafts shops and resident artists. Several of the houses have been renovated by people from Des Moines, Burlington, and elsewhere wishing to make their homes here.

Bonaparte, founded in 1837, is a National Historic Riverfront District and the smallest Main Street Community in the country. Most of the downtown buildings date from the 1850s-1930s, and many have been restored. Separately listed on the National Register are the **Meek Grist Mill** (1878; now a restaurant), the restored **Des Moines River Lock #5** (1852), and the **Aunty Green Museum** (1844), which houses both a museum and the city library.

Keosauqua is the county seat and largest of the towns. The **courthouse**, listed on the National Register, is the oldest in continuous use in Iowa (tours are available). Another structure on the National Register is the brick and stone **Pearson House** (1847), once part of the Underground Railroad. The **Hotel Manning**, still welcoming travelers, is a "Steamboat Gothic Gem" and beloved Iowa landmark.

Two National Register buildings in **Farmington** are the second oldest church west of the Mississippi (1847), now the **Pioneer Museum**, and a limestone structure (1867) that was once home to a carriage manufacturing company. Farmington is also known for its park on lovely **Indian Lake** and its proximity to **Shimek State Forest** (see below).

Two of the best ways to absorb the charm of Van Buren County are by bike and by river. Country roads in most parts of Iowa are good, open, and often interesting—in other words, ideal for bicycling. In Van Buren County the cyclist has the added advantage of being unencumbered by traffic lights. The towns can also be seen from a canoe, kayak, or tube on the Des Moines River, water conditions permitting.

Special Features

Lacey-Keosauqua State Park, one of the largest parks in Iowa, features trails that wind along the hills and dales of the Des Moines River. One part of the park contains 19 mounds built by an ancient Indian group. Many of the park's structures were built by the Civilian Conservation Corps in the 1930s and are now listed on the National Register.

The trails of the **Shimek State Forest**, the largest continuous stand of forest cover in the state, are ideal for hikers and horseback riders in the warmer months, and cross-country skiers and snowmobilers in the winter.

Van Buren County also has eight or so historic towns located away from the river. Several of those in the western part of the county (for example, Cantril and Milton) serve Amish farm communities.

▶ HISTORIC LODGINGS ◀

HOTEL MANNING, *100 Van Buren St., Keosauqua, IA 52565, (800) 728-2718, e-mail: hotelman@netins.net, www.netins.net/showcase/manning.* 1899 "Steamboat Gothic" Iowa landmark, 18 rooms, some private baths, full breakfasts, antiques, spacious lobby with 18-ft ceilings & Vose rosewood grand piano. $

MASON HOUSE INN, *21982 Hawk Dr. (Bentonsport), Keosauqua, IA 52565, e-mail: Stay@MasonHouseInn.com, www.MasonHouseInn.com.* 1846 inn built to serve steamboat travelers, 8 rooms, 1 cottage, private baths, full breakfasts, antiques, 1880 Buck's cookstove, 1882 Estey pump organ. $ to $$ (cottage extra)

Further Information

Villages of Van Buren, *P.O. Box 9, Keosauqua, IA 52565 (800) 868-7822, www.villagesofvanburen.com.*

Directions

From Des Moines, I-35 south to exit 12, IA 2 east to Van Buren County (in southeast Iowa).

Other Charming Iowa Towns

Bellevue
Decorah
Walnut
West Branch

Chapter 16

KANSAS

ABILENE
Population 6,742

If American history were to be packaged into its most memorable and romantic eras, one of them would surely be the brawling cow-town era of the Old West; another would be the subsequent turn-of-the-century period with its Victorian wealth and extravagance. **Abilene** was a prominent member of both eras, and important parts of each have been carefully preserved and blended with the accomplishments of more recent periods to create one of the most charming and interesting towns of the American plains.

Abilene began in 1857 as a tiny village and stagecoach stop. A few years later two strangers arrived in town and very quickly made Abilene a legend: One was the railroad which, moving ever westward, made Abilene its terminus for several years. The second was the cowboy, who herded cattle up from Texas along the legendary Chisholm Trail to meet the railroad. Abilene became a booming cow/railroad town, the "wickedest and wildest town in the west," known for its brawling, boozing, betting, and other end-of-trail diversions.

The town's chapter in Western history, at least the hottest part of the chapter, was actually rather short, lasting only five years (1867 to 1872). As the railroad moved farther west, however, Abilene became anything but a ghost town: New businesses flourished and soon handsome mercantile blocks and Victorian mansions lined the streets.

The town's most famous property, the **Eisenhower Center**, commemorates a man with family and childhood roots in Abilene's Victorian era. Occupying 22 acres, the center includes a museum (1954), Eisenhower family home, library (1962), visitors center, and Place of Meditation, the final resting place of Dwight and Mamie Eisenhower and their first-born son. The museum

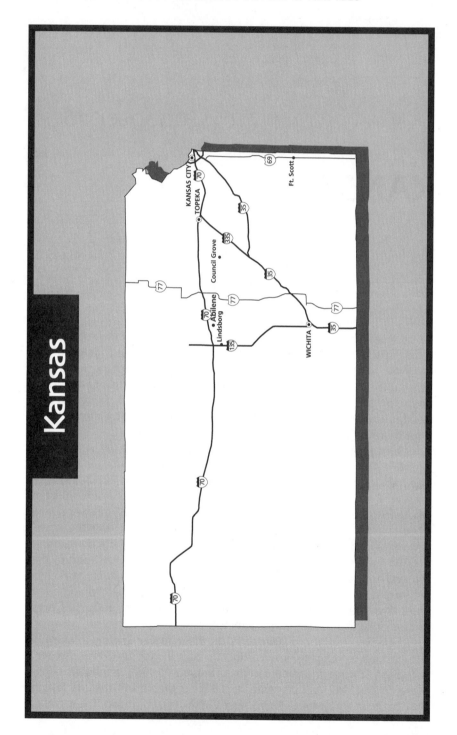

is designed for a self-guided tour through a series of galleries depicting various aspects of Eisenhower's life. Some exhibits are changed periodically to maintain a current relevance.

The best way to enjoy the many mementos of Abilene's Victorian past is with the help of a brochure for a self-guided tour distributed by the Convention and Visitors Bureau (see below). As might be expected, the countless beautiful old homes display a variety of Victorian-era architectural styles. The most prominent homes are the National Register Italianate **Lebold Vahsholtz Mansion** (1880; guided tours by appointment), the center-towered Second Empire/Italianate **Kirby House** (1885, now a restaurant), and the lovely Neoclassical **Seelye Mansion and Museum** (1905). The latter, on the National Register, displays artifacts from a turn-of-the-century patent medicine company (daily tours).

History is also kept alive at the **Dickinson County Historical Museum**, across from the Eisenhower Center, and the adjacent **Museum of Independent Telephony**, which exhibits antique telephones, switchboards, pay stations, and other memorabilia from an early telephone system. The **Vintage Fashion Museum** displays women's, children's, and men's clothing in style from 1870 to 1970.

The arts are represented by the **American Indian Art Center and Gallery**, which features the work of Kansans of American Indian descent, and the **Great Plains Theater Festival**, a year-round professional theater company. The theater stages thrillers, comedies, and musicals and is housed in an 1881 Romanesque church building.

Special Features

The **Abilene & Smoky Valley Railroad Association** offers a 10-mile round trip between Abilene and Enterprise on a 100-year-old wooden coach/diner.

One of Abilene's most popular family attractions is the hand-carved C. W. Parker Carousel, a working carousel that welcomes riders. The carousel is one of many manufactured by a turn-of-the-century Abilene amusement company.
Nearly 3,000,000 cattle were driven from Texas to Abilene during the town's five-year boom period.

▶ HISTORIC RESTAURANT ◀

MR. K's FARMHOUSE RESTAURANT, *407 S. Van Buren, (785) 263-7995.* Abilene landmark & site of President Eisenhower's birthday paddling,

Midwestern cooking—e.g., chicken-fried steak, pan-fried chicken, barbecued brisket, pan-fried catfish, homemade pies. $ to $$

Further Information
Abilene Convention & Visitors Bureau, *Union Pacific Depot, P.O. Box 146, Abilene, KS 67410 (800) 569-5915, www.abilenecityhall.com*

Directions
From Topeka, I-70 west to Abilene; from Wichita, I-135 north to KS 15, north to Abilene

COUNCIL GROVE
Population 2228

The prairie town of **Council Grove** straddles the old **Santa Fe Trail** in the middle of the beautiful **Flint Hills** of central Kansas. The site of the town once afforded water, and also wood from groves of hardwood trees, for the use of soldiers, explorers, and merchant caravans moving west along the Santa Fe Trail. The town itself, established in the late 1850s, was for a while the last supply point on the 780-mile trail.

As you walk or drive along **Main Street**, called **Prairie Plaza** today but once part of the Santa Fe Trail, you will see buildings that were among the last traces of civilization seen by thousands of homesick settlers in the 1860s as they faced west. Much of the early town survives today as a National Historic Landmark District.

The name of the oldest commercial building in town, the **Last Chance Store** (1857), obviously tells something about the store's history. Another of the town's oldest buildings, the **Hays House** (1857), is the oldest continuously operating restaurant west of the Mississippi (see listing below). The structure has doubled over the decades as a mail distribution center, court room, tavern, meeting place for Sunday morning church services, and printing room for the first local newspaper.

Another important structure from pioneer times, the lovely stone **Kaw Mission State Historic Site/Museum** (1850-51) was built as a boarding school for Native American boys and later served as a school for the children of settlers.

Although Council Grove is out on the prairie, there is probably no other town in the country that lists more trees among its historic sites. The **Council Oak**, from which the name of the town arose, was the site of an 1825 council, attended by U.S. officials and Osage chiefs, that agreed to a treaty giving Whites free passage along the Santa Fe Trail. (The tree blew down in a 1958 storm, but the site has been marked by a shrine.)

In addition to the Council Oak there was the **Post Office Oak**, a bur oak that is said to have had a cache in its base where people passing along the trail could leave messages. A third tree was the **Custer Elm** under which legend has it George Armstrong Custer camped while patrolling the trail. (Check with the visitors bureau for the locations of the trunks of these two trees.)

Special Features

KS 177 to the south is one of the state's most scenic routes. Along the way are several little towns that, bypassed by time, are pure Americana. Just outside one of them, Strong City, is the historic **Z-Bar Ranch**, headquarters for the new 10,894-acre **Tallgrass Prairie National Preserve**.

Santa Fe Trail ruts can be seen a few miles west of town, just off U.S. 56. They are on private property, so get instructions from the Visitors Bureau on how to visit them.

▶ HISTORIC RESTAURANT ◀

HAYS HOUSE 1857, *112 W. Main St., (316) 767-5911*. "Oldest restaurant west of the Mississippi" & National Register Historic Landmark, antiques & treasures of local history, original bar, fireplace of native stone; traditional Midwestern cooking—e.g., Crunchy Chicken Salad, steaks, Beulah's Ham, homemade pastries. $$

Further Information

Council Grove Convention & Visitors Bureau, *212 W. Main St., Council Grove, KS 66846 (800) 732-9211, (316) 767-5882, www.councilgrove.com.*

Directions

From Wichita, I-35 north to exit 92, north on KS 177 to Council Grove.

FORT SCOTT
Population 8,362

It seems only fitting that the heartland of America should have one of the country's most beautiful – and beautifully preserved – downtowns. The lawyers, bankers, and socially active women who once moved about **Fort Scott's** streets in their buggies and carriages must certainly have personified

Midwestern middle-class respectability. The setting would have it no other way: 30 miles of brick streets lined by tree-shaded, handsome Victorian homes and awning-shaded, colorfully painted Victorian business blocks. The architecture, while varied, has more depth and age to it than can be dismissed simply as "turn of the century"—some of the buildings go as far back as the Civil War.

At one end of **Main Street** is the **Fort Scott National Historic Site**, a restored 1842 frontier military fort. The only one of its kind in the country, the site comprises 20 buildings, including the hospital, powder magazine, bakery, barracks, and officers' row. Within the buildings are 33 historically furnished rooms. During the summer the fort sponsors weapons demonstrations, an Indian encampment, and other events. Museum exhibits and an audio-visual presentation introduce the visitor to a relatively unknown, but exciting period in America's history.

Other important restorations in the downtown area include the 1873 Gothic-style **Old Congregational Church**, with antique furnishings, and the **Ralph Richards Museum**, an 1893 building displaying turn-of-the-century wedding dresses, railroad memorabilia, antique tools, an old general store, and military artifacts. On the second floor of the museum is a completely furnished Victorian residence with double parlor, library, kitchen, and other rooms.

The downtown area is also the site of two notable memorials, the **Twin Trees Monument** (1965), dedicated to the "Bleeding Kansas" turmoil that occurred before and during the Civil War, and the **20th Century Veterans Memorial** (1990), dedicated to all 20th-century veterans of the U.S. Armed Forces.

Fort Scott's sights may be seen by an hour-long trolley ride (highly recommended). Driving tours, fall foliage tours, antiquing tours, and walking tours are other options.

Special Features

A **U.S. National Cemetery**, one of the 12 such cemeteries designated by President Lincoln, lies on the southeast outskirts of Fort Scott. Established in 1862, and older than the Arlington National Cemetery, the cemetery is the

• A Fort Scott brick business provided 50 million bricks used in the construction of the Panama Canal. Fort Scott brick was also used on the first Indianapolis Speedway.

• The traditional pork steak, fried chicken, and "ham and potato bake" often share the small-town Kansas menu with Midwestern-style cheese burritos and other items of Mexican ancestry.

final resting place of Indian soldiers, Buffalo Soldiers, Civil War veterans, and veterans of more recent wars.

▶ HISTORIC HOTEL ◀

COURTLAND HOTEL (A B&B Inn), *121 E. 1st St., (620) 223-0098, fax (620) 223-1708, e-mail: dngettler@terraworld.net, www.CourtlandHotel.com.* Restored 1906 railroad hotel, 15 rooms, private baths, TV, some phones, expanded Cont. breakfasts, restaurant, family heirlooms, sunny Gathering Room, gift shop, "green-leafy" patio. $

Further Information

Visitor's Information Center, *231 E. Wall St., P.O. Box 205, Fort Scott, KS 66701 (800) 245-3678, (620) 223-3566, fax (620) 223-3574.*

Directions

From Kansas City (KS), US 69 south to Fort Scott.

LINDSBORG

Population 3076

If you look in one direction, the view is of fields and farms, reminiscent of the Midwest. If you look in another, you see the vast spaces of the West. The countryside is incongruous, and sitting in the middle of it all, and adding to the incongruity, is the delightful little Swedish-American town of **Lindsborg**.

Swedish immigrants settling (in 1869) in the **Smoky Hill River Valley** brought with them a commitment to cooperative farming, but also a love and respect for learning and the arts. The value placed on education led to the founding in 1881 of **Bethany College**, known today for its liberal arts tradition and beautiful campus.

The love of the arts has manifested itself in many ways, from woodcarving to folk dancing to the establishment of the 300-voice **Bethany College Oratorio Society**. Most obvious to the visitor are the art galleries, two of which are among Lindsborg's top sites: the **Birger Sandzen Memorial Gallery**, on the campus of Bethany College, which displays works by the widely recognized Swedish-American painter and teacher of art, along with works of other artists; and the **Raymer Center for the Arts**, which includes Lester Raymer's studio, home, and collection of artwork and handmade toys.

The best way to soak up Lindsborg's charm is to wander the old brick streets. The tidy compactness of the town makes a map unnecessary, although one is available from the Chamber of Commerce. Craft shops are especially prominent, along with the art galleries and studios. The emphasis in the shops and restaurants is of course on things Scandinavian: imports, folk art and contemporary crafts, Swedish pastries.

The **Bethany Lutheran Church**, near downtown, has a hand-crafted altar and collection of large oil paintings that give the interior an appearance suggestive of churches in rural Sweden.

Several blocks from downtown is the **Old Mill Museum**, which features Indian and pioneer-day artifacts as well as natural history displays. The museum complex comprises several historic structures, including two on the National Register: the restored 1898 **Smoky Valley Roller Mill** and the **Swedish pavilion** from the 1904 World's Fair.

Special Features

During November and December, Main Street is covered in white lights as Lindsborg lets its Christmas spirit shine. Holiday activities include *Lucia Fest*, "Heritage Christmas," holiday home tours, and a parade.

The panoramic view from **Coronado Heights**, an elevated park and historic site three miles northwest of town, makes it clear that the West is not far away.

> The Dala Horse, a popular form of domestic art in Sweden, was selected by Lindsborg as the symbol of its Swedish heritage.

▶ HISTORIC INN ◀

SWEDISH COUNTRY INN, *112 W. Lincoln St., (785) 227-2985, (800) 231-0266, fax (785) 227-2795, e-mail: info@swedishcountryinn.com, www.swedishcountryinn.com.* Restored turn-of-century bldg., 19 rooms, 2 suites, 1 cottage, private baths, TV & phones, full "traditional Swedish" breakfasts, dining room (breakfast only), handmade Swedish pine furniture, homemade quilts, indoor sauna (massage by appt.), gift shop, bikes. $ to $$

Further Information

Lindsborg Chamber of Commerce, *104 E. Lincoln, Lindsborg, KS 67456 (785) 227-3706, (888) 227-2227, www.lindsborg.org.*

Directions

From Wichita, I-135 north to exit 72 (Lindsborg exit).

Other Charming Kansas Towns

Cottonwood Falls	Wilson
Elk Falls	Yoder

Chapter 17

KENTUCKY

BARDSTOWN
Population 10,374

According to legend, Stephen Collins Foster was inspired by a visit in 1852 to **Federal Hill**, his cousins' home in **Bardstown**, to write *My Old Kentucky Home*, now the Kentucky state anthem and one of the country's most beloved melodies. It isn't clear whether Foster composed the song while in Kentucky or afterward, or whether in fact Foster ever even visited Bardstown. It doesn't really matter, because both Federal Hill and Bardstown look exactly what an "old Kentucky home" ought to look like. Foster couldn't have made a better choice.

Kentucky's second oldest town (1780) and a center of bourbon whiskey production, Bardstown has had its ups and downs (Prohibition was one of its downs). But for reasons relating as much to the townspeople's love of home place as anything, Bardstown has gotten more and more beautiful over the years. The old buildings have been spruced up and restored, the trees have grown bigger and the downtown, although certainly much changed over the decades, looks like it hasn't changed in 150 years. This is a lovely little town that may be closer to the ideal Kentucky home than it was even in Foster's time.

Bardstown has about 200 buildings dating back before 1880. A large number of the older homes were built in the late 1700s and early 1800s. Some are brick, some weatherboarded log, a few frame. Georgian, Federal and, to some extent, Greek Revival styles predominate—the Victorian styles never really caught on.

Two of the most famous homes are open to the public. The first, **Wickland** (1813-1830), home of three governors, may be Kentucky's best

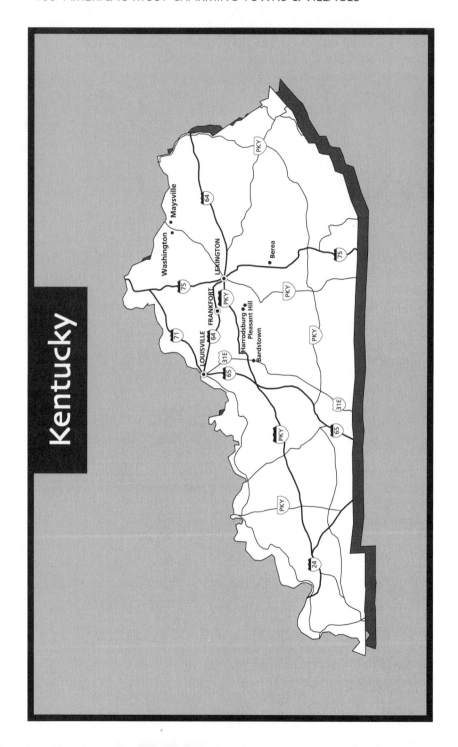

example of Georgian architecture. The second, the stately Georgian **Federal Hill** (1800-1820), now the centerpiece of **My Old Kentucky Home State Park**, is shown by guides in antebellum costume. Close by is the **Civil War Museum**, guardian of Kentucky's largest collection of Civil-War artifacts.

Running a close second behind Federal Hill on the list of historic landmarks is the venerable **Old Talbott Tavern**. Probably built in the late 1700s, the charming brick and stone structure is believed to be the oldest inn in continuous operation west of the Alleghenies. To mention a few who have passed through its doors: King Louis Philippe, George Rogers Clark, Daniel Boone, Queen Marie of Rumania, Henry Clay, General George Patton, Jesse W. James, and John J. Audubon.

The **Basilica of St. Joseph Proto-Cathedral**, the first Roman Catholic cathedral west of the Alleghenies (1819), is another Bardstown landmark. The restored cathedral has several valuable paintings that were donated by Pope Leo XII and Francis I of the Two Sicilies.

Nearby **Spalding Hall** (1826/rebuilt 1837), once a part of **St. Joseph's College** (for young men), is now home to several businesses and two museums. One of the latter, the **Bardstown Historical Museum**, contains Stephen Foster memorabilia, gifts of Louis Philippe and Charles X of France, Jesse James's hat, and Jenny Lind's velvet cape.

Among the items displayed in the **Oscar Getz Museum of Whiskey History**, also in Spalding Hall, is an 1854 E. G. Booz bottle that gave the world the word "booze," and a copy of the liquor license that Abraham Lincoln and his partners held while running a store in Illinois in 1833.

Other buildings of special note in Bardstown include the **McLean House** (ca 1814), one of Kentucky's finest examples of Georgian-style commercial architecture; the 1827 **Presbyterian Church**; and **Roseland Academy** (1820-1830), noted for its three-flight spiral staircase. The **Old County Jails** (1819/1874) were until 1987 the oldest operating jail complex in Kentucky. Guided tours of the buildings, now a bed and breakfast, are available.

Bardstown has two train attractions. Passengers on **My Old Kentucky Dinner Train** dine in elegance against a backdrop of ever-changing scenery. The train departs from the original Bardstown depot. The **Kentucky Railway Museum**, just south of town, offers a 22-mile ride through the scenic Rolling Fork Valley aboard a passenger train powered by a fully restored circa 1905 steam locomotive.

The colorful, costumed cast of the two-hour outdoor musical, The Stephen Foster Story, perform more than 50 of Foster's songs.

Special Features

Three local distilleries (**Heaven Hill**, **Jim Beam**, and **Maker's Mark**) offer interesting tours – and good introductions to local history.

To the northwest of Bardstown is the 14,000-acre **Bernheim Forest**. This lovely area contains trails, ornamental gardens, waterfowl ponds, and hundreds of labeled varieties of trees and shrubs.

John Fitch, inventor of the steamboat, died in Bardstown after years of failed efforts to obtain financial and political support for his invention. Ironically, the steamboat and railroad would eventually hurt Bardstown by drawing growth elsewhere.

▶ HISTORIC INN ◀
TALBOTT TAVERN, *P.O. Box 365, 107 Stephen Foster Ave., (502) 348-3494, e-mail: talbott@bardstown.com, www.talbotts.com.* Oldest Western stagecoach stop in America (1779), 7 rooms, private baths, TV, full breakfasts weekend, Cont. breakfasts weekdays, restaurant, antiques, pub, full of character. $ to $$$

Further Information
Bardstown-Nelson County Tourist & Convention Commission, *P.O. Box 867, Bardstown, KY 40004 (800) 638-4877, www.visitbardstown.com.*

Directions
From Louisville, US 31E/150 south to Bardstown.

BEREA
Population 10,000

Standing in the little park in front of Boone Tavern Hotel in **Berea** is almost guaranteed to bring on feelings of longing and nostalgia. The tulip trees and oaks on the campus across the street have something to do with it. So does the gorgeous white Georgian facade of the hotel, a Kentucky landmark. But it goes beyond that. It is somehow related to what might be called "down home." And Berea has some of the finest of it that our country has to offer.

One of the reasons for this may be that Berea is one of the country's leading centers for the crafting of down-home items. The state in fact has designated Berea the *Folk Arts and Crafts Capital of Kentucky*. It began with the founding in 1855 of the town's centerpiece, **Berea College**, as a place of higher learning for young people, chiefly from Appalachia, who could not afford a college education. Students pay no tuition, and room-and-board costs were — and still are — paid in large part by money earned in the college's labor program. Because ceramics, weaving, woodcraft, broomcraft, and other crafts formed part of the students' work activities, it was inevitable that Berea College and, more generally, Berea would acquire a reputation for quality crafts.

To appreciate the beauty of Berea's crafts, step into the lobby of the **Boone Tavern Hotel** (1909). Although the sheer quality of the work can hide the fact, most of the furniture and furnishings are handmade. The food is also homemade, of course, and let's face it, things like Chicken Flakes in a Bird's Nest, spoon bread, and Southern Pecan Pie can only add to the charm.

Shops offering everything from handmade brooms and patchwork quilts to mountain dulcimers and quality furniture are located in **Old Town** (on N. Broadway) and on campus at The College Square. Some of the work is by local craftspeople, some of it is by students in the college's crafts program. The **Log House Craft Gallery** on Main Street displays student crafts and, on its second floor, the Wallace Nutting collection of early American furniture.

Shopping maps and directories are available in the **Welcome Center**, a restored 1917 railroad depot that has been listed on the National Register.

Special Features

A tour of the loomhouse at **Churchill Weavers**, Berea's first non-college industry, provides an opportunity to watch as some of the most beautiful handwoven fabrics anywhere take form on the handmade looms.

While visiting Berea try your skill at skittles, a handcrafted table-top bowling game. Skittles may be played at the Welcome Center on in the lobby of the Boone Tavern Hotel.

Visitors interested in antiques should explore the 400 block of Chestnut Street.

- Berea College was the first interracial college south of the Mason-Dixon line.
- The Draper Building on the Berea College campus is a reproduction of Independence Hall in Philadelphia.

▶ HISTORIC HOTEL ◀

BOONE TAVERN HOTEL, *Main St., (800) 366-9358, fax (859) 985-3715, e-mail: boonetavern@berea.edu, www.boonetavernhotel.com*. One of Kentucky's best-known inns (1909), 58 rooms, private baths, TV & phones, dining room (Kentucky cooking at its finest), period furnishings, pets (with refundable deposit), gift shop with handcrafts from Student Craft Industries. $ to $$

Further Information

Berea Tourist & Convention Commission, *201 N. Broadway, P.O. Box 556, Berea, KY 40403 (859) 986-2540, (800) 598-5263.*

Directions

From Lexington, I-75 or US 25 south to Berea (45 minutes).

HARRODSBURG/PLEASANT HILL
Population 7335

There are no two other towns in the country that in a single day could provide the visitor with a more thorough and delightful introduction to a state than **Harrodsburg** and **Pleasant Hill**. Harrodsburg, the first permanent English settlement west of the Alleghenies (1774), is one of those places where a beautiful setting and collection of historic attractions have blended to produce a town with a truly distinct character—albeit a very Kentucky one. The **Shaker Village of Pleasant Hill**, just seven miles away, provides one of the finest examples of historic restoration in the country. The village is a National Historic Landmark from boundary to boundary.

The **Harrodsburg/Mercer County Tourist Commission** publishes an exceptionally thorough walking/driving tour guide. Among other things, the booklet begins with a glossary that, with no more than a few minutes' study, is guaranteed to turn the reader into someone with a working knowledge of early American architectural history.

St. Philip's Episcopal Church (1860/61), a Gothic Revival gem, has only one truly centered window, the window back of the altar. For as the designer, the Right Rev. Benjamin Bosworth Smith, taught, "Only Providence is perfect, and man should ever be mindful of such." The Greek Revival **Methodist Parsonage** (ca 1840) has housed more than 60 ministers and their families for over a century and a half.

Beaumont Inn (1845), a major local landmark, was for more than seven decades one of the South's leading female colleges. The building has been owned and operated as a country inn by the same family since 1917. **Morgan Row**, another landmark, is the oldest row house in Kentucky (1807) and the first one constructed west of the Allegheny Mountains.

Old Fort Harrod State Park features an exact replica of the original fort built in 1775. Included on the park grounds are a federal monument dedicated to George Rogers Clark (1934), the oldest pioneer cemetery west of the Alleghenies, and the log cabin in which Abraham Lincoln's parents were married (1806). The Greek Revival **Mansion Museum** (1810 / 1830), also on the grounds, houses exhibits that tell of Kentucky's past, including the Civil

War era when state loyalties were divided between North and South. Craft demonstrations are held in the park during the warmer months.

The Shakers were members of the largest communal society in the country during the 19th century, the *United Society of Believers in Christ's Second Appearing*. Called Shakers because of their ritualistic dance, they were celibate, pacifistic, creative, and hard-working (and obviously had to recruit from the outside).

Pleasant Hill's 33 original buildings and miles of stone fencing are preserved on 2,700 acres of rolling Bluegrass countryside. Among the village's most notable structures are the **Centre Family Dwelling** (1824-1834), which contains a 40-room exhibit of original Shaker crafts and furniture; the **Trustees' Office** (1839), with twin spiral staircases; and the **Meeting House** (1820), where Shaker music is performed.

Special Features

Excursions along the high limestone cliffs of the historic **Kentucky River** can be taken during the warmer months aboard the sternwheeler *Dixie Belle*. The boat departs a short distance from Pleasant Hill, at Shaker Landing.

Filling out the day, evening performances of *Daniel Boone—The Man & The Legend*, an outdoor drama adventure, are held in Harrodsburg during the summer months in the James Harrod Amphitheater.

- Harrodsburg was the site of Kentucky's first law courts, religious service, school, and gristmill.
- The population of Shakers at Pleasant Hill peaked near 500 in the 1830s.

▶ HISTORIC LODGINGS ◀

BEAUMONT INN, *638 Beaumont Inn Dr., (800) 352-3992, fax (859) 734-6897, cmdedman@searnet.com, www.beaumontinn.com*. 1845 inn on National Register, 29 rooms, 2 suites, 2 cottages, private baths, TV & phones, full "Southern" breakfasts, restaurant (famed), antiques, spacious parlors, pool, extensive grounds, Kentucky landmark. $$ to $$$$

SHAKER VILLAGE OF PLEASANT HILL, *3501 Lexington Rd., (800) 734-5611, (859) 734-5411, fax (859) 734-7278, e-mail: info@shakervillageky.org, www.shakervillageky.org*. Guest rooms throughout restored 19th-century Shaker village (National Historic Landmark), 81 rooms including 4 suites & 1 cottage, private baths, TV & phones, breakfast available, restaurant (Shaker & regional foods served family-style), Shaker reproduction furniture, village tours, hiking trails on 2,800 acres of rolling Bluegrass farmland. $ to $$$

Further Information

Harrodsburg/Mercer County Tourist Commission, *P.O. Box 283, 124 S. Main St., Harrodsburg, KY 40330 (859) 734-2364, (800) 355-9192, www.harrodsburgky.com.*

Directions

From Lexington, US 68 southwest to Harrodsburg.

MAYSVILLE/WASHINGTON
Populations 7169/about 500

Located far from the interstates and in a rather remote part of the state, **Maysville** and neighboring **Washington** are certainly among Kentucky's best kept secrets. Each town reached its heyday during an interesting and romantic time in history, and these times are preserved in the form of two picture-postcard historic districts. Steam-driven riverboats still put into Maysville, an old Ohio River town that once went by the name of *Limestone*, and in Washington, sometimes called *Old Washington*, costumed guides escort visitors along flag-stone walks past buildings that may have known Daniel Boone.

Maysville, or Limestone, was founded in 1784, but didn't reach its golden era until a few decades later. A major tobacco market, the town was a hub of riverboat traffic during the middle years of the 19th century. Maysville remains very much alive, but Kentucky's and adjacent Ohio's major centers of commerce did develop elsewhere, and the town was therefore able to preserve some of its inheritance from the old river days.

Established in 1786 as a pioneer post, Washington developed rapidly into one of the more important towns east of the Alleghenies. Although maybe a little larger now than in the 1790s, Old Washington remains a tiny community that looks in many ways like it did 200 years ago.

One of the loveliest (and most photographed) features of Maysville's historic district is a group of **row houses** (ca 1850) that look like a blend of old New Orleans and antebellum Kentucky. The New Orleans flavor is due to the use of iron grillwork by builders who were familiar with Louisiana because of the riverboat trade.

The **Mason County Museum**, now on the National Register, was built as the public library around 1876. The museum uses changing displays and touch exhibits to introduce the visitor to local history. Included are old photos and detailed river dioramas. A genealogical library and an art gallery are also housed in the National Register building. Two other sites of interest in the historic district are the Greek Revival **Mason County Courthouse**, built as a city hall in 1844, and the **National Underground Railroad Museum**, whose exhibits honor the several stations of the Underground Railroad in the Maysville area.

The first stop in Old Washington should be the **Cane Brake**, one of the town's original cabins (1790) and now the visitors' center. In addition to information and historical literature, the center offers an orientation film, guided tours, and a walking-tour map. The historic district lists no fewer than 45 buildings, most built between 1785 and 1812. Four are early buildings that are on tour from the visitors' center: the **Simon Kenton Shrine**, another of the original cabins; **Paxton Inn** (ca 1810), a station on the Underground Railroad; the **Albert Sidney Johnston House** (ca 1797), birthplace of the famous Confederate general; and **Mefford's Station** (ca 1787), a cabin made in part from planks from a flatboat that brought the Mefford family to nearby Limestone. Two churches are also on tour from the visitors' center, the **Methodist Episcopal Church South** (1848), now known as the Old Church Museum, and the Gothic Revival **Washington Presbyterian Church** (1870).

Several buildings that are not part of the guided tours are nevertheless open to the public. One is **Brodrick's Tavern** (1794), Washington's first tavern; another is the 1845 **Washington Hall**, built as a grand hotel.

Many of the historic homes remain private residences. These include the **George Wood House** (ca 1795), the oldest brick structure in Washington; **Cedar Hill** (1807), which hosted two presidents among other prominent Americans; and **Federal Hill** (1800), built by the brother of John Marshall, Chief Justice of the U.S. Supreme Court.

Another residence, the **Marshall Key House** (ca 1807), was where Harriet Beecher Stowe, a visitor in 1833, witnessed a slave auction that inspired her to write *Uncle Tom's Cabin*. The house is now the **Harriet Beecher Stowe Slavery to Freedom Museum**.

Washington's and Maysville's shops offer a variety of items, including antiques. The out-of-town visitor will be especially interested in the handmade and Kentucky-made crafts.

Special Features

The Maysville area boasts 8 of the 13 **covered bridges** remaining in Kentucky. One, the **Goddard Covered Bridge** (1820), is the oldest covered bridge in the state still open to traffic. A map of the bridges is available from the tourism commission (see below).

Woodworkers, blacksmiths, tinsmiths, and other craftspeople demonstrate their talents in the restored village of **May's Lick** (founded 1780s), 8 miles south of Maysville/Washington. The living village is also home to several antique shops.

On August 19, 1782, almost a year after the surrender of Lord Cornwallis at Yorktown, Kentucky militiamen pursuing British and Indian forces were ambushed near the Licking River. Although the ensuing Battle of Blue Licks lasted only a few minutes, some 60 of the Kentuckians were killed. The battle is commemorated at **Blue Licks Battlefield State Park**, south of Maysville/ Washington. In addition to its Pioneer Museum, the park offers camping, swimming, and hiking.

• The Simon Kenton Bridge (1931), which crosses the Ohio River at Maysville, was a prototype of the Golden Gate Bridge in San Francisco.
• The sternwheelers Delta Queen, American Queen, and Mississippi Queen put into Maysville April through November.

Further Information

Maysville-Mason County Tourism Commission, *216 Bridge St., Maysville, KY 41056 (606) 564-9411*; & **Old Washington, Inc. Visitor's Center**, *Washington, KY 41096 (606) 759-7411.*

Directions

From Lexington, US 68 north to Maysville/Washington; from Cincinnati (OH), US 52 south along Ohio River to Aberdeen, OH (across river from Maysville).

Other Charming Kentucky Towns

Augusta
Danville
Olive Hill
Russellville
Shelbyville

Chapter 18

LOUISIANA

ABITA SPRINGS
Population about 1,800

From about 1884 to 1910, New Orleans families used to journey across Lake Ponchartrain to escape the city and the yellow fever epidemics. Resorts in St. Tammany Parish on the north shore of the lake were attractive because of the clean, fresh ozone-rich air emanating from the thick pine forests there. Although the resort towns are still very much around, and continue to attract visitors, most have been altered by the commercial development that follows the automobile. One notable exception is out-of-the-way **Abita Springs**, a village that remains in many ways the delightful little place that it was 100 years ago.

Abita Springs was once an especially popular resort because of its mineral springs. Situated on the banks of the **Abita River**, the **Abita Springs Pavilion** (1888) marks the site of a spring discovered – and enjoyed – by the Choctaw Indians. The town is unique in that its buildings aren't built against one another as in many historic towns. Their wide spacing and location amongst heavy forests give the town a rural, wilderness character.

Many of the buildings are turn-of-the-century "shotgun" houses that once served as second homes for New Orleans's middle classes. There are also "North Shore"-type houses that are variations of the shotguns but that have a projecting section surrounded by galleries on three sides. Adapting to Louisiana's climate, the most dominant features of most of the houses in Abita Springs are the porches.

Abita Springs is for strolling and absorbing. Don't expect much excitement. Here, as elsewhere in the parish, the azaleas, camellias, dogwoods, and other flowers are gorgeous. The **Tammany Trace**, Louisiana's only rail-to-trail

Louisiana

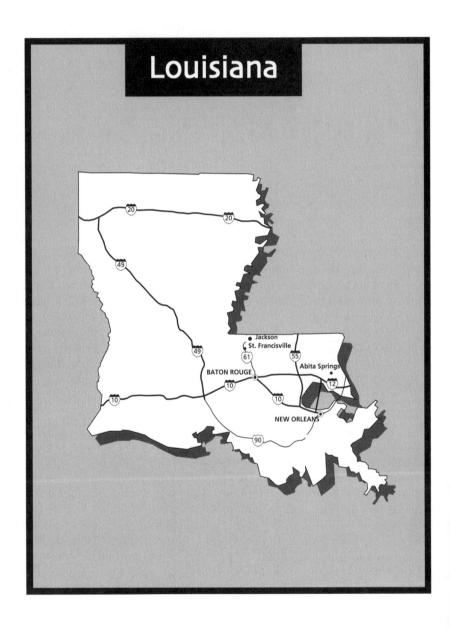

conversion – ideal for joggers, cyclists, rollerbladers, and horseback riders – is open from Abita Springs to **Lacombe** (18 miles).

The best place for shoppers is **Lee Lane** in nearby **Covington**, itself a lovely old town. Here, housed in 19th-century Creole cottages, are unique specialty, antique, and clothing shops.

Special Features

Honey Island Swamp, on the eastern edge of St. Tammany Parish, is one of the most pristine river swamps in the country. Nearly 70,000 acres of the swamp make up a protected wildlife area. Several companies in **Slidell** offer 2- to 4-hour swamp tours, some in environmentally safe craft. The tours provide opportunities to observe alligators, snakes, bald eagles, waterfowl, herons, feral hogs, nutria, otters, mink, and other animals.

Fairview-Riverside State Park south of Abita Springs offers water-skiing, fishing, and crabbing. Under the park's moss-draped oaks is the **Otis House**, built in the 1880s as part of a lumbering camp and renovated in the 1930s to serve as a summer home.

On the grounds of **Fontainebleau State Park**, also south of town, are the ruins of a brick sugar mill built in 1829 by Bernard de Marigny de Mandeville. The park has a swimming pool and a sailboat ramp for launching directly into **Lake Pontchartrain**.

- The Lake Pontchartrain Causeway is the longest over-water highway bridge in the world. It is crossed by millions of vehicles each year.
- The Abita spring water is a critical ingredient of a beer now produced by a successful local micro-brewery.
- The conquest of yellow fever was a major factor in bringing Abita Springs's resort era to an end.

▶ HISTORIC RESTAURANTS ◀

ARTESIA MANOR HOUSE, *21516 Hwy 36, P.O. Box 990, (985) 892-1661, www.artesiarestaurant.com.* In circa 1885 2-story Creole home (National Register) among live oaks & azaleas, contemporary French cuisine—e.g., Poached Gulf Shrimp, Grilled Black Angus Filet Mignon, Sautéed Sweetbreads. $$$

LONGBRANCH COTTAGE, *on grounds of the above.* Cottage from early 1800s, antiques; French, Creole, & Pan-Asian influences in cooking—e.g., Seared Wasabi Glazed Tuna, Chef's Fresh Market Fish, Pan Seared Chicken. $$ to $$$

Further Information
St. Tammany Parish Tourist & Convention Commission, *68099 Hwy. 59, Mandeville, LA 70471 (800) 634-9443, www.NewOrleansNorthshore.com.*

Directions
From New Orleans, Lake Ponchartrain Causeway north to Covington, LA 36 east to Abita Springs.

JACKSON
Population 3,891

Jackson is a gracious old Southern town nestled in the rolling, forested Louisiana countryside east of the Mississippi River and north of Baton Rouge. Established in 1815, the town has 124 buildings on the National Register of Historic Places, the second largest number in Louisiana. Included are a number of Louisiana raised cottages as well as several excellent examples of provincial Greek Revival and Victorian architecture.

As in many small rural Southern towns, the most modest and the most pretentious of the buildings often sit side-by-side, or on the same block. Pamphlets are available for self-guided walking and bicycle tours, and guided group tours may be arranged.

Three homes of special interest are Greek Revival **Milbank** (ca 1836) and restored **Centenaria** (ca 1840), both open for tours by appointment, and **Roseneath** (ca 1832), the town's only full-blown high-style Greek Revival building.

The loveliest buildings from the middle of the 19th century are churches. The **Methodist Church** (ca 1852) and the **Baptist Church** (ca 1860) were both built with brick Gothic Revival basilicas. The **Presbyterian Church** (ca 1852) is of the Colonial style and has finely sculptured windows and the old slave gallery. The **Presbyterian Manse** (ca 1816), now a private residence, was built with wooden pegs rather than nails.

Costumed interpreters conduct walking tours of the **Centenary State Commemorative Area**, the site (1826 to 1908) of the College of Louisiana and, later, Centenary College of Louisiana. Exhibits in an 1837 college dorm and circa 1840 professor's residence offer a glimpse at student life and education in 19th-century Louisiana.

A good overview of the area's rich and exciting history is provided by the **Jackson Museum**. The exhibits include antique cars and buggies, Civil War relics, historic ship models, and a diorama of **Port Hudson Battlefield** (Civil War). The adjacent **Old Hickory Village** contains a cotton gin, cane press, general store, and other structures. A replica of a circa 1860 steam locomotive and touring cars offers visitors a short ride past a variety of scenic and historical sites.

Check with the tourism commission (see below) for information on introductory and customized tours of Jackson and the surrounding country-side.

Special Features

Thirteen miles to the east of Jackson on scenic LA 10 lies **Clinton**, another charming old Southern town with strong historical connections and a fine collection of antebellum and Victorian homes. One of the town's most important buildings is the lovely **East Feliciana Parish Courthouse** (1840), the oldest courthouse in continuous use in Louisiana. **Lawyers' Row** (ca 1840 to ca 1860), which in the 19th century housed some of Louisiana's most skilled lawyers, sits just to the north of the courthouse. Both structures are National Historic Landmarks.

One of the best ways to learn about the history of this region is to spend some time examining the tombstones in the **Old Jackson Cemetery** and the **Clinton Confederate Cemetery State Commemorative Area**.

Tastings of muscadine wines and tours are offered by the **Feliciana Cellars Winery** (Jackson) and the **Casa De Sue Winery** (near Clinton).

• In 1810 the Jackson area became a part of the Republic of West Florida, a country that lasted only 74 days.
• Jackson was once so well-known for its schools and colleges that it was called the "Athens of Louisiana."

Further Information

East Feliciana Parish Tourism Commission, *P.O. Box 667, Jackson, LA 70748 (225) 634-7155, e-mail: tourism1@bellsouth.net.*

Directions

From Baton Rouge, I-110 north to exit 8B, north on US 61 to LA 68, east on LA 68 to LA 10 (and Jackson).

ST. FRANCISVILLE
Population 1,700

A great many of the country's millionaires in the antebellum 1850s lived on plantations along the **Mississippi River** between Natchez and New

Orleans. Quite a number of them had their homes in **St. Francisville** and West Feliciana Parish. The interesting thing is that despite the Civil War, the boll weevil, natural disasters, and changing times, the situation around St. Francisville hasn't really changed very much: The town and parish are still home to many aristocratic old families, intact working plantations, and some of the country's most elegant plantation houses.

St. Francisville sits proudly on bluffs overlooking the Mississippi in the scenic **Tunica Hills** of eastern Louisiana. The area is known as E*nglish Louisiana* because of the ancestry of its settlers (and to distinguish it from *French Louisiana*). The town is steeped in history and has more than 140 structures on the National Register of Historic Places to prove it. Consistent with both the English and Old Southern roots, tradition is important. The old churches and cemeteries are still in use, and dinner is still served with crystal, china, and silver. Especially enduring is the hospitality.

In and around St. Francisville are at least 10 grand plantation homes that are open to the public. Seven are open for tours year-round and three may be toured by appointment. Many second as bed and breakfasts. One of the most gorgeous is **Rosedown Plantation** (1835) with its avenue of moss-draped oaks and magnificent restored gardens. Another is the incredibly beautiful **Greenwood Plantation** house (ca 1830), a Greek Revival mansion surrounded by 28 columns. Within are silver door knobs and hinges and a 70-foot baronial hall. Although smaller than its pre-Civil War 12,000 acres, Greenwood is still a working plantation.

The Gothic **Grace Episcopal Church** (1858-1860), the second oldest Episcopal church in Louisiana, has an especially beautiful interior with fine plaster work and carved double-rowed pews.

A visit to the **Museum of the West Feliciana Historical Society** provides a good introduction to the town. Included in the wealth of information available here are instructions for a mile-long walking or driving loop tour.

Special Features

Audubon State Commemorative Area, to the east of St. Francisville, is the site of **Oakley House**, where John James Audubon completed or began approximately 80 of his bird paintings. The simple but beautiful house was

> • The builders of Rosedown were among the first Louisiana planters to import camellias.
> • Although cotton is certainly still grown in the Delta, many of today's working plantations, including those of West Feliciana Parish, produce cattle, hay, and pecans.

built about 1806 and is listed on the National Register. Oakley's rooms have been restored in late Federal Period style. In addition to the house, there is a restored formal garden, large detached plantation kitchen, plantation barn, two slave cabins, and other facilities.

Further Information

West Feliciana Parish Tourist Commission, *P.O. Box 1548, 11757 Ferdinand St., St. Francisville, LA 70775 (800) 789-4221, (225) 635-6330, www.stfrancisville.us.*

Directions

From Baton Rouge, I-110 north to US 61, north to St. Francisville (30 mins).

Other Charming Louisiana Towns
Clinton
Covington
Franklin
Napoleonville
New Roads
St. Martinville

Chapter 19

MAINE

BETHEL
Population 2,375

Nestled among the scenic **White Mountains** of western Maine, **Bethel** is a village that has appeared on Christmas cards. As you might expect, the village has a National Register historic district, **Broad Street**, lined with 19th-century white clapboard houses that are pure New England (several are now inns – see listings below) and businesses housed in renovated Victorian homes.

The permanent white settlement of Bethel began in 1774 but because of the American Revolution the village grew very little until the 1780s. The oldest house in town, the **Dr. Moses Mason House** (1813), forms part of the Regional History Center of the **Bethel Historical Society**. Next door, and also part of the history center, is the 1821 **O'Neil Robinson House**. Both houses display period furnishings and early murals and offer changing exhibits. Another town landmark, the **Gould Academy**, is a highly respected independent school that was founded in 1836.

Bethel's mountainous setting and proximity to **Sunday River** and other major ski resorts make winter the high season here; the area offers some of the best skiing in the East. The sports calendar is four-season, however. The fishing and hiking are superb, the logging roads are designed for mountain biking, and canoeing opportunities vary from lily-pad paddling to whitewater plunging. The renowned **Bethel Inn & Country Club** has one of the top-ranked golf courses in the Northeast (open to the public).

Special Features
About eight miles north of town is the 1870 **Sunday River Bridge**, one of Maine's most picturesque covered bridges. The bridge is sometimes called,

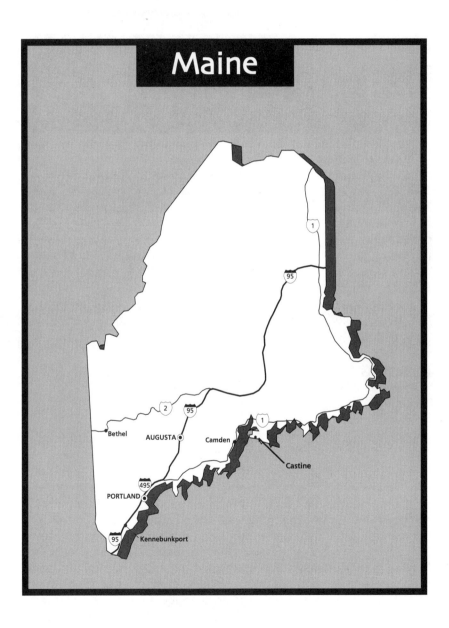

Maine

for obvious reasons, *Artists' Bridge*. **Grafton Notch State Park**, about 14 miles from Bethel, is a mountainous park featuring waterfalls, nature walks, and trail heads for five trails, including the **Appalachian Trail**.

> • The NTL Institute, known for its workshops on leadership development, was founded in Bethel in 1947.
> • The Sunday River Ski Resort offers the only lift-served mountain bike park in the East.

▶ HISTORIC RESTAURANT ◀

THE SUDBURY INN, *151 Main St., P.O. Box 369, (207) 824-2174, (800) 395-7836.* Inn built in 1873, traditional New England menu—e.g., Beef Tournedos ("two petit filet mignon steaks, one in a demi glace, the other in a Great Hill blue cheese sauce, both accompanied by a potato chive cake"), candlelit dining room featuring original tin ceilings & fireplace, full bar, lively pub serving casual fare, entertainment. $$ to $$$ (dining room), $ to $$ (pub)

Further Information

Bethel Area Chamber of Commerce, *P.O. Box 1247, Bethel, ME 04217 (207) 824-2282, (800) 442-5826 for area lodging reservations, www.bethelmaine.com.*

Directions

From Portland, I-495 north to exit 11, ME 26 north to Bethel.

CAMDEN
Population 5,060

Camden is one of those rare places that in real life actually live up to the most romantic of legends. Enticing shops cluster about a picturesque harbor, and time-mellowed New England houses, almost always in white, compete for the prettiest settings along the streets and roads. The grandest or most charming of the houses always seem to have an old sign out front announcing "Antiques" or "Inn." Views of the harbor and bay appear at every turn, and during the warmer months each view includes dozens of white-on-blue sails.

This is sailboat country and to get to know it every visitor should spend at least a couple of hours out on **Penobscot Bay**. Maine needs to be seen from both land and water, weather permitting of course. Camden offers a variety of cruise options on both schooners and motor vessels. Some day trips are as short as an hour, others last all day. For those with more time, overnight, 3-day, and 6-day cruises of the Maine coast are available on classic windjammers. Weekend and week-long courses are offered for visitors wishing to learn how to sail.

Camden's shops, designed as much for the browser as the buyer, tend to shun tee shirts in favor of hand-loomed sweaters and handcrafted jewelry. The restaurants and dining rooms feature some of Maine's most popular products—lobsters, scallops, mussels, clams, haddock, salmon, and swordfish.

Special Features

A road ascends to the top of 900-ft **Mount Battie** in **Camden Hills State Park** just north of town. The views of the bay from the summit are spectacular.

Just down the coast from Camden is **Rockport**, another picturesque harbor village popular with artists and writers.

Nearby **Lincolnville** offers a sandy public beach as well as freshwater swimming and fishing on **Megunticook Lake.**

In Camden it is possible to take a "cruise" on a working lobster boat.

▶ HISTORIC INN ◀

WHITEHALL INN, *P.O. Box 588 (High St.), (207) 236-3391, (800) 789-6565, fax (207) 236-4427, stay@whitehall-inn.com, www.whitehall-inn.com.* Inn with ancestry as 1834 captain's house, "landmark for hospitality" since 1901, 50 rooms, private baths, phones, full breakfasts, dining room with award-winning wine list, period furnishings, parlors, sprawling porches with antique wooden rockers, tennis, shuffleboard. $ to $$$$

Further Information

Camden-Rockport-Lincolnville Chamber of Commerce, *P.O. Box 919, Camden, ME 04843 (207) 236-4404.*

Directions

From Portland, US 1 north (along coast) to Camden.

CASTINE
Population 800

Maybe it's because Castine is a harbor village. Or maybe it's because its many lovely historical homes lend a domestic air. Or maybe it's because its location at the end of a small peninsula and off the main tourist routes gives it a sense of cozy remoteness. Whatever the reason, Castine's mood is personal and intimate. And the setting is beautiful.

Castine began as a series of trading posts and forts shadowed by an ever-changing series of flags (French, Dutch, British, and American). Once American sovereignty was established—and given two British occupations, one during the Revolution and the other during the War of 1812, this could never be taken for granted—the village prospered as a port and shipbuilding center. Later, as the day of the sailing vessel waned, the economy found new life with the arrival of the steamboat and its charge of Victorian summer visitors.

Bordering Castine's streets, especially Main and Perkins, are restored 18th- and 19th-century Georgian and Federal homes and a number of beautiful churches, among them the Gothic **Trinity Chapel** (Episcopal, 1897) and the steepled **Trinitarian** and **Unitarian churches** (1829 and 1790, respectively). Adding variety and color are several Victorian and Edwardian summer homes (or "cottages").

The **Wilson Museum** (1921) displays prehistoric, local Indian, and Victorian-era artifacts. Included in the museum complex are a working blacksmith shop and the restored pre-Revolutionary **John Perkins House**, with late 18th-century furnishings (open to public).

Among the locations marking Castine's early history are the archaeological excavation of France's **Fort Pentagoet** (late 1600s), now a National Historical Landmark, and **Fort George State Park**, the site of the Britain's **Fort George** (1779). Another historic site, **Dyces Head Lighthouse** (1828), offers a commanding view of the Penobscot River—as well as a public path to the water.

The **Maine Maritime Academy**, with buildings dating to 1873, offers undergraduate and graduate courses in ocean and marine-oriented programs. The academy's training vessel, the *T. V. State of Maine*, is berthed at the foot of Main Street. Guided tours of the ship are sometimes available.

Clustered near the waterfront are galleries, restaurants, and quaint shops displaying antiques, gifts, books, and other items. Day-sailing cruises are available for those who can't get enough of Maine's proverbial coastal beauty.

Special Features

Blue Hill, another pretty waterside village, is just a few miles north and east of Castine.

• One of the country's worst naval defeats ever occurred near Castine in 1779 when 40 some American vessels were lost at the hands of a superior British naval force.
• Inhabitants of Castine once included members of the Penobscot Loyalist Society, a group refusing to forswear allegiance to the king. The Castine loyalists were later forced to move to Canada—along with their dismantled houses.

▶ HISTORIC INN ◀

THE CASTINE INN, *Main St., P.O. Box 41, (207) 326-4365, fax (207) 326-4570, e-mail: relax@castineinn.com, www.castineinn.com.* 1898 Italianate inn with wrap-around porch, 16 rooms, 3 suites, private baths, full breakfasts, dining room with hand-painted mural, pub, antiques, art, wood-burning fireplace in sitting room, English gardens, view of harbor. $$ to $$$$

Further Information

Castine Merchants Association, *P.O. Box 329, Castine, ME 04421 (207) 326-4884*; or **Ellsworth Area Chamber of Commerce**, *P.O. Box 267, Ellsworth, ME 04605 (207) 667-5584*

Directions

From Portland, I-95 to Augusta, ME 3 to Belfast, US 1 to ME 175 (1 mi past Bucksport), south on ME 175 (becoming ME 166) to Castine; from Bangor, ME 15 to Bucksport, then as above

KENNEBUNKPORT
Population 1,100

The booklet distributed by the **Kennebunk/Kennebunkport** Chamber of Commerce is a virtual album of lovely photographs. The scenes are as remarkable for their diversity as their beauty. Here are the sea, broad beaches, harbors, boat yards, rocky coasts, tree-shaded village streets, Victorian gingerbread, historic churches, quaint shops, sleigh rides, flowers, and frosty ponds. Some of the most beautiful scenes combine the colors of the sea with the red-violet of the wild rugosa roses that grace the coast.

Kennebunkport is in a sense a collection of colorful places, of images. There's something here for about everyone. But maybe especially for someone who loves the sea and wishes a little seclusion mixed with the charms and comforts of a relaxed old New England town.

Along Kennebunkport's beach, sheltered riverfront, and manicured streets stand the magnificent homes of 18th- and 19th-century sea captains, shipbuilders, and well-to-do summer residents. Many of the homes are now bed-and-breakfast inns—few towns can match Kennebunkport in the number, variety, and quality of its inns. Few, either, can match the experience of the town's innkeepers. Kennebunkport also boasts several restored seaside hotels cut out of another era.

The **Brick Store Museum** (Kennebunk) provides a good introduction to the history of the Kennebunks. The museum's shop features quality reproductions and books on local history and crafts.

Another glimpse at the past is offered by the **Nott House** (1853), a gracious Greek Revival mansion with original furnishings. The house, open to the public, is maintained by the Kennebunkport Historical Society.

With a collection of over 250 trolleys from around the globe, the **Seashore Trolley Museum** bills itself as the oldest and largest transit museum in the world. Among other attractions, the museum offers its visitors a three-mile ride on an antique electric trolley.

The list of activities open to the visitor is as long and varied as the list of views. Many of the historic buildings on **Dock Square** and elsewhere house galleries and artists' studios, as well as a diversity of interesting little shops. For off-shore excursions there are whale-watching, sightseeing, and sailboat cruises. Deep-sea fishing charters can also be arranged. More active pursuits include scuba diving, canoeing on the ponds and streams, golfing, and cross-country skiing. And, of course, hiking or biking along the coast.

Special Features

Just up the coast from Kennebunkport is the picturesque fishing village of **Cape Porpoise**, home port to a fleet of lobster boats. The coastal scenery here is especially beautiful.

The arrival of Santa Claus by lobster boat and candlelight caroling at the **Franciscan Monastery** are among the events of Kennebunkport's *Christmas Prelude*, celebrated the first and second weekends in December.

▶ HISTORIC INN ◀

THE CAPTAIN LORD MANSION, *6 Pleasant St., P.O. Box 800, (207) 967-3141, (800) 522-3141, fax (207) 967-3172, e-mail: innkeeper@captainlord.com, www.captainlord.com.* 1812 country inn on National Register, 15 rooms, 1 suite, private baths, phones, full breakfasts, antiques, working fireplaces, afternoon refreshments, spacious grounds with flower gardens & "Memory" Garden with fountain, one of best in country. $$$ to $$$$

Further Information

Kennebunk, Kennebunkport Chamber of Commerce, *17 Western Ave., Kennebunk Lower Village, P.O. Box 740, Kennebunk, ME 04043 (207) 967-0857, fax (207) 967-2867, www.visitthekennebunks.com* (ZIP for Kennebunkport is 04046.)

Directions

From Portland, I-95 south to exit 3 (Kennebunk), east to Kennebunkport.

Other Charming Maine Towns
Bar Harbor
Northeast Harbor
Wiscasset

Chapter 20

MARYLAND

CHESTERTOWN
Population 4,000

Heir to the second largest collection of Georgian and Federal homes in Maryland, and only a short drive from some of the largest metropolitan areas on the Eastern seaboard (though sheltered from them by Chesapeake Bay), peaceful little **Chestertown** offers a tempting destination for city dwellers seeking an afternoon or weekend's change of pace. Distinctive shops and topnotch eateries and hostelries can only add to the temptation.

Situated on the banks of the Chester River on Colonial Maryland's Eastern Shore, Chestertown-to-be was chartered as a port of entry by the Maryland Assembly in 1706. The town became the seat of Kent County and, as can be seen from the many mansions of successful merchants, prospered. One of the town's centerpieces, **Washington College**, was founded in 1782 and today ranks as the 10th oldest liberal arts college in the country.

Among the most interesting of the many historic brick homes are the **Geddes-Piper House** (ca 1780), a restored townhouse that is now headquarters to the Historical Society of Kent County (restricted summer hours), and the **Hynson-Ringgold House** (1735-1772), called the "Abbey" in Colonial times. Many of the most historic and architecturally interesting houses open their doors to tours in mid-September and mid-December; several are also open as bed and breakfasts.

The **White Swan Tavern**, now a bed and breakfast, is a town landmark with roots dating to before 1733. Just down the street is **Fountain Park**, so called for its ornate 1899 cast-iron fountain. The park is the scene of open-air concerts and arts and crafts exhibits as well as a Saturday morning farmer's market.

Maryland

Two historic churches grace the shaded streets and brick sidewalks of this lovely old town. The first, **Emmanuel Episcopal Church** (1768), is known for its Tiffany window. The second, **Old St. Paul's Church**, is the oldest church in continuous use in Maryland. The church's vestry house, restored, dates to 1766.

Chestertown is designed primarily for two kinds of people: those who seek the spell of another century and those who enjoy exploring quaint little shops—and maybe especially gift, clothing, and antique shops. But the town and its county also attract cyclists, birders, nature enthusiasts, fishermen, and sailors. There are public beaches at **Betterton** and **Rock Hall** (see below), and marinas and boat landings lie in virtually every direction.

Special Features

The waterman's town of **Rock Hall**, southwest of Chestertown, is where George Washington, Thomas Jefferson, and other founding fathers came ashore as they traveled from Virginia to Philadelphia. Today the town's 13 marinas, excellent seafood restaurants, and special water events attract pleasure boaters from all over the Chesapeake. In addition to three very interesting museums, the visitor will find antique and curio shops, artisan and crafts studios, cozy bed & breakfasts, and a restored 1930s ice cream parlor and drug store.

- Actress Tallulah Bankhead is among the notables buried in Old St. Paul's Episcopal Church cemetery.
- General George Washington accepted a place on the Board of Visitors and Governors of Washington College and gave a gift of 50 guineas "as an earnest of my wishes for the prosperity of this seminary."
- According to legend, the body of Sir Peter Parker, a British commander mortally wounded in a skirmish near Chestertown during the War of 1812, was returned to England preserved in a barrel of rum.

▶ HISTORIC HOTEL ◀

THE IMPERIAL HOTEL, *208 High St., (410) 778-5000, fax (410) 778-9662, e-mail: imperial@friendly.com/, www.ImperialChestertown.com.* 1903 hotel (winner of restoration award), 11 rooms, 2 suites, private baths, TV & phones, expanded Cont. breakfasts, acclaimed dining room (with courtyard), authentic period furnishings, Cellar Coffee Bar & Bakery, verandah overlooking sycamore-lined street. $$ to $$$$

Further Information
Kent County Visitor Center, *122 N. Cross St., Chestertown, MD 21620 (410) 778-0416, fax (410) 778-2746, www.kentcounty.com or www.chestertown.com.*

Directions
From Baltimore & Washington, DC, US 50/301 across Bay Bridge, US 301 north to MD 213, MD 213 north to Chestertown.

HAVRE DE GRACE
Population 12,000

A walk through **Havre de Grace** offers two pleasures in one: a tour of an historic old Chesapeake Bay town and a 1 1/2-mile stroll along or near the coast. Almost all of the town's top sights are on a more-or-less straight line between the **lockhouse** on the north and the **lighthouse** on the south. Not surprisingly, most of the sights (the lockhouse and the lighthouse for beginners) have a direct connection with the water.

About 800 (!) structures contribute to the **Havre de Grace Historic District**. The most interesting were built in the Canal (1830-1850) and Victorian (1880-1910) periods. It was during the former that the town became an important link in the country's growing network of railroads and canals; it was during the latter that the town enjoyed the economic benefits of the late industrial age.

Two mansions of special architectural interest are the **Spencer-Silver Mansion** (1896) and the **Vandiver Inn** (1886), both now bed and breakfasts. George Washington stopped several times at the **Rodgers House**, the oldest structure in town (1787). The oldest church in town is **St. John's Episcopal Church** (1809), noted for its simple early 19th-century beauty. Another "oldest" is the **Concord Point Lighthouse** (1827), the oldest lighthouse in the country in continuous use when decommissioned in 1975.

The **Susquehanna Museum of Havre de Grace** includes the restored **locktender's house** (1840) and reconstructed pivot bridge adjoining the lock where mule-drawn canal boats once entered the **Susquehanna & Tidewater Canal**. The **Havre de Grace Decoy Museum**, the town's most popular site and home to valuable collections of decoys, celebrates the "historical and cultural legacy of waterfowling and decoy making on the Chesapeake Bay."

The *Martha Lewis* (1955), a two-sail bateau (or "skipjack"), is the only dredge boat still oystering commercially under sail in the country. Rides and charter excursions are available.

Today Havre de Grace is in what might be termed a "tourism, recreation and retirement" era. The waterfront has several marinas, a boardwalk, and a chain of lovely parks. Historians will write of this era's buildings, too. Among the newest are waterfront condos, structures that many locals believe only serve to enhance the town's charm.

Special Features

The sites of a once-working Harford Count farm are preserved at the **Steppingstone Museum** in **Susquehanna State Park**, northeast of town. The sites include a farmhouse furnished in turn-of-century style and shops that "preserve and demonstrate the rural arts and crafts of the 1880-1920 period."

- The annual Duck Fair, held on the grounds of the decoy museum, features a head-whittling contest, punt-gun demonstration, and duck-&-goose calling contest.
- A $2,000 no-questions-asked reward still awaits the person who returns the original lighthouse lens, missing since 1975 and presumed stolen.

Further Information

Havre de Grace Office of Tourism & Visitor Center, 450 Pennington Ave.., *Havre de Grace, MD 21078 (800) 851-7756, (410) 939-2100, fax (410) 939-8300, www.havredegracemd.com.*

Directions

From Baltimore, I-95 north to exit 89, MD 155 east to Havre de Grace.

ST. MARY'S CITY
(not incorporated)

St. Mary's County, not far south of Washington, D.C., is an agricultural and forested part of Maryland that remains – at least for the present – relatively free of commercial development. Situated on a peninsula bounded by the **Potomac River** on one side and **Chesapeake Bay** on the other, the county is served by highways that go nowhere but the sea. Denied the flocks of tourists that migrate along interstates, the county's restaurants offer seafood at what may be the lowest prices on the Eastern Seaboard north of the Carolinas.

St. Mary's City, in the southern part of the county, was the location of Maryland's first capital (1634-1695) and site of the fourth permanent English settlement in the New World. Although the original town eventually disappeared following the removal of the capital to Annapolis, some of it has been re-created as **Historic St. Mary's City**, a grand 800-acre outdoor history museum and one of America's best-preserved Colonial archaeology sites.

The museum's Visitors Center complex features an exhibit hall, orientation materials, and introductory video. Self-guided walking tours begin here (an audio tour is available to rent). The various exhibit areas are connected by a walking trail system. Here and elsewhere, skits highlighting events in the town's history are acted out by costumed interpreters.

The meticulously reconstructed 1676 cruciform brick **State House** is one of the museum's centerpieces. Another reconstructed 17th-century site, **Smith's Ordinary**, once offered ordinary folk "dyett and drink," lodging, and good-fellowship.

Staff at the **Woodland Indian Hamlet** demonstrate Native American skills. Visitors can try their hand at grinding corn or starting a fire without matches.

The re-created **Godiah Spray Tobacco Plantation** is a living history farm. Complete with livestock and crops, the farm portrays the lives of a middle-class planter family in the 1660s. Farm structures include the one-room main **Dwelling House** (even the middle classes had little privacy in Colonial Maryland), tobacco sheds, and animals pens.

The square-rigged *Maryland Dove*, equipped with 17th-century instruments, is a replica of one of the two ships that carried Leonard Calvert, his settlers, and colony supplies from England. The tiny size of the ship – which was probably used to carry supplies – nicely underscores the extent of the risks the settlers had to face.

Trinity Episcopal Church, adjacent to Historic St. Mary's City, was constructed in 1829 of bricks from the original State House (1676). The **Leonard Calvert Monument** (1890) stands on the church grounds.

Special Features

Point Lookout State Park is located to the south of St. Mary's City at the confluence of Chesapeake Bay and the Potomac River. In the park is the site of Fort Lincoln, a fort built by Confederate prisoners of war. Two memorials honor the 3,364 Confederate prisoners who died here. A Civil War museum is in the Visitor's Center. Cruises to sparsely populated **Smith Island** depart from the park during the summer.

St. Ignatius Church (1785), in St. Inigoes near St. Mary's City, is a Roman Catholic church with magnificent stained-glass windows and altar. The church has one of the oldest cemeteries in the country. The floor of **St. George's Episcopal** (**"Poplar Hill"**) Church (1740), in nearby **Valley Lee**, contains ancient gravestones of four early rectors. Both churches are on the National Register of Historic Places.

The Margaret Brent Memorial honors the first woman in America to request the right to vote in a legislative assembly (1648). The request was denied.

Further Information

Tourist Information Center, *St. Mary's County Chamber of Commerce, 28290 Three Notch Rd., Mechanicsville, MD 20659 (800) 762-1634, (240) 895-4990, www.stmaryscity.org.*

Directions

From Washington (DC), MD 5 south to St. Mary's City.

ST. MICHAELS
Population 1,301

There are ideal retirement communities and there are communities ideal for raising families. Although maybe qualifying for either or both of these, the little harbor town of **St. Michaels** clearly sets the standard for yet a third kind of ideal community: the post-family, pre-retirement community, the perfect place for people who, having raised a family and achieved some degree of professional or business success, wish to change careers and pursue second lives.

St. Michaels is in fact home to many people living "second lives," and it's not hard to understand why. With its narrow streets, pastel-tinted houses, and tidy little gardens, the town is certainly picturesque. It is also gently lapped by a sailboat-trimmed harbor, historic to the tune of 350 years, and remote from, but not too much so (maybe two hours), several East Coast metropolises. The natives welcome newcomers, and the shops, restaurants, and inns range from the solid to the downright upscale. Biking is a favorite travel mode.

The **Chesapeake Bay Maritime Museum**, one of the finest in the country, features an outdoor portion with skipjacks, log canoes, and a restored 1879 lighthouse. The indoor portion has an aquarium of bay life and exhibits that detail, among other things, the history of steamboating on the bay and the impact of migratory birds on the bay's economy, sport, and art.

On the green around which the town was built is **St. Mary's Square Museum** (main building ca 1800), with displays of local memorabilia. The **Cannonball House** (ca 1805), on the square, is a Georgian house whose roof was penetrated by a cannon ball during the War of 1812. St. Michaels's other historic sites include the red brick **Old Inn** (ca 1816) and the restored **Freedom's Friend Lodge** (1883).

Special Features

Sightseeing cruises on **Chesapeake Bay** and the **Miles River** range from the part-day to the overnight, from the narrated historic to the nature-loving.

The incredibly beautiful waterside village of **Oxford**, not far to the southeast, is a smaller but quieter and more sedate relative of St. Michaels.

> • British cannon balls generally overshot the town in the War of 1812 because the forewarned citizens hoisted lanterns to masts of ships and tops of trees.
> • Many visitors to St. Michaels arrive by boat and rent bikes to get around town.

▶ HISTORIC RESTAURANT ◀

208 TALBOT, *208 N. Talbot St., (410) 745-3838*. In 4 small dining rooms in 1870 bldg.; "innovative" American cuisine—e.g., Seared Halibut with Lobster Mashed Potatoes & a Lobster Sauce; reservations recommended. $$$

Further Information

The Talbot County Office of Tourism, 11 North Washington St., *Easton, MD 21601 (410) 770-8000/8091, fax (410) 822-7922, www.tourtalbot.org (ZIP for St. Michaels is 21663.)*

Directions

From Washington (DC), US 50 east (via Chesapeake Bay Toll Bridge) to Easton, MD 33 west to St. Michaels.

Other Charming Maryland Towns

Berlin
Cambridge
Easton
New Market
Oxford
Snow Hill
Solomons

Chapter 21

MASSACHUSETTS

CHATHAM
Population 6,900

Thrust farther out to sea than any other part of Cape Cod—and with the possible exception of the eastern fringe of Nantucket Island, any other part of southern New England— **Chatham** likes to call itself the "First Stop of the East Wind." The sea—and more specifically, fishing and shellfishing—has been important to Chatham pretty much since the arrival of the Pilgrims in 1656. And as can be seen from the catches being unloaded down at the **Chatham Fish Pier**, it still is.

In more recent times the sea has also brought tourists, enough in fact to nearly quadruple the town's population in the summer. Location on Cape Cod would be more than enough to attract visitors, but Chatham itself offers about everything a vacationer might want in a New England town (except, of course, skiing): for the swimmer or beachcomber, town beaches as well as the famous sands and dunes of **Cape Cod National Seashore**; for the harried or overworked, a solid selection of quiet old inns; for the sports-minded, superb salt-water and fresh-water fishing; for the art collector, galleries with works of Cape Cod artists; for the bicyclist, the **Chatham Bike Route** and **Cape Cod Rail Trail**; for the naturalist, nature trails and some of the best birdwatching in New England.

The **Old Atwood House** (1752), owned by the Chatham Historical Society, offers an excellent introduction to the cultural and natural history of the town and Cape. On display are collections of shells, Sandwich glass, antiques, paintings, and other art objects. Changing exhibits use relics and old photographs to recall Chatham's past.

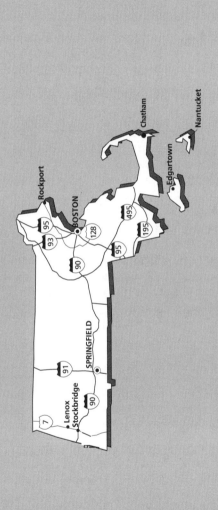

The Railroad Museum, one of New England's best, features a 1910 caboose, exceptional collection of model trains, and wide range of railroad memorabilia. Of special interest to miniaturists is a diorama of the Chatham railroad yards as they looked in 1915. The museum is housed in the depot that served Chatham from 1887 to 1937.

Visitors interested in learning more of Chatham's past will enjoy a tour of the restored **Mayo House**, an 1820 Cape Cod home with period furnishings (check locally for hours). **Chatham's Old Grist Mill** (1797), which once used wind power to grind corn, is another of Chatham's preserved historic treasures.

The Chatham Fish Pier has a visitors' balcony so that the return of the fleet (shortly after noon, depending on tidal conditions) and unloading of the haddock, cod, flounder, lobster, and other catches can be viewed, photographed, and maybe even sketched or painted. Also at the pier is *The Provider* (1992), a monument erected to honor the Chatham fishing industry. The monument's design was selected from some 100 entries in an international competition.

It is only to be expected that a New England town with a long history of tourism should evolve one or two special tourist traditions. And Chatham has done just that. First, visitors love to drive "Down to the Light" and park for an especially grand view of the Atlantic. *The Chatham Light*, or simply *The Light*, refers to the town's 1877 **lighthouse**. A second tradition is heading for Kate Gould Park on Friday evenings during the summer months for a concert by the celebrated **Chatham Band**. The concerts include community singing as well as dance numbers for both children and adults.

Special Features

Guided tours are available of the **Monomoy National Wildlife Refuge** on Monomoy Island. The refuge, one of a chain for migratory waterfowl along the Atlantic Flyway, provides nesting, feeding, and resting grounds for at least 285 species. Boat liveries are also available.

Chatham's summers tend to be cool and prone to morning fogs; the Chamber of Commerce describes the fog as "just another conversation piece." Many believe that the most beautiful season here is Indian summer.

▶ **HISTORIC INN** ◀

CHATHAM WAYSIDE INN, *512 Main St., P.O. Box 685, (800) 391-5734, (508) 945-5550, fax (508) 945-3407, e-mail: info@waysideinn.com,* *www.waysideinn.com*. Renovated & expanded 1860s inn in heart of town, 54 rooms, 2 suites, private baths, TV & phones, variety of dining settings, period furnishings, fireplaces, balconies, pub, heated pool, outside porch areas. $$ to $$$$ (seasonal)

Further Information

Chatham Chamber of Commerce, *2377 Main St., P.O. Box 793, Chatham, MA 02633-0793 (800) 715-5567, (508) 945-5199, www.chathaminfo.com.*

Directions

From Boston, I-93 south to MA 3 (Exit 7), south to Sagamore Bridge over Cape Cod Canal, US 6 east to MA 137 (Exit 11), south to MA 28, east to Chatham center.

EDGARTOWN
Population 3,763 (year-round)

Located seven miles off the Massachusetts coast, **Martha's Vineyard** is in some ways its own little country. Made self-sufficient and independent by their separation from the mainland, the islanders refer to the rest of the world as *off island*. Even the climate is different here: Bathed by the Gulf Stream, the island enjoys cooler summers and milder winters than the rest of New England. When islanders wish a summer home, they buy or build it on another part of the island. Why travel to the mainland when your own little "country" offers six very different towns and a landscape that varies from beaches and wetlands to hills and forests?

Over 350 years old, **Edgartown** is Martha's Vineyard's county seat and oldest town. It is best known for its harbor, filled with sailboats and yachts, and its beautiful old Federal-style whaling captains' homes. Many of the homes can be seen by touring **North** and **South Water Streets**. Some now serve as inns and restaurants.

The 12 rooms of the **Thomas Cooke House** (1765) feature antiques, ship models, costumes, and artifacts of the whaling and early farming industries (tours available). The house is just one of several historic exhibits maintained by the **Martha's Vineyard Historical Society**.

The painstakingly restored **Vincent House** (1672), owned by the **Martha's Vineyard Preservation Trust**, is the oldest known house on the island (open to the public). Also owned by the preservation trust, the six-columned Greek Revival **Old Whaling Church** (1843) has been transformed into a performing arts center.

Few places in our country have as many good restaurants and charming inns per capita as Edgartown. There are no fast-food restaurants nor discount department stores.

Special Features

Each of the towns on Martha's Vineyard has its own character, and no one can agree on which is most charming. In addition to Edgartown, the towns are **Chilmark**, **Aquinnah**, **Oak Bluffs**, **Vineyard Haven**, and **West Tisbury**.

- The spreading pagoda tree on South Water Street was brought to Edgartown as a seedling from China in the early 19th century.
- Old box pews that are entered through little doors still occupy the Federated Church (1828).
- Early 19th-century camp meetings of the Methodists helped pave the way for the development of a summer resort industry.

▶ HISTORIC INN ◀

THE DAGGETT HOUSE, 59 N. Water St. (Edgartown), (800) 946-3400, (508) 627-4600, fax (508) 627-4611, www.thedaggetthouse.com. Inn comprising three historic properties, incl. 1660 tavern & early 1800s whaling captain's home; 31 rooms incl. 2 suites, private baths, TV & phones, "traditional New England country" breakfasts, candlelit dining in ca 1660 dining room, antiques, hidden stairway, harbor & garden views. $$$ to $$$$ (summer), $$ to $$$ (value season)

Further Information

Martha's Vineyard Chamber of Commerce, Beach Rd., P.O. Box 1698, Vineyard Haven, MA 02568 (508) 693-0085, E-mail mvcc@vineyard.net, www.mvy.com (Zip for Edgartown is 02539.)

Directions

Year-round ferries from **Woods Hole** (MA) carry passengers and cars (car reservations recommended—even required on certain dates in season). Seasonal passenger ferries sail from **New Bedford**, **Falmouth**, **Onset**, and **Hyannis,** MA; and from **Montauk**, NY, and **New London**, CT. The island is also connected via regularly scheduled plane service to Boston, Hyannis, Nantucket, New Bedford, Providence, New York City, and Washington, D.C.

LENOX
Population 5,600

When a village nestled in a **Berkshires** valley has a summer performing arts schedule rivaling that of many large cities, it should be obvious why by November its inns are nearly booked solid for the following summer. Many of the towns listed in this guide can boast of art galleries, summer stock productions, concerts, and other celebrations of the arts. None, however, possesses the cultural splendor of **Lenox's** billings:

There is first of all the **Tanglewood Estate**, site of the **Shed**, the internationally famous summer stage of the **Boston Symphony Orchestra**. Also at Tanglewood are the handsome, modern **Seiji Ozawa Hall** (chamber music), and the **Hawthorne Cottage**, a reproduction of the small farmhouse where in 1850-51 Nathaniel Hawthorne wrote several books.

There is also the 1,200-seat concert hall of the **Berkshire Performing Arts Theatre** of the **National Music Center**, where top artists perform every genre of American music. A major music library, a hands-on museum, and a home for retired performers are among the projects planned for the center.

Then there is **The Mount**, Edith Wharton's 1902 summer estate (now the **Edith Wharton Restoration**). The Mount is home to *Shakespeare & Company*, a festival with performances of Edith Wharton, Henry James, and Shakespeare in two indoor and two outdoor theaters.

Lenox also has its off-stage attractions. In addition to one of the finest and most romantic collections of inns in the nation, there are eight or nine art galleries and some of the best shopping in western Massachusetts. Tucked among the woods and hills about Lenox are estates built as summer houses by late 19th- and early 20th-century East Coast millionaires. Most of the houses remain private and their magnificence must therefore be admired from the distance. Some have been converted to inns (see below).

The development of cross-country ski areas and the proximity to great downhill skiing are adding winter to the list of Lenox's most popular seasons.

But irrespective of season, and beyond the onstage and offstage, Lenox is a place of quiet beauty and refinement. It's a place to relax amongst reminders of a more gracious time. One senses that Wharton and James and others of their era still choose to linger here.

Special Features

The grounds and miles of trails of the 1,112-acre **Pleasant Valley Wildlife Sanctuary** north of Lenox provide a beautiful all-season retreat for people as well.

Among the attractions at the **Berkshire Scenic Railway Museum** are model railroads and a 10-minute train ride.

> Tea is served between performances staged in the drawing room at The Mount.

▶ HISTORIC LODGINGS ◀

In addition to an excellent selection of B&Bs and small inns, Lenox boasts a number of larger inns, many of them full-service. These were often built in the 19th century as elegant country houses, or "Berkshire Cottages." They include the **Apple Tree Inn**, **Blantyre**, **Cornell Inn**, **Gables Inn**, **Rookwood Inn**, **Village Inn**, and **Wheatleigh**.

Further Information

Lenox Chamber of Commerce, *P.O. Box 646, Lenox, MA 01240 (413) 637-3646.*

Directions

From Springfield, I-90 (Massachusetts Turnpike) west to Interchange 2, US 20 north to MA 183, MA 183 into the village.

NANTUCKET ISLAND

Population approximately 7,000 (year-round)

Now and then history and nature collaborate to produce an ambiance so distinctive and compelling that it has to have a name. The usual practice is to select the name of the town most closely associated with the ambiance. **Nantucket** is a good example. For many Americans "Nantucket" refers to more than a town or island: It refers to fishing boats and wharves and surf, to old shingled houses with potted flowers, to candlelit dinners in 18th-century dining rooms, to harbors and lighthouses and models of old ships.

Nantucket is all of this, and more. The town is also a leading art colony, a major yachting and recreational fishing center, a living museum (the entire island is a historic district). And the beaches are some of the best in the country, if not the world.

The importance of whaling to Nantucket's history is highlighted by the engaging exhibits of the **Whaling Museum** (1847), one of Nantucket's top sites. The restored Greek Revival **Hadwen House** (1845), built by a whale-oil merchant, and the elegant decor and furnishings within offer another glimpse of what whaling once meant to Nantucket (open to public).

The **Oldest House** (1686) provides a good example of the late 17th-century house plan of the Massachusetts Bay Colony (tours). Built a few decades later, the **Macy-Christian House** (1723) combines the Colonial style of its inhabitants with the late 19th-century revival of its most recent owners (tours).

For a magnificent view of Nantucket Town and Island, climb the tower of the **First Congregational Church** (open to public). Another church, the **Unitarian Universalist Church** (also open), houses the town clock and 1810 bell in its gold-domed tower. The church's interior is decorated with trompe l-oeil painting.

Special Features

The **Nantucket Life Saving Museum** is a re-creation of the original station built by the U. S. Life Saving Serving in 1874. Picnickers are attracted by the scenic location (open to the public).

- The Old Mill (1746) still grinds corn during favorable weather. The mill is the sole survivor of four that once served the island.
- The two-story Old Gaol (1805), made of logs fastened with iron bolts, may have been the first jail in the U.S. to allow prisoners to go home at night.
- Nantucket Memorial Airport is the second busiest commercial airport in Massachusetts (after Boston's Logan International).

▶ HISTORIC LODGINGS ◀

ACCOMMODATIONS ET AL, *11 India St., (508) 228-0600, (800) 992-2899, fax (508) 325-4046, e-mail: RHInn@aol.com www.robertshouseinn.com.* Group of restored 18th- & 19th-century inns & cottages, 60 rooms & 5 suites, 3 cottages, private baths, TV & phones, Cont. breakfasts, antiques & canopy beds, fireplaces, harbor views, packages. $$$$ (private baths) $$$ (shared baths)

Further Information

Nantucket Island Chamber of Commerce, *48 Main St., Nantucket Island, MA 02554 (508) 228-1700, fax (508) 325-4925, www.nantucketchamber.org* Contact the Chamber of Commerce for a copy of their very colorful and comprehensive annual guide.

Directions

Comfortable ferries, some operating year-round, serve Nantucket from **Hyannis** (MA). Cars require reservations, but passengers and bicycles do not.

Visitors are discouraged from bringing cars to the tiny island. Several major as well as local airlines have regularly scheduled flights from a variety of East Coast locations.

ROCKPORT
Population 7,432

Rockport's harbor is one of the most picturesque on the Eastern seaboard. Anyone who enjoys paintings and watercolors of American fishing villages and harbor scenes has seen the harbor in a gallery somewhere. Indeed, an old red shack on Bradley Wharf has been so popular with art students that it has been nicknamed *Motif No. 1*. Many of the famous names in American art, including Winslow Homer, Edward Hopper, and Fitz Hugh Lane, placed their easels at or near Rockport Harbor at some stage in their lives.

Rockport is designed for walking. The main and back streets of the town are bordered by many fine homes built between 1692 and 1864, most in the 1700s. Many are adorned with shutters, fan lights, and old-fashioned gardens. Also along the streets is a goodly collection of studios and galleries. Of special note (and popularity) are the diverse exhibits in the galleries of the **Rockport Art Association**.

The harbor, **Headlands**, and beaches, including a couple right in town, are ideal for hiking and strolling (the Chamber of Commerce publishes a guide that describes three short in-town walks originating from Dock Square). Wildflowers abound in the area's waysides, salt marshes, and ponds. Birdwatchers spot not only the upland birds of New England, but also a wide selection of shore and sea birds. Island cruises and informative whale-watching and lobstering trips are available for those looking to the water.

Special Features
Halibut Point State Park affords splendid views of Ipswich Bay and, on a clear day, points in New Hampshire and Maine. Closer at hand in the park are tidal pools and a beautiful water-filled granite quarry.

- Rockport became the American landfall of the trans-Atlantic cable in 1884.
- Rockport granite was used in the construction of New York's Woolworth Building, New Orleans's Federal Reserve Bank, Philadelphia's Kensington National Bank, and dozens of other structures in the U.S. and elsewhere.

A house constructed of approximately 100,000 copies of Boston newspapers may be visited at nearby **Pigeon Cove**. The house and its furniture, also made of newspapers, required some 20 years to "build."

Note: Rockport has been "dry" since 1856, when some 200 women hatcheted the kegs and poured the contents into the streets. Bring your own paper bag.

▶ HISTORIC INN ◀

EMERSON INN BY THE SEA, *1 Cathedral Ave., (978) 546-6321, (800) 964-5550, fax (978) 546-7042, e-mail: info@EmersonInnByTheSea.com, www.emersoninnbythesea.com.* Inn (originally on stagecoach route) from 1846-1912, transformed to Greek Revival seaside resort hotel in 1912, 34 rooms & 2 suites, private baths, TV & phones, full breakfasts (warm months) or expanded Cont. breakfasts (cooler months), turn-of-century Grand Café with ocean-front dining, antiques & reproductions, deluxe rooms with spa tubs & private balconies, 139-ft verandah, massage, day spa, heated salt-water pool, landscaped gardens, nature trail, snorkeling, diving, shuttle to train/village, Ralph Waldo Emerson once a visitor. $$$ to $$$$

Further Information

Rockport Chamber of Commerce, *P.O. Box 67, Rockport, MA 01966 (978) 546-6575, (888) 726-3922, fax (978) 546-5997, e-mail: lesadept@shore.net, www.rockportusa.com.*

Directions

From Boston, US 1 north to MA 128, MA 128 east to exit 9, MA 127 north to Rockport.

STOCKBRIDGE
Population 2,311

The oldest village improvement society in the United States, the Laurel Hill Association, was formed in **Stockbridge** in 1853. The goal of the association, the oldest preservation society in the U.S., was and remains to "glorify God's grandeur by gracefully combining Art and Nature." Stockbridge is also home to the oldest private land trust in the country, The Trustees of Reservations, founded in 1891. The townspeople of Stockbridge were clearly among the first in the nation to draw attention to the beauty of the past, and to the need to protect it.

Given the village's cultural heritage and beauty, the interest in preservation isn't really surprising. For instance, the buildings and architectural styles along Main Street combine to create one of the most picturesque village scenes in the country. The street is the kind of main street that small American towns are supposed to have – which is probably why Norman Rockwell chose to portray it in his famous painting, *Stockbridge Mainstreet at Christmas*.

Among the structures along the street are the famed **Red Lion Inn** (1773, rebuilt 1897; on the far right of Rockwell's painting), the **Cat and Dog Fountain** (1862), the Greek-Revival **Stockbridge Town Hall**, and the **Stockbridge Library**, one of the oldest libraries in western Massachusetts (original part built in 1864). On the lower level of the library is a history museum and research center, known as the Historical Room.

Then there are the *Cottages*, summer homes built during the closing years of the 19th and beginning of the 20th centuries by the barons of America's post-Civil War industrialization. Although many of the mansions have since disappeared, enough remain to add color and an Old World sense of aristocracy to Main Street and the other byways in and round the village (see also Lenox). Most are private, but several of the most important – along with a few earlier, Colonial houses – are open to the public.

The oldest house of these is **Mission House** (1739), the home of John Sergeant, first missionary to the Stockbridge Indians. The restored house has period furnishings and a warm Colonial garden. Other historic – and beautiful – homes include:

Naumkeag (1885) is one of the village's best-known Cottages. The 26-room gabled mansion, built by an ambassador to England, boasts a collection of Chinese porcelain, elegant furnishings, and especially lovely gardens. Although built much earlier (1820s), the Federal-style **Merwin House** displays late 19th- and early 20th-century furnishings. The house and its peaceful grounds also go by the name of *Tranquility*.

Chesterwood is the name of the studio (1898) and Colonial Revival summer home (1901) of sculptor Daniel Chester French. One of the country's foremost artists, it was French who created the *Minute Man* (1875) in Concord, Massachusetts, and the seated *Abraham Lincoln* (1922) in the Lincoln Memorial in Washington, D.C. Chesterwood is home to nearly 500 pieces of sculpture, as well as to gardens and rolling woodlands.

The **Norman Rockwell Museum**, dedicated to a man unrivaled as a perceiver and illustrator of American charm, contains Rockwell's studio and the world's largest collection of original Rockwell art. Architect Robert A.M. Stern has skillfully fashioned Colonial elements to create a new museum building that is itself a masterpiece of American charm. The museum's 36 acres of scenic grounds are available for picnicking and relaxation.

Stockbridge's shops display American and European items ranging from paintings and antiques to gourmet foods, contemporary glass, candles, and hand-knit sweaters. During the summer months the renowned **Berkshire Theatre Festival** presents classic, contemporary, and children's theater.

Special Features

For a healthy hike leading up to three-state mountain views, ask for directions to the nearby historic Ice Glen area.

The 15-acre **Berkshire Botanical Garden**, northwest of town, features plantings of primroses and conifers, herb garden, rose garden, ponds, woodland walks, and in general, quiet beauty.

West Stockbridge, less frequented than Stockbridge and Lenox, is another charming Berkshires village.

▶ HISTORIC INN ◀

THE RED LION INN, *30 Main St., (413) 298-5545, fax (413) 298-5130, e-mail info@redlioninn.com, www.redlioninn.com.* Famed landmark (est. ca 1773), 83 individually decorated rooms and 25 suites in main inn & nearby guest houses, some private baths, TV & phones, elegant main dining room, Widow Brigham's Tavern, The Lion's Den Pub, antiques, fitness center, flower-laden courtyard, heated pool, gift shop, golf privileges, packages. $$ to $$$$

Further Information

Stockbridge Chamber of Commerce, *P.O. Box 224, Stockbridge, MA 01262 (413) 298-5200.*

Directions

From Springfield, I-90 west to Interchange 2, MA 102 west to Stockbridge.

Other Charming Massachusetts Towns

Concord
Great Barrington
Hyannis
Sheffield
Williamstown

Chapter 22

MICHIGAN

FRANKENMUTH
Population 4,408

Frankenmuth, Michigan's *Little Bavaria* is one of the more unusual of our country's towns. Gabled and towered Bavarian buildings dot the landscape, giving the town a romantic European appearance. At the same time, landscaped parkland and the American love of detached construction put distance among the buildings, giving the town a spacious American appearance. The colorful Bavarian-inspired architecture of many of the structures, including the glockenspiel tower and covered bridge, is delightful. At the same time, many of the visitor attractions along the two-mile business stretch could exist only on this side of the Atlantic. A tug of war exists between the authentic and the copied, with charm the sometimes victor.

In 1927 a Frankenmuth restaurant began serving chicken dinners family-style. Word got around and by the 1940s "Frankenmuth-style" chicken was attracting people from as far away as Detroit. The use of Bavarian-style architecture made its appearance around 1948. Today, two restaurants serve over 2,000,000 dinners, mostly chicken, annually. And the architecture is more popular than ever.

Unlike many towns with more natural sources of charm, Frankenmuth has plenty to keep all members of the family busy. Tours of woolen mills, woodcarving shops, a restored grist mill, and a brewery inform and entertain at the same time. Among the many interesting shops is one specializing in pewter, another that boasts the world's largest outdoor cuckoo clock, and yet another that displays thousands of dollhouse miniatures in over 100 room settings.

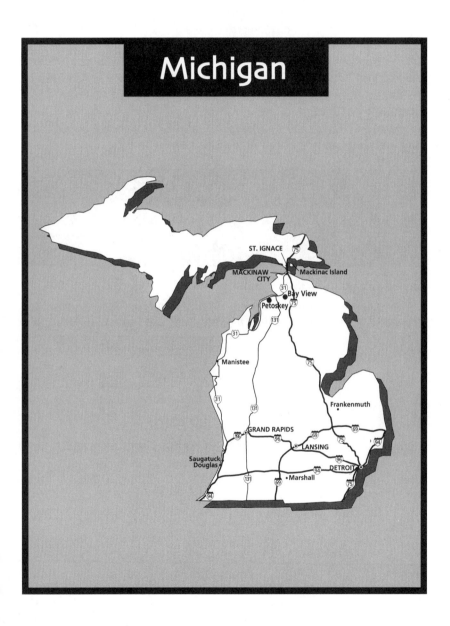

Bronner's Christmas Wonderland, the world's largest Christmas store, offers 500 different styles of Nativity scenes, 260 decorated trees, 200 styles of nutcrackers, and over 50,000 unique trims and gifts.

For those tiring of the commercial, there are guided tours of Gothic **St. Lorenz Lutheran Church** (1880). The church has a 167-foot steeple, vivid stained-glass windows, and a carved baptismal font that is a replica of the font in the original St. Lorenz Church in Bavaria.

Special Features

Frankenmuth boasts two large full-service Bavarian-style lodges, the **Bavarian Inn Lodge** and **Zehnder's Bavarian Haus**.

> • "Franken" refers to the province in Bavaria from which the town's settlers came, and "Muth" means "courage" in German.
> • Three million people visit Frankenmuth each year.

Further Information

Frankenmuth Convention & Visitors Bureau, *635 S. Main St., Frankenmuth, MI 48734 (989) 652-6106, (800) 386-8696, www.frankenmuth.org.*

Directions

From Detroit, I-75 north to exit 136, MI 83 east and north to Frankenmuth.

MACKINAC ISLAND
Population maybe 550 year-round

The stately **Grand Hotel**, white with yellow awnings. The magnificent Victorian "cottages" lining the **West** and **East Bluffs**. The red geraniums against the white clapboards and fence pickets. The purples, lavenders, and whites of the lilac trees in the spring. The sound of horses and carriages. The neatness, cleanliness, and civility. Above all, the blue waters of **Lake Huron**, everywhere. **Mackinac** (MACK in awe) Island offers spectacular views and a glorious diversity of images.

Strategically located between **Lakes Huron**, **Michigan**, and **Superior**, Mackinac Island has been a special place for centuries. The Indians, the French, the English, and finally the Americans all passed through. The island slipped from beneath one flag to another, but always without bloodshed. The history, the beauty, and the pollen-free environment began to attract steamships in the latter half of the 19th century, and Mackinac Island became a resort. Most visitors came to spend a few days. A few, the wealthy, built cottages so that they might spend the summer.

More than 80 percent of the island is now a state park. The island is closed to motor vehicles (except for snowmobiles in the winter, and even these are restricted). All travel is by foot, bicycle, or horse. Horse-and-carriage taxi service is available, as are tours and "drive yourself" hourly rentals. There are also private liveries and an abundance of bicycle liveries.

The most important of the historic sites is **Fort Mackinac** (1780), a **Mackinac State Historic Park** and National Historic Landmark. Given by the U.S. Government to the State of Michigan in 1895, the fort is manned by "soldiers" who portray the military life of the Victorian 1880s. The fort comprises 14 restored buildings, including the **Soldiers' Barracks**, **Post Hospital**, the **Guardhouse**, and the **Officers' Stone Quarters**. The latter was built with 4-foot-thick walls and is one of Michigan's oldest buildings. Each building tells its own special story using exhibits, multi-media programs, costumed reenactments, and period craft demonstrations. There are also concerts.

The 1817 **Robert Stuart House**, the home of an Astor Fur Company manager, is now a museum displaying local artifacts, including records of the American Fur Trading Company, and period rooms. The displays of the **Beaumont Memorial** describe the famous 1820s experiments of Dr. William Beaumont, who furthered knowledge of the human digestive system by examining the stomach of a man with a gunshot wound in the abdomen. Other historic buildings include the 1830 **Mission Church**, the three-story **Indian Dormitory** (now a museum with period furnishings), and the **McGulpin House**, a restored Canadian log residence.

Even visitors staying elsewhere should spend some time at the majestic **Grand Hotel** (1877). Non-registered guests may stroll the 600-foot verandah, enter and explore the hotel (until 6:00 p.m., admission fee), and after obtaining a special guest pass, wander the Grand Hotel gardens. Luncheon may be taken at any of six restaurants. Tea is served mid-afternoon, dinner is accompanied by music of the hotel's orchestra, and music and demitasse follow in the parlor. The bar atop the tower has one of the finest views on the island. An orchestra plays in the evening: There are few experiences so romantic as going by carriage up to the ballroom of the Grand Hotel for an evening of dancing (dress code after 6:00 p.m.).

If you like pure white snow, clear blue skies, tranquility and stillness, consider visiting Mackinac Island in the winter. A number of businesses remain open to serve cross-country skiers, snowmobilers, and sleigh riders. Ferry boats continue until after the holidays (this is a wonderful place to spend Christmas) and airplane service from S**t. Ignace** is available after the straits freeze. Check with the Chamber of Commerce for information on transportation, lodging, and snow conditions.

Special Features

A bicycle or carriage tour around the island on MI 185 (8.1 miles) includes such sights as Arch Rock, a natural limestone arch that stands nearly 150 feet above the water; Lover's Leap, a 145-foot limestone pillar; and Devil's Kitchen, a cave with a spectacular view of the Lower Peninsula and **Mackinac Bridge**.

Mackinac Island's beautiful lilacs, among the oldest and biggest in North America, were introduced in the 1600s by French missionaries. The annual **Mackinac Island Lilac Festival**, held in mid-June, hosts numerous cultural as well as hometown-style events (e.g., hay rides).

• It should come as no surprise to learn that Mackinac Island's MI 185 is the only state road in Michigan that has never had an automobile accident.
• More than 800,000 people visit Mackinac Island each year.

▶ HISTORIC HOTELS ◀

GRAND HOTEL, *Mackinac Island, (906) 847-3331, (906) 847-3259, www.grandhotel.com.* Michigan landmark est. 1877, 385 rooms, 7 suites, private baths, TV & phones, full breakfasts, 6 restaurants in variety of settings, antiques, orchestra, afternoon tea, 660-ft verandah, gardens, spectacular views, heated pool, golf, tennis, putting green, sauna. $$$$ (per person based on double, MAP)

THE ISLAND HOUSE, *1 Lakeshore Dr., P.O. Box 1410, (906) 847-3347, (800) 626-6304, fax (906) 847-3819, e-mail: info@theislandhouse.com, www.theislandhouse.com.* Hotel est. in 1852, Michigan Historic Site, 94 rooms, 3 suites, private baths, TV & phones, full breakfasts, restaurant, indoor pool, large verandah overlooking Straits of Mackinac, packages. $$ to $$$$

Further Information

Mackinac Island Tourism Bureau, *P.O. Box 451, Mackinac Island, MI 49757 (906) 847-6418 or 3783, (800) 454-5227, www.mackinacisland.org* .

Directions

Commercial air service is available to the island, but most people prefer to go by ferry, departing from either **Mackinaw City** or **St. Ignace**. The ferry ride is itself an experience. Among the many spectacular views is that of the 5-mile-long **Mackinac Bridge** that connects Michigan's lower and upper peninsulas.

MANISTEE
Population 6,968

"The Victorian Port City of Manistee" can be reached by air, land or, if you prefer, by cruise ship or sailboat or canoe. The shores of Lake Michigan border the town's west side, to the east is **Manistee Lake** (and the Manistee National Forest), and through the heart of town flows the **Manistee River**.

Manistee's heyday came in the years after the Civil War when, thanks to the vast pine forests, the town became one of Michigan's most important lumbering centers. Seeing no virtue in frugality, the lumber barons built elegant Victorian mansions and a downtown business district that, today, displays what is probably the finest collection of Victorian commercial buildings in Michigan.

The Romanesque **First Congregational Church** (1892), listed on the National Register, was designed by noted Chicago architect William LeBaron Jenney. Two of the 36 stained-glass windows are Tiffany and two others were displayed at the 1893 Columbian Exposition (tours by reservation). Another National Register church, **Our Saviour's Church** (1868/69), is the oldest Danish-American Evangelical Lutheran Church in America. It has a hand-carved pulpit and Viking ship and is topped by an octagonal spire with finial weathervane (tours by reservation).

The **Ramsdell Theatre** (1903), on the National Register, is acoustically one of the best in the U.S. Among other things, the theater boasts its original thunder machine and an act curtain by Walter Burridge, who designed the sets of the original stage production of *The Wizard of Oz* (tours available).

An especially popular place, in part because visitors are always welcome, is Manistee's Romanesque Revival **Fire Hall** (1889). Now a State Historic Site, the structure hasn't undergone usage or design alterations since it was built and is reputed to be one of the oldest continuously operating firehouses in the state (open for tours).

The 1882 **Babcock House** features period furniture, Oriental rugs, unusual automatic musical instruments, and the original gas light system (guided tours).

There are several ways to explore the Victoriana. Probably the most leisurely and rewarding is a stroll down **River Street**, the main street, followed by a stroll back along the lovely **Manistee Riverwalk**. Both parallel the river, and each other, and do what some of the most charming byways in the world do, twist and turn. A tour aboard a 1900s-replica trolley (hourly) is another option. A brochure outlining a self-guided tour through Manistee's historic neighborhoods is available from the Chamber of Commerce (see below).

Wednesday evening concerts on the river's edge are held in the beautiful Victorian **Gazebo Bandshell** (1991) during the summer months. A variety of performances by the **Manistee Civic Players** delight audiences at the Ramsdell Theatre.

Special Features

But a few blocks from downtown, the white sand beaches of **Lake Michigan** provide a beautiful backdrop for swimming, picnicking, enjoying nature, or just plain lazing.

Chartering and other marine services are available for those seeking coho and chinook salmon, lake trout, steelhead, brown trout, and large, yellow lake perch.

Hiking, boating, cross-country skiing, and other recreational opportunities abound in the some 80,000 acres of the **Manistee National Forest** just east of Manistee.

- Boat watching is a favorite Manistee pastime. Freighters often pass through the center of town on the Manistee River.
- The North Pier Catwalk (1880), on the National Register, is one of five remaining pier catwalks on the entire coast of Lake Michigan.
- James Earl Jones began his career at the Ramsdell Theatre.

Further Information

Manistee Area Chamber of Commerce, 11 Cypress St., *Manistee, MI 49660 (231) 723-2575, (800) 288-2286, www.manisteecountychamber.com.*

Directions

From Grand Rapids, I-96 west to US 31, US 31 north to Manistee.

MARSHALL
Population 7459

Fountain Circle in **Marshall** is without qualification one of our country's grandest circles. Anchored in the center by a Greek Revival Fountain and surrounded by a set of handsome buildings, the circle looks like the product of a marriage between a lovely Continental city and a prosperous Midwestern town. The adjacent streets continue the flavor, except that a little of New England seems to get into the mixture as well.

It was once assumed that Marshall would become the capital of Michigan – moving the capital from Detroit to Marshall was in fact written into the original state constitution. However, when in 1847 the state legislature voted on the matter, Marshall lost by just one vote and Lansing was chosen.

As a kind of consolation prize, and a considerable one at that, the battle's loser went on to become one of Michigan's most beautiful towns. Today, with 867 designated buildings, Marshall is the largest National Landmark District in the country in the "Small Urban" category.

The Chamber of Commerce's self-guided tour brochure includes no fewer than 144 buildings and 49 historic markers! Several of the houses and sites are open to the public during the **Annual Historic Home Tour** on the first weekend after Labor Day.

The **Honolulu House Museum**, on Fountain Circle, was built by a Chief Justice of the Michigan Supreme Court to resemble the mansion he had occupied in Honolulu as U. S. Consul to the Sandwich (Hawaiian) Islands. A blend of Italianate, Gothic Revival, and Polynesian influences, the house has received a number of awards for the recent restoration of the paint-on-plaster wall and ceiling decorations.

Also on Fountain Circle are the lovely stone **Town Hall** (1857), built as a stage coach stop and livery stable, and the **National House Inn** (1835), the first brick building in the county and the oldest operating inn in Michigan (see below).

Throughout the historic district, but especially along the streets to the east and north of Fountain Circle, is a virtual museum of 19th- and early-20th-century American residential architecture. Most of the homes have been restored. The shade trees for which Michigan's towns are well-known make touring the streets especially pleasurable.

Special Features

Marshall's **Michigan Avenue**, designated a "Historic Heritage Route" by the state of Michigan, ranks as one of the finest (and healthiest) main streets in the country. A shopping guide is available from the Chamber of Commerce. Abundant parking is available behind the shops. •

• The 1839 Greek Revival Governor's Mansion was built on the hopeful assumption that Marshall would become Michigan's capital.

• In the 1840s members of Marshall's leading families were sued and heavily fined for their efforts to prevent slave hunters from returning an escaped slave to his former owner in Kentucky.

▶ HISTORIC INN ◀

NATIONAL HOUSE INN, *102 S. Parkview (on Fountain Circle), (269) 781-7374, fax (269) 781-4510, e-mail: innkeeper@nationalhouseinn.com, www.nationalhouseinn.com*. Restored 1835 stagecoach stop on National Register, 15 rooms, private baths, TV & phones, full breakfasts, restaurant, antiques, massive open-hearth fireplace, afternoon tea, sitting garden, gift shop. $$$

Further Information

Marshall Area Chamber of Commerce, *424 East Michigan Ave., Marshall, MI 49068 (269) 781-5163, (800) 877-5163, www.marshallmi.org.*

Directions

From Detroit, I-94 west to exits 110 or 112 (Marshall exits); from Lansing, I-69 south to exit 36.

PETOSKEY/BAY VIEW
Population 6,056

Back in the days before the three-car family and air-conditioned house, residents of large Midwestern cities could escape the summer's heat and humidity—and pollen—by boarding a train or steamboat and traveling up to the clear waters and rolling forests of northern Michigan. Two favorite destinations were **Petoskey** and **Bay View**, adjacent resort communities on Lake Michigan's beautiful **Little Traverse Bay**.

Chartered in 1879, Petoskey started as both a lumbering center and a resort. The town's first passenger train arrived in 1873 and the first brick hotel (still in operation—see Stafford's Perry Hotel below) opened in 1899. Next door, tiny Bay View was founded as a summer retreat in 1875 by the Methodist Church. The village was (and remains) noted for its programs of lectures, concerts, and Sunday evening vespers; it is now a National Historic Landmark with more than 440 cottages, most dating to before 1890.

The many **Victorian buildings** make leisurely walking tours of Petoskey and Bay View appropriate—and very enjoyable. (Check with the visitors bureau—see below—for walking-tour brochures.) One of downtown Petoskey's most important structures is the **Little Traverse History Museum**, once the passenger depot (1892) for the Chicago & West Michigan Railroad. Exhibits in the Richardsonian Romanesque structure include memorabilia associated with author Ernest Hemingway and historian and journalist Bruce Catton. The Italianate **Symons General Store** (1879), also downtown, was Petoskey's first brick building. The oldest building in Petoskey is the timbered **St. Francis Solanus Indian Mission** (1859; closed).

Boyne Country (which includes Petoskey and Bay View) offer a near-limitless range of recreational pursuits. Petoskey's **Gaslight Shopping District** is respected throughout the upper Midwest, and beyond. Bay View has a substantial summer calendar of musical and theatrical performances. More than 25 public courses beckon the golfer, and a lovely slice of Lake Michigan shoreline plus several good-sized inland lakes invite swimmers, boaters of all kinds, and water enthusiasts in general. Public fishing sites provide access to trout, bass, walleye, salmon, and steelhead. Those seeking more unique pursuits might enjoy hunting for morel mushrooms, or maybe *Petoskey Stones* (fossilized coral).

Sometimes billed as the "Midwest's favorite winter destination," Boyne Country has more than 120 downhill ski runs and several hundred kilometers of groomed cross-country trails. There are also sledding hills and excellent facilities for skating, snowmobiling, and ice fishing. The apres-ski scene is reputed to be the best between New England and the Rockies.

Special Features

Boyne Country has a wealth of scenic—and quiet—**back roads**. Many are ideal for bike tours.

Varying from the bright reds and oranges of the maples and oaks to the yellows of the birches and basswoods, northern Michigan's **autumn foliage** is among the country's most spectacular. Five fall tours ranging in length from 45 minutes to 2 1/2 hours are described in a special brochure distributed by the Convention and Visitors Bureau.

• A downtown parking lot has been enlivened by a half-block-long mural that depicts historic Petoskey and incorporates actual areas of the downtown.
• The Petoskey area provided lumber for the rebuilding of Chicago after the Great Fire of 1871.

▶ HISTORIC LODGINGS ◀

STAFFORD'S BAY VIEW INN, *2011 Woodland Ave., P.O. Box 3, (231) 347-2771, (800) 258-1886, fax (231) 347-3413, e-mail: bayview@staffords.com, www.staffords.com.* 1886 inn on Little Traverse Bay, Michigan Historic Site, 31 rooms, private baths, full breakfasts, dining room, antiques, wicker & chintz sunroom, bayside gardens, in heart of the Bayview Assoc., bikes. $$ to $$$$

STAFFORD'S PERRY HOTEL, *Bay & Lewis sts., (800) 456-1917, (231) 347-4000, fax (231) 347-0636, e-mail: perry@staffords.com, www.staffords.com.* 1899 hotel in Gaslight District, 80 rooms, private baths, TV & phones, restaurant with multinational menus, antiques, live music in Noggin Room, balconies, al fresco dining in summer, golf packages. $$ to $$$$

Further Information

Petoskey-Harbor Springs-Boyne Country Visitors Bureau, *401 E. Mitchell St., Petoskey, MI 49770, (800) 845-2828, (231) 348-2755, www.boynecountry.com.*

Directions

From Grand Rapids, US 131 north to Petoskey.

SAUGATUCK/DOUGLAS
Population 954/1,040

With a combined population of less than 2,000, the snug Lake Michigan harbor villages of **Saugatuck** and **Douglas** boast 35 bed and breakfasts, 30 art galleries, 3 golf courses (including Michigan's second oldest), a **Chamber Music Festival**, and a summer stock theater. They are also home to **Oxbow**, the summer camp of the internationally respected Chicago Institute of Art.

Saugatuck and Douglas are the kinds of places where bed and breakfasts place illustrated histories of Great Lakes steamers on coffee tables. Appropriately, the *SS Keewatin*, a 1907 Canadian Pacific Railway passenger liner, is moored here as a museum. Guided tours allow a glimpse of the comfort once enjoyed by steamship travelers on the Great Lakes. Turning to the present and future, Saugatuck has been instrumental in bringing cruise ships back to the Great Lakes and, indeed, was one of the ports to receive the first foreign luxury cruise liner to sail the lakes in some 50 years!

The two villages share one of the 10 best harbors in the U.S., and that means some world-class Great Lakes sailing. The villages also share beautiful unspoiled beaches and, not far away, towering dunes. In the waters outside the harbor, sports fishermen pull in salmon, trout, walleye, and perch.

Touring options are unusually broad: bicycle, dune buggy, paddlewheeler, cruise boat, ice skates, horse and buggy, hot-air balloon (etc.).

Special Features

The dunes of **Saugatuck Dunes State Park**, just north of the villages, provide beauty and challenge for hikers and cross-country skiers.

Oval Beach, across the Kalamazoo River, has been named by several organizations one of the top beaches in the country.

> • The old hand-cranked ferry still carries passengers across the Kalamazoo River to Oval Beach Road.
> • The Goose Festival (third weekend in October) in nearby Fennville celebrates the return of 300,000 Canada Geese.
> • The townspeople are openly proud of the fact that nearly all—if not in fact all—of their businesses are locally owned.

Further Information

Saugatuck/Douglas Convention and Visitor's Bureau, *P.O. Box 28, Saugatuck, MI 49453 (616) 857-1701, www.saugatuck.com (ZIP for Douglas is 49406.)*

Directions

From Chicago, I-94 east to I-196 (near Benton Harbor, MI), I-196 north to exit 36 (Saugatuck/Douglas exit).

Other Charming Michigan Towns

Allegan
Calumet
Gaylord
Grand Haven
Lexington
Romeo
St. Clair
South Haven

Chapter 23

MINNESOTA

GRAND MARAIS
Population 1,353

Grand Marais is a picturesque little harbor town situated on one of the most beautiful shorelines in the United States, the **North Shore of Lake Superior**. Walk along Grand Marais's beach or scan the harbor from the deck of a boat offshore and you can't help but respect the sheer vastness of the northlands.

Beyond the town lie miles of mountains and forests, largely undeveloped, and beyond these is the **Boundary Waters Canoe Area Wilderness** (or **BWCAW**), a natural area that stretches for 150 miles in Minnesota and along the Canadian border. Then there is **Lake Superior**, an inland sea so great that you have to drive 1,026 miles just to get around it! It is uncrowded here.

Start your visit to Grand Marais with a tour of the shops. Then stroll along the harbor and out to the lighthouse. Finally, by all means take a couple of hours to explore the tiny peninsula most aptly named **Artists' Point**. The views from here of Lake Superior and its renowned shoreline are magnificent.

If you have several days to spend in this beautiful area, consider a guided canoe trip, or maybe enrollment in a class at the **North House Folk School** and/or **Grand Marais Art Colony**. The latter offers week-long classes in watercolor, oils and acrylics, pottery, and other media

One of the best places to turn for indoor entertainment is the **Arrowhead Center for the Arts**, home of the Grand Marais Playhouse, North Shore Music Association, and Grand Marais Art Colony. The playhouse presents plays, concerts, and other events and shows during its summer season.

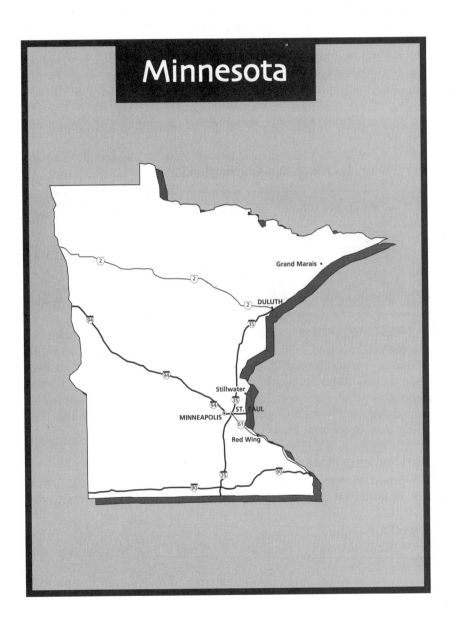

Minnesota

Special Features

MN Highway 61 along the North Shore of Lake Superior is one of the most scenic routes in the country. From Duluth to the Canadian border, and beyond, rugged cliffs and thick forests vie for attention with grand expanses of blue water.

The **Gunflint Trail** connects Grand Marais with the eastern entrance to the Boundary Waters Wilderness. The black-topped highway winds for 58 miles through and around the wooded hills and glacial lakes of one of the country's great wilderness regions. Check with the Grand Marais Area Tourism Association in Grand Marais for information on events, lodging, dining, and shopping.

Motor vessels make daily passenger runs between Grand Portage (farther up the coast) and **Isle Royale National Park**.

- Northeastern Minnesota's shape has earned it the nickname, "Tip of the Arrowhead."
- Grand Marais is the ideal place to come for a second spring after the spring flowers of more southern climes have begun to fade.

▶ HISTORIC INN ◀

NANIBOUJOU LODGE, *20 Naniboujou Trail, (218) 387-2688, fax (218) 387-2688, e-mail: info@naniboujou.com, www.naniboujou.com.* Exclusive 1920s private club converted to inn, National Register, 24 rooms, private baths, dining room, antiques, Great Room with largest native-rock fireplace in state & colorful Cree-Indian designs, pine-walled guest rooms, afternoon tea, hiking to waterfall on shore of Lake Superior. $ to $$

Further Information

Grand Marais Area Tourism Association, *P.O. Box 1048, Grand Marais, MN 55604 (888) 922-5000, (218) 387-2524, www.grandmarais.com.*

Directions

From Duluth, MN 61 northeast 110 mi (along Lake Superior) to Grand Marais.

RED WING
Population 16,211

You'd think that having a historic town tucked amongst the scenic bluffs and forests of the upper Mississippi would be enough. Not for the people of **Red Wing**. Apparently believing that everyone wins when nature and humankind work to complement each other, the people of Red Wing have added some 33 parks and hung 326 flowering baskets from the downtown lampposts. The result is a stunning union between an already handsome downtown and one of the most beautifully landscaped riverfronts in the U.S.

It doesn't hurt either that the historic preservation board has the authority to say "no" to about any downtown construction that doesn't remain true to the middle of the 19th century (1858 to be exact). The results of the board's efforts can be enjoyed by one of three walking tours—brochures are obtainable at the visitors center or front desk of the St. James Hotel (listed below). Twenty-six of the sites along the way are on the National Register of Historic Places.

One of the most visited of the sites is the restored **T. B. Sheldon Auditorium Theatre** (1904), the first municipal theater in the country. The Renaissance Revival theater presents a varied slate of attractions year round. Probably most important to the visitor is a public tour and multi-media program on Red Wing's history.

Boathouse Village is one of Red Wing's most famous attractions. Located on the Mississippi in **Bay Point Park**, the "village" consists of boat storage houses that ride up and down on poles, adjusting to the water's level. The poles are called *gin poles*, because gin bottles were tied to them and hidden in the water during Prohibition. The place is very popular with photographers and artists.

What with the stores downtown, over 20 retail and other shops in the **Pottery Place Mall** (itself a National Historic Building), and the **St. James Hotel Shopping Court**, Red Wing offers fabulous shopping.

Red Wing has a number of scenic views of the **Mississippi**, and the visitor has an array of sightseeing options. By all means the most time-honored is the 600-foot climb to the top of dramatic **Barn Bluff**. Henry David Thoreau made this climb in 1861 and wrote glowingly of the views. Today there are marked paths and stairways to make the climb easier. Another beautiful view, this time of Red Wing as well as the river, can be reached by driving up to **Memorial Park**. In addition to the views, there are hiking trails and caves to explore.

In 1890, 98 people perished on the excursion boat "Sea Wing" in a storm on Lake Pepin, downriver. The tragedy is marked by a memorial in Levee Park.

▶ HISTORIC HOTEL ◀

ST. JAMES HOTEL, *406 Main St., (800) 252-1875, fax (651) 388-5226, www.St-James-hotel.com.* Restored 1875 hotel on National Register, 61 rooms, private baths, TV & phones, 2 restaurants, antiques, shopping court. $$ to $$$$ (seasonal)

Further Information

Red Wing Visitors & Convention Bureau, *406 Main St., Suite A Red Wing, MN 55066 (800) 498-3444, www.redwing.org.*

Directions

From St. Paul, US 61 south to Red Wing.

STILLWATER
Population 15,350

Stillwater is the kind of town you feel you've seen before. The feeling is a warm one, a very positive case of *deja vu*. It's probably because the town is an amalgam of charming old towns everywhere, towns that many of us visited or passed through as children. There's a beautiful river, and up the hill from the river a turn-of-the-century main street. Yet farther up steeple spires and hints of old houses rise above the trees. Sets of steps link the steeples and the houses with the downtown below.

A first glance suggests that most of the older buildings are turn-of-the-century. Many of them are, but some, especially those on the National Register of Historic Places, go back much further, to the 1840s-1870s. Among the structures of special interest are the predominantly Italianate **Washington County Historic Courthouse** (1867-70), the oldest standing courthouse in the state, and the early Federal-style **Warden's House** (1853), the residence of 11 wardens for the adjacent **Territorial/State Prison** (1851; only remnants remain).

The new (1993) **Stillwater Depot, Logging and Railway Museum** recalls the lumber and rail history of the town. The museum is the home of the 1940s dinner train, the *Minnesota Zephyr*, which offers a three-hour excursion along the bluff-rimmed **St. Croix**. The stern-wheeler, *The Andiamo*, offers river excursions, and the *Stillwater Trolley* offers historical tours. Check with the Chamber of Commerce for a self-guided walking/driving tour.

Special Features

The **St. Croix River**, a National Wild and Scenic River, is designed for boating. Canoeing and kayaking are popular north of town. To the south sailboats, speedboats, houseboats, and yachts navigate the river to its junction with the Mississippi. Tour boats are available in Stillwater, as are cafes, bars, and shops that cater to boaters. And, of course, fishing is great in this part of the world.

- In the mid 19th century, all transportation, mail, and shipping to and from Stillwater depended on the steamboat.
- Believing that a state prison would offer more employment than a state capitol, many Stillwater people back in 1851 sought the prison. And they got it.
- The Stillwater-Houlton (WI) Lift Bridge (1931) is one of two remaining vertical-lift bridges in Minnesota.

Further Information

Greater Stillwater Chamber of Commerce, *106 S. Main St., P.O. Box 516, Stillwater, MN 55082 (651) 439-7700, www.ilovestillwater.com.*

Directions

From St. Paul, I-94 east to MN 95, MN 95 north (along river) to Stillwater; also, I-35E north to MN 36, MN 36 east to Stillwater (20 to 30 mins); from Minneapolis, I-35W north to MN 36, MN 36 east to Stillwater.

Other Charming Minnesota Towns

Afton
Grand Rapids
Lanesboro
Mantorville
New Prague
Northfield

Chapter 24

MISSISSIPPI

HOLLY SPRINGS
Population 7,957

Holly Springs has an antique square of colorfully painted storefronts and, on the streets just off the square, one of the finest collections of antebellum houses in the South. On seeing the houses, the visitor is going to have three questions, at least. First, where did all the wealth come from? Second, how did so many antebellum mansions get through the Civil War unscathed (especially because Union forces were thick in these parts)? And third, who lives in them?

In answer to the first, much of the wealth arose from land transactions made during the cotton real-estate boom of antebellum days. Many of those who prospered were (surprisingly) lawyers. Also, the town was settled by a number of well-to-do families from Virginia and the Carolinas.

Second, General Ulysses S. Grant was headquartered here for a period during the Civil War. The story goes that when Confederate General Van Dorn occupied the city, Mrs. Grant pleaded with Van Dorn to respect the privacy of her bedroom—and, incidentally, her husband's private papers. The general obliged and, later returning the favor, General Grant ordered that the town not be torched.

Third, the houses are in demand because many people, often young couples, wish the experience of restoring them. It doesn't hurt either that Holly Springs, just 34 miles from Memphis, attracts families who would rather live away from the big city.

The sheer number and variety of 19th-century mansions make Holly Springs a living museum (although most houses are closed to the public, see below). A brief but representative sampling of the homes includes:

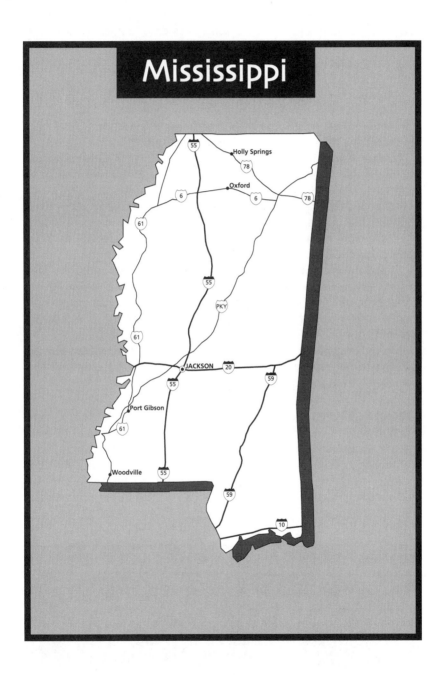

Mississippi

Dunvegan (1845), a one-story Greek Revival home furnished with Empire and Regency antiques and decorated in many rooms with painted murals. Dunvegan's style of architecture is sometimes described as "English basement."

Grey Gables (1839-1849), an Italianate house noted for its magnificent spiral stairway and hand-cut Bohemian glass windows.

Montrose (1858), a Greek Revival mansion with a graceful circular stairway, parquetry floors, and beautiful cornices (open by appointment). The arboretum on the grounds, with 50 specimens of native trees, has been designated the **Mississippi Statewide Arboretum**.

Walter Place (1859), a magnificent mansion combining Greek Revival and Gothic Revival elements. It was here that General and Mrs. Grant lived during their stay in Holly Springs.

Maps and walking tours are available through the tourism office (104 E. Gholson Ave.). Special group tours of homes, churches, and other buildings may also be arranged through the CoC. Many of the homes are open to visitors during the Annual Pilgrimage, the third weekend in April.

The **Kate Freeman Clark Art Gallery** houses over 1,200 still lifes, portraits, and landscapes by the gifted Holly Springs student of William Merritt Chase. Refusing to sell even one painting, Clark willed all of her work to Holly Springs. Only a few of her paintings are on display at any time (open by appointment).

On display at the imposing **Marshall County Historical Museum** are such diverse items as Chickasaw Indian artifacts, relics from the Civil War and War of 1812, vintage costumes, and antique toys.

Special Features

Birdwatchers, hikers, and lovers of wildlife (and human history) will enjoy a visit to **Strawberry Plains Audubon Center**, a 2,500-acre cotton plantation about four miles north of town. Bequeathed to the National Audubon Society in 1982, the plantation includes a massive Federal-style brick house that was completed in 1851, burned in the Civil War, and, over a century later (1968-73), fully restored to its former grandeur.

• Federal troops used the basement of the First Presbyterian Church as a stable for their horses.

• Rust College was established in 1866 to educate newly freed slaves. The college's library is named after the Mississippi-born singer Leontyne Price.

An hour or so in the 1837 **Hillcrest Cemetery** can be both an informative and moving experience. Here Victorian cast- and wrought-iron fences enclose old burial plots, and marble and granite obelisks commemorate not only Confederate generals but victims, young and old, of the 1878 yellow-fever epidemic.

Further Information
Holly Springs Chamber of Commerce, *148 E. College Ave., Holly Springs, MS 38635 (662) 252-2943, www.visithollysprings.org.*

Directions
From Memphis (TN), US 78 southeast to Holly Springs.

OXFORD
Population 10,026

Oxford is home to several nationally renowned authors. Endowed by the literary heritage of William Faulkner, served by a major state university, and given character by one of the most colorful (and beautiful) squares in small-town America, Oxford seems designed for the writer.

The courthouse and much of the surrounding square were looted and burned by Federal troops in 1864. Some buildings survived in whole or in part, however, and others were rebuilt. Today the magnificently restored and maintained square is home to the "new" **courthouse** (rebuilt 1873), the **Oxford City Hall** (1885), the oldest continuing department store in the South (1897), and a nationally renowned bookstore, housed in one of the first buildings built after the Civil War. And a host of interesting shops and restaurants.

The walking-tour brochure distributed by the tourism council lists four tours, one focusing on the square area and three on Oxford's other historic areas. One of the latter, the area north of the square, embraces a number of structures dating back to the 1830s. One of the oldest and best known is the **Barksdale-Isom House** (1838-1843), a large planter-style house built of native timber and handcrafted by Indians and slaves (open by appointment).

The area south of the square contains homes from the mid and late 19th century. By all means the most famous is **Rowan Oak** (1848), the home bought and renovated by William Faulkner. Set in a grove of oak and cedar trees, the house was Faulkner's office, home, and quiet refuge from 1930 until his death in 1962. The house, preserved as it was when the Nobel Prize winner died, is open to the public.

The buildings along or near **University Avenue** make up Oxford's fourth historic area. Here are the **University Museums**, a complex of museums noted for excellent collections of 18th- and 19th-century scientific instruments, Southern folk art, Greek and Roman antiquities, and paintings by Oxford folk artist Theora Hamblett. Of special interest on the nearby **University of Mississippi** campus is the restored Classical Revival **Barnard Observatory building** (1848), which houses the **Center for the Study of Southern Culture** (exhibits).

A guide to Oxford's some 13 antique shops is available at the visitor's center.

> • The building at 520 N. Lamar, built in 1875, was designed by James and Alexander Stewart, designers of three state capitols and the Savoy Hotel in London.
> • Don't expect to find lodgings in or near Oxford when Ole Miss has a home football game.

▶ HISTORIC RESTAURANT ◀

DOWNTOWN GRILL, *110 Courthouse Sq., (601) 234-2659.* In 1888 National Register bldg with wrap-around upstairs balcony; Southern dishes—e.g., Catfish Lafitte or Stuffed Pork Tenderloin with Wilted Spinach & Cheese Grits; piano bar; historic photographs; memorabilia. $$ to $$$

Further Information

Oxford Tourism Council, *107 Courthouse Sq. (City Hall), P.O. Box 965, Oxford, MS 38655 (662) 234-4680, (800) 758-9177, www.touroxfordms.com.*

Directions

From Memphis (TN), I-55 south to exit 243, MS 6 east to Oxford.

PORT GIBSON
Population 1,810

According to legend, General Grant proclaimed **Port Gibson** "too beautiful to burn." Whether because of Grant's proclamation or some other reason, the town on **Little Bayou Pierre** was spared. More than a century later it became the first town in Mississippi to be designated a National Historic District. It is one of the South's most beautiful and historic little towns.

Settled around 1788, Port Gibson was chartered as a county seat in 1803. The place was a wide-open frontier town for a spell, but rather quickly succumbed to the advances of civilization. It acquired, for example, the state's first library (1818), second newspaper, and third Masonic Lodge.

Union soldiers crossed the Mississippi River near here in 1863 in what was the largest amphibious landing of troops prior to World War II. The Union victory at the ensuing Battle of Port Gibson, fought a few miles west of town, helped pave the way for the Confederate loss of Vicksburg.

Both within the city and out in the country are many lovely historic homes. Several are open for tours, some daily (such as the 1901 Queen Anne **Bernheimer House**) and others seasonally, and may offer bed-and-breakfast accommodations. Several others open their doors during the annual spring pilgrimage.

A number of unique homes are located on Church Street. The **Englesing Home**, an 1817 Federal-style cottage, boasts the state's oldest formal garden. Another, the **Gage House** (1830-1850), has a two-story brick dependency that once contained slave quarters and the home's kitchen.

Also known as the *City of Churches*, Port Gibson's **Church Street** is graced by no fewer than eight churches. The **First Presbyterian Church** (1859) is known for the gilded hand that tops its steeple, and also for its chandeliers, originally on the famous Mississippi River steamboat, the *Robert E. Lee*. **Temple Gemiluth Chessed** (1891) is the state's oldest synagogue, and the only one of its architectural style in Mississippi.

Port Gibson in the early 20th century (1906-1915) comes alive in a collection of old photographs, *Picturing our Past*, on exhibit at the city hall. The pictures are unique in that hints of technological and social change co-exist with reminders of the traditional Old South.

Mississippi Cultural Crossroads operates a (mostly) African-American quilting workshop and the children's **Peanut Butter and Jelly Theater**. Quilts, and art work by both children and adults, are on display and for sale.

Special Features

Southwest of town are the haunting ruins of **Windsor**, the largest antebellum house ever built in Mississippi (1859-1861). Spared by the Yankees, the mansion was destroyed by fire from a cigarette in 1890. Only the 23 columns remain.

Grand Gulf State Park, northwest of town, comprises Confederate forts **Coburn** and **Wade**, several restored buildings, and a museum containing Civil War memorabilia and a collection of horse-drawn vehicles.

Southwest of town near the Mississippi River is the ghost town of **Rodney**. Once a busy river town, Rodney was vacated following a shift in the course of the river. The town's **Presbyterian Church** was built in 1829. Do not attempt a visit before checking locally for instructions.

▶ HISTORIC LODGING ◀

ROSSWOOD PLANTATION, *2513 Red Lick Rd. (Lorman 39096), (601) 437-4215, (800) 533-5889, fax (601) 437-6888, e-mail: whylander@aol.com, www.rosswood.net.* 1857 Greek Revival mansion (1849 plantation) on 100-acre estate, National Register, 4 rooms, private baths, TV & phones, full breakfasts, antiques, fireplaces, refreshments, gift shop, tours, pool & spa, canoeing & fishing in lake. $$ to $$$

▶ HISTORIC RESTAURANT ◀

RESTORATION CAFÉ, *212 Carol St., (601) 437-3186.* Classically rustic café in circa 1839 bldg. on street used by Gen. Grant and troops; "healthy" Southern folk cuisine ("quzeen"), incl. sandwiches & wraps, unique salads, soups, homemade bread & desserts; also, antiques, coffees, tea blends, jellies & jams, gift items. $ (lunches), $$ (Sunday dinner)

Further Information

Port Gibson-Claiborne County Chamber of Commerce, *P.O. Box 491, Port Gibson, MS 39150 (601) 437-4351, fax (601) 437-8667.*

Directions

From Vicksburg, US 61 south to Port Gibson.

WOODVILLE
Population 1,393

Woodville hasn't changed in 100 years. Not much is happening here today, and people say that not much will be happening tomorrow, either. Many like it that way, and that includes the traveler in search of old out-of-the-way Southern towns that aren't going anywhere.

Woodville is the classic antebellum Southern town. Like most other small Southern towns, but contrary to common knowledge, the homes of the black people, who make up well over half the population, share the streets more or less equitably with the homes of the whites. The old oak and magnolia trees shade a number of beautiful houses and churches built during the first decades of the 19th century. The churches are among the oldest in Mississippi. Several of the antebellum homes bear the columns of classic Greek Revival.

The homes and churches are best toured with the aid of a brochure obtainable at the **Wilkinson County Museum**. The **Woodville Baptist Church** dates from 1809, and the **Woodville Methodist Church** and **St. Paul's Episcopal Church** go back to the 1820s. (St. Paul's was the church attended by the family of Jefferson Davis, President of the Confederacy.) Many of the historic homes are located on **Church Street**. The Wilkinson County Museum offers small and large group tours of historic sites and/or nature areas that are not normally open or accessible to the public. The tours include a picnic or lunch/dinner in a home *(for more information, write to the address below or call the museum director at 601-888-3177).*

Just one mile east of town (on MS 24) is a house that may be visited without joining a tour – **Rosemont Plantation House**, the family home of President Jefferson Davis. Built about 1810 by Davis's parents, this lovely house is centered about a large hall that opens onto front and back galleries. The house was home to five generations of the Davis family and has many of the family's furnishings.

Special Features

About 14 miles west of town on the **Pinckneyville Road** is an old-fashioned general store, called **Pond Store** (1881), that is straight out of the old rural South. The adjacent pond, which gave the store its name, was dug generations ago as a watering hole for animals hauling cotton and other produce to steamboats waiting at **Fort Adams**, just to the west. Tours of the store are available by appointment.

Next to Pond Store is the **Clark Creek Nature Area**, with over 1,200 acres of steep bluff woodlands and winding trails. The state natural area has seven waterfalls, one of them 50 feet high, and is popular with hikers. A park ranger is on duty.

• Ft. Adams, an old port city, was a Mississippi River entry point into the United States prior to the Louisiana Purchase (1803).

• Military personnel attached to Ft. Adams built homes in the area of Pond Store following the Revolutionary War. Several of these homes, now over 200 years old, still stand.

• "The Woodville Republican" is Mississippi's oldest newspaper (est. 1824).

▶ HISTORIC LODGING ◀

DESERT PLANTATION, *411 Desert Lane, Woodville (18 mi from Woodville) or P.O. Box 877, St. Francisville, LA (70775), (877) 877-1103, e-mail: info@desertplantation.com.* 1812 home on 1,000-acre plantation, National Register, 4 rooms, private baths, full "country" breakfasts, dinners by appt., period furnishings, some pets, pool, refreshments on verandah. $$ to $$$

Further Information

Wilkinson County Museum, *P.O. Box 1055, Woodville, MS 39669 (601) 888-3998.*

Directions

From Jackson, I-20 west to exit 1b (Vicksburg), US 61 south (via Natchez) to Woodville.

Other Charming Mississippi Towns

Bay St. Louis
Carrollton
Corinth
French Camp
Kosciusko
Meadville
Pass Christian

Chapter 25

MISSOURI

ARROW ROCK
Population 79

The National Historic Landmark of **Arrow Rock** has become a weekend retreat for many Kansas Cityans (and others). It's all there, enough for two full but restful days: a quiet and picturesque historic site that can be leisurely toured with or without a guide; a 19th-century Main Street with interesting antique, gift, and specialty shops; craft demonstrations; a top summer repertory theater; good food; a park with an exercise-inviting hiking trail; and a choice of several delightful bed & breakfasts.

It was at Arrow Rock that the **Santa Fe Trail** crossed the **Missouri River**. Westbound explorers and traders paused at the Arrow Rock Spring, and in 1829 some of them decided to settle and found a town. There are a few Victorian houses, but the early date of settlement means that many buildings are of the Federal style, a style uncommon this far west. Many of the older buildings make up the **Arrow Rock State Historic Site**.

The most prominent building in the historic site is the **Old Tavern** (1834), a two-story Federal-style brick building that houses a restaurant (see listing below). The most historic of the houses is the small Federal-style dwelling (1837) of **George Caleb Bingham**, the nationally renowned artist. Other historic sites include a mid-1800s **gunsmith shop** and a **newspaper office** with antique presses. Displays at the **state historic interpretive center** highlight these and other town landmarks (open year round).

Musicals, comedies, and a sprinkling of classic dramas are offered in rotating repertory from June through October at the 420-seat **Arrow Rock Lyceum Theater**, Missouri's oldest professional repertory theater.

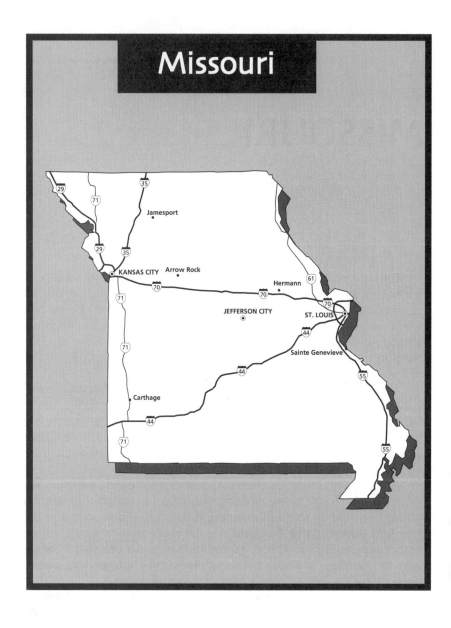

Special Features

The recently restored **Prairie Park**, an 1845/49 Greek Revival mansion several miles out in the country, is one of Missouri's premier properties. The house, listed in the National Register, was built by the son of Dr. John Sappington, the physician who popularized the use of quinine for treating malaria. Check locally for tour information.

▶ HISTORIC RESTAURANT ◀

HISTORIC ARROW ROCK TAVERN, *302 Main St., (660) 837-3200.* 1834 brick tavern believed to be oldest restaurant in continuous operation west of Mississippi; traditional country fare—e.g., fried chicken or country ham, grilled steaks or elk or pork chops; reservations requested. $$

Further Information

Arrow Rock Area Merchants Association, *P.O. Box 147, Arrow Rock, MO 65320 (660) 837-3305, www.arrowrock.org.*

Directions

From Kansas City, I-70 east to exit 89, K Hwy. north to MO 41, MO 41 north to Arrow Rock; from St. Louis, I-70 west to exit 98, MO 41 north to Arrow Rock.

CARTHAGE
Population 10,747

Enriched by lead and zinc mines, marble quarries, and flour mills, **Carthage** had by the end of the 19th century more millionaires per capita than any other city in the country. Much of the wealth remains, as a drive by the beautifully preserved Victorian homes on **Grand Avenue** and **S. Main Street** will make clear. The town's maple-lined streets are especially lovely in the fall. They're not bad in the spring, either, when the dogwoods are in bloom.

A tour brochure distributed by the Convention and Visitors Bureau provides full architectural histories and color photos for a sample of 20 of the Victorian homes. Dating from the last three decades of the 19th century, the houses represent all major Midwestern Victorian styles. Good examples are the 1870 Italianate **Spencer House**, the magnificent Chateauesque 1887 **Hill House**, and the 1873 **Italian Villa**, known as "Wetzel's Folly."

Two homes, **Kendrick Place** and the **Phelps House**, offer tours. One of the oldest buildings in the Carthage area, Kendrick Place (1849) has been restored to its pre-Civil War appearance. The 1890s Classical Revival Phelps House has 10 fireplaces and a hand-operated elevator that serves all floors between the basement and the third-floor ballroom.

On the square downtown is the magnificent Romanesque Revival **Jasper County Courthouse** (1894/95). Listed on the National Register, the courthouse has several first-floor exhibits of Indian artifacts and mineral specimens from the region's mining days. The building also contains a 1976 mural, *Forged in Fire*, that depicts Carthage's history.

The **Powers Museum** provides a glimpse at local history and the arts; a variety of changing exhibits are featured. As its name indicates, the **Carthage Civil War Museum** tells the story of the role played by Carthage in the Civil War. Included among the exhibits are a diorama and a large mural, both of the Battle of Carthage.

The **Precious Moments Chapel**, southwest of town, was created by artist Samuel J. Butcher. The nondenominational chapel is noted for its murals, carvings, and 15 stained-glass windows, all of the Precious Moments motif. Sharing the beautifully landscaped grounds with the chapel are a gallery, restaurant, gift shop, flower gardens, fountains, and scenic overlooks.

Special Features

About 10 miles south of Carthage is the **George Washington Carver National Monument**, birthplace and childhood home of the renowned educator, botanist, agronomist, and artist. Born a slave, Carver achieved national prominence for his innovative agricultural research.

To the east of Carthage lies the small town of **Sarcoxie**, "Peony Capital of the World" and home of the **Gene Taylor Library and Museum**.

• The first major land battle of the Civil War occurred in Carthage on July 5, 1861.
• A statue of Carthage's Marlin Perkins, host of TV's "Wild Kingdom" series, is located in Central Park.

Further Information

Carthage Convention and Visitors Bureau, *107 E. Third St., Carthage, MO 64836 (417) 359-8181, fax (417) 359-9119, www.visit-carthage.com.*

Directions

From Springfield, I-44 west to exit 18, US 71 north to Carthage.

HERMANN
Population 2,754

Hermann was founded by the German Settlement Society of Philadelphia in 1836 (settled 1837). It's believed that the founders selected this lovely spot on the **Missouri River** because it reminded them of their native Rhine. The original plans called for a large city that would preserve German culture. The city obviously never materialized, but the townspeople's commitment to preserve their German traditions survived. Picturesque little Hermann remains German, consciously so.

Vineyards, part of Hermann's Rhineland heritage, were planted during the town's earliest years, and grape growing eventually became an important part of the area's economy. Today there are four wineries, each offering daily tours. The oldest, **Stone Hill Winery** (1847), has been declared a National Historic District. At the turn of the century, Stone Hill was the third largest winery in the world. Forced by Prohibition to grow mushrooms (in its vast cellars) rather than grapes, the winery was reopened in 1969; in 1989 it became the first Missouri winery since Prohibition to be awarded an international gold medal. The winery has the largest underground arched cellars in the United States.

Another historic winery, the **Hermannhof Winery** (1852), has a magnificent festhalle. The winery's stone wine cellars and winery building are on the National Register of Historic Places.

The streets of the **Hermann Historic District** (the town has two historic districts) are lined with tidy German-American homes and gardens. Two of the houses are preserved as the **Deutscheim State Historic Site**: the German Neoclassical **Pommer-Gentner House** (1842), with furnishings from the 1840s, and the **Strehly House and Winery** (1844), a German Vernacular house furnished in the 1860s-1880s style.

The **German School Building** (1871) **Museums** provide a comprehensive and fascinating look at Hermann's history. Among the museums' exhibits are a handmade wooden wine press, circa 1835 wood cloth-printing blocks, and boat models and other items depicting the town's river history. One of the museums features dolls and toys from the late 1890s, another displays a handmade Rococo Revival bedroom set of solid walnut (open April-October).

The **White House Hotel** (1868) is a three-story brick building, with two-story wing, featuring 15-foot ceilings, arched hallways, and an iron-railed widow's walk. The hotel contains 36 rooms with furnishings and decorations from the late 19th century. The kitchen still has its original cook stove (guided tours).

Hermann abounds with art galleries, antique shops, and quaint craft and gift shops. Crafts include quilts, afghans, handwoven baskets, and handcrafted wood items. Black-powder guns, vintage lighting, and European giftware are among other items displayed in the shops.

Special Features

The rolling **Missouri River Valley** and the foothills of the **Ozarks** to the south combine to make **MO 19**, which passes through Hermann, an especially scenic highway.

- The Gasconade County Courthouse (1896-1898) was the gift of a local merchant (!)
- Octoberfest, held the first four weekends in October, features a Showboat Theatre, craft demonstrations, German bands and folk dancing, and lots of food, beer, and wine.

▶ HISTORIC INN ◀

WHITE ROSES B&B, *311 Market St., (573) 486-9094, (800) 458-4095, e-mail: carol@ktis.net, www.whiterosesbandb.com*. Three-story 1850s bldg. in historic district, National Register, 5 rooms, private baths, full breakfasts, antiques, library, screened porch with hammock. $$$ to $$$$

▶ HISTORIC RESTAURANT ◀

VINTAGE RESTAURANT, *1110 Stone Hill Hwy. (at Stone Hill Winery), (573) 486-3479*. In original stable & carriage house of historic winery, German & American specialties—e.g., German-style Schnitzel, German Onion Tart, German Chocolate Pie. $$ to $$$

Further Information

Hermann Tourism Group & Welcome Center, *312 S. Market St., Hermann, MO 65041-1058 (800) 932-8687, (573) 486-2744, www.HermannMo.com*.

Directions

From St. Louis, I-70 west to exit 175, MO 19 south to Hermann.

JAMESPORT
Population 570

Jamesport is set in the picturesque rolling countryside of northwestern Missouri. The village is surrounded by beautiful old farms, mature woods, and winding rivers. Horses and buggies are common to the roads.

There are really two Jamesports, one complementing the other. The first is the village, a few streets of antique shops and old homes where everyone knows everyone else and no one bothers with street addresses or last names. The second is the surrounding countryside, dotted with Amish farms and country stores.

The village, tiny though it may be, has 16 antique shops and 26 craft and specialty shops. There's an old-fashioned soda fountain, of course. And there are places to sit and relax, quiet places where in the evening only fireflies and whippoorwills disturb.

Although not settling in Jamesport until the early 1950s, the Amish now farm much of the rich land around the village. Amish families also operate several country stores and greenhouses along the highways. The stores sell everything from fabrics and handmade quilts to homemade noodles, jellies, and jams (closed Thursdays and Sundays). Bus tours of the stores and Amish countryside are available.

Special Features
The countryside around Jamesport, like that of much of Missouri, is rich in pastoral beauty. Invest a couple of hours in exploring the climbs and curves of the back roads.

The little county seat of **Gallatin**, 8 miles west, boasts an 1887 squirrel-cage jail.

- The Amish maintain seven one-room parochial schools in the Jamesport area.
- Visitors need to remember that picture-taking goes against Amish religious beliefs.

▶ HISTORIC INN ◀
COUNTRY COLONIAL B&B, *Main & East streets, P.O. Box 46, (660) 684-6711, (800) 579-9248, www.jamesport.net or www.jamesportmo.com. Restored 1894 hotel with double verandahs, 3 rooms, private baths, full breakfasts, antiques, study, baby grand piano, flower garden with fish pond & patio. $ to $$*

Further Information

Jamesport Community Association, *P.O. Box 215, Jamesport, MO 64648 (660) 684-6146, www.jamesportmo.com.*

Directions

From Kansas City, I-35 north to exit 61, MO 6 east to Jamesport.

STE. GENEVIEVE
Population 4,411

The first thing the visitor approaching **Ste. Genevieve** notices is that the town is nestled in a valley (in an old riverbed in fact) near the **Mississippi River**. The second – if not the first – is that the town is dominated by a tall steeple (of the 1876 **Church of Ste. Genevieve**). The third and fourth are that the church and its steeple share the middle of the town's square with a relatively small old **courthouse** (1821), and that the square is surrounded by 19th-century step-gabled brick storefronts. The most important discovery, however, comes with a stroll down the streets leading off the square. For here lies one of the largest collections of 18th-century houses in the country.

Established between 1725 and 1750 by French settlers, Ste. Genevieve is the oldest town in Missouri. More than 50 of the 18th-century homes built by the settlers survive; many have been restored. Some are private residences and others are house museums (see below). Among them are three of the only four remaining houses in North America of poteaux-en-terre construction (built on poles placed vertically in the ground, with no foundation).

The 19th-century brick buildings on (and off) the square were built by immigrants from southern Germany. These together with the French Colonial buildings form an historic district noted for its craft shops, antique galleries, boutiques, and restaurants.

The two logical starting points for a tour of the district are the Tourist Information Office and the **Ste. Genevieve Museum**. The former provides information for a self-guided walking tour, including take-out cassette tapes. The latter contains collections of local memorabilia. Of note are prehistoric Indian relics, Spanish land grants, and artifacts from the **Saline Creek Salt Works**, Missouri's first industry.

Seven structures, six homes and one inn, are of special architectural and/ or historic interest:

The **Guibourd-Valle House** (ca 1806) has elegant furnishings and an attic with hand-hewn oak beams. Outside are a courtyard, rose garden, and old stone well (costumed tour guides).

The **Felix Valle House** (1818), a state historic site, is a Federal-style limestone building with early Empire furnishings and original mantels. Inside is an authentically restocked mercantile store. On the grounds are an attractive garden and original brick and frame outbuildings.

The **Bolduc House** (1770), an authentically restored Creole structure, has original 18th-century furnishings, frontier kitchen, and 18th-century culinary and medicinal herb gardens (open to public).

The **Bolduc-LeMeilleur House** (1820), a frame structure with brick nogging, is furnished with early Federal pieces. The house has early 19th-century herb and scented gardens (open to public).

The **Green Tree Inn** (1792) was the first inn and tobacco shop west of the Mississippi. The inn features original walnut shutters and woodwork and a triangular fireplace that opens into three rooms (under restoration).

The poteaux-en-terre **Amoureaux House** (1792), once the home of a French nobleman, may be the oldest building in Missouri (prearranged group tours only).

The **Bequette-Ribault House** (1808) is another of the four remaining poteaux-en-terre structures in North America (not open to public).

Special Features

Hawn State Park, southwest of Ste. Genevieve, features pine trees, azaleas, and a 10-mile backpacking trail.

• A town square divided into two parts by a street (as in Ste. Genevieve), with one part housing a government building and the other a church, indicates Spanish ancestry. (And indeed, the territory west of the Mississippi was held by Spain from 1762 to 1800.)
• According to legend, the posts used for poteaux-en-terre construction were soaked in arsenic prior to use to repel termites.

▶ HISTORIC INN ◀

THE INN ST. GEMME BEAUVAIS, *78 N. Main St., (573) 5744, (800) 818-5744, fax (573) 883-3899, e-mail: buffin@msn.com, www.bbhost.com/innstgemme*. 1848 Greek Revival inn in historic district, oldest continually operated inn in Missouri, 4 rooms, 9 suites, 1 cottage, private baths, TV, 4-course breakfasts (choice of 8 entrees), antiques, fireplaces, fresh flowers, very large garden with gazebo & fountain. $$ to $$$$

▶ HISTORIC RESTAURANT ◀

OLD BRICK HOUSE, *Third & Market streets, (573) 883-2724*. In oldest brick bldg. west of Mississippi River (1785-1805), ambiance, American cooking—e.g., seafood, fried chicken, liver dumplings, 40-oz steaks. $ to $$

Further Information

Ste. Genevieve Tourist Information Office, *66 S. Main St., Ste. Genevieve, MO 63670 (573) 883-7097, (800) 373-7007, www.saintegenevievetourism.org.*

Directions

From St. Louis, I-55 south to either exit 154 (and US 61 south to town) or exit 150 (and MO 32 east to town).

Other Charming Missouri Towns
Bethel
Kimmswick
Rock Port
Steelville
Weston

Chapter 26

MONTANA

FORT BENTON
Population 1,660

As the head of navigation on the Missouri River and the West's innermost port, **Fort Benton** was destined to encounter some colorful and rowdy days. And the days came: The town was a fur-trading post, the eastern staging post of the **Mullan Trail** (completed in 1859) connecting with Fort Walla Walla in Washington, a steamboat landing for the Gold Rush of the 1860s, and the southern terminus of the **Whoop-Up Trail** (1870/83), along which flowed whiskey and other goods into western Canada. Only with the 1880s did calm and respectability finally come to town.

Today people drive 150 miles across the sweeping wheat fields of central Montana to spend the day in this historic town. Others select *the Birthplace of Montana* to retire to. All it takes to understand why is a stroll along **Front Street**, now peaceful but once infamous for its "bloodiest block in the West." Separating the street from the Missouri is the steamboat levee, site of the **Lewis and Clark State Memorial** (1976). Staked here and there are signs telling about the days when the levee was crowded with boats, freight, and ox and mule teams. Lovely old cottonwoods and various conifers shade the riverbank and **Old Fort Park**, resting place for the remains of **Old Fort Benton** (1847; under restoration).

Bordering the street are historic buildings, some of them brick and most from Fort Benton's Golden Years, the early 1880s. The imposing **Grand Union Hotel** is one of Montana's oldest (1882). Now a National Historic Landmark, the Grand Union was once the most luxurious hostelry between Minneapolis and Seattle. The **Old Firehouse**, on the National Register of Historic Places,

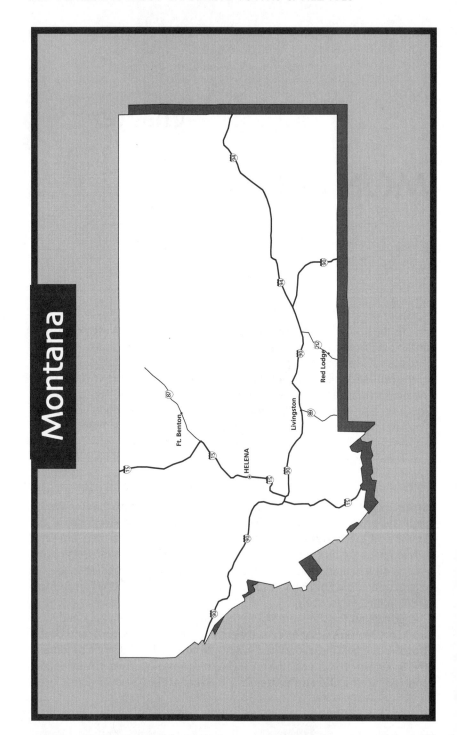

dates from 1883. The building housed a steam-powered engine and other firefighting equipment shipped from the East by steamboat.

Built about the same time (1880) but located a few blocks from the river is the recently restored Norman Gothic **St. Paul's Episcopal Church** (visitors welcome). The displays of the **Fort Benton Museum of the Upper Missouri** center on the history of the Fort Benton region from the 1840s until 1887. A second museum, the **Museum of the Northern Great Plains**, depicts the history of the homestead era and the region's farming practices.

Special Features

The *Benton Belle*, a replica of an 1890s riverboat, offers daily excursions on the **Missouri River**.

The scenery and abundant wildlife of some 150 miles of the unspoiled upper Missouri River, designated a Wild and Scenic River, can be seen by canoe (rentals are available) and 3- to 5-day guided boat tours.

• People continue to visit the profile monument and marker over the grave of the dog Shep, who spent 5 1/2 years meeting every train at Fort Benton after his master's body was taken away by train in 1936 for burial back East. Although many tried to befriend Shep, the dog faithfully waited for his master's return until killed, ironically, by a train.

• Another of the sites on Fort Benton's levee is a replica of the keelboat "Mandan," built for the movie "The Big Sky." Yet another levee site is the hull of the small steamboat, "Baby Rose" (1900).

Further Information

Fort Benton Chamber of Commerce, *P.O. Box 12, Fort Benton, MT 59442 (406) 622-3864.*

Directions

From Helena, I-15 north to exit 280 (Great Falls), US 87 northeast to Ft. Benton.

LIVINGSTON
Population 7,500

Robert Redford's selection of Livingston as the setting for his movie, *A River Runs Through It*, was entirely appropriate. The beautiful **Yellowstone River**, the longest free-flowing river in the lower 48, runs right through town. And with no fewer than 436 residential and commercial structures listed on the National Register, and the facades of some 20 buildings on **Main Street** restored to their original designs, much of Livingston should and does look like an early 20th-century Montana town.

One of Livingston's principal landmarks is the grand old **Northern Pacific Railroad depot**. The turn-of-the-century depot was designed by the same firm that designed New York's Grand Central Station. Recently restored at a cost of $800,000, the building is now a museum known as the **Livingston Depot Center**.

Lying among four mountain ranges, some of them snow-capped all year, and astride a world-class river, Livingston has attracted artists, writers, actors, and musicians. Despite the tiny population, the town and its county boast two resident theater companies, the Blue Slipper and the Firehouse 5. The works of local artists are displayed in more than a dozen fine galleries. Some of the art is traditional, centering on Western, wildlife, and angling scenes; much of it, however, is contemporary. Many of the galleries carry pottery, Montana porcelain, basketry, and jewelry.

Special Features
The Yellowstone River is world-famous for its fishing. The river is also ideal for boating, floating, and kayaking. Both whitewater and scenic trips lasting from a half-day up to a week are available through commercial raft companies.

> • The fabulous flyfishing scenes in "A River Runs Through It" were filmed on the nearby Gallatin and Yellowstone rivers.
> • Livingston is the original and only year-round entry to Yellowstone National Park.

▸ HISTORIC HOTEL ◂
MURRAY HOTEL, *201 W. Park St., (406) 222-1350, e-mail: murrayhotel@ycsi.net, www.murrayhotel.com.* Restored 1904 railroad hotel on National Register, 30 suites, private baths, TV & phones, Cont. breakfasts, Murray Café, Murray Lounge, antiques, some pets, marble staircase, hot tub on roof, views of 3 mountain ranges, Hollywood celebrities among guests. $ to $$$

Further Information
Livingston Area Chamber of Commerce, *303 E. Park St., Livingston, MT 59047 (406) 222-0850, fax (406) 222-0852, www.yellowstone-chamber.com.*

Directions
From Billings (MT), I-90 west to exits 332 or 333 (Livingston exits); from Yellowstone National Park and Gardiner (MT), US 89 north to Livingston.

RED LODGE
Population 2,300

Winding through the highest driveable points in both Montana and Wyoming, the 65-mile **Beartooth Scenic Byway** is one of the country's, indeed the world's, most beautiful highways. At one end of the byway is the northeastern gateway to **Yellowstone National Park**. At the other end is **Red Lodge**, an old western town tucked Hollywood-style below spectacular mountains and big blue Montana skies.

Nearly all of Red Lodge's downtown district has been added to the National Register of Historic Places. The district includes many stone and brick buildings, their facades restored, dating from the 1880s to 1915. Especially interesting are the original railroad station house (1889) and a group of buildings, known as *Old Town*, that formed the town's business center from 1886-1893.

Among the displays at the **Carbon County Historical Museum** are rodeo memorabilia, the town's first telephone switchboard, and the homestead cabin of John Johston, known as "Liver Eatin' Johnson," on whose story the movie *Jeremiah Johnson* was based.

Red Lodge is the site of one of the country's foremost summer festivals, the **Festival of Nations**. The ancestry of the festival can be traced to the 1880s when the discovery of coal attracted hundreds of Finnish, Italian, Scandinavian, and other miners to Red Lodge. Later, about 1949, the Festival of Nations was established to help the various cultural groups learn more about each other.

Each day of the 9-day August festival is assigned to a different culture. There are dances, songs, parades, and other entertainment along with information on cooking, crafts, customs, and languages. On the evening of the day assigned to the Scots, for example, bagpipes, kilts, and dancers fill the streets and bars until the last watering hole closes. It's international learning and party time.

As for outdoor forms of recreation, Red Lodge is a four-season paradise. There's downhill skiing at **Red Lodge Mountain Ski Area**, cross-country skiing at **Red Lodge Nordic Center**, white-water rafting trips, bicycling, horseback riding, golfing, and fantastic trout fishing.

> • Around 1886 there were four men to every woman in Red Lodge.
> • Although just 65 miles long, the Beartooth Scenic Byway will demand at least 2 1/2 to 3 hours of your time—you'll simply not want to speed past the views of the glaciers, snow-capped mountains, and alpine lakes and plateaus.

▶ HISTORIC HOTEL ◀

THE POLLARD HOTEL, *2 N. Broadway, P.O. Box 650, (800) 765-5273, fax (406) 446-0002, e-mail: pollard@pollardhotel.com, www.pollardhotel.com.* Restored 1893 hotel, 39 rooms, private baths, TV & phones, expanded Cont. breakfasts, restaurant, antiques, health club with hot tubs & sauna, racquetball. $ to $$$$

Further Information

Red Lodge Area Chamber of Commerce, *601 N. Broadway, P.O. Box 988, Red Lodge, MT 59068 (406) 446-1718.*

Directions

From Billings, I-94 west to exit 434 (Laurel exit), US 212 south to Red Lodge.

Other Charming Montana Towns
Bigfork
Big Timber
Stevensville
Virginia City
Whitefish

Chapter 27

NEBRASKA

MINDEN
Population 2,940

The cozy little Nebraska prairie town of **Minden** fits about every romantic notion of what a wholesome American hometown ought to be. In the middle of the town square is an old and imposing courthouse with a magnificent white dome. Around the square are businesses and, with a nod to the past, no fewer than seven antique shops. Not far from the square is an area of beautiful homes, some with more rooms than really make sense, built by Minden's Victorian-era doctors and lawyers. Finally, there are the farms with their rich irrigated cornfields.

Minden has something else, though, that makes the town just a little different from other prairie towns: A few blocks north of the square is the **Harold Warp Pioneer Village**, one of the top museums of its kind in the country. Within the some 26 buildings of this award-winning museum are exhibits employing 50,000 items to trace the development from 1830 onwards of everything from lighting and bath tubs to motorcycles and musical instruments. Included are the oldest internal combustion engine (1876), the oldest jet airplane (1942), an 1890 combine pulled by 30 horses, and the first "Kelvinator" refrigerator (1925).

Among the museum's buildings are several historic structures situated about a village green. Included are Minden's first church (1884), an original livery stable complete with harness shop, and an authentic replica of a sod house. The museum also presents daily weaving, broom-making, and other craft demonstrations.

The 1891 **Minden Opera House** (National Register) has been completely renovated to serve as a community center. The center includes an art gallery

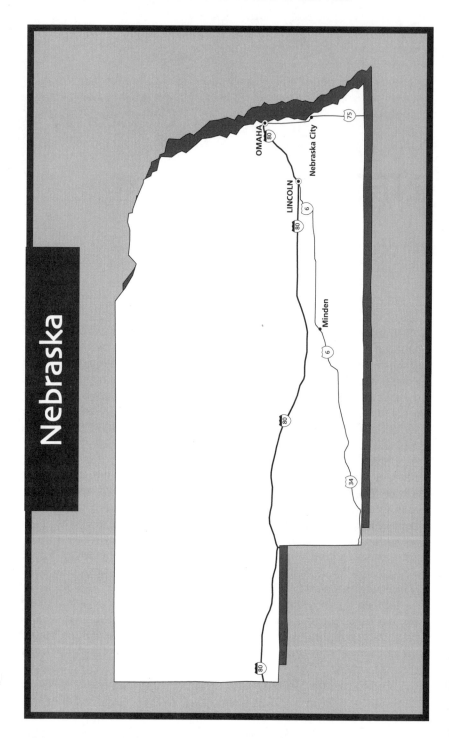

Nebraska

OMAHA

LINCOLN

Nebraska City

Minden

and the handsome **Ruth Armstrong Theatre**. The latter is graced by a ceiling mural that holds 2,500 fiber-optic lights.

Earning Minden the nickname *The Christmas City*, the square and the **Kearney County Courthouse**, especially the dome, are strung every Christmas with 10,000 lights. The lights are turned on as the climax of a Christmas pageant held the last Saturday night in November and the first two Sunday nights in December (the lights are also on every evening from the first production of the pageant until New Year's Day).

Special Features

Fort Kearny State Historical Park northwest of Minden was once an outpost on the **Oregon Trail**. The park features several re-created structures, including a stockade, along with period artifacts.

Fort Kearny State Recreation Area north of town is the site of the sandhill crane spring migration. Nature lovers especially will enjoy the 5-mile hike/bike trail.

Christmas lights were first strung on the courthouse dome in 1915. For many years the bulbs were colored by hand dipping.

Further Information

Minden Chamber of Commerce, *509 N. Colorado Ave., P.O. Box 375, Minden, NE 68959 (308) 832-1811, www.mindenne.com.*

Directions

From Omaha, I-80 west to exit 279, NE 10 south to Minden.

NEBRASKA CITY
Population 7,280

The old Missouri River town of **Nebraska City** has a town center that nicely demonstrates how the old and the new can work together. Perceiving the benefits of encouraging downtown retail development, the community planted the area with trees and flowers and added Victorian park benches and period streetlights and trolleys. The result is a beautiful and healthy old-new downtown.

Set among apple and cherry orchards and heir to over 300 properties on the National Register of Historic Places, Nebraska City has long been a special kind of place. A good way to see the town is to park your car (free parking) and hop a trolley. (The Chamber of Commerce distributes a map showing the city's many attractions.)

Among the historic homes served by the trolley is the 10-room **Wildwood Period House**, a Gothic Revival house of 1860s vintage (open to the public), and the **Taylor-Wessel-Nelson House**, considered the finest example of Greek Revival architecture in Nebraska. The latter is now home to the Nebraska City Historical Society and may be seen by appointment. Other important sights on the tour are the very Victorian 1880s **Farmers Bank**, winner of the President's National Preservation Award, and the **Old Freighter's Museum**, headquarters of an 1859 freight company and now a history museum (open by appointment).

Best times to visit the town's three orchards are during blossom time, usually the first week of May, and at harvest time, beginning around mid-September. The most famous of the orchards is the **Arbor Day Farm** (a National Historic Landmark), named in honor of and forming part of the original estate of the founder of Arbor Day, J. Sterling Morton. Barns from the early 1900s, apple sorting and packing, and cider making are among the sights open to visitors.

The elegant 52-room Colonial Revival **Morton Mansion** is the central feature of adjacent **Arbor Lodge State Historical Park and Arboretum**. A large variety of native trees and shrubs may be seen on the mansion's grounds.

Mayhew Cabin and Historical Village features a cabin reputed to be the oldest surviving structure in Nebraska (ca 1852). Beneath the cabin is a cave that was once a station on the **Underground Railroad**. Also on the property are 18 buildings from various periods in Nebraska City's history.

Special Features

The **Meriwether Lewis Steamboat Museum of Missouri River History**, river cruises, and various cultural events add to the charm of **Brownville**, an old steamboat port and one of Nebraska's oldest settlements, downriver from Nebraska City.

• Nebraska City is a major antique center.
• Escaping slaves were fed cornbread and water and allowed to spend the night at John Brown's Cave before resuming their trip north.

Further Information

Nebraska City Tourism & Events, 806 1st Ave., Nebraska City, NE 68410 (402) 873-3000, www.nebraskacity.com.

Directions
From Omaha, US 75 south to Nebraska City.

Other Charming Nebraska Towns
Arthur
Brownville
Gothenburg
Valentine

Chapter 28

NEVADA

EUREKA
Population 1,200

A sign welcoming visitors to **Eureka** announces that "You Are Entering the Loneliest Town on the Loneliest Road in America." Even though the townspeople will hasten to note that their home is not truly lonely, they readily admit that it is remote. Situated in the middle of the Nevadan desert, a round-trip automobile excursion to the city (Carson City or Reno in this case) takes about eight hours. And that's counting only driving time. There are few towns in this book where the surrounding "countryside" has changed so little since the first white settlers arrived—Eureka is fortunately in no immediate danger of being engulfed by a sprawling suburbia. The air will hint of sagebrush for many years to come.

Following the discovery of silver in 1864 and the development of smelters a few years later, Eureka boomed into Nevada's second largest city, with a population of over 9,000. There were 100 saloons, dozens of gambling houses, an opera house (see below), and everything else you'd expect in a classic 19th-century mining camp. There was even a Chinatown. On the unromantic side were the soot and pollution from 16 smelters, earning the town the nickname "Pittsburgh of the West." Even though the big boom was over by 1890, mining activity continued to surface on and off over the years, and in fact the town is currently enjoying a boom.

Many of the buildings fronting Eureka's streets were built of brick or volcanic stone in the 1870s and 1880s. Although some are vacant, most continue to house hotels, cafes, bars, shops, and other mercantile establishments. The original pressed-tin ceilings can still be seen in several. A few are private residences. A brochure for a self-guiding tour, published by the Eureka

Nevada

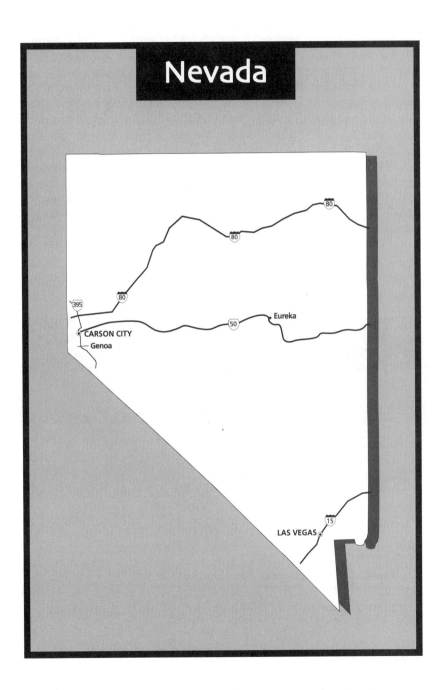

County Economic Development Council, provides an excellent way to get to know them.

On display at the **Sentinel Museum** (1879) are the presses and equipment of the *Eureka Sentinel Newspaper*, published between 1870 and 1960. Mementos from other areas of Eureka's past are also exhibited.

The **Eureka County Courthouse** (1879-1880), the town's most important historic structure, once ranked second only to the courthouse in Virginia City as the grandest in the state. The judge's bench in the courtroom (second floor) was made of Spanish cedar. The building continues in use as a courthouse.

The **Eureka Opera House and Theatre** (1880), another enduring landmark, once served as the community auditorium as well as an opera house and theater. Renovated, it is now a convention and cultural arts center. The quaint **St. James Episcopal Church** was built in 1872 to accommodate miners from England.

Special Features

With the silhouettes of distant mountain ranges acting to dramatize their colors, Eureka's **desert sunsets** are breathtaking.

In 1879 six Italian charcoal burners were killed and another ten wounded by a posse in a dispute over the pricing of charcoal. The event, Eureka's most historic, is known as the Charcoal War of 1879.

▶ HISTORIC HOTEL ◀

THE JACKSON HOUSE, *11 S. Main St., (775) 237-5577, fax (775) 237-5155, e-mail: eurekainn@eurekanv.org*. Restored 1880s hotel, 8 rooms, 1 suite, private baths, TV, expanded Cont. breakfasts, restaurant, saloon, antiques, parlor, broad second-floor balcony, recipient of restoration award. $ to $$

Further Information

Eureka County Economic Development Council, *701 S. Main St., P.O. Box 14, Eureka, NV 89316 (775) 237-5484, fax (775) 237-5175*; also, **Eureka Chamber of Commerce**, *11 N. Main St., P.O. Box 1078, Eureka, NV 89316 (775) 237-5544, fax (775) 237-7438.*

Directions

From Carson City, US 50 east to Eureka.

GENOA
Population 250

A picturesque Old West town tucked in the foothills of the **Sierra Nevada**, **Genoa** is neither the skeleton of a late 19th-century mining town nor a 20th-century resort with glittering casinos. Genoa (accent on second syllable) is very much a 19th-century town, the oldest non-Indian settlement in Nevada in fact, but its careful preservation is very much 20th century, as are its comforts.

Genoa's Old West credentials are impressive. The town was established in 1851 as a trading post, known as **Mormon Station**, that served as a resting place and provisioning station for fur traders and prospectors dreaming of silver or gold. From 1855 until 1916 the town was a county seat, and in 1860 and 1861 it was a stop on the Pony Express.

Today Genoa has nearly 30 buildings listed on the National Register of Historic Places. Construction dates include every decade from the 1850s onward into the early 20th century. The buildings served, and in some cases continue to serve, as guest houses, stores, homes, a dance hall, a Masonic Hall, even a health spa.

By all means the best known and most photographed of the buildings is the charming **Genoa Courthouse** (1865). Now the **Genoa Courthouse Museum**, this lovely brick building served as a courthouse until 1916, then as a school until 1956. The museum has a diversity of exhibits, including the original courtroom, a period schoolroom, a blacksmith shop with hand-forged tools, and antique ranching/farming items, including snowshoes for a horse.

Across the street from the courthouse is a replica of Mormon Station. The replica and historical exhibit inside make up **Mormon Station State Park**. Just down the street is another popular site, the **Genoa Saloon**, allegedly the oldest bar in Nevada (1850s).

The **Carson Valley** can be toured by bicycle, but hot-air ballooning and soaring (world-class) are also exciting ways of getting around.

> The townspeople make some 4,500 pounds of candy in preparation for the annual "Candy Dance," held the last weekend in September. Now attracting thousands of visitors, the Candy Dance started in 1919.

▶ HISTORIC HOTEL ◀

DAVID WALLEYS'S RESORT, HOT SPRINGS, SPA, *2001 Foothill Rd., P.O. Box 158, (775) 782-8155 (ext. 8127), fax (775) 782-2103, e-mail: banquet@quintusresorts.com, http://davidwalleys.com/intro.htm*. Established as elegant spa & hotel in 1862, currently undergoing restoration to 19th-century glory, 72 rooms, 72 suites, 4 cottages (historic), private baths, TV & phones, two restaurants & lounge, antiques, hot mineral springs & spas, pool, tennis, fitness center, gift shop, Mark Twain & Presidents Grant and "Teddy" Roosevelt among guests. $$ to $$$$

Further Information

Carson Valley Chamber of Commerce, *1513 US 395 N, Gardnerville, NV 89410 (775) 782-8144, (800) 727-7677 (ZIP for Genoa is 89411.)*

Directions

From Reno, US 395 south (through Carson City) to Genoa Ln., west to Genoa.

Other Charming Nevada Towns
Lamoille
Unionville
Virginia City

Chapter 29

NEW HAMPSHIRE

EXETER
Population 9556

Founded in 1638 and located on a tidal river, railroad line, and major highways, **Exeter** possesses the kind of sophistication that comes with centuries of contact and commerce with peoples from other parts. The town not only has a long, but also a rich history, one distinguished by individualism and Revolutionary rebellion and patriotism.

Exeter's architectural diversity gives tangible expression to its worldly wisdom and long history. Buildings from every era line the town's streets. The best way to explore the architecture is by foot (the Exeter Historical Society publishes a brochure for walking tours). A good starting point is **Front Street**, bordered by an exceptional collection of handsome Federal-style houses. The 1798 **Congregational Church** is also on this street.

The attractive campus of historic **Phillips Exeter Academy** (1781), also on Front Street, has more than 100 buildings. The 1970 library by Louis Kahn and the ornate 1897 Gothic church are of special architectural interest.

Elsewhere is the **Ladd-Gilman House** (1721), a national landmark that is now the **American Independence Museum**. Included in the museum's collections are one of three Purple Hearts awarded by George Washington, handwritten documents of General and President Washington, and one of the 24 surviving original copies of the Declaration of Independence.

The older part of the **Gilman Garrison House** was built in the mid 1600s of hewn logs. Originally a garrison, the structure was remodeled in the 18th century. Period furnishings include Daniel Webster's desk. (open to the public)

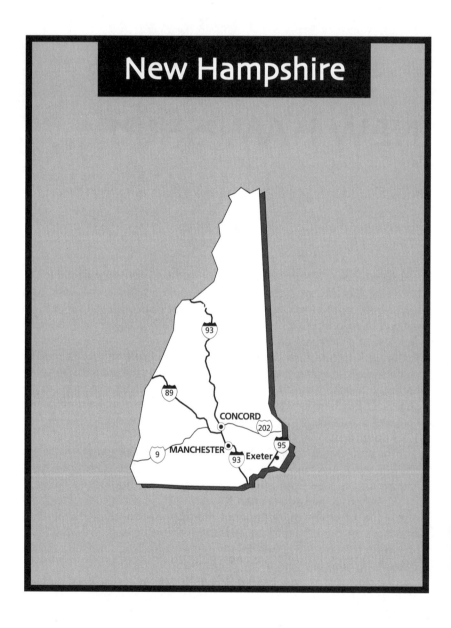

New Hampshire

Visitors may want to add some of Exeter's specialty shops to their itineraries. Among the offerings are fine old books, unique gifts for children, and imported foods.

• The IOKA Theatre (1915) is one of the oldest movie theaters in the country still in operation.
• In 1776 New Hampshire became the first of the colonies to adopt an independent state constitution.

Further Information
The Exeter Area Chamber of Commerce, *120 Water St., Exeter, NH 03833 (603) 772-2411, www.exeterarea.org*

Directions
From Manchester, NH 101 east to exit 9, right onto Rte. 27 into downtown Exeter

Other Charming New Hampshire Towns
Center Harbor
Hancock
Jackson
Jaffrey
Peterborough
Sugar Hill

Chapter 30

NEW JERSEY

CAPE MAY
Population 4,668

One of the country's premier Victorian seaside resorts, **Cape May** is among the elite of America's charming towns. If in your mind's eye you can replace the cars with carriages, and the shorts and jeans with bustles and parasols, you can see the town pretty much the way it was. Gorgeous Victorian homes and inns still grace the streets, and visitors still relax on verandahs or stroll the sidewalks and seaside promenade. The views and breezes from the sea are timeless, of course.

No one has yet explained the lure of the sea, but Cape May is surviving proof that, whatever its nature, that lure has been around for many generations. The town was known as a resort when New Jersey was still a British colony. Steamship service between Cape May and Philadelphia began in the early 1800s and was soon followed by regular railroad service. Over the years the resort has entertained a number of presidents and other prominent people – including John Philip Sousa and Congressman Abraham Lincoln. Thanks to the growth of Atlantic City in the early 20th century, Cape May stopped developing and became forever fixed in the colorful closing decades of the 19th century.

Cape May's National Historic Landmark District has over 600 preserved Victorian buildings, a number impressive by any standard. The buildings display an unusually wide variety of architectural styles and ornamentation. A stroll among them is a pleasure any time, including after dark, when the streets are lit by gas lamps. There are maps for self-guided walking tours, and visitors wishing guided tours will be dazzled by the number of options.

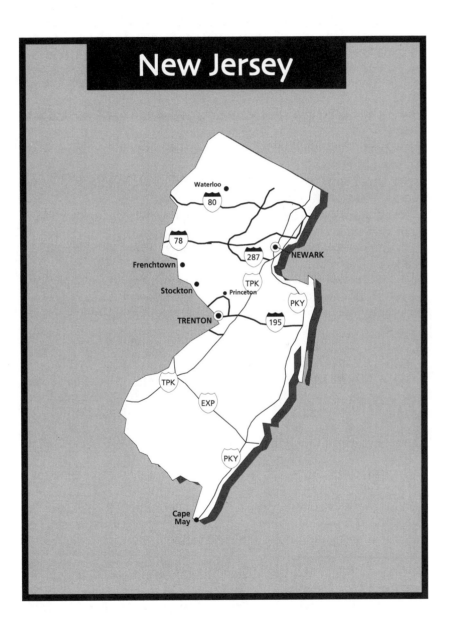

The **Emlen Physick Estate** (1881), an 18-room Stick-style mansion designed by Frank Furness, is one of the most important of the historic homes. The house and its Eastlake-style furniture may be seen by tour. Many of the most interesting of the other historic houses are now bed-and-breakfast inns.

Cape May's attractions are hardly confined to Victorian homes and inns. The **Cape May Point Lighthouse** (1859) guards the shipping lanes between Delaware Bay and the Atlantic Ocean. Now a museum, the lighthouse features displays on its history as well as a 199-step spiral staircase leading to a spectacular view.

Cold Spring Village, north of town, is a re-created 19th-century South Jersey farm village. Included among the restorations are an old jailhouse, an 18th-century inn, a country store, and a restaurant. There are also craft shops and demonstrations.

Special Features

The **Cape May Bird Observatory** is widely known for its many entertaining programs and bird-watching opportunities.

The **Cape May Whale Watch and Research Center** offers cruises for whale- and dolphin-watchers.

Historic **Lewes, Delaware** is only 70 minutes away on the Cape May-Lewes Ferry. The ferry offers daily service; during July and August twilight and moonlight cruises are also offered. Passengers may walk, bicycle, or drive aboard.

▶ HISTORIC LODGINGS ◀

THE MAINSTAY INN, *635 Columbia Ave., (609) 884-8690, www.mainstayinn.com.* 1872 Italianate villa built as gentlemen's gambling house (in 3 bldgs.), 9 rooms, 7 suites, private baths, some phones & TV, expanded Cont. (summer) & full breakfasts (rest of year), antiques, some fireplaces, elegant afternoon teas, 3 community parlors, some private porches, wrap-around verandah, gardens with fountain. $$ to $$$$

THE VIRGINIA HOTEL, *25 Jackson St., (609) 884-5700, (800) 732-4236, fax (609) 884-1236, e-mail: virginia@virginiahotel.com, www.virginiahotel.com.* 1879 hotel renovated as European-style boutique hotel, 24 rooms, private baths, TV & phones, Cont. breakfasts, award-winning restaurant, fireplace in front parlor, verandahs, glass-enclosed porches off parlors, intimate garden, central location. $$$ to $$$$

Further Information

Chamber of Commerce of Greater Cape May, *P.O. Box 556, Cape May, NJ 08204 (609) 884-5508.*

Directions
From Philadelphia/Camden, I-76 south to NJ 42, south to Atlantic City Expwy., Atlantic City Expwy. to Garden State Pkwy., south on Rt. 109 to Cape May.

FRENCHTOWN
Population 1,528

New Yorkers (and others) seeking a picturesque little river town where the days are relaxed and the nights quiet are discovering **Frenchtown** on the Delaware. It isn't everyday that you can find such a place, especially one just 60 minutes out of New York City.

Frenchtown was on the map, although not necessarily by that name, as far back as the mid-18th century, when a ferry crossed the **Delaware** at this point. During its earlier years the town saw a gristmill, a manufacturer of spokes and wheels, a railroad, even a poultry industry. Around 1875 things began to slow down, however, and the town took a long nap. Then, 20 years or so ago, charm-loving kinds of people began to rediscover the place, and the restorations, art studios, boutiques, and antique shops began to appear.

Although Frenchtown remains quiet, there is more to do than admire the setting, charming though it may be. Sophisticated shoppers will find what they're looking for off the brick sidewalks of the antiqued **Bridge Street**. And sportsmen of all ages can find what they're looking for in or on the waters of the Delaware River. The Delaware is a *play river*, meaning that it's great for canoeing, tubing, fishing, and other river sports.

Special Features
The bed of the old railroad has been converted to a first-class hiking/biking path.

> Frenchtown was named after an aristocratic European settler who apparently never bothered to tell the locals that he originated in Switzerland rather than France.

Further Information
Frenchtown Visitors Bureau, *P.O. Box 425, Frenchtown, NJ 08825 (800) 989-3388.*

Directions
From Newark, I-78 west to exit 15, County 513 south to Frenchtown (12 miles).

PRINCETON
Population 14,203 (borough)

Stroll down Nassau Street on a warm spring day. Or maybe on an autumn football day when the colors are orange and black. Then cross the street and spend some time exploring the campus. Finally, wander over to the graduate school. You'll find that parts of both **Princeton** and **Princeton University** could have been transplanted from England—Cambridge would be a good bet. You'll also find that the university's campus is indisputably one of the finest in the world. And you'll understand why some might be tempted to vote Princeton the most beautiful town in the United States.

Facing Nassau Street is **Nassau Hall,** in almost every sense Princeton's heart, and one of the country's most hallowed places. The largest academic structure in the Colonies when completed in 1756, the building saw service as the meeting place of New Jersey's first legislature in 1776, as a barracks and a hospital during the Revolutionary War, and as home to the Continental Congress in 1783. To list those who have walked its halls would be to compile an index for a book on American history. Within its walls today are Memorial Hall, honoring the university's war dead, and the faculty room, modeled after Britain's House of Commons.

The university's buildings represent a range of architectural styles and, as might be expected on an Ivy League campus, are often the work of top architects. Structures that may have greatest appeal to the romantic are those of the "Collegiate Gothic" style. One of these, the non-denominational **University Chapel** (1928), is among the largest university chapels in the world; of special interest are the French pulpit and lectern and the American stained-glass windows. The **Graduate School** (1913), with its magnificent tower and lovely quadrangles, provides another splendid example of the Collegiate Gothic style.

Displayed about the campus are the **Putnam Sculptures**, a large collection of modern outdoor works by internationally renowned artists. Other campus sites that merit a visit are the **Art Museum** and the **Woodrow Wilson School of Public and International Affairs**.

Princeton's many lovely and historic homes justify a special tour in their own right. The starting point should be the charming red brick home (ca 1766) of the **Historical Society of Princeton** on Nassau Street. The house boasts many original Colonial details such as wide-plank floors and a grand stairway. The society's museum offers changing exhibits on Princeton history.

Other homes on the tour should include **Morven** (1755), home of Richard Stockton (signer of the Declaration of Independence) and until recently the official residence of New Jersey's governors; and the grand Greek-Revival **Drumthwacket** (1835, enlarged 1890s), official residence of the state's current governors. Both homes are open to the public, although on a restricted schedule or by appointment.

Another home open to the public, the **Thomas Clarke Farmhouse** (ca 1772), is located in **Princeton Battlefield State Park**, where General Washington defeated the British in 1777. The rooms have period furnishings. Among the many other important Princeton houses (privately owned) are the **Woodrow Wilson Houses** (1836 and 1895); **Westland** (1854), once home to Grover Cleveland; and Albert Einstein's home (ca 1840).

The historical society offers guided tours (Sundays at 2:00 p.m.) as well as brochures for self-guided walking tours. Check at the Frist Student Center on Washington Road for information on campus tours.

Special Features

In nearby **Rocky Hill** is the homestead (ca 1710) that served as General Washington's headquarters in 1783 and where the general wrote his *Farewell Orders to the Armies*. The dwelling and attendant buildings now form the **Rockingham State Historic Site**. Rooms are furnished in period style.

In the days before the Civil War, Princeton University was popular with wealthy Southern as well as Northern families. The Civil War subsequently and consequently set close friends and classmates against one another.

▶ HISTORIC INN ◀

NASSAU INN, *10 Palmer Sq., (609) 921-7500, (800) 8.NASSAU, fax (609) 921-9385, e-mail: sales@nassauinn.com, www.nassauinn.com.* "Hotel located in the heart of downtown Princeton since 1756," National Register, 203 rooms & suites, private baths, TV & phones, Yankee Doodle Tap Room with mural by Norman Rockwell, some pets, fitness center, across from university in Palmer Square (with shopping/dining). $$$$

Further Information

Chamber of Commerce of Princeton Area, *216 Rockingham Row, Princeton Forrestal Village, Princeton, NJ 08540 (609) 520-1776, fax (609) 530-9107*; or **Historical Society of Princeton**, *Bainbridge House, 158 Nassau St., Princeton, NJ 08540 (609) 921-6748, www.princetonhistory.org.*

Directions

From Trenton, US 1 north to Princeton turnoff; from Newark (and New York City), New Jersey Tpk. south to exit 9, follow signs to US 1, south to Princeton turnoff.

STOCKTON
Population about 600

No more than three miles up the Delaware from Lambertville, **Stockton** consists of a couple of historic inns, a wonderful old railroad station, a couple of craft shops, and maybe one grocery store. There are some interesting old homes on the side of the hill, but you won't see much of them from the main road (NJ 29). A narrow, old-fashioned truss bridge connects the little town with Pennsylvania across the Delaware. Situated as it is alongside the Delaware, the old **Delaware and Raritan (D & R) Canal**, and an old railroad bed turned hiking/biking trail, Stockton is about as likely to be visited today by hikers, bikers, and canoeists as by motorists.

Stockton began as a ferry town in the 18th century. The canal and then the railroad came in the 19th century. Now, with the ferry and railroad gone and the canal (actually a feeder for the main canal) long empty of commercial craft, the town survives on its charm and attractiveness as a home for people commuting to New York City and Philadelphia.

On the northern edge of town is the **Prallsville Mills** section of the **D & R Canal State Park**. Here, clustered on the canal, are an 1877 gristmill (open to the public), a 1794 linseed-oil mill, a sawmill, and several other historic structures. The beginning of the canal is a few miles farther north, at a point now occupied by the **Bull's Island** section of the state park. The park offers excellent canoeing, boating, fishing, hiking, and birdwatching. Approximately 70 feet wide and 8 feet deep, the canal is ideal for canoeing – and safer than the adjoining **Delaware River**.

Special Features
The old railroad-bed trail leads south to **Trenton** and north to **Frenchtown** (see selection). Whether on the trail, canal, or river, Stockton is an excellent place to "put into" for food, supplies, and rest.

Sergeantsville, four miles northeast of Stockton, is the site of **Green Sergeants Bridge**, New Jersey's last covered bridge.

> The Delaware and Raritan Canal was dug by hand by Irish immigrants between 1830 and 1834.

▶ HISTORIC INN ◀
THE STOCKTON INN, *1 Main St., P.O. Box C, (609) 397-1250, fax (609) 397-8948, e-mail stocktoninn@snip.net, www.stocktoninn.com.* 1710 stone home, 3 rooms & 8 suites, private baths, TV & phones, restaurant with

fireplaces & alfresco dining in terraced garden pavilion, bar, entertainment, reproductions, wishing well. $ to $$$$ (Note: It was about this inn that Richard Rodgers and Lorenz Hart wrote the song about "a small hotel, with a wishing well.")

Further Information
Delaware River Mill Society, *P.O. Box 298, Stockton, NJ 08559; also,* **Asst. Innkeeper**, *Stockton Inn, 1 Main St., Stockton.*

Directions
From Trenton, NJ 29 north along Delaware River to Stockton.

WATERLOO VILLAGE
Population a handful

Situated as it is in a valley alongside a beautiful winding river (the **Musconetcong**) and remains of an old canal, it's hard to believe that picturesque **Waterloo Village** is only minutes from the outer banks of New Jersey's suburbs (it's near the town of **Stanhope**). But it is, even though the setting is rural, in fact as well as appearance.

Deserted as the railroad, iron furnaces, and history in general moved elsewhere, tiny Waterloo Village never emerged from the 18th and 19th centuries. The village was an iron town in the 18th century—the forge in fact provided cannonballs for the Revolutionary effort—and then prospered as a canal town in the 19th century. By the 20th century, however, the place was largely forgotten. Then, after World War II, Waterloo Village was "discovered," restored and opened to the public (1964).

Now a National Historic Site, Waterloo Village embraces over 30 restored structures. A canal museum, working gristmill, blacksmith shop, and sawmill provide excellent glimpses at the commercial and industrial life of another day. Other structures include the 1876 **Wellington House** (now a museum), the **Methodist Church** (1859), and several homes that remain private residences. The village also contains an early farmstead and a re-created **Lenape Indian village**. Period-attired guides and craftspeople explain the architecture and history and demonstrate various crafts.

As part of its new life, Waterloo Village has become a center for the arts. Top artists perform everything from classical music and opera to jazz and rock as part of the **Waterloo Concert Series**. Also on the calendar are Civil War re-enactments, arts & crafts festivals, antiques fairs, and Irish, Scandinavian, and other festivals.

Special Features

Like Waterloo, nearby **Stanhope** was once a forge town, iron-producing center, and port on the **Morris Canal**. The town has many beautiful old houses.

The grounds of Waterloo provide an excellent setting for a family picnic.

> Waterloo is the most intact village along the Morris Canal.

Further Information

Waterloo Foundation for the Arts, Inc., *Village of Waterloo, 525 Waterloo Road, Stanhope, NJ 07874 (973) 347-0900, www.waterloovillage.org*

Directions

From New York City, I-80 west to exit 25, follow signs to Waterloo

Other Charming New Jersey Towns
Batsto
Clinton
Flemington
Lambertville
Salem

Chapter 31

NEW MEXICO

HILLSBORO/KINGSTON
Population 200/30

Few Americans have heard of the old mining towns of **Hillsboro** (gold) and **Kingston** (silver). Indeed, there are New Mexicans who have never heard of these tiny spots.

Both villages are tucked away far out on the rolling high desert of southwestern New Mexico. The road that leads to them eventually winds its way through the **Black Range** to the west, but there's nothing in particular on the other side of the mountains—except more spectacular scenery. Overhead the skies are true blue, and the waters coming down from the mountain are sparkling.

Although Hillsboro is on the desert, its **Main Street** passes through a natural grove of old cottonwood trees. Among the trees are several quaint shops, an art gallery, and a bed and breakfast. It's easy to see why movies and commercials have been filmed here. The town also has an old church (1882) that's still in use, the ruins of the old courthouse (the county seat was moved elsewhere in the early 1940s), and on its outskirts, apple orchards, the reason for the town's annual **Apple Festival** (Labor Day weekend). There's also a small museum, the **Black Range Museum**, that displays gold-mining artifacts dating from about 1875 to 1900.

Nothing much remains of tiny Kingston, nine miles down the road, but an old brick assay office, the **Victorio Hotel** (now a private residence), and a few other historic buildings. And a grand setting!

Special Features

Straddling as they do the **Geronimo Trail Scenic Byway**, Hillsboro and

New Mexico

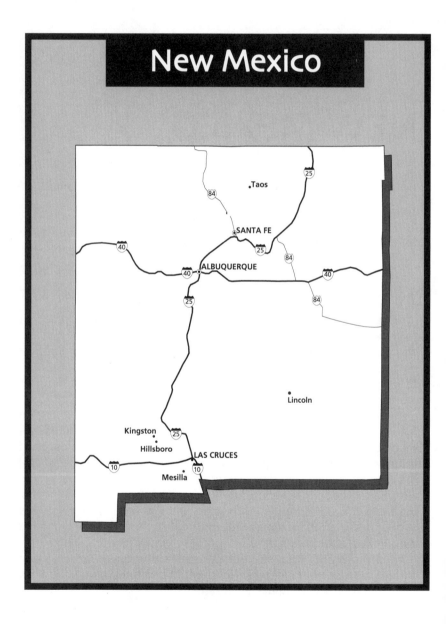

Kingston are within convenient excursion distance of the **Black Range Scenic Area**, the **Gila Cliff Dwellings National Monument**, the **City of Rocks State Park, Caballo Lake State Park, Elephant Butte Lake State Park**, and several early New Mexican communities.

- Ted Turner's Ladder Ranch is located between Hillsboro and Truth or Consequences (to the east).
- Corpses used to be kept in the basement of the Victorio Hotel in Kingston until the spring thaw made burial possible.

▶ HISTORIC RESTAURANT ◀

HILLSBORO GENERAL STORE & COUNTRY CAFÉ, *Main St., P.O. Box 427, (505) 895-5306.* Store in continuous operation since 1879; National Register; Southwestern menu & traditional café-style food; Bumbleberry Pie, Hillsboro Hot Dog, Huevos Rancheros among specialties; historic memorabilia; locally crafted gifts. $

Further Information

Black Range Business Association, *P.O. Box 155, Hillsboro, NM 88042 (505) 895-5686.*

Directions

From Albuquerque, I-25 south to exit 63, NM 152 west to Hillsboro/ Kingston; from El Paso, I-10 north to I-25, I-25 north to exit 63 (and as above).

LINCOLN
Population 130

Little **Lincoln** is situated in a remote valley in one of the prettiest corners of New Mexico. To the north are the starkly beautiful **Capitan Mountains** and to the south the forested foothills and snow-tipped peaks of the magnificent **Sacramentos**. Pastoral in the foreground, rugged on the horizon, the setting is unmistakably Western.

Lincoln's history was also unmistakably "Western," at least for a few months in the late 19th century. (And for the traveler seeking a romantic glimpse of the Old West, a few months are probably more than sufficient.) In 1878, rivalry between two mercantile operations erupted into open conflict when a member of one group was murdered by a sheriff's posse. This sparked a 6-month battle, later known as the **Lincoln County War**, that culminated in a 5-day shootout. The bloodshed didn't end there, for three years later one of the participants in the war, William Bonney (a.k.a. Billy the Kid), now an outlaw, killed two deputies in his legendary escape from the courthouse jail.

The town's one street is now paved, and there are a few cars about (and one public telephone). But except for these few changes, Lincoln remains pretty much as it was in the late 1800s. Eleven of the town's adobe and stone structures comprise the **Lincoln State Monument**. Five of the buildings are museums:

The **Old Lincoln County Courthouse** and the **Anderson-Freeman Visitors Center & Museum** acquaint the visitor with Lincoln's colorful, often multiethnic history. History is also on exhibit at the **Tunstall Museum**; the focal point here is the **Tunstall Store**, equipped with original 19th-century merchandise and furnishings. Also open to the visitor are the Greek Revival **Dr. Woods House** and the **Montano Store**.

Two other structures of special note are the 1887 **San Juan Mission** and the **torreon** (tower) built to protect early settlers from Apache attacks. Lodgings, restaurants, galleries, and craft shops, all housed in historic buildings, are sprinkled throughout the village.

Lincoln is small enough to explore by foot. Stagecoach tours offer another option.

Note: I wish to thank Drew Gomber for providing some of the information for this selection. Mr. Gomber is historian for the **Hubbard Museum of the West** in nearby Ruidoso Downs.

Special Features

Eight scenic miles to the west is historic **Fort Stanton**. The fort was once home to Colonel Kit Carson (1862), the Buffalo Soldiers (1869-1889), Lieutenant "Black Jack" Pershing (1887-1891), and other American heroes. The fort has been used for a variety of purposes since its service as a military installation, among them a sanitarium for the merchant marine (1899-1952) and an internment camp in World War II. Check locally for visitation times.

Capitan, 12 miles down the road from Lincoln, is home to **Smokey Bear Historical Park** and **Smokey Bear Museum**.

Nestled in the valleys of Lincoln County are the quaint mountain village of **Cloudcroft**, the popular resort towns of **Ruidoso** and **Ruidoso Downs**, and the ghost town of **White Oaks**. Art galleries abound in these and other towns and villages.

Further Information

Historic Lincoln, *P.O. Box 98, Lincoln, NM 88338 (505) 653-4025.*

Directions

From Albuquerque, I-25 south to exit 139 (San Antonio), US 380 east to Lincoln; from El Paso (TX), US 54 north to US 380 (Carrizozo), east to Lincoln.

MESILLA
Population 1,975

The Mexican-American town of **Mesilla** (*little table*) nicely fits the romantic stereotype of the Old Southwest: a plaza, a mission-style church, and of course, old one-story adobe buildings that front directly on the street. Many of the buildings are the same that lined the streets nearly a century and a half ago. Thanks to a zoning ordinance, the original scale of the town and the architectural character of the buildings are carefully preserved.

Also known as *La Mesilla* and *Old Mesilla*, Mesilla has a history that even Hollywood would have difficulty matching: Apache attacks, shootings, the trial of Billy the Kid, cockfights, caravans on the **Chihuahua Trail**, the ratification of the Gadsden Purchase (1854), arrivals and departures of the **Butterfield Overland Mail and Stage Line**. Prospering as a transportation center on a major route to the West Coast, and as a supply center for ranching and mining operations, Mesilla grew from a small settlement in the late 1840s to the largest town between San Antonio and San Diego in the 1880s. Then the inevitable happened: The railroad went to Las Cruces instead of Mesilla. Mesilla was left to wither.

San Albino Church, originally built in 1855 and rebuilt in 1906, overlooks the **plaza**. The church offers masses in Spanish as well as English. Many of the adobe buildings about the plaza now house galleries, boutiques, unique shops, and restaurants (see below). The plaza area is where strolling, shopping, and sightseeing all blend together. The shops offer an excellent selection of Indian and Southwestern handmade jewelry, Kachinas, and Southwestern art and fashions.

About three blocks off the plaza is the **Gadsden Museum**, a house museum shown by guided tour. The museum features possessions, including the famous Gadsden Purchase painting, of the Albert Jennings Fountain family, a family prominent in Mesilla Valley history.

Special Features

During harvest time, chilies, melons, tomatoes, and other produce can be bought at roadside stands along **NM 28** (south) and other highways in the **Rio Grande Valley**.

Nearby **Las Cruces** has two interesting historic districts of its own. The streets of the **Mesquite Street Original Townsite Historic District** are lined with traditional adobe houses tinted with pastels or left in natural shades of beige. Turn-of-the-century houses and other buildings displaying a range of architectural styles, including Spanish-Pueblo Revival and Mission Revival, occupy the **Alameda Depot Historic District**. Between the two districts are the museums of the **Cultural Complex**. One of these houses exhibits on area history, while another, the **Las Cruces Museum of Fine Art and Culture**, specializes in local and regional contemporary art.

> • The Mesilla Valley is known throughout New Mexico for its chiles. Strings of red chilies, called "ristras," are often hung for decoration.
> • The wooden beams that support the roofs of adobe buildings are "vigas." The vigas, exposed on the ceiling, are an important element in New Mexican interior decoration.

▶ HISTORIC RESTAURANTS ◀

DOUBLE EAGLE RESTAURANT, *2355 Calle de Guadalupe (on the plaza), (505) 523-6700*. In 1848 adobe home with gold-leafed ceilings & Baccarat crystal chandeliers; Continental cooking with New Mexico influence—e.g., Green Chile Cheese Wontons & Pineapple Jalapeno Salsa, Banana Enchiladas, Chicken Mesilla; steaks & seafood; haunted; hand-carved oak Imperial Bar. $$ to $$$

LA POSTA DE MESILLA, *just off plaza (P.O. Box 116), (505) 524-3524*. In 1840s Butterfield Stage Bldg., National Register, "Serving Mexican food and steaks since 1939," Tostada Compuesta Cups (introduced by La Posta in 1939) & Sour Cream Enchiladas among favorites, specialty margaritas, popular. $ to $$

Further Information

Las Cruces Convention & Visitors Bureau, *211 N. Water St., Las Cruces, NM 88001 (800) 343-7827, www.lascrucescvb.org; also*, **Old Mesilla Association**, *P.O. Box 1005, Mesilla, NM 88046*.

Directions

From El Paso (TX), I-10 west to exit 140 (Las Cruces), NM 28 south to La Mesilla.

TAOS
Population 6,213

Taos is a delightful alternation between ambiance and art. The alternation is almost literal, with attention swinging between strolls along adobe streets and visits to world-class galleries. The ambiance is itself only one step away from art. The walled gardens with their hollyhocks, arched entries, and antique wooden doors have been the subjects of thousands of paintings and watercolors. An old adobe house with blue window frames and sashes and potted pink geraniums can bring out the artist in anyone.

There's more even than the ambiance to induce the artist, however. There are the mountains, always changing in hue and brightness, and mesas, rivers, and forests whose beauty seems only to increase with each change in season. Then there's that New Mexico light, with its special purity. Mix all of this together with the creative traditions of New Mexico's three principal cultures – Native American, Hispanic, and Anglo – and you have one of the world's major art centers.

Taos has 80 plus art galleries! Work varies from traditional to contemporary, and from the pure to the blended and interbred. In one shop you'll find pottery with intricate geometrical decoration from the Acoma pueblo, in the next will be handcrafted contemporary jewelry with shapes and colors defying any description beyond "Southwestern" and "spectacular."

Top exhibits of Taos's art history can be found in the **Millicent Rogers Museum** and the **Harwood Foundation Museum**. The former is distinguished by its collection of Southwestern native American jewelry, textiles, pottery, kachina dolls, painting, and basketry. The latter is operated by the University of New Mexico and features works by Taos artists from 1898 to the present. Two other superb art collections are displayed in the **Fechin Institute**, the historic home of Russian emigre artist Nicolai Fechin, and the **Ernest Blumenschein Home and Museum**, built in the 1700s and furnished as it was when the artist lived there (1919 to 1960).

The exhibits of the **Kit Carson House and Museum**, a National Historic Landmark, chronicle the history of Taos as well as the life of the legendary Kit Carson. The house was built in 1825 and has exposed ceiling beams (*vigas*) and 30-inch adobe walls. Some of the rooms are furnished in period style.

The massive adobe buttresses of the **San Francisco de Asis Church** (early 1700s) have made the church a popular subject for many artists, including Georgia O'Keeffe. The beautiful interior is famous for its Spanish religious carvings.

The **Taos Pueblo** is one of Taos's, and indeed the country's, top sites. Composed of multi-story adobe buildings, the pueblo is the finest example of Pueblo architecture anywhere and has inspired the Pueblo Revival style now popular throughout the Southwest. Centuries old and now a World Heritage Site, the pueblo is still inhabited.

The Taos area is virtually synonymous with outdoor recreation. Nearby **Taos Ski Valley**, **Red River**, **Sipapu**, and **Angel Fire** offer some of the finest skiing in the U.S. There is also world-class white-water rafting on the **Rio Grande**. Fishing, mountain biking, and hiking opportunities abound.

Special Features

The period rooms of the **Hacienda de Martinez** (ca 1804) open onto two courtyards (*placitas*). As a visit here will show, Spanish Colonial haciendas were self-sufficient villages surrounded by windowless walls to protect against occasional Comanche and Apache raids.

The panoramic **Rio Grande Gorge Bridge**, the second highest suspension bridge in the country, stretches 1,200 feet across and 650 breathtaking feet above the river.

> Contemporary Taos cooking is a creative blend of Mexican, Southwestern Spanish, Continental, and California cuisines.

▶ HISTORIC LODGING & DINING ◀

THE HISTORIC TAOS INN, *125 Paseo del Pueblo Norte, (505) 758-2233, (fax) (505) 758-5776, e-mail: taosinn@newmex.com, www.taosinn.com.* 19th-century adobe bldgs. est. as inn in 1936, National Register, 33 rooms & 3 suites, private baths, TV & phones, Doc Martin's Restaurant with seasonal patio dining, Adobe Bar, Spanish-Colonial antiques & handmade furniture, many fireplaces, private courtyard rooms, seasonal heated pool, indoor whirlpool, live entertainment. $$ to $$$$

INN ON LA LOMA PLAZA, *102 La Loma Plaza, Box 4159, (800) 530-3040, fax (505) 751-0155, e-mail: laloma@VacationTaos.com, www.VacationTaos.com.* Walled Pueblo Revival hacienda dating to 1800, National Register, 7 rooms, private baths, TV & phones, full breakfasts, antiques, some pets, original art, handcrafted furniture, fireplaces, high ceilings, hand-carved vigas, private entrances, private patios/decks, afternoon appetizers, hot tub, fountains, mountain views. $$ to $$$$

TOUCHSTONE INN & SPA & GALLERY, *110 Mabel Dodge Ln., P.O. Box 1885, (505) 758-0192, fax (505) 758-3498, e-mail: Touchstone@Taosnet.com, www.Touchstoneinn.com.* Ca 1795 adobe hacienda, 9 rooms, private baths, TV & phones, full breakfasts, dining room (guests only), art, Southwestern furniture, whirlpool, massage, garden, fountains, labyrinth. $$ to $$$$

APPLE TREE RESTAURANT, *123 Bent St., (505) 758-1900, www.appletreerestaurant.com.* In 1903 2-story adobe building incorporating much older adobe structure; American-New Mexican fare, fresh fish, vegetarian dishes; award-winning wine list; summer patio dining & winter by the fireplace. $$

Further Information
Taos County Chamber of Commerce, *P.O. Drawer I, Taos, NM 87571 (800) 732-8267, www.taoschamber.com* **Note**: The **Taos Visitor Center** on Paseo del Pueblo Sur is open seven days a week.

Directions
From Albuquerque, I-25 north to exit 282 (Santa Fe), US 84 north to Espanola, NM 68 north to Taos.

Other Charming New Mexico Towns
The Acoma Pueblo
Capitan
Cimarron
Cloudcroft
Galisteo
Las Vegas
Madrid
San Felipe Pueblo

Chapter 32

NEW YORK

CAZENOVIA
Population 3,007

The similarity of **Cazenovia** to a scenic New England village is something visitors frequently note, especially as they drive down the hill and into town. Dating as far back as the early 1800s, the buildings downtown are of brick or stone with quaint contrasting white or cream door and window surrounds. Listed as a Historic District on the National Register, the downtown area is pure picture-postcard. Of special interest is **Lincklaen House** (ca 1835), one of the most gracious of the country's old inns. Inside are high ceilings, carved moldings, Colonial chandeliers, and large fireplaces (visitors are welcome). The rest of the village, primarily residential, consists of stately old homes, tree-lined streets, and lovingly maintained lawns and gardens.

Lorenzo, just south of town, is a stately full front-gabled Adam mansion built in 1807. Preserved as the **Lorenzo State Historic Site**, the house has original furnishings, reproduction wallpapers & fabrics, formal garden, and magnificent views of the lake and surrounding hills.

Cazenovia's rolling setting is also very reminiscent of New England. The village is nestled at the foot of lovely **Cazenovia Lake**, popular with sailboaters. Country inns and cider mills dot the landscape. With winter comes first-class snowboarding and downhill and cross-country skiing (there are numerous groomed trails), and a little later, maple sugaring.

Special Features
At **Chittenango Falls State Park**, just four miles from town, the water plunges 167 feet over ledges and boulders.

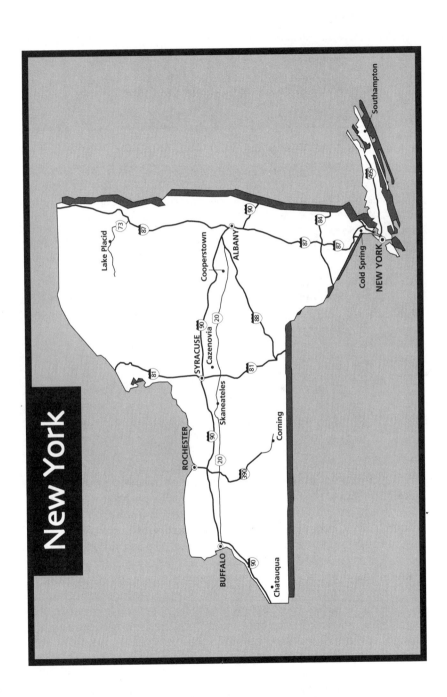

One of the best ways to take in the local scenery is to make the 10-mile drive around Cazenovia Lake.

Many of Cazenovia's residents work in Syracuse, 25 hilly minutes away.

▶ HISTORIC HOTEL ◀

LINCKLAEN HOUSE, *79 Albany St., (315) 655-3461, fax (315) 655-5443, www.LincklaenHouse.com.* Restored 1835 hotel, 23 rooms & 6 suites, private baths, TV & phones, Cont. breakfasts, dining room & courtyard restaurant, tavern, some antiques, small pets, individually stenciled rooms, atrium, afternoon tea, President & Mrs. Cleveland among famous guests. $$ to $$$$

Further Information

Greater Cazenovia Area Chamber of Commerce, 59 Albany Street, *Cazenovia, NY 13035 (315) 655-9243, fax (315) 655-9244, (888) 218-6305, www.cazenoviachamber.com.*

Directions

From Syracuse, NY 92 southeast to Cazenovia.

CHAUTAUQUA
Population 350 to 10,000

The **Chautauqua Institution** was founded on the shores of **Chautauqua Lake** in 1874 as a summer school for Sunday-school teachers. A pioneer in adult education, the institution soon expanded to include other summer schools. Along the way lodgings ranging from cottages to grand hotels were built to house students and a wide range of other visitors. Today Chautauqua Institution, a National Historic Landmark, is a self-contained Victorian village. The beautifully restored 1881 **Athenaeum Hotel** (see listing below) is one of the many buildings that in and of themselves would justify a visit here.

During the 9-week season of programming, extending from late June to late August, admission is by gate ticket. In addition to the lodgings, the grounds are sprinkled with restaurants, shops, art galleries, a library, and a broad array of educational and recreational facilities. Many of the activities are designed for children as well as adults. The gate ticket is good for all events and activities except opera and theater performances (for which separate tickets must be purchased). Special 3-, 4-, and 7-night vacation and cultural packages that combine lodgings (American or European plan) and gate tickets are available by reservation.

The arts are represented by a symphony orchestra; opera, dance, and theater companies; chamber music concerts; art exhibits; film festivals; and concerts by popular entertainers. Dozens of 1-day, 1-week, 9-week, and other courses offer instruction in everything from sailing and investment to writing and piano. Also, distinguished speakers deliver lectures on such topics as philosophy, politics, and religion.

> Admission to the grounds is open when the institution is not in session; many – but not all – of the hotels, restaurants, and other facilities are closed, however.

▶ HISTORIC HOTEL ◀

THE ATHENAEUM, *P.O. Box 66, (800) 821-1881, fax (716) 357-2833, e-mail: athenaeum1881@hotmail.com, www.athenaeum-hotel.com.* Restored Victorian hotel (1881) on grounds of Chautauqua Institution, 157 rooms & suites, private baths, both Cont. & full breakfasts, grand buffet lunch & 5-course dinner included, elegant dining room (jacket at dinner, no tipping), antiques, facing Chautauqua Lake, next to amphitheatre, tennis & golf nearby, lawn games, nature walks. $$$$ (open late June to late August—check dates)

Note: The visitor may choose among a variety of accommodation options on Chautauqua's grounds – for information call (716) 357-6373.

Further Information

Chautauqua Institution, *Chautauqua, NY 14722 (800) 836-2787*; or **Chautauqua County Visitors Bureau**, *P.O. Box 1441, Chautauqua, NY (800) 242-4569, www.tourchautauqua.com.*

Directions

From Buffalo, I-90 south to exit 60, NY 394 east to Chautauqua.

COLD SPRING
Population 2,000

If you take the Hudson Railroad north from New York City along the Hudson River, you'll soon enter a region where the river and the Appalachian Mountains meet. Along an especially beautiful stretch of the river in this region, about 50 miles from Manhattan, the train stops at **Cold Spring**, one of the most picturesque little towns in the **Hudson Valley**.

The National Register of Historic Places describes the town as "one of the best-preserved 19th century townscapes in the Hudson River region...." **Main Street** is flanked by shade trees and an array of charming storefronts. There are more than a dozen shops catering to collectors and lovers of antiques and memorabilia. There are also shops selling books, chocolates, nautical gifts, handcrafted jewelry, hand-knitted Irish sweaters, dried flowers, gourmet foods, and unique clothing. There are also some good pubs. And Cold Spring, neighboring **Garrison**, and the surrounding region are renowned for their excellent restaurants.

Cold Spring was a foundry town during the Revolutionary and Civil Wars. A variety of exhibits from those and other days in the town's history are on display in the **Foundry School Museum** – an 1850s schoolhouse and museum of the **Putnam County Historical Society**.

Just south of town and with a sweeping view of the Hudson is **Boscobel** (1804), a fully restored and outstanding example of New York Federal domestic architecture. Inside the house is a superb collection of Federal furniture and decorations (guided tours). On the grounds are an herb garden, orangerie, and rose garden.

Nature enthusiasts are drawn to Cold Spring for several reasons. One of them is the **Constitution Marsh Wildlife Sanctuary**, operated by the National Audubon Society, south of town (canoe tours available). Another is the **Manitoga Nature Preserve**, an 80-acre nature center with beautiful woodlands and waterfalls (self-guided tours). Hikes along country roads and cruises on the **Hudson River** (from **West Point**) are also great ways to enjoy the area's natural attractions.

Special Features

Four miles south of Cold Spring is **Garrison**, another charming Hudson River town – and one also served by the Hudson Railroad. The **Garrison Art Center** houses a gallery and schedules a variety of art classes.

The **United States Military Academy** at West Point is south of town across the river. West Point's Visitors Center offers tours of and information on the academy. The best way to reach West Point is via the Bear Mountain Bridge nine miles south of Cold Spring.

- Cold Spring's name is believed to have originated with a reference to the local spring by General George Washington.
- The Hudson Gorge is a true fjord as it passes through Cold Spring.

Further Information

Cold Spring/Garrison Area Chamber of Commerce, *P.O. Box 36, Cold Spring-on-Hudson, NY 10516 (845) 265-3200, www.hvgateway.com; also,* **The Putnam County News & Recorder**, *86 Main St., Cold Spring, NY (845) 265-2468.* Note: Don't confuse with the town of Cold Spring Harbor on Long Island's north shore!

Directions

From New York City, US 9 north to Cold Spring (across from West Point).

COOPERSTOWN
Population 2,500

At latest count the **Cooperstown** area had about 73 bed-and-breakfast inns, possibly the largest number per capita in the country. Some overlook the shores of beautiful **Otsego Lake**, others grace the geranium-laden streets of the historic district, and yet others are tucked along the winding roads and creeks of the surrounding countryside. They cater to every budget, mood, and personality, and vary from quaint cottages to working farms to Victorian mansions. And they exist for good reason, for even without its lake, rolling hills, forests, and lovely old farms, Cooperstown's arts calendar and world-class sights would make the little town one of the most charming and interesting resorts in the United States.

As with the bed and breakfasts, Cooperstown probably has the largest number of museums per capita in the country. The "Big Three" are the **National Baseball Hall of Fame and Museum**, the **Farmers' Museum**, and the **Fenimore Art Museum**.

The **Hall of Fame** was founded in 1939 to honor the game's heroes and to serve as the game's historian by assembling, preserving, and displaying information and memorabilia. More than 6,000 items are on display. A multi-media show is presented continuously in the museum's new 200-seat theater.

The **Fenimore Art Museum** (1930s), a grand columned mansion on the shore of Lake Otsego, has three floors of galleries featuring outstanding collections of folk, academic, and decorative arts. There is also a gallery displaying memorabilia associated with novelist and social critic James Fenimore Cooper. A new wing houses the **Eugene and Clare Thaw Collection of American Indian Art**, one of the finest in the country. The Fenimore House is home to the museum and offices of the **New York State Historical Association**.

Life in rural upstate New York during the 19th century is recalled by the buildings, artifacts, and craft demonstrations of the **Farmers' Museum**. Included on the picturesque grounds of the museum complex are the **Main**

Barn and the **Village Crossroads**, a collection of buildings comprising a general store, druggist, church, tavern, working farm, and other historic structures.

Cooperstown's other museums include the **American Baseball Experience**, the only baseball wax museum in the country, and the **Fly Creek Cider Mill** (ca 1856), a water-powered mill that uses equipment dating from the late 19th and early 20th centuries.

Everything from jazz to chamber music is performed by top artists during the winter season of the **Cooperstown Concert Series**. In the summer there are the renowned **Glimmerglass Opera** and the **Leatherstocking Theatre**. The visual arts are represented by shows at the **Cooperstown Art Association** and the **Smithy-Pioneer Gallery** (in Cooperstown's oldest building, 1786), as well as by numerous fine craft, antique, and gift shops on Main Street.

Cooperstown's recreational options include walking, bicycle, and boat tours; water sports on Lake Otsego, challenging golf, and of course, fun at one of the baseball games or batting ranges. The **Clark Sports Center** includes a complete gymnasium, swimming and diving pools, bowling alleys, racquetball courts, and rock climbing wall.

Because parking in Cooperstown is limited, consider parking in a perimeter parking area (free) and riding the trolley about town.

Special Features

At **Glimmerglass State Park** on the north side of the lake is **Hyde Hall** (1817/1835), a 50-room mansion with two grand public rooms, two libraries, two kitchens, and several dozen other rooms. Although undergoing restoration, the mansion is open daily in summer, weekends during spring and fall, and by special tour at other times.

The **Cherry Valley Museum** (1832) in the historic village of **Cherry Valley** northeast of Cooperstown features a unique collection of local memorabilia.

- Cooperstown was founded by and named after the father of James Fenimore Cooper, author of the "Leather-stocking Tales."
- Almost 400,000 visit the National Baseball Hall of Fame each year.
- On the Sunday before Thanksgiving over 100 local residents turn out to decorate the 44 light poles on Main Street for Christmas. Others get ready for Santa's arrival the day after Thanksgiving by preparing his Victorian cottage. The afternoon concludes with a complimentary buffet at the venerable "Pit," Cooperstown's oldest tavern.

▶ HISTORIC HOTEL ◀

THE INN AT COOPERSTOWN, *16 Chestnut St., (607) 547-5756, e-mail: the inn@telenet.net, www.innatcooperstown.com*. Restored 1874 Second Empire hotel (designed by Henry Hardenbergh) in heart of historic district, National Register, 16 rooms, 1 suite, private baths, TV in sitting rooms, expanded Cont. breakfasts, antiques, sweeping verandah with rocking chairs, recipient of preservation awards, rated one of best. $$ to $$$$

Further Information

Cooperstown Chamber of Commerce, *31 Chestnut St., Cooperstown, NY 13326 (607) 547-9983, fax (607) 547-6006, www.cooperstownchamber.org.*

Directions

From Albany, US 20 west to NY 80, NY 80 south to Cooperstown.

CORNING
Population 11,938

Nestled on the banks of the **Chemung River** and surrounded by the rolling woodland of southwestern New York, **Corning** has a scenic setting. Home to the headquarters of Corning Incorporated, a Fortune 500 company, it also has a sound economic base. And to complete the list, it has an active downtown/historic district and a town plan that encourages walking. The car is often left home, and sidewalk visiting and old-fashioned friendliness are the beneficiaries.

The **Market Street Historic District** is a four-block area of fine old commercial buildings that have been restored to a late 19th-century appearance. The district's brick sidewalks are lined with shade trees and a colorful collection of specialty shops, restaurants, antique stores, and – in case the visitor forgets this is Corning – glass-blowing shops. There's also a restored 1880 ice cream parlor and the beautiful new **Riverfront Park** (a gift of Corning Incorporated).

The **Corning Museum of Glass** is one of the great museums of the world. Using some 35,000 objects representing 3,500 years of glassmaking, the museum depicts all aspects of glass, including its history, uses, manufacture, and service as an art form. In addition to the colorful exhibits, the museum campus comprises the eye-dazzling Carder Gallery, the GlassMarket, and a fascinating do-it-yourself workshop (all day, everyday).

The **Rockwell Museum**, another top attraction, is housed in an historic Romanesque Revival building. The museum has superb collections of American Western art, Carder Steuben glass, and antique toys. Films and changing exhibitions are also featured.

Centering more on local and regional history, the **Benjamin Patterson Inn Museum Complex** boasts an impressive collection of restored structures. Foremost among them is the furnished 1796 **Benjamin Patterson Inn**, a former stagecoach stop. Others include the log **DeMonstoy Cabin** (1784), the authentically furnished one-room **Browntown School** (1878), and a replica of the 1868 **Starr Barn**.

Special Features

The **National Soaring Museum**, located between Corning and Elmira, focuses on aviation history. Featured are the country's largest glider and sailplane collection, a cockpit mockup, and films on soaring. A glider field and scenic overlook are adjacent.

- The Corning area is one of the best in the country for soaring.
- Much of today's Corning is the result of a major reconstruction effort undertaken after the devastating flood of 1972.

Further Information

Greater Corning Area Chamber of Commerce, *1 Baron Steuben Pl., Corning, NY 14830 (866) 463-6264, www.CorningNY.com.*

Directions

From Rochester, I-390 south to I-86, I-86 east to Corning.

LAKE PLACID
Population 2,600 (village), 8,600 (township)

Host to the Olympic Winter Games of 1932 and 1980, and situated among the mountains and lakes of the lovely Adirondacks, **Lake Placid** is a place of scenery and spectacular sports facilities. **Main Street's** sophisticated shops and restaurants add a cosmopolitan air. Yet the charm of Lake Placid only begins with the setting. For arising from the sports complexes, and echoed by the hillsides, is the nostalgic kind of charm that comes with grand memories, memories of gold-medal achievements and cheers and national anthems.

Lake Placid is as complex as its charm. There are many Lake Placids, and all have to be sampled if the town is to be known. Each sports facility is its own village. Even the lake is too complex to be grasped by a glance. Unless you have time to spare, take some kind of organized tour. The bus tours are good, the 1-hour narrated boat cruise wins raves from visitors, and the **Lake Placid Olympic Site Tour** (sponsored by Eastman Kodak Company) offers a convenient, comprehensive self-guided motor tour of the sports complexes. For a geographical overview, scan the region from a scenic flight.

One of the most active of the sports complexes is the **U.S. Olympic Training Center**, where visitors are free to watch as athletes from all over the country train. The **Olympic Center**, another complex open to visitors, is the largest indoor ice facility in the world. Figure skaters, hockey players, and speed skaters train on the center's rinks. At the **Olympic Jumping Complex** even watching can be breathtaking as athletes train on the 90- and 120-meter ski jumps. Training takes place all year, with plastic matting replacing snow in the warmer months.

The **Lake Placid Sinfonietta** concerts, held weekly during the summer, are among the most popular of Lake Placid's many cultural events.

Special Features

On a clear day the summit of **Whiteface Mountain** offers one of the most spectacular panoramic views in the country. Drive the 5-mile **Whiteface Mountain Veterans Memorial Highway** (in **Wilmington**) to the parking area near the summit, then complete the climb by a short hike or by a unique elevator ride through the heart of the mountain.

The internationally famous figure skater Sonja Henie won a gold medal in 1932 for her performance in the Olympic Center.

Further Information

Lake Placid Convention & Visitors Bureau, *216 Main St., Olympic Center, Lake Placid, NY 12946 (800) 447-5224, www.lakeplacid.com.*

Directions

From Albany, I-87 north to exit 30, NY 73 northwest to Lake Placid.

SKANEATELES

Skaneateles (pronounced scan ee AT las) lies at the top of a gorgeous lake by the same name. The village and the lake complement each another, the one enhancing the already remarkable beauty of the other.

Skaneateles's **downtown** is an historic district containing numerous brick buildings constructed in 1835 to replace wooden structures destroyed in a fire. Brick-lined sidewalks and cast-iron lampposts complete the scene to produce something out of an old photo album. Trees, hanging floral arrangements, and hand-painted storefronts give the photo color. Proud of the beauty and vitality of the downtown, the village has been successful so far in keeping shopping malls at bay.

In the surrounding neighborhoods are faithfully restored and landscaped homes dating from the early 1800s onward. Here as well as downtown, the streets are notable for the attention given to maintenance, cleanliness, and historic authenticity.

Skaneateles Lake is one of the most beautiful and popular of New York's **Finger Lakes**. The 16 x 1 1/2-mile lake has crystal-clear water, with a through-the-water visibility of 25 feet (the lake has New York's highest water-quality rating). The lake is ideal for virtually all water sports, including scuba diving. The village has two waterfront parks, one for swimming and one for enjoying the scenery. Both are great for family recreation.

Special Features

Sightseeing, lunch, Sunday brunch, and dinner **cruises** offer one way to tour the lake. Driving or biking around the lake offer others.

Woven among the Finger Lakes of central New York is some of the most beautiful countryside in the nation. Whenever possible, get off the main highways and explore it.

Friday-evening gazebo concerts and Sunday-afternoon polo matches form part of Skaneateles's entertainment calendar.

▶ HISTORIC INN ◀

SHERWOOD INN, *26 W. Genesee St., P.O. Box 529, (315) 685-3405, e-mail: info@thesherwoodinn.com, www.thesherwoodinn.com.* Inn with beginnings as 1807 stagecoach stop, 24 rooms, private baths, TV & phones, Cont. breakfasts, 2 restaurants, tavern, antiques, panoramic lake view. $$ to $$$$ (in-season)

Further Information

Skaneateles Chamber of Commerce, *P.O. Box 199, 22 Jordan St., Skaneateles, NY 13152 (315) 685-0552, www.skaneateles.com.*

Directions

From Syracuse, I-81 south to exit 15, US 20 west to Skaneateles.

SOUTHAMPTON

Population 4,023 (village)

Esteemed for decades as a resort of the celebrated and very wealthy, **Southampton** is renowned for its grand estates and beautiful beaches. Although once thought of as a summer beach colony, the village has become a "community for all seasons," offering a wide range of recreational activities, shops, restaurants, and cultural outlets. The year-round population, which in the past consisted mainly of tradespeople and former fishermen and farmers, increased as various professional people were drawn by the area's successful marriage of cultural sophistication and natural beauty. Reminding that this is still resort territory, however, the population swells during the summer months when thousands flock to enjoy the trendy, affluent, and artsy mood that represents the summer "Hamptons."

The **Southampton Historical Museum** comprises a number of sites, including **Captain Rogers' Homestead**, a grand two-story whaling captain's house (1843). The house's exhibits include a sea captain's bedroom, a Colonial bedroom, Indian relics, and antique toys, costumes, china, etc. Among the displays on the grounds are a furnished one-room schoolhouse, a carriage shop, a post office and country store housed in a pre-Revolutionary barn, and a village street from a century ago.

The restored **Old Halsey Homestead** (1648), another of the museum's possessions, is Southampton's oldest surviving house, and indeed the oldest English frame house in New York State. The house contains authentic 17th- and 18th-century furnishings. Outside is a Colonial herb garden and border gardens.

Yet another structure belonging to the historical museum is the restored **Elias Pelletreau Silversmith Shop** (built ca 1686; used by three generations of silversmiths from 1750 to 1820). Pieces of Pelletreau silver, very rare, are highly valued by collectors of early American silver.

The Parrish Art Museum (1898), housed in a handsome Italianate structure, features 19th- and 20th-century American art, collections by William Merritt Chase and Fairfield Porter (two renowned artists/late residents of Southampton), Renaissance pieces, and other works. The permanent collection includes more than 2,000 pieces.

The shingled **St. Andrew's Dune Church** was originally a Life Saving Station built by the U.S. Government (in 1851). A church since 1879, the building's walls and windows (by Tiffany) have beautifully inscribed Biblical passages. On the grounds are remnants of old shipwrecks.

Southampton boasts many sophisticated boutiques, art and craft galleries, and gourmet food shops. It is also home to the country's oldest department store, **Hildreth's** (established 1842). The Southampton region (and the southern coast of Long Island in general) is blessed with miles of beautiful beaches and dunes. Beach access can be a problem, however, so check in advance with an innkeeper or the Chamber of Commerce.

The Southampton area harbors attractive farms that abound with vegetables and fruits. Eastern Long Island is rapidly becoming an influential wine region and Southampton has several vineyards that offer tours, tastings, and sales. The region is ideal for hiking, biking, and rollerblading (bike and Rollerblade rentals are available).

Lodging reservations are a must during the summer months and restaurant reservations are recommended (although some restaurants do not accept reservations during the summer months).

Special Features

Westhampton Beach, **Sag Harbor**, **East Hampton**, and other picturesque coastal towns are just a few miles away. Each presents its own unique view of the Hamptons.

The **Southampton Cultural Center** offers art education programs, children's activities, chamber-music concerts, and art exhibitions. Another cultural center, the **Bay Street Theatre** in Sag Harbor, stages literary readings, musical events, and plays throughout the year.

Several oceanside state parks are located at the eastern tip of Long Island, among them **Montauk Point State Park**, site of the 1795 **Montauk Lighthouse**.

- A locally published tour of antique shops and sources lists no fewer than 82 establishments!
- Eastern Suffolk County is dotted with 18th- and 19th-century windmills. All are of English design.

▶ HISTORIC LODGING ◀

MAINSTAY, *579 Hill St., (631) 283-4375, fax (631) 287-6240, e-mail: elizmain@hamptons.com, www.themainstay.com.* Structure dating to 1870s, once a country store, some private baths, some TVs, expanded Cont.

breakfasts, antiques, 2-bedroom & spacious master suites, pool, garden, walking distance to village & beach. $$ to $$$$

Further Information
Southampton Chamber of Commerce, *76 Main St., Southampton, NY 11968 (631) 283-0402, fax (631) 283-8707, e-mail: info@SouthamptonChamber.com, www.SouthamptonChamber.com.*

Directions
From New York City, I-495 (Long Island Expwy.) east to Exit 70, south on Manorville/County Road 111 to NY 27, east past Southampton College to Southampton/North Sea Rd. exit, south to Main Street.

Other Charming New York Towns
Annandale-on-Hudson
East Hampton
Hammondsport
Hudson
Rhinebeck
Wyoming

Chapter 33

NORTH CAROLINA

BEAUFORT
Population 4,032

Sometimes the sights are themselves active, and then sightseers need only linger passively by to enjoy them. And so it is along the old waterfront of the picturesque port and county seat of **Beaufort**. Sailboats bob at anchor or dock, dinghies and harbor cruise boats come and go, sailors talk of shrimping, restaurants smell of fresh seafood, and street musicians entertain.

Settled around 1710, and once the target of attack by pirates, Beaufort is North Carolina's third oldest town. Proud of their history, the people of the town have done much to preserve and restore their architectural heritage. As with the waterfront, much of the town's history can be enjoyed with little effort—the harbor area from the deck of a cruise boat, the streets from the seat of an English double-decker bus.

The **Beaufort Historic Site** comprises several restorations. One of the most prominent, the **Joseph Bell House** (ca 1767), provides an excellent example of early Beaufort architecture. The house has 18th-century furnishings. The **Josiah Bell House** (ca 1825), another restoration, has a beautiful side garden maintained by the Garden Club.

The oldest surviving public building in the state, the **Carteret County Courthouse** (1796), has authentic furnishings and boasts among its posses-sions an original thirteen-star American flag. Other restored structures include the circa 1829 **Carteret County Jail** and a circa 1859 **apothecary shop**. The **Safrit Historical Center** welcomes and orients visitors to the historic site.

The **North Carolina Maritime Museum**, one of Beaufort's top sites, displays boats and boat models, outstanding shell collections, and other exhibits concerned with the maritime and natural history of the North Carolina

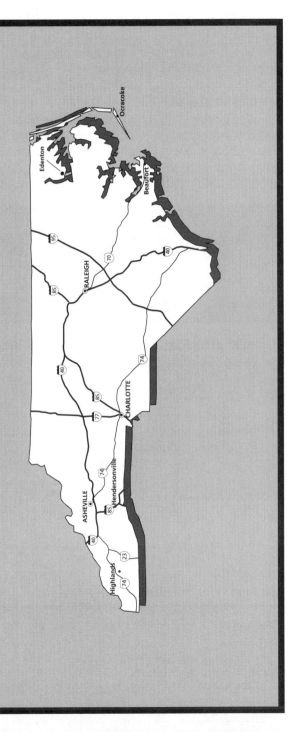

North Carolina

coastal region. The museum also offers field trips, lectures, and other programs.

Among the graves of the **Old Burying Grounds**, which date to 1731, are those of victims of the Indian Wars.

Special Features

Wild herds of ponies, with ancestors dating back to Colonial times, are Beaufort's most novel attraction. **Carrot Island** and **Bird Shoals**, which form part of a nature reserve system and are visible from Beaufort's waterfront, are home to many species of birds, some endangered, as well as to the ponies. Check locally for information on ferry service to the sites.

> • Ann and Queen Streets were named for Queen Anne, who ruled at the time the town was surveyed in 1713.
> • Hurricanes in the late 19th century eventually drove as many as 600 people from nearby Shackleford Banks, now part of the Cape Lookout National Seashore.

Further Information

Carteret County Tourism Development Authority, *P.O. Box 1406, Morehead City, NC 28557 (800) 786-6962, www.sunnync.com (ZIP for Beaufort is 28516.).*

Directions

From Raleigh, US 70 southeast to Beaufort.

EDENTON
Population 5,000

Retirees searching for the perfect place to live often end up with a North Carolina address. Many who do so settle in Hendersonville or Highlands (see selections) or other mountain communities in the western part of the state. Those preferring to be near the water and, at the same time, longing for the charm of a bygone era are more likely to look to Beaufort (see selection) or **Edenton**, a historic and architectural gem sometimes called "the South's prettiest town."

Lying on little Edenton Bay on the northern shore of **Albemarle Sound**, Edenton is very much near the water. And the town is certainly in a position to evoke the charm of bygone eras: The second largest port in the Colonies in the early 1700s and capital of North Carolina Colony until 1743, Edenton (incorporated 1722) had a collection of fine homes and other buildings long before North Carolinians even thought of breaking with the king. An eventual decline in commercial importance combined with a relatively remote location—and local commitment to preserving traditional ways—ensured that this charming bit of the past would survive.

Today Edenton has a lovely tree-lined historic district of handsome 18th-, 19th-, and early 20th-century buildings. Bordering the district at its southern end are waterfront parks with picture-postcard views of the bay and sound. People who have retired here talk with pride about the area's friendliness, safety, and absence of traffic congestion.

Edenton's business district offers the shopper a variety of boutiques and collections of antiques and—remembering North Carolina's tradition of fine cabinet-making—reproductions. The sports-minded will find marina services and two golf courses.

Special Features

Some of the finest beaches in the world are in North Carolina's famous **Cape Hatteras National Seashore**, an hour or so to the east of town.

Two plantations with beautifully restored houses are a short driving distance from Edenton. One, **Hope Plantation** (ca 1803), features the frame Federal-style home of North Carolina statesman David Stone. The second, **Somerset Place**, is a complex consisting of a fine verandahed house (ca 1830), outbuildings, and grounds; it was once one of the largest plantations in North Carolina. Both plantation houses are open to the public and are furnished in period style.

> After the Great Lakes, Albemarle Sound is the largest body of fresh water in the country.

▶ HISTORIC INN ◀

THE LORDS PROPRIETORS' INN, *300 N. Broad St., (800) 348-8933, fax (252) 482-2432, e-mail: stay@edentoninn.com, www.edentoninn.com.* Five bldgs. dating from 1801 on 2 acres in historic district, 16 rooms, 2 suites, private baths, TV & phones, full breakfasts, dining room, antiques, large patio, extensive open spaces. $$$ to $$$$

Further Information

Chowan County Tourism Development Authority, *116 E. King St., P.O. Box 245, Edenton, NC 27932-0245 (252) 482-3400, (800) 775-0111, fax (252) 482-7093, www.edenton.com.*

Directions

From Raleigh, US 64 east to US 17, north to Edenton; from Portsmouth (VA), US 17 south to Edenton.

HENDERSONVILLE/FLAT ROCK
Population 10,420

With its mild and healthful climate and glorious mountain scenery, **Hendersonville** is a retreat, and it has been for close to 200 years. Maybe longer, because the Cherokees are believed to have come here to seek solitude long before the arrival of any Europeans.

Rice and indigo plantation owners from Charleston and other lowland towns once built summer homes in the Flat Rock area just south of here so that their families could escape the heat, humidity, and malaria of the coastal region (see also Pendleton, SC). The plantation families were followed by Georgians and Floridians seeking to escape the yellow fever epidemics. Later, victims of tuberculosis and other chest ailments were attracted by the region's altitude. Maintaining the tradition, retirees from the East and Midwest wishing to escape the cities and cold winters began settling here in the 1940s and 1950s.

Hendersonville is today as popular as ever as a place to escape to. The air and water are pure, crime is low, and the pace of life easy. The town is one our grandparents or great grandparents could have lived in. The country is rural, a place where people watch birds or go on wildflower walks.

There are two historic districts, one in **Flat Rock**, three miles south, and the other in Hendersonville. The Flat Rock historic district is older, dating back to the summer days of antebellum planters. Hendersonville grew as businesses developed to serve those retreating to the area, and so its district dates to a later stage of the 19th century.

Many of the summer homes built by privileged Charlestonians and others from the coastal region remain in private hands as estates and can only be seen from the distance, if at all. There is one most notable exception to this rule, however: **Connemara** (ca 1838), the farm where Carl Sandburg and his family lived for 22 years. Now the **Carl Sandburg Home National Historic Site**, the home and grounds of the beloved American poet are open to the public. The house is kept very much like it was when Sandburg lived there, and numerous hiking trails lead to a functional goat barn and to panoramic views of lakes, rolling hills, and in the distance, the **Blue Ridge Mountains**.

Another structure from the days of the Southern aristocracy open to the public is the Episcopal **Church of St. John in the Wilderness**, in Flat Rock. The church was built in 1833 as a chapel for the estate of an English-born family.

Later, it was turned over to the Episcopal Diocese and, in 1852, doubled in length. The church has been entered in the National Register.

Woodfield Inn, built in Flatrock in 1852 as "The Farmers Hotel," served as the first stagecoach stop on the Old Indian Trial and, later, as a Confederate military post during the Civil War. Soldiers are reported to have hidden gold and jewelry in a secret room that is still accessible. The inn has been placed on the National Register. (See lodging listing below.)

The historic **Hendersonville Depot** (1879) is now home to the 420-square-foot **Apple Valley HO Scale Model Railroad**. The model has over 600 feet of track, more than 100 switches, and a variety of scenic, rural, and industrial landscape features. The depot's exterior paint has been restored to its original color. Celebrating another mode of transportation, the **Western North Carolina Air Museum** exhibits restored and replica antique airplanes. Included in the collection are a 1930 Curtis Robin and a 1936 Piper J-2 Cub.

Ten blocks long, Hendersonville's **Main Street** has 194 businesses. The late 19th-century buildings, many with restored storefronts, house antique shops, upscale clothing shops, bakeries, and coffee shops. The solid retail presence combined with creative landscaping and frequent colorful sidewalk events give the street a vibrancy that most main streets lost decades ago. (Much of the town's outlying commercial development also has an attractive park-like appearance, thanks again to careful planning and planting.)

An alternative form of shopping is offered at the **Henderson County Farmer's Curb Market**, in operation for more than 75 years. Here there are garden-fresh vegetables, baked goods, afghans, and aprons, all home-grown or homemade.

Hendersonville's recreation scene is consistent with that of a community that has no fewer than seven banks on Main Street. There are several well-known golf courses, each unique, and others are being built (many are open to the public). Comedy, classic, musical, whodunit, and other kinds of hits from the Broadway and London stages are presented each summer at the **Flat Rock Playhouse**, one of the ten best summer stock theaters in the country. Other productions are offered by the **Hendersonville Little Theater** and the **Belfry Players**. Inquire at the visitors center for information on these and other events, including performances of mountain music.

Special Features

North of town lies the **Johnson Farm**, a fine example of a late 19th- and early 20th-century mountain farm, now a hands-on museum. The elegant home and other buildings were handmade from bricks fired on-site from river mud. (National Register; admission)

Chimney Rock Park, 20 minutes east of Hendersonville, offers an eye-dazzling 75-mile view of the rugged western North Carolina landscape. Within the park are a 400-foot waterfall, rock formations, and nature trails.

> The Hendersonville area ranks as the seventh largest apple producer in the country. And, yes, there's an annual apple festival (September).

▶ HISTORIC INNS ◀

THE WAVERLY INN, *783 N. Main St., (800) 537-8195, fax (828) 692-1010, e-mail: innkeepers@waverlyinn.com, www.waverlyinn.com.* 1898 inn on National Register, 13 rooms, 1 suite, private baths, TV & phones, full breakfasts, antiques, refreshments, rocking chairs on verandah. $$ to $$$$

WOODFIELD INN, *US 25 2 miles S, P.O. Box 98 (Flat Rock 28731), (800) 533-6016, fax (828) 693-0437, e-mail: info@woodfieldinn.com, www.woodfieldinn.com.* Oldest operating inn in N.C. (ca 1850), National Register, 18 rooms, private baths, TV, full breakfasts, restaurant, antiques, antebellum atmosphere, on 23 acres, wedding gazebo & formal gardens, sweeping verandah. $$$ to $$$$

Further Information

Visitors Information Center, *201 S. Main St., Hendersonville, NC 28792 (800) 828-4244, www.historichendersonville.com,*

Directions

From Asheville, I-26 south to exit 18A (Hendersonville exit),

HIGHLANDS
Population 948 (village only)

Tucked in the middle of a national forest in western North Carolina's Blue Ridge Mountains, **Highlands** is a place of mountain streams and waterfalls, dogwood and rhododendron, autumn brilliance, craft shows and superb shopping. There are no theme parks, chain restaurants, factory outlets, or video arcades. Highlands is a place for lovers of nature.

Established in the 1870s, Highlands was known by the 1880s as a health resort and refuge from the heat of Southern summers. With a cool average altitude of 4,118 feet, the little town became a summer hideaway for the affluent from the South, especially Atlanta. For Atlanta's privileged, Highlands became synonymous with "summer mountain retreat." Many built second homes here, expensive second homes. They still do. As a result, the village is surrounded by a twisting maze of gorgeous gated estates and country-club communities.

The wealth of Highlands's summer residents is reflected in the merchandise in the shops, the restaurant menus, and the many fine country clubs. It's indeed possible that Highlands has the largest number of excellent restaurants per capita in the United States. The town boasts a multitude of boutiques and quaint shops. Some offer art, others antiques, and yet others hand-made items of wood, iron, fabric, etc. Shop windows display music boxes, custom-designed jewelry, porcelain, Oriental rugs, bird and even bat (!) houses.

The cultural scene is similarly rich. The **Performing Arts Center** hosts speakers, productions of the **Highlands Community Players**, and music events, while the **Highlands Playhouse** stages professional productions in its hilltop theater. Each year music lovers make their way here to attend the highly respected month-long **Highlands Chamber Music Festival**. Local artists display their works in the **Bascom-Louise Gallery**, located in the Hudson Library, as well as in private galleries.

It is nature, however, that dominates Highlands. The **Highlands Nature Center** features indoor wildlife exhibits, botanical gardens, and seminars and lectures. The area around Highlands is known for its mountain trails, challenging golf courses, and trout-fishing streams. Of very special note are the waterfalls. At least seven sizable falls are located within a few miles of town. (Visitors are cautioned to view the falls from a distance and not to climb them.)

Special Features

Franklin, 16 or so miles northwest of town, is famous for its gem mining. Visitors are invited to mine for rubies, sapphires, and other stones. The drive to Franklin (**US 64**) is one of the most scenic in North Carolina.

▶ HISTORIC INN ◀

HIGHLANDS INN, *420 Main St., P.O. Box 1030, (828) 526-9380, (800) 964-6955, e-mail: Info@Highlandsinn-nc.com, www.Highlandsinn-nc.com.* Renovated 1880 inn on National Register, 29 rooms, 6 suites, 2 cottages, private baths, TV, full breakfasts, restaurant, antiques, Colonial stenciling, private rock garden, front porch overlooking Main St. $ to $$$$

Further Information

Highlands Visitor Center, *P.O. Box 404, Highlands, NC 28741 (828) 526-2112, fax (828) 526-0268, www.highlands-chamber.com.*

Directions

From Asheville, I-26 south to exit 9, NC 280 southwest to US 64 (near Brevard), US 64 west to Highlands.

OCRACOKE
Population 700

A quiet and relaxed way of life continues among the picturesque **Outer Banks** houses and live-oak trees that cluster about the pretty little harbor. Unless there's a rush on to catch the next ferry, there's no reason to hurry. The bicycle is the best way to get around town. This is one of the Atlantic Coast's true treasures!

Located on **Ocracoke Island** in the middle of **Cape Hatteras National Seashore**, **Ocracoke Village** relaxes next to 17 miles of unobstructed oceanfront. Because buildings may not be built near the ocean, the shops and restaurants stick close to the village. Just down the beach is the photogenic **Ocracoke Lighthouse** (1823), the oldest lighthouse still in operation in North Carolina.

One of the most popular ways to tour Ocracoke Island's beaches is by horseback.

Special Features

Day trips are available to **Portsmouth**, an abandoned village on nearby Portsmouth Island. Some of the village has been restored under the supervision of the National Park Service.

- The waters and coves hereabouts were once the haunt of Edward Teach, otherwise known as Blackbeard, and other pirates.
- Four Royal Navy sailors killed near here in 1942 are buried in the village's British Cemetery.

Further Information

Outer Banks Chamber of Commerce, *P.O. Box 1757, Kill Devil Hills, NC 27948 (252) 441-8144, www.outerbankschamber.com (ZIP for Ocracoke is 27960.)*

Directions

Toll ferries connect Ocracoke with the mainland at **Cedar Island** (crossing time approximately 2 1/4 hours) and **Swan Quarter** (approximately 2 1/2 hours). Reservations for the toll ferries are strongly recommended. The ferry to **Hatteras Inlet** (approximately 40 minutes) is free. Call (252) 928-3841 for reservation and schedule information.

Other Charming North Carolina Towns

Bath
Brevard
Cashiers
Dillsboro
Manteo
Saluda

Chapter 34

NORTH DAKOTA

FORT RANSOM
Population 111

Fort Ransom is a quaint little Norwegian-American village nestled in the scenic **Sheyenne River Valley** of southeastern North Dakota. Along its recently paved main street are buildings with rosemaling, inside as well as out, and on the wooded slopes of the valley above the main street, houses climb apparently without pattern. This is the kind of place that yearns to be painted and photographed. It is the site of a major arts and crafts festival.

Of special interest in the village is the **Ransom County Historical Museum**, which houses exhibits and artifacts from Fort Ransom's pioneer years. Nearby are the restored one-room **Bear Creek Schoolhouse** and the **T.J. Walker Historical Site** (1882), consisting of a mill, barn, and residence.

Fort Ransom is remote from the interstates and beaten tourist route – it may be the only community in this guide that isn't served by at least one state highway. Yet the village is almost literally surrounded by scenic and recreational attractions: One mile south, at the **Fort Ransom Historic Site**, are the archaeological remains of a log fort that was used from 1867 to 1872 to guard a settlement trail and the **Northern Pacific Railroad**, then under construction.

One mile north is **Fort Ransom Ski Area**, popular with downhill skiers. Two miles north is beautiful **Fort Ransom State Park** (see below). Three miles southeast is the 509-acre **Sheyenne State Forest**, great for canoeing and snowshoeing. And traversing the village is the 46-mile-long **Sheyenne Valley Snowmobile Trail**.

As if all of this weren't enough, the area is rich with old farmsteads, reminders of the Norwegian farm families who settled here in the 1870s and 1880s.

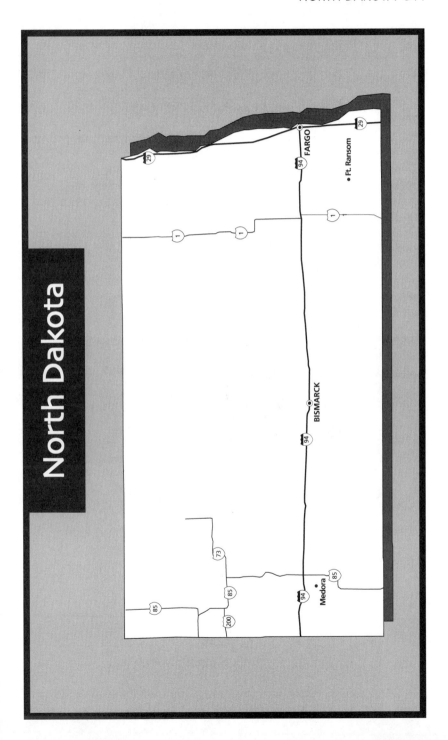

Special Features

Fort Ransom State Park features camping, picnicking, horseback riding, bird watching, hiking, cross-country ski trails, canoe and kayak rentals, and a canoe campsite. There is also a scenic overlook that provides spectacular views of the Sheyenne River Valley. Because of the many habitats, over 140 species of birds may be seen at the park.

The park is best known, however, for its **Fort Ransom Sodbusters Days**, get-togethers in July (second full weekend) and September (weekend after Labor Day) that attract thousands with turn-of-the-century plowing and threshing demonstrations, displays of antique farm equipment, quilting, ice-cream making, farm-style cooking, and other early farming and household re-creations.

The best way to tour the Sheyenne River Valley is to drive the **Sheyenne River Valley Scenic Byway/Backway**, a National Scenic Byway. The route, which passes through Fort Ransom, extends between Valley City (on I-94) and Lisbon (to the south). The byway, or northern half, is paved, whereas the backway, or southern half, is gravel. The route is marked by signs showing a buffalo silhouetted in the sunset.

- The original buildings of two early homesteads (1879 and 1884) have been incorporated as part of Fort Ransom State Park.
- The Sheyenne Valley Snowmobile Trail is maintained with funds from snowmobile registrations, required in North Dakota.

Further Information

Fort Ransom State Park, *5981 Walt Hjelle Pkwy., Fort Ransom, ND 58033 (701) 973-4331, www.state.nd.us/ndparks.*

Directions

From Fargo, I-29 south to exit 48, ND 46 west to Ransom County 58, Ransom County 58 south – look for the signs.

MEDORA
Population about 101

There are few better ways to recapture the spell of a small 1800s cattle town than to stroll **Medora's** boardwalks. Along the way are restored buildings like the **Rough Riders Hotel** (1884) and original buildings like **St. Mary's Catholic Church** (1884) and the **Billings County Courthouse** (1913; now a museum). The spell isn't hurt by the awesome beauty of one of the country's finest Western settings – the **North Dakota Badlands**. Nor the knowledge that Theodore Roosevelt once rode these parts. Nor the electric replicas of gas street lights.

Medora was named for the wife of the Marquis de Mores, a French aristocrat who in 1883 founded the town. de Mores came to Dakota Territory to seek his fortune in the cattle and meat-packing industry. The fortune was never made and the family was seldom seen here after 1886, but during his stay the marquis built a town and a legacy.

de Mores is best remembered today through his 26-room frame summer home, or *chateau*, which overlooks Medora. The house, along with the stables and several other outbuildings, is now the **Chateau de Mores State Historic Site**. Most of the furnishings are European and American antiques, some of them summer-cottage rustic, original to the family.

The **Medora Musical** is a grand spectacle of music, dancing, comedy, and variety acts that pay patriotic tribute to Theodore Roosevelt's "Bully Spirit." The show, performed by professional entertainers, is presented in a 2,750-seat amphitheater reached by a large outdoor escalator. The amphitheater is positioned to offer a breathtaking view of the Badlands. While here, inquire about tickets to one of North Dakota's major eating events, the **Pitchfork Steak Fondue**.

Special Features

Medora is the entrance to the **South Unit** of the **Theodore Roosevelt National Park**, a park known for its Badlands scenery and wildlife, including buffalo, wild horses, and elk. A visitors center, museum, and Roosevelt's **Maltese Cross Ranch cabin** are near the entrance.

Several miles north in the park is the **Peaceful Valley Ranch**, an old dude ranch and now a park concession that offers a variety of horse-back trail rides. The rides vary in length from 1 1/2 hours to all day. Several journey to the park's **Petrified Forest** and **Painted Canyon**. A trail ride is a must for those who have the time.

• In addition to Theodore Roosevelt and the Marquis de Mores, Medora has attracted such notables as silent-screen star Tom Mix and Marie, Queen of the Rumanians.
• General George Armstrong Custer camped just a few miles south of Medora's site in 1876 on his way to Little Big Horn.

▶ HISTORIC HOTEL ◀

ROUGH RIDERS HOTEL, *downtown Medora, (701) 623-4422, (800) Medora-1, fax (701) 623-4494, e-mail: medora@medora.com, www.medora.com.* Restored 1880s hotel operated by the Theodore Roosevelt Medora Foundation, 9 rooms, private baths, TV & phones, rustic dining room with good wine selection, antiques. $$ to $$$

Further Information

Site Supervisor, *Chateau de Mores State Historic Site, P.O. Box 106, Medora, ND 58645 (701) 623-4355;* also, **Medora Chamber of Commerce**, *P.O. Box 186, Medora, ND (701) 623-4910* and **Theodore Roosevelt National Park**, *P.O. Box 7, Medora, ND (701) 623-4466.*

Directions

From Bismarck, I-94 west 140 mi to exit 24 (Medora exit).

Other Charming North Dakota Towns
Devils Lake
Kenmare
Walhalla

Chapter 35

OHIO

BERLIN
Population 1,000

Maybe about half of all Amish people in the world have their farms in the rolling countryside around **Berlin** (accent on first syllable) and other towns and villages in this part of east central Ohio. It goes without saying that the countryside is picturesque: Amish farms are traditional American farms, with big barns and proper farmhouses. Shunning the modern, the Amish drive buggies rather than cars and use kerosene lamps rather than electric lights. They love the handmade and the home-baked. It's no coincidence that several other towns in this guide lie in or close to Amish areas (the villages of Van Buren County, Iowa; Jamesport, Missouri; and Lewisburg and Lititz, Pennsylvania).

People have been heard to say that "Lancaster County, Pennsylvania is like the Disneyworld of Amish; Berlin is the real thing." The some 70 businesses in and around the town are locally owned, and the area's volume of business is too small to pose much danger to the countryside. Although "country" malls, "country" markets, "country" stores, and other "country" businesses that capitalize on country charm occasionally dot the main highways, visitors find Berlin's back-road landscapes pleasantly untouched.

A guided tour of **Behalt**, a 10-foot by 265-foot cyclorama, offers a good and very enjoyable introduction to the Amish and Mennonite peoples. The enormous painting traces the history of these people from their beginning in 1525, in Zurich, Switzerland, to the present.

Another way to learn about the Amish is to visit an Amish farm that's open to the public. One choice is **Schrocks' Amish Farm and Home** east of town (on Rte. 39). Here visitors may tour two Amish homes, pet farm animals, have a buggy ride, and otherwise take a somewhat romantic look at the Amish lifestyle.

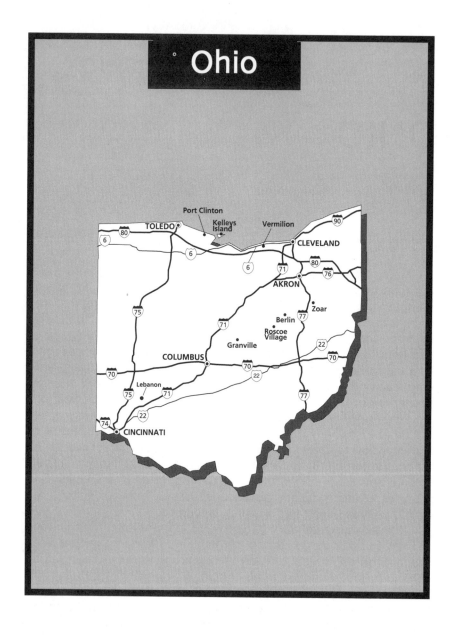

A large number of Berlin stores sell locally crafted furniture, often of oak. The town is also a good place to shop for fine quilts. Food shops offer delicious locally made cheeses, ice creams, and pastries.

Another way to shop for local foods and crafts is to travel the back roads. Many Amish farms have shops. This is also a good way to meet the Amish and to learn more about their farms.

Special Features

Farmerstown, **Charm**, **Mount Hope**, and **Kidron** are among the most charming and unspoiled of the area's towns and villages.

- Remember that the Amish regard the photograph as a sign of vanity, something forbidden by the Bible.
- Founded in 1816, Berlin had a population of 75 by the time of the 1830 census.

Further Information

Amish Country Visitors Bureau, *P.O. Box 177, Berlin, OH 44610 (330) 893-3467, www.visitamish.com.*

Directions

From Akron, I-77 south to exit 83, OH 39 west to Berlin.

GRANVILLE
Population 5,000 plus

Granville's settlers came from Massachusetts and Connecticut in the opening years of the 19th century. They brought with them their New England ways, including some of their architecture. Even today their heritage can be seen – and felt – in Granville. But there are also strong Midwestern elements here, and the fusion of the New England with the Midwestern has produced a lovely village.

Granville is a place to relax, to stroll, to think or read. It's also the place for the Midwesterner seeking a meal in a gorgeous old inn - the **Buxton Inn**, for example, which is Ohio's oldest continuously operated inn housed in its original building (1812; see below). The restored facades and beautiful landscaping along **Broadway**, Granville's main street, maintain a New England flavor, with maybe a little Continental color thrown in. As is true of central Ohio in general, Granville's trees and shrubs seem especially lush.

The **Robbins Hunter Museum**, housed in an 1842 Greek Revival mansion, displays 18th- and 19th-century American, European, and Oriental antiques in 11 furnished rooms. The grounds are maintained by the Granville Garden Club. Collections of hand tools, costumes, and other artifacts from settlement days are on exhibit at a second museum, the stone **Granville Historical Society Museum**. The museum is the oldest (1816) of more than 100 buildings on the National Register of Historic Places. A third museum, the brick Italianate **Granville Life Style Museum and H.P. Robinson House**, features a state-of-the-art 1949 kitchen as well as Victorian furnishings and a collection of 19th-century photographs.

The chapel and 11 other campus buildings of **Denison University**, a private liberal arts and sciences college, are listed on the National Register. The lovely campus should be part of every tour of Granville.

Special Features

Licking County has paved old railroad routes to construct trails for walkers, bikers, skaters, and skateboarders.

▶ HISTORIC INN ◀

THE BUXTON INN, 313 E. Broadway, (740) 587-0001, fax (740) 587-1460, www.BuxtonInn.com. Restored 1812 stagecoach tavern on National Register, 25 rooms, private baths, TV & phones, expanded Cont. breakfasts, dining room, period antiques, fountains & formal gardens, 4 restored bldgs. on grounds, floral displays (light displays winter). $$

Further Information

Granville Area Chamber of Commerce, P.O. Box 135, Granville, OH 43023 (740) 587-4490, www.granville.oh.us.

Directions

From Columbus, OH 16 or 161 east to Granville.

KELLEYS ISLAND
Population 200

For many years, even before the Civil War, excursion steamers plied the waters of the Great Lakes. One of the ports of call was the **Village of Kelleys Island** on the shores of the largest American island in **Lake Erie**. Today the boats are smaller, but Kelleys Island is still a port of call, and an especially pleasant one at that.

Following a common scenario, the charm of Kelleys Island is due in part to "undevelopment." At the turn of the century the island was home to numerous wineries, limestone quarries, orchards, and logging and fishing industries. The population was four times what it is today. Then the industry began to disappear, and the 2,800-acre island became relatively undeveloped (one third of it now belongs to the state). Rich in flora and fauna as well as reminders of another day, the island is today known for its quiet and relaxed atmosphere and is listed in its entirety on the National Register of Historic Places.

The island has two unique state memorials. The first, the **Glacial Grooves**, discovered back when there was blasting in the quarries, has been described as the most spectacular example of glacial carvings in the country. The second, **Inscription Rock**, contains pictographs inscribed by Erie Indians hundreds of years ago.

Cars are permitted here, but many visitors rent bikes or golf carts and tour the island at a pace more befitting the setting. Hiking is also popular, and the island has nature trails that boast fossils (very popular these days) and abandoned quarries as well as a diversity of bird species. Other activities include summer swimming, winter ice fishing, and year-round wine tasting.

Special Features

The 352-foot **Perry's Victory and International Peace Memorial**, commemorating Commodore Perry's victory over the British fleet in the War of 1812, is located in nearby **Put-in-Bay**. There is daily summer boat service to Put-in-Bay from Kelleys Island.

> Datus and Irad Kelley purchased the island for $1.50 an acre in the 1830s.

▶ HISTORIC RESTAURANT ◀

Kelleys Island Wine Co., *Woodford Rd., (419) 746-2537.* Tuscan-style dining room in 19th-century vineyard, Italian fare, imported & domestic cheeses served with fresh fruit & crusty warm French bread & house mustard, wine-tasting room, gourmet deli, outdoor seating with acres to roam. $

Further Information

Kelleys Island Chamber of Commerce, *P.O. Box 783, Kelleys Island, OH 43438 (419) 746-2360, www.kelleysislandchamber.com.*

Directions

You can get to Kelleys Island by island-hopping cruisers out of **Sandusky**, by ferries and cruisers from **Marblehead** (another charming village), and by air from Sandusky and **Port Clinton** (see selection). And, of course, by private boat.

Check with the Chamber of Commerce for schedules. No matter how you get there, do allow at least four or five hours, preferably several days.

LEBANON
Population 13, 700

Lebanon is the kind of town that an expatriate from the Midwest could easily long for. Quiet streets and mature trees. Porch swings and overhanging eaves. A nicely preserved downtown with brick sidewalks, linden trees, and a handsome slice of the 19th century. Lots of history (settled 1796). A major antique center.

The Golden Lamb, an imposing brick landmark that began as a two-story inn and coach stop in 1803, is Ohio's oldest hotel and restaurant (see below). Its halls have echoed the voices of 10 presidents and such other dignitaries as Mark Twain, Henry Clay, and Charles Dickens. Also a museum, the hotel has antique-furnished rooms and an outstanding collection of Shaker pieces and Currier and Ives prints (open to diners and guests).

Glendower State Memorial, a mansion built between 1836 and 1840, displays one of Ohio's finest examples of Greek Revival architecture. The interior is furnished with Empire and Victorian pieces.

One of the best county museums in the country, the **Warren County Historical Society Museum** houses collections ranging from the paleontological and archaeological to the Victorian, folk art, and horse-drawn (including a magnificent sleigh). On the third floor is the Robert and Virginia Jones Shaker Gallery, an outstanding collection of Shaker furniture, spinning wheels, and other memorabilia.

The **Turtle Creek Valley Railway** offers passengers a 14-mile, approximately 1-hour trip through the Ohio countryside. The tracks follow an old stage coach route and 1880 railroad bed. Complete with a 1950s diesel/electric locomotive, 1930 passenger coaches, and gondola car with open-air seating, the train offers Saturday, Sunday, and mystery dinner tours as well as longer rides.

Over 30 antique and specialty shops dot Lebanon's downtown streets. What with several good eateries and an old-fashioned soda fountain serving as additional incentives, it's understandable why shoppers from nearby cities love to head this direction for a day of browsing.

Not least among Lebanon's attractions is a location that makes the town ideal as a vacation center. To the south is Cincinnati, one of the country's truly unique cities; only a few miles from Lebanon, on the northern fringes of Cincinnati, are two of the nation's top recreation parks, **Paramount's Kings Island**, with world-class roller coasters, and **The Beach**, a premier water park. A scenic river popular with rafters and canoers (see below) and a series of lakes and state parks offering boating, swimming, hiking, and camping lie to the east. Also to the east are the rolling woods and pastureland of pretty southern Ohio, a rural landscape designed for a little relaxed motoring.

Special Features

Boasting more than 35 antique shops of its own, **Waynesville**, a charming little town just up the highway, is sometimes called the *Antiques Capital of the Midwest*..

Just east of Lebanon is the **Little Miami Scenic State Park & Bike Trail**, a 50-mile linear park on the east bank of the **Little Miami River**. Canoe and raft liveries are located at several points along the river.

Overlooking the Little Miami Valley, **Fort Ancient State Memorial** is the site of a very large hilltop enclosure built by prehistoric Indians. A museum focuses on the earthwork as well as on Ohio's Indian heritage.

Nearby Waynesville was the birthplace of branch banking (1877) and home of the originator of the Stetson hat.

▶ HISTORIC INN ◀

THE GOLDEN LAMB, *27 S. Broadway, (513) 932-5065, fax (513) 934-3049, e-mail: presetar@goldenlamb.com, www.goldenlamb.com*. Oldest inn in Ohio—in continuous operation since 1803, 17 rooms & 1 suite, private baths, TV, Cont. breakfasts (Sun.-Thurs.), 4 dining rooms (locally popular), Black Horse Tavern, antiques, historical exhibit rooms. $ to $$

Further Information

Lebanon Area Chamber of Commerce, *25 W. Mulberry St., Lebanon, OH 45036 (513) 932-1100, fax (513) 932-9050.*

Directions

From Cincinnati, I-71 north to South Lebanon exit (exit 28), north on OH 48 to Lebanon; also, I-75 north to Lebanon exit (exit 29), east on OH 63 to Lebanon; from Dayton, I-75 south to exit 29, east on OH 63 to Lebanon; also, OH 48 south into downtown Lebanon.

PORT CLINTON
Population 7,106

Port Clinton is an old fishing town with a colorful waterfront, beautiful trees, and lovingly maintained buildings from the last decades of the 19th and early decades of the 20th centuries. The houses sport a variety of hues. The town is also a summer resort and gateway town, a place on the way to **Catawba Island**, to **South Bass Island** way out in Lake Erie, and to anywhere else in or on Lake Erie where boats can go. Port Clinton is where fishing and sightseeing trips begin. It is one of those towns whose appeal is based in part on anticipation.

Nicknamed the *Walleye Capital of the World*, the port was once a center for commercial fishing, boat building, and various industries related to the water. Although commercial fishing remains, many of the water-based industries have given way to water-based recreations. Thanks to civic pride and the efforts of the regional planning commission, the town has become a delightful little lakeside resort with a touch of class and an unmistakable, though unpretentious, upscale ambiance.

Sailors and other visitors will find Port Clinton's attractive downtown amply stocked with shops and restaurants. There are several structures of historic interest here as well. One is the venerable **Island House Hotel**, now restored (listed below). Another is the magnificent sandstone Romanesque Revival **courthouse**, listed on the National Register of Historic Places. Of special interest are the murals on the upper floors depicting **Ottawa County's** history.

Bounded by beaches on one side and a series of lovely homes on the other, **East Perry Street** offers one of the few places on the southern shore of Lake Erie where the beauty of the lake can be enjoyed from the seat of a car.

- The Portage River Lift Bridge, linking downtown to western Ottawa County, was designed by a female engineer in the late 1920s. It seems that the program printed for the bridge's dedication listed the engineer only by first initial and last name, whereas all men involved with the project were listed by their first as well as last names. The bridge, carefully preserved, still operates to allow boats to pass out to Lake Erie.
- The Port Clinton Lighthouse (1874) guided ships for 90 years.
- Movie stars used to stay at the Island House Hotel while outfitting their classic wooden Matthews yachts, built in Port Clinton.

Foremost among Port Clinton's recreations are fishing and boating. Charters are available for the pursuit of smallmouth bass, walleye, perch, and other lake fish. There are also marinas and outfitters for private boaters. For sightseers in general, there are excursion boats serving the resort and "party" village of Put-in-Bay on South Bass Island.

▶ HISTORIC HOTEL ◀

THE ISLAND HOUSE, *102 Madison St., (800) 233-7307, (419) 734-2166, www.islandhouseinn.com.* "Lake Erie's Centennial Hotel," est. 1886 & restored 1986, 38 rooms, private baths, TV & phones, expanded Cont. breakfasts, 2 restaurants, bar, antiques, some pets. $ to $$$$ (seasonal)

▶ HISTORIC RESTAURANT ◀

MON AMI, *3845 E. Wine Cellar Rd., (419) 797-4445, (800) 777-4266, www.monamiwinery.com.* In 1872 limestone winery; American menu—e.g., prime rib, crab cakes, house salad; wine-tasting bar; live entertainment weekends; guided tours of vaulted cellars; gift shop. $$ to $$$

Further Information

Ottawa County Visitors Bureau, *Lake Erie Islands Regional Welcome Center, 770 S.E. Catawba Rd., Port Clinton, OH 43452 (800) 441-1271, (419) 734-4386, fax (419) 734-9798, www.lake-erie.com.*

Directions

From Toledo, OH 2 east to Port Clinton.

ROSCOE VILLAGE
Population about 500

Roscoe Village is a little canal community cut from the 1830s. The village is an authentic restoration, not a reconstruction; a living community, not a museum. The sidewalks are brick and the lampposts and signs antique. Guides wear 1830s clothing. Period crafts are demonstrated and the products sold in quaint shops. There's an inn and lovely perennial gardens. Some of the restorations are private homes. The population is almost exactly what it was in the 1830s.

Adding to the realism is a 1 1/2-mile restored section of the old **Ohio and Erie Canal** in nearby **Lake Park**. Tours of the canal aboard a horse-drawn replica of an 1800s canal boat are one of the park's most popular attractions (45 minutes).

Founded in 1816, Roscoe Village was from the 1830s to the 1860s a busy canal port. The railroad and, terminally, a disastrous flood in 1913, drove the little village into oblivion. Following a scenario almost exactly that of Waterloo Village in New Jersey (see selection), the town was rediscovered in 1968 and restoration of its buildings begun. Roscoe Village was to become Ohio's – and one of the country's – premier restored villages.

The **Visitor Center & Exhibit Hall** feature miniature dioramas and a wide-screen high-tech theater presentation on early transportation. Within the village are several living history buildings, including a working 19th-century print shop, a blacksmith shop, an 1825 working man's home, the kitchen and rooms of a doctor's home, and the **Toll House**, whose exhibits demonstrate 19th-century building techniques as well as modern restoration techniques. The separately administered **Johnson-Humrickhouse Museum** is noted for its collections of Native-American, early American, and Oriental artifacts. The museum is also home to a variety of 19th- and 20th-century American and European decorative art treasures.

The **Living History Tour** gives the visitor a glimpse of what life was like in an 1800s community.

Special Features

New to Lake Park is a professionally designed playground, the **Playvilion**, with a dozen towers, pirate ship, canal boat, sand canal, and more.

Coshocton, just across the Muskingum River, has a beautifully restored downtown area. South of Roscoe Village in Muskingum County is **The Wilds**, the largest private land preserve in the world. Built on 9,154 acres of reclaimed land, the preserve is designed to protect rare wildlife. The land may be toured by car or tram.

Food baskets may be purchased at nearby **Rainbow Hills Vineyards** and enjoyed with a glass or bottle of wine by the pond or on an outdoor deck in the woods behind the winery.

• Roscoe Village's Whitewoman Street got its name from a white captive, Mary Harris, who was married to an Indian and lived in the area in 1750.
• The Muskingum River is the only river that both begins and ends within Ohio.

▶ HISTORIC RESTAURANT ◀

THE OLD WAREHOUSE RESTAURANT, *400 N. Whitewoman St., (740) 622-4001*. In restored 1838 canal warehouse, American cooking featuring char-grilled entrees, family-style dining. $ to $$

Further Information

Roscoe Village Foundation Marketing & Public Relations Dept., *381 Hill St., Coshocton, OH 43812 (800) 877-1830, (740) 622-9310, www.roscoevillage.com.*

Directions

From Cleveland, I-77 south to exit 65, US 36 west to Coshocton (and Roscoe Village); from Columbus, OH 16 east to Coshocton.

VERMILION
Population 11,127

Vermilion is sometimes described as a "New England seaside community" and a home of steamship captains. The reference to New England is given in quotes because Vermilion isn't of course in New England, but no qualification is needed for the reference to the steamship captains: More than 50 Great Lakes captains made their homes here in the latter part of the 19th century.

An active Lake Erie port as far back as the early 1800s, many of Vermilion's people, and their homes, had New England roots. The roots can still be seen in a downtown waterfront area that has been restored as **Harbour Town 1837**. Here are gracious captains' homes, the old **Town Hall**, the old **Opera House**, and numerous specialty shops and unique restaurants. You can also see the town's roots in the lovely white Cape Cod homes nestled on the lagoons of the **Vermilion River**.

The two floors of the **Inland Seas Maritime Museum** tell the fascinating story of the Great Lakes using paintings, photographs, models, and artifacts. The museum features a simulated ship's bridge and a replica of the **Vermilion Lighthouse**.

Reflecting its popularity with fishing and recreational craft, Vermilion has an excellent small-boat harbor. The town also has several fine beaches. Sail and power boat rentals, fishing charters, and bicycle rentals provide good ways to enjoy this charming "New England" port city and summer resort.

▶ HISTORIC RESTAURANT ◀

CHEZ FRANCOIS, *555 Main St., (440) 967-0630, www.chezfrancois.com.* In 1840 "sail loft" on Vermilion River; National Register; French philosophy with focus on seasonal specialties; Lobster Bisque, Beef Wellington, Soft Shell Crab among specialties; hand-hewn wood ceiling and brick walls & floor; riverfront café dining. $$$ to $$$$

Further Information

Vermilion Chamber of Commerce, *5495 Liberty Ave., Vermilion, OH 44089 (440) 967-4477*

Directions

From Cleveland, OH 2 or Ohio Turnpike west to OH 60, north to Vermilion

ZOAR VILLAGE
Population 199

The streets of the picturesque little village of **Zoar** are entering the 21st century looking in good measure like they did in the first half of the 19th century. Just how this happened is a little piece of classic American history.

Persecuted for their religious beliefs in Germany, a group known as German Separatists immigrated to the United States and founded the town of Zoar – named for Lot's Biblical town of refuge – in 1817. Finding themselves unable to provide for themselves and to pay for their new land, the Zoarites chose to pool their individual properties and operate as a commune. The commune prospered, and by the middle of the century the *Society of Separatists of Zoar* had acquired assets valued at more than $1 million. Among their holdings at one point were four boats on the Ohio & Erie Canal (see Roscoe Village selection).

Economic and social factors were eventually to plague the group, however, and in 1898 the Society disbanded. During the years following, members of the younger generations left to seek brighter futures elsewhere, and outsiders bought and restored the buildings as members of the older generations died. Ten of the buildings have been restored by the Ohio Historical Society. Prominent among the other restorers have been families from Canton, just a few miles to the north.

Five of the historic buildings are log cabins; the rest are two-floor structures, some brick and some frame (but filled with brick masonry, or nogging). The solid old-world construction of the buildings has added to their value and encouraged restoration efforts.

Visitors should first stop by the **Zoar Store** (1833) to purchase tour tickets and to see an introductory video. Reproductions of 19th-century wares are also sold here. (Note – tours are only offered during warmer months.)

The historic district comprises 12 blocks. The most imposing of the buildings maintained by the **Ohio Historical Society**, and therefore open to the public, is the **Number One House** (1835-1845), a Georgian-style house that was the home of Zoar Society leader Joseph Baumeler and several other families. Among the historical society's other properties are the bakery (1845), tin shop (1825), blacksmith shop (1834), wagon shop (1840), and garden and greenhouse (1835).

Zoar may be best known for the beauty of the formal **community garden**. The garden occupies an entire village square and is arranged with geometric precision according to a Biblically-inspired pattern.

The old **Town Hall**, now a museum maintained by the **Zoar Community Association**, displays old photos, tinware, furniture, and other Zoar memorabilia (open Mondays-Thursdays). The majority of buildings are private residences, shops, restaurants, and bed and breakfasts. The 1868 **schoolhouse** (usually closed) and 1853 **Meeting House** (now United Church of Christ) are among the village's most handsome buildings.

- Because there is no home delivery, Zoarites treat the post office as a common meeting place.
- Men and women possessed equal political rights in The Society of Separatists of Zoar.

▶ HISTORIC TAVERN ◀

THE ZOAR TAVERN, *162 Main St., P.O. Box 509, (330) 874-2170, fax (330) 874-3903, e-mail: zoartavn@tusco.net, www.Zoar-tavern-inn.com.* 1831 home built by village doctor, 3 rooms & 1 suite, private baths, TV & phones, Cont. breakfasts, restaurant, antiques, hand-hewn beams, private gardens. $ to $$

Further Information

Zoar Village State Memorial, *P.O. Box 404, Zoar, Ohio 44697 (330) 874-3011, (800) 874-4336, www.ohiohistory.org/places/zoar or www.zca.org.*

Directions

From Cleveland, I-77 south to exit 93 (Bolivar), OH 212 south to Zoar.

Other Charming Ohio Towns
Bath
Bellevue
Milan
Oberlin

Chapter 36

OKLAHOMA

GUTHRIE
Population 10,518

At high noon on April 22, 1889 a pistol was shot and thousands dashed across the border into Oklahoma to claim free land in the central part of the state. Some went by train, others by horseback, wagon, or foot. In the morning **Guthrie** consisted of not much more than a train depot; by evening there was a tent and wagon city of some 10,000 *Boomers*. From 1890 until 1907 Guthrie was the territorial capital of Oklahoma, and from 1907 to 1910 the state capital. Then the capital was moved to Oklahoma City, and Victorian Guthrie stood still.

Embracing 400 city blocks and more than 1,300 pre-1910 buildings, Guthrie today has one of the largest urban historic districts in the United States. Virtually every building from the 19th century survives. Much more than a museum, the beautifully restored downtown is alive with shops, restaurants, an original saloon, and turn-of-the-century trolleys. A carriage can frequently be seen conveying newlyweds to the **Harrison House** (see below).

Guthrie is home to seven quite unique museums. Site of Oklahoma's first daily newspaper, the **State Capital Publishing Museum** features turn-of-the-century printing equipment. The **Oklahoma Frontier Drug Store Museum**, a turn-of-the-century pharmacy, is furnished with wooden drug-store fixtures and antique wall cabinets with pharmacy memorabilia. Among the displays is a 1910 wooden telephone booth. Yet another museum, the **Oklahoma Territorial Museum**, is a showcase of territorial and early statehood artifacts.

Dominating Guthrie's skyline, the **Scottish Rite Masonic Temple** boasts stained-glass windows, an elegant marble atrium, two theaters, a ballroom, reading salons, and a Gothic library. Many rooms re-create important periods of architecture, including Egyptian, Assyrian, Pompeiian, Italian Renaissance,

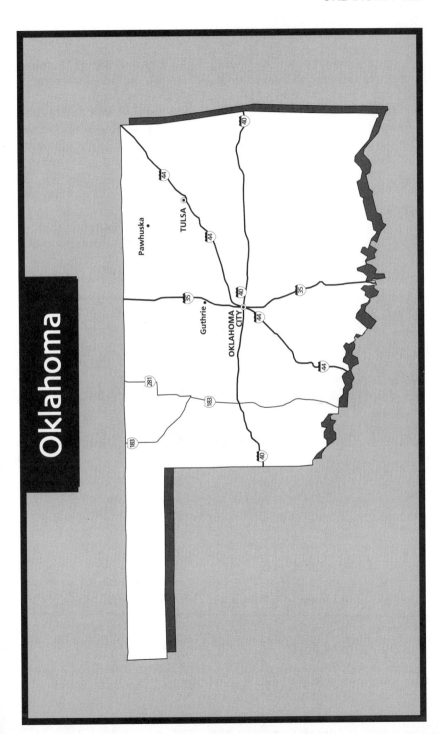

and Robert Adam. The structure is the largest Scottish Rite temple in the world (open to the public).

Rounding out the list of museums are the **Oklahoma Sports Museum** and the **National Four-String Banjo Hall of Fame Museum**, which features "America's premier collection of vintage banjos."

A cultural center today as it was in territorial days, Guthrie has the only full-time professional theater in Oklahoma: The **Pollard Resident Theatre Company** performs classic and contemporary plays and musicals 11 months each year. As for music, the sound of bluegrass and western swing livens the stage of Byron Berline's **Double Stop Music Hall**.

Special Features

The **National Cowboy Hall of Fame and Western Heritage Center** is about 25 miles south of Guthrie in Oklahoma City. The museum features the Old West with paintings, statuary, portraits of TV and film stars, life-size settings, stagecoaches, and other exhibits.

- When the "89ers" reached Guthrie, they found that many of the choicest properties had been claimed by people who had sneaked in before the rush. These, and eventually all Oklahomans, came to be known as "Sooners."
- A Guthrie city directory published several months after the rush listed 39 doctors and surgeons, 40 restaurants, and 46 grocery stores.

▶ HISTORIC LODGING ◀

HARRISON HOUSE, *124 W. Harrison St., (800) 375-1001, (405) 282-1000, www.machtolff.com.* Two restored turn-of-century bldgs., 20 rooms, private baths, phones, full breakfasts, period furnishings, small pets, elevator, theater package. $ to $$$

▶ HISTORIC SALOON ◀

THE BLUE BELLE, *224 W. Harrison St., (405) 260-2355.* Western saloon where Tom Mix bartended (1902-04), character, hamburgers & sandwiches. $

Further Information

Guthrie Convention & Visitors Bureau, *P.O. Box 995, Guthrie, OK 73044 (800) 299-1889, (405) 282-1947, fax (405) 282-0061, www.guthrieok.com.*

Directions

From Oklahoma City, I-35 north to exit 157 (Guthrie exit).

PAWHUSKA

Population 3,825

Up in northern Oklahoma and far from the interstates stretches a region of grassland hills known as the **Osage**. The landscape is reminiscent of the High Plains, although these don't begin for more than another 100 miles to the west. Home to a few ranchers and a sprinkling of little towns, the area hasn't been known to many since the oil-boom days of the 1920s.

Although small, **Pawhuska** is the seat of **Osage County**, capital of the **Osage Indian Nation**, and the largest town for miles. Part of the town's charm is that it doesn't seem to belong. A downtown filled with mostly brick turn-of-the-century and 1920s buildings (89 of them on the National Register) might belong in many places, but not in a valley among the vast expanses of the **Osage Hills**.

The best way to see Pawhuska is to park your car and, as with most charming towns, explore the downtown by foot. Unlike most charming towns, however, the downtown here is still being discovered by outsiders. It's the original. There are a few art galleries and antique and curio shops, but too few (as yet) to impart a touristy flavor. The most historic of the buildings include the **Immaculate Conception Catholic Church** (1887), noted for its beautifully colored stained-glass windows, and the **Constantine Theatre**, opened in 1914 as a grand playhouse after conversion from a hotel built in the mid-1880s. Both structures may be toured by appointment.

The **Osage Tribal Museum**, part of the **Osage Agency Campus**, boasts a collection of over 2,000 rare photographs of early Osage Indians and the town of Pawhuska. The museum, the oldest continually operated tribal museum in the country, is situated on a hill overlooking the town and can be reached by car or by foot using a stairway leading from downtown.

Exhibits of the **Osage County Historical Museum** include a monument to the country's first Boy Scout Troop (established in 1909), two Santa Fe Railroad cars that once served Pawhuska, and a restored one-room school-house.

Just seven miles north of town starts Pawhuska's (and Oklahoma's) most important old-new attraction, the Nature Conservancy's recently established **Tallgrass Prairie Preserve**. The purpose of the preserve is to restore a native American tallgrass prairie ecosystem. The preserve, now totaling over 36,000 acres, may be visited by following a marked drive. Along the way are scenic overlooks where visitors may step out of their cars and take a closer look at the flora and fauna, including perhaps some of the recently reintroduced

American bison. Information is available at the Pawhuska Visitors Center (Chamber of Commerce) as well as at the preserve headquarters.

Special Features

Taking a nature walk at **Osage Hills State Park** northeast of Pawhuska offers an especially enjoyable way to become acquainted with the starkly beautiful Osage.

One of the finest Western museums in the country, the **Woolaroc Museum and Wildlife Preserve**, is just a 30-minute drive east of Pawhuska. The museum and preserve are the legacy of a 3,600-acre ranch built by the founder of the Phillips Petroleum Company in the 1920s. The museum is celebrated for its artwork, including paintings by Frederic Remington and Charles Russell, and its outstanding collections of Navajo blankets, Colt Paterson firearms, and other Indian and Western art and artifacts.

Lake Pawhuska, three miles west of town, is a winter trout-fishing lake. Camp sites and other facilities are available.

> • Until the Allotment Act of 1906 the Osage Indians roamed the prairies as they wished and held the land in common.
> • Under President Ulysses S. Grant's "Church Policy," the Quakers were given charge of the country to which the Osage Indians were assigned. However, many of the Indians were (and are) members of the Roman Catholic Church because of an earlier contact with that church.

Further Information

Pawhuska Chamber of Commerce & Visitors Center, *222 W. Main St., Pawhuska, OK 74056 (918) 287-1208, E-mail: chamber@mmind.net.*

Directions

From Tulsa, OK 11 north to OK 99, OK 99 north to US 60, US 60 west to Pawhuska.

Other Charming Oklahoma Towns
Elk City
Freedom
Hominy
Sulphur

Chapter 37

OREGON

ASTORIA
Population 10,069

Astoria is in some ways a small American edition of a Scottish port city. In the background are hazy, brooding mountains; closer in are patches of rich green and, in the foreground, the waters of a large estuary, or firth. The city also has a long maritime history, just as do Scottish cities.

The **Astoria Column** up on **Coxcomb Hill** is especially reminiscent of Edinburgh, a Scottish city known for its classical hilltop memorials. The 125-foot column makes an ideal first stop on a visit to Astoria. Dedicated in 1926 and patterned after the Trajan Column in Rome (erected in 114 A.D.), the column bears a pictorial frieze commemorating landmark events in Astoria's history. Inside is a 164-step circular staircase leading to a breathtaking view of the lower **Columbia River** and the **Pacific Ocean**.

Salmon canneries and logging, fishing, and shipbuilding industries turned Astoria into a lively boom town in the late 1800s (the town was apparently also a notorious shanghaiing port), and Astoria's Victorian homes remain a tangible reminder of those times. Many of the homes are now bed & breakfast inns.

Perhaps the best known of the houses is the 1885 **Capt. George Flavel Mansion**, now a museum of the **Clatsop County Historical Society**. Among the house's many outstanding features are six handcrafted fireplace mantels, each carved from a different hardwood and accented by a different imported tile surround.

The Clatsop County Historical Society also maintains two other museums, the **Uppertown Firefighters** and the **Heritage**. Among the fire-fighting memorabilia on display at the former are fire engines that range from the

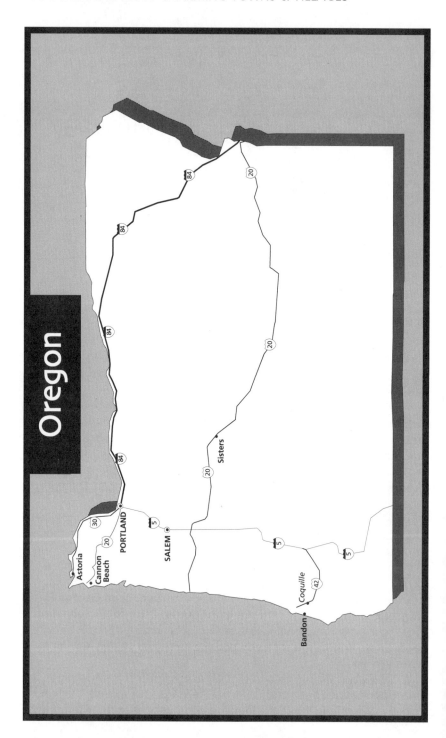

hand-pulled to the motorized. The Heritage Museum, housed in Astoria's old Neoclassical city hall (ca 1904), has exhibits tracing the natural and cultural histories of Astoria and the Columbia River.

Astoria is blessed with one of the finest marine museums in the world, the **Columbia River Maritime Museum**. In the Great Hall, designed with a soaring waveform, and in seven exhibit galleries are displays on fishing and whaling, steamboating and sailing, history and adventure. Some of the exhibits are real-life vessels, including the West Coast's last seagoing lighthouse, now a floating National Historic Landmark. The museum has recently added an award-winning orientation film that dramatically illustrates the fury and dangers of the notorious Columbia River Bar.

A beautifully restored 1914 electric trolley offers a narrated tour along the city's new four-mile **Astoria River Trail**.

Special Features

Nearby **Fort Stevens Historic Area & Military Museum** offers Civil War re-enactments, historical tours, and scenic views of the Columbia River. Fort Stevens was the only military installation in the continental U.S. to be fired on by the Japanese in World War II (June 21, 1942). The park includes miles of ocean beaches and the skeleton of a British sailing ship that ran aground in 1906.

Fort Clatsop National Memorial, just south of town, is where Lewis and Clark spent the winter of 1805-06 before returning to report on their expedition to President Jefferson.

The mouth of the Columbia River provides some of the finest fishing in the world. Boat charters are available.

- Known as the "Graveyard of the Pacific," the region around the mouth of the Columbia River has seen the loss of more than 100 ships and 2,000 small craft.
- Over four miles long, the Astoria Bridge is the longest continuous truss span bridge in the world.

▶ HISTORIC HOTEL ◀

ROSEBRIAR HOTEL, 636 14th St., (800) 487-0224, (503) 325-7427, fax (503) 325-6937, e-mail: rbhotel@pacifier.com, www.rosebriar.net. Renovated turn-of-century home & convent, 9 rooms & 2 suites, 1885 cottage, private baths (some whirlpools) TV & phones, full breakfasts, antiques, some fireplaces, refreshments, verandah, scenic views, packages. $ to $$$$

▶ HISTORIC RESTAURANT ◀

CAFÉ UNIONTOWN, *218 W. Marine Dr., (503) 325-8708*. In 1907 bldg. overlooking river; on Uniontown Alameda; fresh Northwest Oregon cuisine; Fish & Chips, Dry Aged Filet Mignon, Willapa Bay Oysters among specialties; live music. $$$ (main entrees)

Further Information

Astoria-Warrenton Area Chamber of Commerce & Visitor Center, *P.O. Box 176, Astoria, OR 97103 (800) 875-6807, (503) 325-6311, fax (503) 325-9767, www.oldoregon.com.*

Directions

From Portland, either US 30 or US 26 northwest to Astoria.

BANDON
Population 2,770

Within the city limits of **Bandon** (or **Bandon-by-the-Sea**) is one of the most beautiful beaches on the West Coast. Rock-studded and with smooth white sand, it may be the most beautiful between Alaska and Acapulco. At least the locals think so. Off shore are spectacular rocks, or *seastacks*, home to seals and other animals. Bandon also has a river, the **Coquille**, and two national wildlife refuges within its limits.

Bandon's **Old Town** embraces a colorful collection of art galleries and craft shops. Not only do visitors admire and/or shop for arts and crafts, they watch the works take shape as quilters, silversmiths, glass blowers, and others display their skills. Some of the shops are in historic buildings that were fortunate enough to escape devastating fires in 1914 and 1936. Cranberry products are among the items unique to Bandon's shops – one shop offers free samples of cranberry candy.

Even considering its marine location, Bandon offers the visitor an unusually wide variety of activities. Seal watching and, in season, whale watching are popular. (Don't disturb seal pups resting on the shore—their mothers may reject them.) Birdwatching is also popular—puffins, for example, can be seen in the spring on **Elephant** and **Table Rocks**. Fishing, both dockside and deepwater, is excellent. So are clamming and crabbing. Crab rings as well as fishing gear can be rented.

Among the many other beach activities are kite-flying, horseback riding, and tidepooling. Beachcombing is rewarded with finds of driftwood, petrified wood, agate, and jasper. Windsurfing is popular on the ocean, river, and local lakes; there's a windsurfing school south of town.

Special Features

Several tempting tour sites for the beach- and shopping-weary: a seafood processing plant, the 100-year-old **Bandon Cheese Co.** (winner of a national award for sharp cheddar), a cranberry bog (seasonal), the **Bandon Historical Society Museum**. Check with the Chamber of Commerce for details.

Hundreds of free-roaming birds and animals may be met, petted, filmed, and talked to at **West Coast Game Park** south of town.

> The restored Coquille River Lighthouse (1896) is probably Bandon's most photographed landmark and one of the few American lighthouses ever to be rammed by a ship (in 1903).

Further Information

Bandon Chamber of Commerce, *300 Second St. SE, P.O. Box 1515, Bandon, OR 97411 (541) 347-9616, fax (541) 347-7006.*

Directions

From Portland, I-5 south to exit 120, OR 42 west either to Coquille (and 42S to Bandon) or to US 101 (and south to Bandon).

CANNON BEACH
Population 1,425

In one of its travel guides, the State of Oregon publishes a photograph of the Oregon coast taken from Ecola State Park. The view is breathtakingly beautiful. The little seaside resort of **Cannon Beach** appears in the picture, but because it is so overwhelmed by its setting you may have to look twice to see it. Snow-topped mountains, wooded headlands, vast golden beaches, enormous rocks jutting from the water, and of course, that spectacular Pacific surf. You can feel the wind off the sea. The beauty was noted on paper as early as 1806 when Captain William Clark described the views as "the grandest and most pleasing prospects which my eyes ever surveyed...."

It was these "prospects" that would eventually nurture the development of Cannon Beach. Conceived by the beauty of its setting, it was inevitable that the little town would grow up with strong artistic leanings, and so it's hardly surprising that Cannon Beach has become one of Oregon's top **art colonies**, with some 25 fine galleries and studios.

Although art may be Cannon Beach's foremost human-made attraction, there are others of note. Tops among these is **Tillamook Rock Lighthouse**

(1879/80), located one mile off-shore from Ecola Point (and best viewed from Ecola State Park—see below). A major work of art in its own right, the lighthouse was decommissioned in 1957, renovated, and designated a National Historic Monument. In 1995 the lantern room was converted to a celebrity internment area. The lighthouse and the rock on which it stands were designated a wildlife refuge in 1993.

Colorful shops, restaurants, and flower gardens mingle with the galleries and studios both downtown and in midtown to the south. Visitors interested in learning more about the town's past will find a variety of exhibits—including old photos and audiovisual interviews of long-time residents—at **History House**, headquarters of the Cannon Beach Historical Society.

Rugged 235-ft **Haystack Rock** ranks tops among the area's many natural attractions. One of Oregon's most photographed landmarks, the rock is a federally protected marine garden, home to a diverse variety of birds and intertidal animals. Starfish, crabs, large green anemones, and other interesting creatures inhabit the tide pools; among the birds nesting on the rock above is the colorful tufted puffin. Cameras only, though—no life form may be removed from within 300 meters of the rock.

At low tide a magnificent walkable beach meanders for nine miles from north to south of town. It is here that those wishing to relax may watch the waves and wildlife, or maybe engage in a little beachcombing. More active beach pursuits include hiking, jogging, and kite flying. Bicycle and horseback riders may choose between the beach and the famed **Oregon Coast Trail**.

The **Coaster Theater Playhouse** offers a year-round program of plays, musicals, and concerts. The art exhibits—and of course the many shops and restaurants—offer other forms of indoor recreation.

Special Features

Viewpoints, picnic tables, beach access, flowers, and other attractions may be found in a dozen or so **Cannon Beach area parks**. The best known, **Ecola State Park**, offers commanding views of the ocean and Coast Range. This day-use park, just north of town, has acres of grass and trees for hiking, relaxing, socializing, etc.

North Coast Oregon Menus feature fresh seafood (especially salmon, sole, halibut, crab, shrimp, & oysters), fresh meat from the Willamette Valley, organically grown fruits & vegetables from local farms, and, of course, Oregon wines.

Some of the larger anemones in the Haystack Rock tide pools may be 50 to 100 years old.

Further Information
Cannon Beach Chamber of Commerce, *2nd & Spruce, P.O. Box 64, Cannon Beach, OR 97110 (503) 436-2623, fax (503) 436-0910*, "http://www.cannonbeach.org" *www.cannonbeach.org.*

Directions
From Portland (80 mi), US 26 to US 101 (Oregon Coast Hwy), south to Cannon Beach.

SISTERS
Population 1,080

Sisters is a tribute to what can happen when a spectacular setting is complemented with human planning and imagination. Overlooked by the snow-capped peaks – including those of the **Three Sisters** – of central Oregon's **Cascade Range**, and bordered by forests of towering ponderosa pines, Sisters's setting would itself guarantee the town high marks.

But what makes the little town so special is its Old West flavor. Originally because of special incentives, and more recently a building code, buildings in the downtown area conform to an 1880s' architectural style. The building code also restricts elevations to 30 feet or less, thereby preserving the panoramic views of the Cascades. The result is a business district with charm and character—the kind of place where people linger even when they've got nothing particular to buy.

· The range of goods in the shops is impressive for a small town (although Sisters serves an area of several thousand). Bordering the Western streets are galleries, boutiques, and an especially interesting and diverse array of gift and specialty shops.

Sisters opens onto an outdoor paradise. There are no fewer than ten public and private golf courses within 25 miles of town! The region's many unspoiled rivers, lakes, and streams provide opportunities for sailing, boating, swimming, rafting, and fishing. The mountains and forests beckon horseback riders, hikers, and climbers. For the winter months there are two major downhill ski areas and hundreds of trails for cross-country skiing, snowshoeing, and snowmobiling. The snowmobile trails rank among the best in the country.

The Sisters area is dotted with resorts and campgrounds. Several outfitters cater to those planning trips into the wilderness.

Special Features

The approximately 100-mile loop of a National Scenic Byway begins just west of town. One part of it, **McKenzie Highway** (**OR 242**), is closed in the winter. Check locally for routing and road conditions.

The crystal-clear **Metolius River** emerges from the ground at the base of **Black Butte** in **Camp Sherman**, a community northwest of Sisters. The 42-degree water forms one of the largest spring-fed rivers in the country.

> Many of the peaks in the nearby Cascades are potentially active volcanoes, especially South Sister and Mt. Bachelor.

▶ HISTORIC RESTAURANT ◀

BRONCO BILLY'S RANCH & SALOON, *190 E. Cascade Ave., P.O. Box 1287, (541) 549-7427, www.broncobillysranchgrill.com.* In renovated 1912 hotel; steaks, seafood, The Caballero (voted Oregon's best burger), Mexican specialties, barbecue; Western décor; deck dining (seasonal); Western saloon. $ to $$

Further Information

Sisters Area Chamber of Commerce, *P.O. Box 430, Sisters, OR 97759 (541) 549-0251, www.sisterschamber.com.*

Directions

From Portland, I-5 south to exit 233 (Corvallis), US 20 east to Sisters.

Other Charming Oregon Towns

Hood River
Jacksonville
Newberg
Yachats

Chapter 38

PENNSYLVANIA

BELLEFONTE
Population 6,358

Visitors sometimes arrive expecting the **Big Spring** in **Bellefonte** to be another Old Faithful. They shouldn't. The Big Spring doesn't gush, or do anything else very dramatic—in fact, it can't even be seen because it's been covered. Still, adjacent to the (now-covered) spring is pleasant **Talleyrand Park**, with gazebo and foot bridges, where people stroll on Sundays and listen to concerts by local musicians. A nice place to relax awhile.

Bellefonte is a relaxed kind of town in general. Maybe it's because the town's growth leveled off around the turn of the century and a little of the way of life of another century still lingers. The old residential streets as well as downtown share in the attitude.

The walking-tour brochure distributed by the Chamber of Commerce is in fact an 1874 city map with 45 little numbers superimposed to show the more important sites. The map's message is clear: A lot of what was Bellefonte in 1874 is still around.

Throughout the town are fine old buildings, with the accent on fine as much as old. Especially noteworthy are the early **Georgian buildings**. A beautiful example is the gray-stone, white-shuttered 1815 **Potter Home**. This lovely building now houses an interesting historical museum. Other notable structures include the handsome Gothic Revival **Brockerhoff Hotel** (1864/1865), the largely classical **Hastings Mansion** (1840s), and the flamboyant but picturesque **Crider Exchange Building** (1872).

Visitors who enjoy strolling shaded streets flanked by 19th-century mansions should include Linn, Curtin, and North Allegheny streets in their tour.

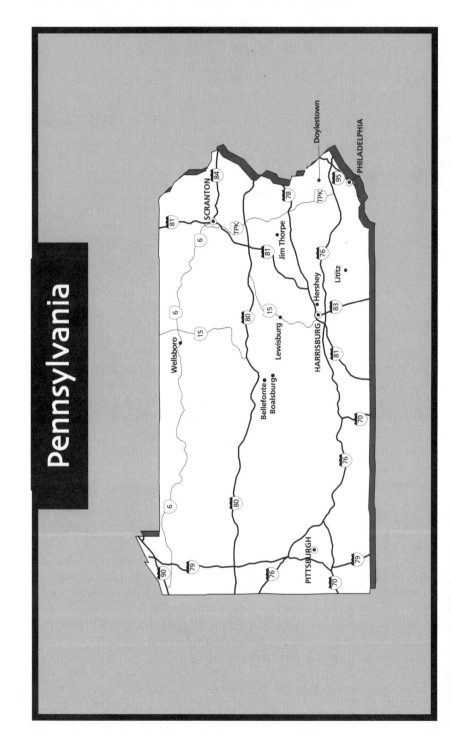

For the evening, the **Garman Opera House**, a restored 1890s theater, stands ready to entertain with the latest movie releases.

Special Features

At the old brick **Train Station** the **Bellefonte Historical Railroad** offers seasonal excursions aboard its two rail diesel cars. The excursion to **Curtin Village**, a 19th-century ironworks village with restored furnace and 1831 ironmaster's mansion, is particularly recommended (weekends).

- Bellefonte ("beautiful fountain") started out as Big Spring, but was renamed after "Big Spring" was visited by the French statesman, Talleyrand, in exile in America from 1794 to 1796.
- Bellefonte was one of the first towns in the world to have electricity (1884).

▶ HISTORIC RESTAURANTS ◀

THE GAMBLE MILL TAVERN & RESTAURANT, *160 Dunlap St., (814) 355-7764.* In restored grist mill with origins in 1786; National Register; eclectic menu—e.g., Seafood Strudel, Bluegrass Beef Filet, Butternut Ravioli; inviting lunch menu; atmosphere of old wood & brick & stone; bar. $$ to $$$

SCHNITZELS TAVERN, *315 W. High St., (814) 355-4230.* Authentic German dining in 1868 hotel, variety of homemade sausages & baked goods, Keller atmosphere, outdoor dining overlooking creek. $$

Further Information

Bellefonte Intervalley Area Chamber of Commerce, *320 W. High St. (Train Station), Bellefonte, PA 16823 (814) 355-2917, fax (814) 355-2761, www.bellefontechamber.org.*

Directions

From Scranton/Wilkes-Barre, I-81 south to I-80, west to exit 23, PA 150 south to Bellefonte.

BOALSBURG
Population 2,206

Quiet, shady sidewalks nudging friendly old two-story houses. Black shutters against white on some houses, lots of gingerbread on others. Picket fences and potted flowers. People chatting on broad, cool porches. Shops and other businesses just a stroll down the tree-canopied street. A romanticized image of the 19th-century small American town, true, but maybe one that's not far off the mark. **Boalsburg** is living proof of that.

Settled by families of Scots-Irish background in 1808, Boalsburg came of age during the 19th century. Major action—including the establishment of Penn State's ancestor at nearby State College—tended to bypass the town, however, and Boalsburg was able to retain much of its 19th-century townscape and flavor.

The furnishings of nine generations of the Boal family, the town's founders, may be seen in the family home (1789), now the **Boal Mansion Museum**. On the mansion's grounds are several interesting 18th- and 19th-century structures, but of very special note is the **Columbus Chapel**, which contains religious and secular heirlooms, some dating as far back as the 1400s, that belonged to Christopher Columbus and his family. Described as "the strongest link with Columbus in the USA," the chapel was inherited by a member of the Boal family and moved to the family estate from Spain in 1909.

Every tour of Boalsburg must begin, end, or resume with a walk down picturesque Main Street. Here is the **Boalsburg Heritage Museum**, housed in an 1825 home, featuring a gallery as well as pieces from old homes in the area. Here also is **Duffy's Tavern**, a handsome stone stagecoach tavern (1819; see below). And here also are little establishments that will delight shoppers, window as well as serious, with their selections of antiques, gifts, quilts, gourmet items, cookware, and seasonal crafts.

Special Features

State College, home of the **Pennsylvania State University** (1855), is only three miles from Boalsburg. Points of interest on the attractive campus include the administration building, **Old Main** (rebuilt 1929), and its land-grant frescoes by Henry Varnum Poor; the **Creamery**, renowned for its ice creams; and several important museums, including the **Palmer Museum of Art**.

▶ HISTORIC TAVERN ◀

DUFFY'S TAVERN, *113 E. Main St., (814) 466-6241, www.duffystavern.com.* Tavern & stagecoach stop est. in 1819; antiques; American menu—e.g., Sautéed Lump Crab Cakes, Pan-seared Elk Rib-eye Steak; Duffy Burger popular for lunch. $$$ (dinner)

Further Information

Centre County/Penn State Country Convention & Visitors Bureau, *800 E. Park Ave. (State College, PA 16803-6707) (814) 231-1400, (800) 358-5466, fax (814) 231-8123, www.visitpennstate.org (ZIP for Boalsburg is 16827.)*

Directions
From State College, US 322 east to Boalsburg.

DOYLESTOWN
Population 8,575

Doylestown is not a suburb, but neither is it a small rural town. It isn't a tourist spot, but it *is* a spot that many tourists like to visit. Philadelphia isn't far away, but neither is the famed **Bucks County** countryside with its time-mellowed stone farmhouses. Doylestown is a "Main Street" community, with hanging baskets and historic streetlights, but the charm belongs to a real town, a town where families are raised and groceries bought.

Doylestown's 250 years of history, its selection as the county seat of Bucks County, its location and interesting architectural admixture, these and other factors have contributed to an unusually rich cultural heritage and diversity. James A. Michener, Pearl S. Buck, and Oscar Hammerstein II are a few of the creative and accomplished who over the years have chosen to make their homes here.

The town is probably best known for the three unique concrete structures that make up the **Mercer Mile**. The first, **Fonthill Museum** (1908-1910), is the 44-room home built by eccentric millionaire and Renaissance man Henry Chapman Mercer to display his 900 prints and eye-dazzling tile collection. The seven-level building, with no fewer than 32 stairwells and 200 windows of varying size and shape, was inspired by European castles and aided in its design by a good dose of imagination. Fonthill is a National Historic Landmark (guided tour).

The **Mercer Museum** (1913-1916), the second member of the Mercer Mile and also a National Historic Landmark, displays a fabulous collection of more than 50,000 early American tools and other objects. At least 60 Early American trades are represented by the exhibits.

The third building, the **Moravian Pottery and Tile Works** (1912), is a living history museum where decorative tiles and mosaics are produced much as Mercer produced them 90 years ago (self-guided and guided tours).

The **James A. Michener Art Museum of Bucks County**, located in reconstructed buildings of the Bucks County prison, houses a superb collection of 19th- and 20th-century regional American art. The museum is also noted for its outdoor sculpture garden and its permanent exhibition, *James A. Michener: A Living Legacy*, celebrating the famous author's career. The new **Mari Sabusawa Michener Wing** features 12 distinguished Bucks County artists.

Special Features

Just 15 minutes away is **Green Hills Farm**, the 1835 stone farmhouse and 60-acre estate of Nobel and Pulitzer prize-winner Pearl S. Buck (guided tours).

A couple of days can be spent touring lovely **Bucks County**. Among the attractions are storybook farms, wineries, 12 covered bridges, renowned antiquing, historic **New Hope**, and the gardens, shops, and restaurants of **Peddler's Village**.

- Concern over the possibility of fire led Henry Mercer to construct the buildings of the Mercer Mile of reinforced concrete.
- The 60-acre Henry Schmieder Arboretum at Delaware Valley College is little-publicized but well worth a visit.

▶ HISTORIC HOTEL ◀

DOYLESTOWN INN, *18 W. State St., (215) 345-6610, fax (215) 348-9940, www.DoylestownInn.com.* Restored 1902 hotel in heart of town, National Register, 11 rooms & 1 suite, private baths, TV & phones, Cont. breakfasts, tavern, elegant period furnishings, 4-story center atrium with skylight, elevator, unique turn-of-century turret. $$$ to $$$$

Further Information

Bucks County Conference & Visitors Bureau, Inc., *3207 Street Rd., Bensalem, PA 19020 (888) 359-9110, fax (215) 642-3277, www.ExperienceBucksCounty.com.*

Directions

From Philadelphia, PA 611 north to Doylestown. **Note**: Regular train service is available from Center City and other Philadelphia stations.

HERSHEY
Population 11,860

Hershey's ancestry is very different from that of other towns in this guide. For one thing, almost all of the town is less than 100 years old. For another, this town is a company town, a *planned* company town. This is where Milton Hershey built the world's largest chocolate manufacturing plant between 1903 and 1905. Hershey built a new community around his factory; deliberately avoiding the usual anonymous company town, however, he chose instead to create a "real home town." And somewhere along the line – 1900 is as good a year as any – Hershey was born.

It's hardly surprising that the major sites of this company town all bear the name Hershey. What is more surprising is that some of the most impressive sites were built during the Depression as part of Milton Hershey's attempt to provide jobs.

At **Hershey's Chocolate World Visitors Center**, cars take passengers on a 12-minute tour that explains the chocolate-making process. A food court, souvenir shops featuring chocolate items, and a cafe ensure that not only the brain gets nourished here.

Hersheypark is an attractive 110-acre theme park that really does have something to please everyone. There are more than 60 rides, some of them state-of-the-art. For those uninterested in mechanical thrills, the park offers shows, strolling performers, theme areas that include nostalgic American and 17th- and 18th-century English and German villages, restaurants, and the 11-acre **ZooAmerica North American Wildlife Park**. The zoo features five environments, including an indoor collection of animals and plants native to the Sonoran Desert.

The **Hershey Museum's** exhibits chronicle the history of Hershey's chocolate industry and community. Other exhibits highlight Native American and Pennsylvania German cultures. Children may touch the past in the hands-on Discovery Room.

The lovely 23-acre **Hershey Gardens** (est. 1937) features collections of unusual plants, an All-America Rose Selections display garden, old-fashioned roses, a Japanese garden, and, new for 2003, the Children's Garden. The Butterfly House allows visitors to learn about these lovely creatures and their environment.

Hershey also has one of the country's grand old cinemas, the **Hershey Theatre** (1933). Clouds appear to move among the stars on the elaborate ceiling.

A 45-minute trolley tour of Hershey's sites is offered year-round.

- The Hershey Rose Gardens attracted more than 20,000 visitors on opening day in 1937.
- Founders Hall, on the Milton Hershey School campus, is capped by the largest unsupported dome in the Western Hemisphere.

▶ **HISTORIC HOTEL** ◀

THE HOTEL HERSHEY, *100 Hotel Rd., (717) 533-2171, fax (717) 534-8887, e-mail: TheHotelHershey@HersheyPa.com, www.TheHotelHershey.com.*

1930s-era Mediterranean-style luxury hotel on 300 acres, 234 rooms & 22 suites, private baths, TV & phones, famed Circular Dining Room and The Fountain Café, period furnishings, spa "chocolate treatment," formal gardens, fountains, reflecting pools, woodlands, golf. $$$$

Further Information

For more information, call 800-HERSHEY or visit www.HersheyPA.com .

Directions

From Harrisburg, US 322 east to Hershey.

JIM THORPE
Population 5,048

The brick and stone towers, steeples, and gables peering from the mountain valley look almost Old World. The narrow, meandering Victorian streets reinforce the impression. But it isn't clear what part of the Old World the town might belong to, and besides, some of the architecture is certainly American. What is clear is that for people who love charming towns, **Jim Thorpe** is a real find.

With roots deep in anthracite coal, canals, the railroad, county government, and later, tourism, **Mauch Chunk** (pronounced MAWK CHUNK; now Jim Thorpe) prospered throughout the 19th century, especially in the period between the 1850s and 1890s. Much of the prosperity was converted directly into grand homes and public buildings. The town declined, however, in the early 20th century, in parallel with the decline of the coal industry. In an act of hope and a desire to win publicity and tourists, the town in 1954 offered the widow of the famous 1912 Olympic athlete Jim Thorpe a proper burial and memorial for her husband in exchange for the use of his name.

The visitor's first order of business should be by all means a walking tour of the historic district. A good starting point is the **Jersey Central Railroad Station** (1888), which now houses the **Tourist Welcoming Center**. The station has a unique end tower that helps contribute to the town's quaint appearance.

A more prominent tower highlights the rough-faced sandstone **Carbon County Courthouse** (1893). The building's main courtroom is noted for its oak paneling and stained-glass skylight. Yet another prominent tower belongs to the Gothic Revival **St. Mark's Episcopal Church** (1869). The church's stunning interior, open for tours, is distinguished by Tiffany windows, an ornate baptismal font, and an English Minton tile floor.

Millionaires Row and **Stone Row** are picturesque old residential structures. The former, built between 1860 and 1890, consists of homes of families made wealthy by old Mauch Chunk's industries. The latter (also mid-1800s) contains 16 individualized three-story rowhouses built for employees of the Lehigh Valley Railroad. Renovated or undergoing renovation, many of the homes in both rows now house art galleries and studios, antique and specialty shops, apartments, cafes, and B&Bs.

Overlooking downtown and by all means the most imposing of the 19th-century homes is the 20-room **Asa Packer Mansion** (1860). The rooms of the Italianate mansion, open to the public, are furnished with such items as an ancient Egyptian chair and a solid ebony Steinway grand piano.

Jim Thorpe is known today for its cultural calendar and collection of good studios and galleries. As the Mauch Chunk Historical Society puts it, the town has become a "magnet for people involved with the arts, looking for an economic, emotional, and spiritual haven from the urban experience."

There are several ways to enjoy the surrounding **Pocono Mountains**: hiking or biking the 16-mile old **Switchback Railroad bed**, rafting down the **Lehigh River** (guided tours), and taking a scenic train excursion along the Lehigh River. When the mountains are snow-covered, they can be enjoyed by downhill and cross-country skiing, tobogganing, and snowmobiling.

Special Features

Flagstaff Park offers a panoramic view of Jim Thorpe and the Pocono Mountains.

The 20-ton granite **Jim Thorpe Mausoleum** is just east of town on PA 903.

June is the month for the annual **Laurel Festival of the Arts**, a two-week program of chamber-music concerts. Late September and early October bring the **Art Walk**, a festival of the visual arts that includes the juried Sacred Mountain Art Show.

> Also among the furnishings of the Asa Packer Mansion is a chair that belonged to Robert E. Lee and a chandelier that was copied for use in the movie "Gone with the Wind."

▶ HISTORIC HOTEL ◀

THE INN AT JIM THORPE, *24 Broadway, (570) 325-2599, (800) 329-2599, fax (570) 325-9145, e-mail: innjt@pkl.net, www.innjt.com*. Restored New Orleans-style hotel dating to 1840s, National Register, 34 rooms & 11 suites, private baths (some whirlpools), TV & phones, expanded Cont. breakfasts midweek & full hot buffet breakfasts weekends, The Emerald

Restaurant, Molly Maguire's Pub, antiques, some fireplaces, game room, exercise room, balcony. $$ to $$$$

Further Information

Carbon County Office, Pocono Mountain Vacation Bureau, *P.O. Box 27, Jim Thorpe, PA 18229 (570) 325-3673; also, Mauch Chunk Historical Society of Carbon County, 14-16 W. Broadway, P.O. Box 273, Jim Thorpe (570) 325-4439.*

Directions

From Philadelphia, I-476 (Pennsylvania Tpk. NE Ext.) north to Interchange 34, US 209 west to Jim Thorpe.

LEWISBURG
Population 7,615

The streets of historic **Lewisburg** are bordered by beautiful old buildings that open directly onto the sidewalks. The buildings are generally brick and display a diversity of decorations and facades that were added, according to the fashion of the period, subsequent to their construction. Between the sidewalks and the streets are period street lamps. Various little gardens, sometimes planted between buildings and sometimes in windowboxes and elsewhere, add color. Many of the buildings, especially those along **Market Street**, house businesses and, upstairs, apartments. The area is so lively – and at the same time charming – that space is in demand.

An old canal and **Susquehanna River** town, with roots in the 18th century, Lewisburg flourished first in the 1820s and 1830s, then again in the middle of the 19th century, and yet again in the 1920s. A number of Federal-style buildings were constructed during the first period of growth; during the second and even more prosperous period, the architecture was Federal Revival, a style similar to but more spacious than the original. The growth of the 1920s occurred largely in what were then the outskirts of town, and so the older buildings were largely protected.

Many downtown storefront facades were added at the turn of the century, and a number of buildings, including the Art Deco **Campus Theatre** (downtown), ably represent the architecture of the 20th century. Today, 54 19th- and 20th-century structures, and groups of structures, of special architectural and/or historic interest line the streets.

Two of the most important homes have been converted to history museums. The first, the **Packwood House Museum**, was a late 18th-century log tavern that evolved into a three-story Victorian hotel. The rooms now display a wide variety of early Pennsylvania and American decorations and other artifacts. The second museum is the **Slifer House Museum**, a restored 20-room Italianate mansion (1861) with a wrap-around verandah and gracious lawn (tours).

Bucknell University, a private liberal-arts college, has long been a part of Lewisburg – in fact, the first commencement was held in 1851. One of the buildings on the beautiful hillside campus is the state-of-the-art, 1200-seat **Weis Center for the Performance Arts**. The center presents top artists in the fields of music, theater, and dance.

Lewisburg is a major center in central Pennsylvania for the arts. Of special interest is an 1883 mill that has been restored and converted to an antique marketplace. Here over 200 dealers display their wares.

Special Features

Scenic PA 45, which intersects Lewisburg, wanders through a variety of charming communities. The villages of **Mifflinburg** and **Millheim** are especially attractive.

- The original name of Lewisburg was Derrstown, after the town's founder, Ludwig Derr. The town was probably renamed for a Pennsylvania governor or cabinet member.
- Lewisburg's three globed streetlights, unique to the town, are still cast from the original mold from a local foundry.
- Lewisburg has one of the lowest crime rates in the country.

▶ HISTORIC RESTAURANT ◀

ELIZABETH'S—AN AMERICAN BISTRO, *412 Market St., (570) 523-8088, www.elizabethsbistro.com*. Restaurant in 1860 bldg. serving innovative American cuisine—e.g., Roasted Lemon Bay Chicken, Corn Crusted Salmon, Filet of Beef with Portabella Mushrooms; European-style breads baked daily. $$ to $$$

Further Information

Susquehanna Valley Visitors Bureau, *81 Hafer Rd., Lewisburg, PA 17837 (800) 525-7320, www.visitcentralpa.org.*

Directions

From New York City, I-80 west to exit 210A (just across Susquehanna River), US 15 south to Lewisburg.

LITITZ
Population 8,280

The old Moravian town of **Lititz** nicely illustrates what is turning out to be the next stage in the evolution of many of our country's charming towns – the home away from the city. Blessed with a well-preserved 18th-century historic district (and many fine homes from the next two centuries, too), and located not many country miles from several urban centers, Lititz has become a popular place to live for people who work in Lancaster, Harrisburg, even Philadelphia. As is so often true of adopted towns, newcomers to Lititz like to restore old houses and attend crafts shows and weekend band concerts in the park.

Lititz was founded in 1756 by members of the Moravian Church and remained a closed religious community until the mid-1800s. Then, in the mid-1900s a major preservation effort began as people realized that a priceless 18th-century treasure lay along East Main Street. Now, 50 years later, a stroll down **Main Street** is a stroll into the past, but because the splendidly preserved buildings are still in use, the stroll is into a past that is still very much a part of the present.

Two buildings open to the public are the **Johannes Mueller House** (1792), a living museum of a Moravian home and workplace, and the **Schropp House** (1793) next door, now the **Lititz Museum**. Also on Main Street is the restored house (original from 1871) where General John A. Sutter, of California Gold Rush fame, spent the last seven years of his life. The house has been restored. Sutter was buried in the church cemetery behind **Moravian Church Square**.

The shop adjoining the **Peter Kreider House** (1784) was the site of America's first pretzel bakery. Still in the pretzel business, the bakery is one of the most popular stops on Main Street (outlet, tours of old bakery).

Linden Hall, the oldest girls' boarding school in the country, is also in the historic district. The school's Sisters' House and Linden Hall were built in 1758 and 1767, respectively.

Special Features

An entertaining history of American candy-making is on display at the **Wilbur Chocolate Company's Candy Americana Museum**. There is also a candy shop.

The **Heritage Map Museum** displays hundreds of original maps from the 15th to the 19th centuries. The museum was created for "lovers of history, science, geography and art."

Marietta and **Strasburg** are two other very charming Lancaster County towns.

• The country's first commercial pretzels were made in the bakery adjoining the Peter Kreider House, known as the "Pretzel House."

• Lititz Springs Park is the site of one of the oldest annual 4th of July celebrations in the country.

▶ HISTORIC INN ◀

GENERAL SUTTER INN, *14 E. Main St., (717) 626-2115, fax (717) 626-0992, e-mail: BrophyInn@aol.com, www.generalsutterinn.com.* Inn est. in 1764, 12 rooms & 2 suites, private baths, TV & phones, full breakfasts, The 1764 Restaurant, Z-A Café, Pearl's (Victorian bar), antiques, pets, parlor, courtyard with Civil War fountain. $$ to $$$

Further Information

Lititz Historical Foundation, *509 S. Broad St., Lititz, PA 17543 (717) 627-3374*; **Pennsylvania Dutch Convention & Visitors Bureau**, *501 Greenfield Rd., Lancaster, PA 17601 (800) 723-8824, (717) 299-8901, fax (717) 299-0470.*

Directions

From Harrisburg, I-76 east to exit 20, PA 72 south to Manheim, PA 772 to Lititz.

WELLSBORO
Population 3,430

The **Allegheny Plateau** of north central Pennsylvania is one of the most rugged and scenic areas of the eastern United States. It is also one of the least populated – and least known. Its most dramatic geographic feature is the spectacular *Grand Canyon of Pennsylvania*, a winding 50-mile-long, 1,000-foot-deep gorge. Its most beautiful little town is **Wellsboro**.

Wellsboro is a community of wide boulevards, gas lights, lovely large homes, and stately old elms and maples. The town is sometimes described as "New England-like". The mood is decidedly relaxed and friendly, the kind of place where a shopping trip becomes a social event.

The townspeople are openly proud of their **Main Street**, a beautifully manicured boulevard lined with nicely preserved Victorian buildings. One of the elms along the way dates back to the 1700s. On the public square, or **The Green**, is another object of pride – a fountain with the delightful bronze statue

Wynken, Blynken and Nod (1938). Next to the fountain is a plaque bearing Eugene Field's famous poem.

Two of Wellsboro's most handsome buildings are the 1835 **county courthouse**, facing The Green, and the 1894 **First Presbyterian Church**. The "**Lincoln Door House**" has a front door that was an 1858 gift from Abraham Lincoln to the owners; the door came from a building in Springfield, Illinois. The **Wellsboro Cemetery** (1855) has many historic tombs and a beautiful setting.

The **Tioga County Historical Society Museum** is located in the **Robinson House** (ca 1820, with 1840s' additions), listed on the National Register. Originally a tavern, the museum features an 1892 Estey organ and items associated with the life of author George Washington Sears, known by the Indian name of Nessmuk. In the **Museum Annex**, a replica of the Greek Revival 1864 First National Bank, are a 1923 Model T Ford truck and various military, home-making, dressmaking, and millinery exhibits.

The seat of a county with 100 miles of stocked streams, seven lakes, and abundant state forests and parks, Wellsboro is one of Pennsylvania's most popular sporting centers. Summer sports include boating, fishing, golfing, and horseback riding. With the winter come downhill and cross-country skiing, snowmobiling, ice fishing, and skating. The canyon is perfect for white-water rafting and canoeing when the spring waters are up. Hiking enthusiasts will enjoy the **Pine Creek Rail Trail** in the canyon's basin.

Special Features

The streams and lookout points of the **Pennsylvania Grand Canyon** begin just a few miles out of town. Self-guided driving tours through the area are aided by a series of directional arrows of different colors.

> The statue of "Wynken, Blynken and Nod" was the work of Mabel Landrum Torrey. A marble version of the work may be seen in Denver's Washington Park.

▶ HISTORIC HOTEL ◀

THE PENN WELLS HOTEL & LODGE, *Main St., P.O. Box 158, (717) 724-2111, (800) 545-2446, fax (717) 724-3703, e-mail: pennwell@prolog.net, www.pennwells.com.* Hotel dating to 1869 & modern lodge, 73 rooms & suites, private baths, TV & phones, 19th-century dining room with linen & silver, lounge, period furnishings, some pets, pool, fitness room, playground, packages. $ to $$

Further Information
Wellsboro Area Chamber of Commerce, *P.O. Box 733, Wellsboro, PA 16901 (570) 724-1926, www.wellsboropa.com.*

Directions
From Rochester (NY), I-390 south to NY 17, NY 17 south to US 15 (near Corning), US 15 south to US 6 (Mansfield), US 6 west to Wellsboro.

Other Charming Pennsylvania Towns
Chadds Ford/Kennett Square
Harmony
Hanover
Marietta
Meadowcroft Village (Avella)
Mechanicsburg
New Hope
Old Economy Village (Ambridge)
Punxsutawney
Shippensburg
Strasburg
Volant

Chapter 39

RHODE ISLAND

WATCH HILL
Population 500

Watch Hill, a Historic Landmark Community, is really three villages in one, and there are plenty of breathtaking views of the Atlantic for all of them. The first is a seaside resort, a place where families have been coming for beachside holidays since the 1840s. The second is a charming little harbor village where Westerly people come to shop for a special gift or enjoy a lunch by the sea.

The third is a colony, founded in the late 1800s, of summer homes owned by a tightly-knit group of American aristocrats. The great Victorian homes, or *cottages*, are elegant but sprawl more casually than their cousins in nearby Newport. Although the occupants and the interiors of the mansions are usually inaccessible, the grand exteriors, the winding roads linking them, and the magnificent ocean views are there for everyone to enjoy.

One of Watch Hill's logos is a bronze statue of **Ninigret**, chief of Rhode Island's branch of the **Niantics**, the tribe that once occupied this area. The statue, sculpted in Paris in 1914, overlooks the harbor.

Watch Hill's most unique attraction is the **flying-horse carousel**, the oldest merry-go-round in the country (built prior to 1879). The still-operating steeds, once water-powered but now motor-driven, are suspended by chains from a large turning wheel and "fly" out when in motion. The **Watch Hill Lighthouse**, now a museum, was built in 1858 to replace an earlier structure (special summer hours).

Special Featuress
The **Napatree Point Conservation Area** occupies a spit of land that extends west from Watch Hill one-half mile into **Little Narragansett Bay**.

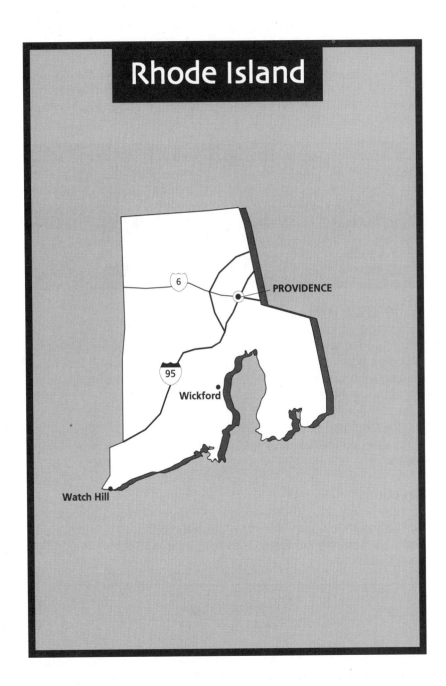

Rhode Island

6

PROVIDENCE

95

Wickford

Watch Hill

Although the area is privately owned, beachcombers, bird watchers, and nature lovers in general are welcome. The ruins of a **fort** built during the Spanish-American War may be explored at the end of the point.

Westerly's 14-acre **Wilcox Park** (1898) is home to a Tree Walk, Colonial Theatre's Shakespeare-in-the-Park, Virtu Outdoor Art Festival, and the 200-member Chorus of Westerly's Summer Pops. The park, named in the National Register of Historic Places, features lush gardens, statuary, and a goldfish pond.

- Every year dozens of people get married in the lovely non-denominational Watch Hill Chapel (1875).
- The nearby Misquamicut Golf Club is one of the oldest in the country (1895; private).
- Summer homes that once dotted Napatree Point were washed to sea in a 1938 hurricane. The area has never been rebuilt.

▸ HISTORIC INN ◂

WATCH HILL INN, 38 Bay St., (800) 356-9314, (401) 348-8912, fax (401) 596-9410, www.watchhillinn.com. Inn with history dating to 1845, 13 rooms & 3 suites, private baths, TV & phones, Cont. breakfasts, seasonal restaurant, antiques, on hill overlooking Little Narragansett Bay, short walk to beaches & seaside shopping. $$ to $$$$

Further Information

Greater Westerly-Pawcatuck Area Chamber of Commerce, 1 Chamber Way, Westerly, RI 02891 (800) 732-7636 (ZIP for Watch Hill is 02891.)

Directions

From Connecticut, I-95 north to exit 92 (in Connecticut), CT 2 south to RI 78, RI 78 south (becoming Airport Rd. after crossing US 1) to end, left on Watch Hill Rd.; from Providence, I-95 south to exit 1, RI 3 south to RI 78, proceed as above.

WICKFORD
Population 2,750

Located on a harbor stirred by colorful fishing boats, private yachts, and quahog skiffs (the *quahog* is a type of clam), **Wickford Village's** shops would make a perfect setting for a TV commercial showing people loading an SUV with a just-acquired antique or work of art.

Wickford is an unspoiled New England fishing village with tree-lined streets and memories going back to Colonial times. Many of the village's late 18th- and early 19th-century houses survive. A few are bed and breakfasts. There are also a number of 19th-century summer houses.

One of the most venerated of Wickford's possessions is the Old **Narragansett Church** (1707, moved 1800), the oldest Episcopal church in the northern United States. The church has box pews, a slave gallery, a silver communion set that was a gift from Queen Anne, and the oldest church organ (1680) in North America. A much "younger" church, the Romanesque Revival **St. Paul's**, was built in 1847.

Although not far from Providence, Wickford remains essentially rural, in character as well as setting. The age of the village can be appreciated by noting that several generations of English settlers had lived here before the word "Revolution" was even spoken. There were once even grand plantations in the area that were worked by slaves and indentured servants (although in 1774 Rhode Island became the first colony to outlaw the importation of slaves).

Special Features

Smith's Castle, just north of Wickford, is one of the oldest plantation houses in the country (1678; with 18th- and 19th-century additions). The furnished house and its lovely Colonial, waterfront, and cutting gardens may be seen by guided tour (check locally for hours).

The birthplace of **Gilbert Stuart**, famous for his portraits of George Washington (and many, many others), is five miles south of Wickford. Among the features of the authentically restored house (1751) are corner fireplaces, wooden door latches, and hand-blown window panes. The house is also the site of the country's first snuff mill (still operative; guided tours), a fish ladder, and a partially restored grist mill.

• The Wickford Art Festival is one of the oldest art shows in the country.
• Many visitors to Wickford arrive by boat.

▶ HISTORIC RESTAURANT ◀

HOOFFINFEATHERS CARRIAGE INN, *1065 Tower Hill Rd. (N. Kingstown), (401) 294-2727, (800) 884-6242.* In 200-year-old carriage house & stable; Hereford Filet Mignon, Provencal Grilled Shrimp, Lobster Sauté, Apple Orchard Chicken among specialties. $$ to $$$

Further Information

North Kingstown Chamber of Commerce, *8045 Post Rd., N. Kingstown, RI 02852 (401) 295-5566, www.northkingstown.com (ZIP for Wickford Village is 02852.)*

Directions

From Providence, I-95 south to exit 9, RI 4 to Wickford exit; from NYC and Connecticut, I-95 north to exit 5, RI 102 south and east to Wickford.

Other Charming Rhode Island Towns

Chepachet

Kingston Village

Little Compton

North Scituate

Chapter 40

SOUTH CAROLINA

ABBEVILLE
Population 5,840

Abbeville is a beautiful old Southern town (founded 1758) situated in the rolling countryside of Upcountry South Carolina. The townspeople consciously and successfully cling to a traditional small-town life style. Visiting is in, hurrying is out, and many businesses close on Wednesday afternoons (and Sundays, of course). In recent years Mennonite families from the North have been acquiring area farms. The inevitable result has been an increasingly prosperous and beautiful countryside.

At the center of the **Abbeville Historic District** is a picture-postcard town square. The square is bordered by brick-paved streets and businesses with facades carefully restored to their turn-of-the-century appearance. Traditional hardware stores sit cheek by jowl with antique and chic specialty shops.

Among the buildings on the square is the magnificently restored **Opera House** (1908), pride of the town. Early in the 20th century, when Abbeville was a railroad stopover for road shows, the three-balconied Opera House hosted such vaudeville stars as Fanny Brice, Jimmy Durante, and Groucho Marx. Now in the second chapter of its life, the elegant theater is home to the year-round productions of the professional **Opera House Players**.

Next door to the Opera House is a 1903 inn, originally called the Eureka, that once served drummers of the textile trade as well as touring actors and traveling theatre companies. The inn was completely restored in 1984 and reopened as the **Belmont Inn** (see below).

A wonderful walking town, Abbeville boasts many gracious 19th-century homes, both antebellum and postbellum, and no fewer than 36 churches. The most historic of the homes is the **Burt-Stark House** (ca 1840), a plantation

South Carolina

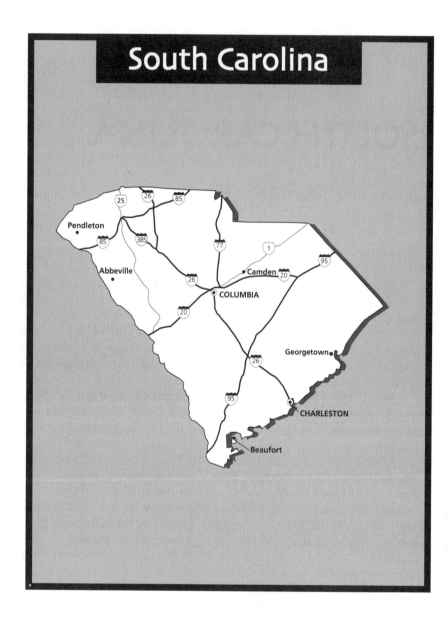

house where Confederate President Jefferson Davis stayed on his retreat from Richmond at the end of the Civil War (the house may be toured by appointment.) The lovely Gothic Revival **Trinity Episcopal Church** (1860) has hand-carved woodwork, a working 1860 John Baker Tracker organ, and a stained-glass chancel window that was made in England.

Abbeville has two interesting museums. The **Abbeville County Museum**, housed in the three-story county jail (1850s), features artifacts from the town's more than two centuries of history. The **Abbeville County Library** is home to the **Poliakoff Collection of Western Art**, an excellent collection of contemporary Native American ceramics, weavings, and other art objects.

Abbeville may be seen by two self-guided tours (north and south) or by one of three guided tours—check with the Chamber of Commerce.

Special Features

The nearby town of **Due West** is home to beautiful **Erskine College**, the oldest denominational liberal arts college in South Carolina (1839). Much of this charming little town is on the National Register of Historic Places.

Located on **Richard B. Russell Lake** 13 miles away, **Calhoun Falls State Park** offers water sports and, in the spring, spectacular displays of redbuds and dogwoods.

- Site of the first organized meeting to adopt an Ordinance of Secession, and the final meeting place of the Confederate Council of War, Abbeville was "the birthplace and the deathbed of the Confederacy."
- The Abbeville Courthouse Square is an excellent example of how historical preservation can be used to revitalize the economy of a small town.
- The chancel window of Trinity Episcopal Church made it safely through the Union blockade of Charleston.

▶ HISTORIC HOTEL ◀

BELMONT INN, *104 E. Pickens St., (864) 459-9625, (877) 459-8118, e-mail: belmontinn@wctel.net, www.belmontinn.net*. Renovated 1903 hotel on National Register, 24 rooms, private baths, TV & phones, Cont. breakfasts, restaurant, period furnishings, elegant lobby, verandah, Spanish-style architecture, theater packages. $

Further Information

Greater Abbeville Chamber of Commerce, *107 Court Sq., Abbeville, SC 29620, (864) 366-4600*.

Directions

From Columbia, I-26 north to exit 54 (near Clinton), SC 72 south (via Greenwood) to Abbeville.

BEAUFORT
Population 10,718

Sometimes described as an "undeveloped Charleston," **Beaufort** (BYUU fert) has become a favorite retirement spot for corporation presidents, prominent writers and artists, and senior military personnel. It's not difficult to understand why. The picturesque coastal town is blessed with one of the most beautiful historic districts in the country, excellent restaurants, twelve naturally beautiful golf courses, a variety of cultural opportunities, great fishing, bountiful sunshine, and access to miles of unspoiled beaches.

Early in the 19th century indigo and, later, long staple sea-island cotton, brought wealth to area planters, and magnificent homes to Beaufort's streets. Many of the homes and plantations still survive because Beaufort was occupied by Union forces early in the Civil War and the town and nearby plantations were spared.

Old Point, part of the **Beaufort Historic District**, contains over 150 antebellum homes, many with lovely landscaped gardens. A setting for several films, the enchanting area is made to order for leisurely walking or bicycling. The verandahed white homes, the moss-draped live oaks, and the splashes of color added by the roses, camellias, azaleas, and other flowers produce at times an almost impressionistic effect.

One of Beaufort's historic houses is open to the public: the Federal-style **John Mark Verdier House** (ca 1790), noted for its fine interior details. The Marquis de Lafayette was a guest in the house in 1825. Other beautiful old homes (private) include the Greek Revival **Joseph Johnson House** (1859), the early 19th-century frame **Henry Farmer House**, the double-verandahed **Tidalholm** (ca 1853), and the Greek Revival **George Parsons Elliott House** (1844).

St. Helena's Episcopal Church is one of the oldest churches (1724) still in use in the United States. The building was used as a hospital during the Civil War. The **Beaufort Museum**, once an arsenal, was constructed of brick and tabby in 1798 (rebuilt 1852). The Gothic Revival structure features prehistoric shark teeth, fossils, early Indian pottery, and Civil War and plantation memorabilia.

Both local tradition and retiree interest have fostered a number of cultural organizations. Among them, the **Beaufort Orchestra Guild**, the **Beaufort Little Theatre**, the **University of South Carolina at Beaufort's seasonal music program**, and the **Byrne Miller Dance Theatre**.

There are many ways to enjoy the natural beauty of Beaufort's southern coastal setting. Fishing (offshore, surf, or pier) is a favorite pastime; boat rentals and private charters are available. Nearby beaches offer swimming and shelling. The **Beaufort River** can be viewed by a stroll or jog along the sea wall promenade of the **Henry C. Chambers Waterfront Park**. The area boasts many tennis courts and, as noted, beautiful golf courses.

Special Features

The 5,000-acre **Hunting Island State Park**, 16 miles from Beaufort, offers over three miles of unspoiled beaches. Within the park is the 132-ft **Hunting Island Lighthouse**, built in 1875 to replace a lighthouse (1859) destroyed during the Civil War to keep Union forces from using it. Built of cast-iron sections so that it could be disassembled and moved as the beach eroded, the lighthouse was moved to its present location in 1889. (self-guided tours)

Nearby **Port Royal**, one of the state's earliest settlements, has a 1,260-foot boardwalk.

Legend has it that the flat tombstones of St. Helena's Episcopal Church were used as operating tables during the Civil War.

▶ HISTORIC RESTAURANT ◀

THE BEAUFORT INN RESTAURANT & WINE BAR, *809 Port Republic St., (843) 521-9000.* In 1897 home, later an inn; regional American cuisine with local ingredients featuring (e.g.) fresh seafood & Black Angus beef; in heart of historic downtown; highly rated. $$ to $$$

Further Information

The Greater Beaufort Chamber of Commerce & Visitors Center, *P.O. Box 910, 1106 Carteret St., Beaufort SC 29901, (843) 524-3163, www.beaufortsc.org (ZIP for Beaufort is 29902.)*

Directions

From Charleston, US 17 south to US 21 (Gardens Corner), US 21 south to Beaufort; from I-95 southbound, US 17 (exit 33) north to US 21, US 21 south to Beaufort; from I-95 northbound, SC 170 (exit 8) north to Beaufort.

CAMDEN
Population 6,696

Rare indeed is the old Southern town, especially one in the Deepest part of the South, whose history can be discussed without dwelling on the War Between the States. Created by order of King George II in 1733, **Camden** was a Revolutionary War town. And the town's fame as a horse training and breeding center, although certainly with 19th century roots, belongs more to the 20th century.

The original Camden was a British stronghold during part of the Revolutionary War, fortified with a stockade wall and six small surrounding forts. Although they won the nearby **Battles of Camden** and **Hobkirk Hill**, the British took heavy losses at the latter and evacuated Camden, setting fire to the fortifications as they left. In recent years, excavations at the site have uncovered the remains of the old town, its fortifications, a large powder magazine, and the foundation for the **Kershaw-Cornwallis House**, headquarters for General Cornwallis and other officers during the 1780-81 British occupation.

The excavations provided the basis for **Historic Camden**, a 92-acre partial reconstruction and park. In addition to several reconstructed fort sites, this unique Revolutionary War park features miniature dioramas, a model of the original town, a narrated slide presentation, and nature trails.

The park also has a number of interesting historic buildings that have been moved to the site from other locations. The jewel of the park, however, is the reconstructed Kershaw-Cornwallis House. The exterior of this house is an exact replica of the original 1780 Georgian-style mansion. The inside, with period furniture, is modeled after the interiors of Charleston houses of the same period.

The **Camden Historic District**, not to be confused with Historic Camden, is an oak-shaded area of more than 60 lovely homes and other buildings. Many of the houses are beautifully-maintained, privately-owned mansions that date from the 19th century (Camden came through the Civil War largely untouched). Of special interest in the district is the Greek Revival **Bethesda Presbyterian Church** (ca 1822), designed by Robert Mills, South Carolina's most prominent architect and designer of the Washington Monument in Washington, D. C.

The Chamber of Commerce has information on walking, driving, taped, and special guided tours of the district.

Special Features

Horses are second only to textiles in importance to Camden's economy. There are two major training centers for horses, one for steeplechase training and the other for flat-race training. There are also two major equestrian events, the **Carolina Cup Steeplechase** and the **Colonial Cup International Steeplechase**. Both take place at the **Springdale Race Course**.

• Many of the roads around Camden are dirt rather than paved in deference to the unprotected feet of the horses.
• The horse industry was started during the 1920s in large part by well-to-do Northerners who were attracted by the area's beautiful homes and mild winter climate.

Further Information

Kershaw County Chamber of Commerce, *724 S. Broad St., P.O. Box 605, Camden, SC 29020 (803) 432-2525, (800) 968-4037.*

Directions

From Columbia, I-20 northeast to exit 98, US 521 north to Camden.

GEORGETOWN
Population 9,912

Whether viewed culturally or geographically, there wasn't just one Old South: There were several, each represented by one or two cities and several towns. One Old South, known as the *Lowcountry*, stretched across the coastal regions of Georgia and South Carolina. It had a long history, reaching back to the earliest years of the 18th century, and was distinguished by its gentility, linkage to the sea, and African and French as well as British heritage. It boasted an American aristocracy, and an economy based on slavery. Its capital cities were Charleston and Savannah. Foremost among its towns was **Georgetown**.

Founded in 1729, Georgetown is South Carolina's third oldest city. Surrounded by large rice and indigo plantations and lying on the banks of the Sampit River with direct access to the open seas, the town became a thriving port with a complement of fine 18th- and 19th-century homes, churches, and public buildings. During the 1800s slaves made up some 85% of the area's population. As with many Southern communities, the town's fortunes have swung up and down since the Civil War; two of its mainstays today are tourists and retirees.

Over 65 Georgetown properties have been listed on the National Register. Georgian, Federal, and Classical and Greek Revival architectural styles predominate, but a sprinkling of New England and other influences add variety. The Greek Revival **Rice Museum** building, the town's lovely centerpiece, is in fact the **Old Market Building** (ca 1842) topped with the town clock and bell tower (ca 1845). Dioramas and other exhibits in the museum focus on the history of the area's rice and indigo production.

Another museum, the **Kaminski House Museum** (ca 1769), displays a number of valuable antiques, including 18th-century pieces made in Charleston. The house enjoys a commanding view of the Sampit River. **Prince George Winyah Episcopal Church** (ca 1747; steeple, 1824) was built of bricks used as ballast in British ships. The earliest inscriptions in the churchyard (ca 1735) go back to 1767.

The **Harborwalk** is a charming boardwalk that meanders along the Sampit River for 1,500 feet. Here and there along its north side are the back entries of shops and restaurants that lie on Georgetown's colorful Front Street.

Georgetown County is dotted with grand plantation houses, resorts, beaches, and other attractions—several are listed below. Reflecting this, Georgetown and its county offer a wide array of organized walking, tram, and boat tours. For those preferring to go it alone, there are maps, brochures, and books about local history (check with the Chamber of Commerce). Opportunities to catch seafood—surf fishing, deep-sea fishing, crabbing, shrimping, clamming—are second only to the many opportunities to eat it.

Special Features

Rivers in the Georgetown area are lined with dozens of restored **rice plantations**. Some of them are resorts or bed-and-breakfasts; others may be viewed during a spring plantation tour. Two of the most beautiful are open to the public: **Hampton Plantation** (ca 1735), once visited by George Washington, and **Hopsewee Plantation** (ca 1740), built by Thomas Lynch, a signer of the Declaration of Independence.

The grounds of Brookgreen Plantation have evolved into the lovely **Brookgreen Gardens**, where over 500 stunning 19th- and 20th-century American figurative sculptures are displayed among some 2,000 species and subspecies of plants. There is also a 23-acre wildlife park (open to the public).

• Some believe that nearby Pawleys Island/Litchfield is the oldest resort area in the United States.

• Local restaurants serve a melange of Low Country cooking, traditional Southern cooking, and creative American cuisine. Low Country cooking, known for its African as well as European ancestry, features local ingredients, especially fresh seafood.

▶ HISTORIC RESTAURANT ◀

RIVER ROOM RESTAURANT, *801 Front St., (843) 527-4110.* In historic 1888 bldg. overlooking harbor; seafood—e.g., Shrimp & Grits, Crab Cakes, Herb Crusted Grouper; also chicken, steaks, pasta; historic papers on display. $$

Further Information

Georgetown County Convention & Visitors Bureau, *P.O. Box 1776, Georgetown, SC 29442 (800) 777-7705, (843) 546-8436.*

Directions

From Charleston, US 17 north to Georgetown; from Myrtle Beach, US 17 south.

PENDLETON
Population 3,314

The wealthy of the Old South tended to divide their lives between two beautiful worlds: The pillared plantation of novel and screen and the less familiar summer retreat. In South Carolina the former was usually *Low Country*, meaning coastal and often not far from Charleston. The latter was usually *Up Country*, in the higher and cooler elevations of the western part of the state. **Pendleton**, in the foothills of the **Blue Ridge Mountains**, was a favorite Up Country summer retreat (see also Hendersonville, NC).

The town, listed in its entirety on the National Register of Historic Places, is centered about a delightful village green set with period streetlamps and shaded park benches. On the streets about the green stand many lovely homes from the late 18th and early 19th centuries. Some of the finest restaurants in this part of South Carolina are also here.

The first stop for the visitor should be **Hunter's Store** (1850), headquarters for the Pendleton District Historical, Recreational and Tourism Commission. The center offers everything from cassette tape tours in English and French to art exhibits, local crafts, and a book shop.

Fronting on the **village green**, across from Hunter's Store, is the peaceful old **Farmers Society Hall** (1826), town landmark and the oldest continuously used farmers hall in the country. Perhaps the most prominent member of the **Pendleton Farmers Society** (in essence an agricultural club) was U.S. vice president and statesman John C. Calhoun.

St. Paul's Episcopal Church (1822) has most of its original furnishings. Few of the region's early settlers were in fact Episcopalians—but many of the coastal families summering in the town were. The gravestones in the churchyard read like a South Carolina history book. Many famous South Carolinians are also buried near the **Old Stone Church**, an early Presbyterian church (1802) on the road between Pendleton and Clemson.

In the country just outside town are several old plantation homes; some of them have also served as summer homes. Two, **Ashtabula** (1820s) and four-story **Woodburn** (ca 1830), are now house museums.

Special Features

Fort Hill plantation house (ca 1806), home of John C. Calhoun, and **Hanover House** (1716), a transplanted Low Country French Huguenot home, are on the campus of **Clemson University**, just 3 1/2 miles away. Both houses are open to the public.

• Several of the streets in Pendleton's historic district bear the names of blacks who have contributed with special distinction to the town and region's heritage.
• The presence of an Episcopal church in non-Episcopal Upcountry is usually a good sign that the area was once a summer refuge for (Episcopal) Low Country planters.

Further Information

Pendleton District Historical, Recreational & Tourism Commission, *125 E. Queen St., P.O. Box 565, Pendleton, SC 29670 (864) 646-3782, (800) 862-1795.*

Directions

From Atlanta, I-85 northeast to exit 14 (in SC), SC 187 north to Pendleton; from Charlotte (NC), I-85 southwest to exit 19 (in SC), US 76/SC 28 north to Pendleton.

Other Charming South Carolina Towns

Cheraw
Edgefield
McClellanville
Walhalla

Chapter 41

SOUTH DAKOTA

DEADWOOD
Population 1,830

A heated night life, Old West saloons, and busy gambling parlors have been especially prominent during two periods in **Deadwood's** history. The first, the wild period of the 1870s and 1880s, was triggered by the discovery of gold in the **Black Hills**. Prospectors, claim jumpers, prostitutes, gunfighters, gamblers, hell-raisers, and opportunists breathed fire in **Deadwood Gulch**.

Law and Order amounted to an occasional vigilante court. Those were the days when a Jim McCall could kill a Wild Bill Hickok and get by with it (at least for a while), and a Calamity Jane could boast that she captured the killer when in fact she never did.

The second of the colorful periods began in the 1980s and is in full swing at this moment. In the 1980s Deadwood decided to legalize gambling (maximum wager $5.00) and use 4% of the profits for historic restoration. The town also decided that all restoration, whether funded by gaming or private moneys, would be closely supervised by Deadwood's **Historic Preservation Commission**.

The result is a National Historic Landmark with a cobblestoned **Main Street**, period street lights, trolleys, buried utilities—and more than 80 Old-West-style gaming halls! The best of the first wild period is back, and the worst is buried with Wild Bill Hickok, Calamity Jane, Potato Creek Johnny, and the rest up in **Mount Moriah Cemetery**.

Not that the gambling halls offer the only game in town. Three museums offer good glimpses of Old Deadwood. The exhibits at the **Adams Memorial Museum**, or "Deadwood's attic," include the biggest gold nugget ever found in the Black Hills. The **House of Roses Historic Home**, on the National

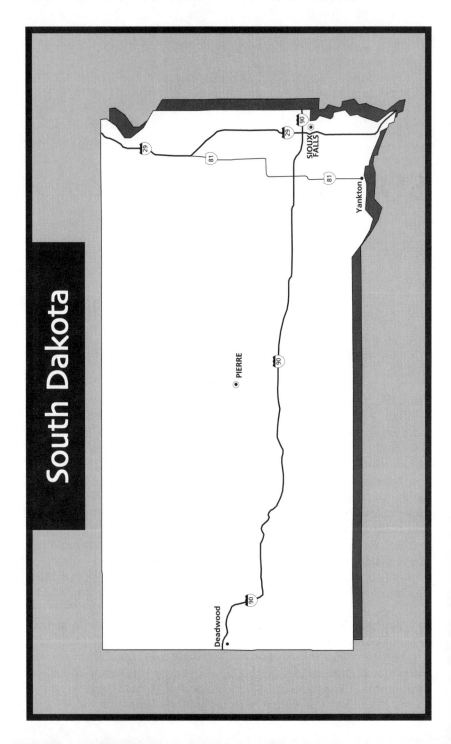

Register, boasts no fewer than 27 rooms of Victoriana. And the **Ghosts of Deadwood Gulch Wax Museum** displays some 72 life-size figures in 19 haunted settings.

Farther afield, several golf courses and ski resorts offer their own varieties of recreation.

Special Features

Tours of the **Broken Boot Gold Mine** (operated by the Deadwood-Lead Chamber of Commerce) include a guided trip through timbered tunnels and huge underground "rooms" (or stopes) of an historic mine.

Just a few winding miles up the road is mile-high **Lead** (pronounced Leed), another charming town and also on the National Register. Here are a narrow turn-of-the-century Main Street and Victorian houses, modest to mansion, clinging to steep hillsides. One of the top sights is the **Black Hills Mining Museum**, with interesting displays and a walk-through replica of a gold mine.

> • During its earliest years Deadwood was destroyed three times, twice by fires and once by a flash flood.
> • Founded in 1876, the Homestake Gold Mine in Lead is the oldest continuously operated gold mine in the world.

▶ HISTORIC HOTELS ◀

THE BULLOCK HOTEL, *633 Main St., (605) 578-1745, (888) 428-5562, e-mail: hub@mato.com, www.bullock-hotel.com.* Restored 1895 city landmark, 36 rooms & 2 suites, private baths, TV & phones, restaurant, period furnishings, elegant gaming parlors & polished staircases, gift shop. $ to $$$

HISTORIC FRANKLIN HOTEL, *700 Main St., (800) 688-1876, http://deadwood.net/franklin.* 1903 hotel on National Register, 80 rooms & 6 suites, private baths, TV & phones, restaurant, period furnishings, gaming halls, gift shop, columned porch & sun verandah. $

Further Information

Deadwood Chamber of Commerce & Visitors Bureau, *735 Main St., Deadwood, SD 57732 (800) 999-1876, (605) 578-1876.*

Directions

From Rapid City, I-90 west to exit 30, US Alt. 14 west to Deadwood.

YANKTON
Population 13,300

Yankton has clean air, no traffic jams, low crime, arts programs, and excellent schools; in other words, it's a model American hometown. Part of the town's appeal lies in its success in blending the old with the new. For while Yankton works to mold a town that will be as proud of its 21st-century heritage as its 19th, this descendant of an old riverboat town and capital of **Dakota Territory** (1861 to 1883) also respects and preserves its historical heritage.

Third Street, Yankton's main street, is protected as part of a National Register Historic District, but the size of the town demands more business space, and so there is also a modern shopping mall. New houses are built, but the town maintains guard over the many lovely homes from the 1870s and 1880s that grace the historic district. New industry is courted, but balanced against the new are a goodly number of old, established businesses.

The same blending of old and new can be seen – and heard – in **Riverside Park**. Here music from a blues or rock concert (for example) in the amphitheater echoes off the walls of a nearby replica of the **Dakota Territorial Capitol**. Here also the traditional and the contemporary mingle at the annual **Yankton Riverboat Days and Summer Arts Festival**, held the third weekend in August.

Given its location on the **Missouri River**, Yankton is popular with those seeking to trace the footsteps of Lewis and Clark. On the fourth weekend of August the community holds a **Lewis and Clark Festival** where reenactors, artists, and others help history come to life.

The **Dakota Territorial Museum** is filled with reminders and artifacts of Yankton's territorial days. Included in the museum complex are a rural schoolhouse, **Great Northern Railway Depot** (1892-1893), blacksmith shop, an 1870 parlor, and an office replica of Dakota Territory's first governor.

Special Features
Just four or so miles down the Missouri is the beautifully developed **Lewis and Clark Recreation Area**. The area is located on the banks of **Lewis and Clark Lake**, a 33,000-acre reservoir that stretches for 30 scenic miles along the Missouri River. The lake and recreation area boast a marina, boat rentals, sandy beaches, excellent camping, biking trails, and fishing.

French fur traders were in the Yankton area as early as the 1780s and 1790s, several years before Lewis and Clark came through in the early 1800s.

Further Information
Yankton Area Chamber of Commerce, *218 W. Fourth St., P.O. Box 588, Yankton, SD 57078 (800) 888-1460, (605) 665-3636, www.yanktonsd.com.*

Directions
From Sioux Falls, I-29 south to exit 26, SD 50 west to Yankton.

Other Charming South Dakota Towns
Hot Springs
Milbank
Pierre
Spearfish

Chapter 42

TENNESSEE

GREENEVILLE
Population 15,198

Greeneville, and East Tennessee in general, has an ambiance that doesn't quite seem to belong to most of the rest of Tennessee, nor to North Carolina just across the border. It is partly mountain, partly Southern, and partly something else, something rooted in pride and self-determination.

Greeneville has always had a mind of its own. The town was once the capital of the **State of Franklin**, a state that because of a complex piece of history existed for a few years in the 1780s but was never recognized by the U.S. Congress. Less than a century later, Greeneville sided with the Union in the Civil War, even though the region is in the South.

Greeneville's downtown historic district has rolling tree-lined streets bordered by lovely antebellum homes and churches of the Federal and Greek Revival styles. The brick sidewalks and absence of power lines (buried) contribute to the beauty. The district embraces more than 35 structures. One of them is an authentic reconstruction of the capitol of the *Lost State of Franklin*. Others include the **Greene County Stone Jail** (1838/1882), the Federal-style **Valentine-Sevier House** (1820), and the **Sevier-Lowry House** (1790s), the oldest structure in Greeneville.

Several of the structures make up the **Andrew Johnson National Historic Site** (Johnson was the 17th president of the United States): the **Visitor Center Complex**, which includes Johnson's tailor shop, a museum, and the president's 1830s house; the **Homestead**, Johnson's home from 1851 until his death in 1875; and the **national cemetery** where Johnson and his family are buried.

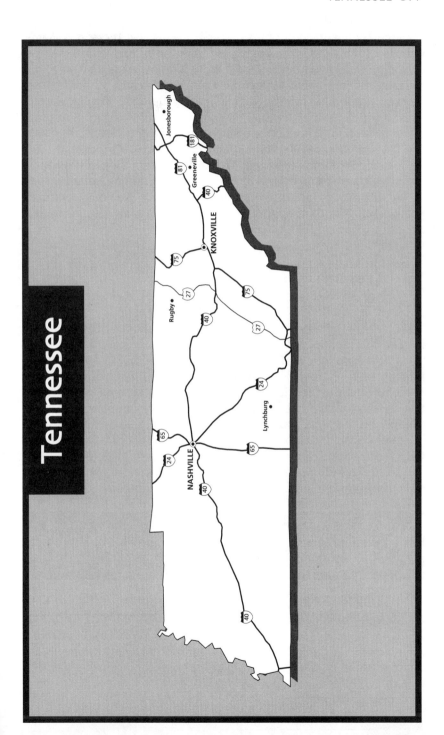

Probably the grandest of the homes is the restored **Dickson-Williams Mansion** (1815-1821), known as the *Showplace of East Tennessee*. The circular staircase, which rises three full flights, provides elegant tribute to the craftsmanship of the two Irishmen who designed and built the house. Davy Crockett, Andrew Jackson, the Marquis de Lafayette, and Henry Clay were all guests here.

The historic district includes three churches of special beauty: the 1860s Greek-Revival **Greeneville Cumberland Presbyterian Church**, the 1850 white-frame **St. James Episcopal Church** (which has the oldest organ in Tennessee), and the 1848 Federal-style **First Presbyterian Church**.

A $12-million renovation of **Morgan Square**, a late 19th-century railroad hotel district, was completed in early 1996. On the "new" square are the General Morgan Inn and Conference Center (see below), a reception area, a restaurant, and numerous specialty shops.

Special Features

A beautifully illustrated booklet detailing four back-road day trips may be obtained at the Green County Partnership/Chamber of Commerce (see below). The award-winning booklet will appeal to everyone from the nature lover to the Civil War buff.

The **Andrew Johnson Presidential Library** is on the campus of **Tusculum College**, the oldest college west of the Alleghenies (1794/1818), located just east of Greeneville (check locally for directions). Books printed as far back as the 16th century are housed in the Rare Book Room of the Special Collections Library (access by special permission only). Nine of the college's structures have been established as the **Tusculum College Historic District**. Campus tours are available.

Davy Crockett's Birthplace State Historic Area is east of town on TN 351 (near Limestone).

> Andrew Johnson was the only senator of a Southern state to reject secession from the Union.

▶ HISTORIC INN ◀

GENERAL MORGAN INN, *111 N. Main St., (423) 787-1000, (800) 223-2679, fax (423) 787-1001, www.generalmorganinn.com.* "East Tennessee's Premier Historic Hotel" created from 4 late 19th-century railroad hotels, 51 rooms & 1 suite, private baths, TV & phones, 3 dining rooms, bar, some pets, high ceilings & period mahogany furnishings, down comforters; golf, history, & romance packages. $$

Further Information

Greene County Partnership, *115 Academy St., Greeneville, TN 37743-5601 (423) 638-4111, fax (423) 638-5345, www.greenecountypartnership.com.*

Directions

From Knoxville, I-40 east to I 81, northeast to exit 23, US 11-E east to Greeneville.

JONESBOROUGH
Population 4,380

Many charming towns can transport the visitor to another era, but they do so with varying degrees of believability and authenticity. **Jonesborough** is among those that do it most believably and authentically. The sidewalks are brick, there are no stoplights downtown, even the power and telephone lines are hidden underground. Here you enter another time, and a beautiful time it is. At night the street lights, which look like gaslights, illuminate with a rare softness. Drive down **Main Street** after dark and you'll know that Jonesborough takes its history seriously.

Jonesborough was founded in 1779 and is Tennessee's oldest town. Its historic district, with over 150 structures, was the first in Tennessee to be listed on the National Register. The town's history is closely linked with the lives of many notable Americans, including three presidents—Andrew Jackson, James Polk, and Andrew Johnson. Records indicate that Andrew Jackson fought several duels here.

The **Jonesborough-Washington County History Museum**, with over 30 professionally designed exhibits, is housed within the **Historic Jonesborough Visitor Center**. The center offers guided walking tours, brochures for self-guided tours, and information on horse-drawn carriage tours. The **Discover Jonesborough's Times and Tales Tour**, which brings the town to life through stories and anecdotes, has been honored with two prestigious awards (reservations a must).

The place where the presidents stayed, and often conducted official business, was the **Chester Inn** (1797), now restored and painted in authentic (of course) shades of cream and russet. The inn was built on the **Great Stage Road** from Washington, D.C. and is Jonesborough's second oldest building.

The oldest building is the **Hawley House** (1793, with 1818 additions), a log home that today is also a bed and breakfast (see listing below). Among the many other historic homes are the three brick row houses making up **Sisters Row** (ca 1820), built by Samuel Jackson for his three daughters. The brick was handmade on site, and although the houses are very similar, each has a distinctive fanlight and other features.

Jonesborough has several interesting antebellum churches. One of them is the Greek Revival **Presbyterian Church** (1840s), with a slave gallery and original pews and pulpit. Another is the **Baptist Church** (1850), a church with exceptionally rare and beautiful hand-painted etched-glass windows.

This beautiful little town is best seen on foot or by horse-and-surrey tour.

• Each October The Storytelling Foundation International sponsors the highly respected National Storytelling Festival.
• The country's first abolitionist paper, "The Emancipator," was published in Jonesborough in 1820. Jonesborough was later a Union stronghold.

Note: Like many communities in this part of the country, Jonesborough is dry. BYO!

Further Information

Historic Jonesborough Tourism Cooperative, *111 W. Main St., Suite 202, Jonesborough, TN 37659 (877) 913-1612, www.historicjonesborough.com.*

Directions

From Knoxville, I-40 east to I 81, I 81 to exit 23, east on TN 11E.

LYNCHBURG
Population 361

Nestled among the hills, hollows, and springs of south central Tennessee, **Lynchburg** is virtually synonymous with the **Jack Daniel Distillery**, the oldest registered distillery in the United States (1866). The visitor's itinerary is relatively short, but very pleasant: After making reservations for mid-day dinner at **Miss Mary Bobo's Boarding House** (just off the square; see below), walk over to the visitors center of the distillery for an especially interesting and informative tour. Regular tours include visits to the **Barrelhouse**, the original 19th-century office, and **Cave Spring** (responsible for a major ingredient of the whiskey). The steps in whiskey-making, including the distillery's famous charcoal-mellowing process, are explained.

After the tour, it's Miss Mary Bobo's for "dinner." The afternoon can be spent napping, browsing through the shops, and relaxing on a bench in the town square. Whittling is still a favorite pastime in the square, and visitors are welcome to take a seat and watch (this may be one of the few places in the country where it's perfectly safe to sit next to a stranger with a knife).

The **Moore County Courthouse** (1883), on the square, was built of bricks made by the people of Lynchburg. On the lawn is a monument (1927) honoring the county's Confederate soldiers.

About the square are little shops that sell white-oak barrels, art, Jack Daniel memorabilia, needlework, antiques. There's even a hardware where locals – and visitors – can pass the time with a game of checkers. One of Lynchburg's most popular products (after the whiskey) is the **Tipsy Cake** (made with the whiskey, of course).

The **Ledford Mill & Tool Museum**, east of town, is home to an old gristmill (1884) and collection of 18th- and 19th-century wood-working tools.

> The water produced by Cave Spring is pure lime-stone water, always 56 degrees cool and virtually iron-free.

▶ HISTORIC RESTAURANT ◀

MISS MARY BOBO'S BOARDING HOUSE, *925 Main St., (931) 759-7394.* Mid-day dinner served family-style in old home; est. 1908; traditional Tennessee cooking featuring home-style meats, home-grown vegetables, & homemade pies & cobblers; reservations a must. $

Further Information

Lynchburg & Metro Moore County Chamber of Commerce, *P.O. Box 421, Lynchburg, TN 37352 (931) 759-4111.*

Directions

From Nashville, I-24 south to Manchester, TN 55 southwest to Lynchburg.

RUGBY
Population about 75

Although residing in the rough-and-ready wilderness of Tennessee's **Cumberland Mountains**, **Rugby's** settlers formed literary and theatrical groups, played tennis, and dressed for afternoon tea. Their English village had as many as 70 buildings and a population of around 350 (in 1884). Today only 22 of the gabled buildings survive, but they form what the National Trust calls one of the "most authentically preserved historic villages in America." Nestled among tall trees near a river gorge, it is also one of the prettiest.

It all began in 1880 when English author and social reformer Thomas Hughes established the community as an experiment in cooperative agrarian living. Part of the purpose of the community was to provide a place for the landless younger sons of Britain's landed gentry to learn and practice manual and agricultural trades.

The community wasn't designed to be exclusively English. Some of the settlers were American.

The experiment was not to succeed - drought, harsh winters, a typhoid epidemic, fire, and maybe a little too much tennis and tea drinking all took their toll. Many of the colonists left and in a decade or two the village drifted into a small farming community. Revival of the village began in 1966, when **Historic Rugby** set about preserving, restoring, and exhibiting some of the colony's remaining buildings. The entire village is now listed on the National Register of Historic Places.

Several of the buildings, all painted in their original Victorian colors, may be toured. One of them, the **Schoolhouse Visitors Center**, contains exhibits that chronicle the history of the village. Another, the Gothic Revival **Christ Church Episcopal** (1887), has the original hanging lamps and 1849 rosewood organ. The **Thomas Hughes Library**, unchanged since it opened in 1882, has some 7,000 original volumes of Victorian fiction and non-fiction. **Kingstone Lisle** (1884), the delightful rural Gothic Revival cottage built for Rugby's founder, contains original Rugby furnishings. Most of the surviving homes, now private residences, are normally closed. However, many are open during the **Rugby Pilgrimage**, held every other year during the first weekend in August.

The **Rugby Commissary Museum Store** is divided into two shops, both truly unique. One carries traditional crafts and British foods, among other items. The other specializes in Victorian gifts and area history books.

Special Features

In the Rugby vicinity are the **Big South Fork National River & Recreation Area**, **Frozen Head** and **Pickett** state parks, and the **Obed Wild & Scenic River area**. These and other facilities offer hiking, biking, horseback riding, seasonal rafting, remote river canoeing, fishing, and camping.

The popular **Rugby Festival of British & Appalachian Culture** is held every May.

• Thomas Hughes, author of "Tom Brown's Schooldays," devoted much of his time to helping the English working classes.
• The trails built by the colonists down to the river are still in use.

▶ HISTORIC LODGING ◀

NEWBURY HOUSE B&B, *P.O. Box 8, (423) 628-2441, fax (423) 628-2266, e-mail: rugbytn@highland.net, www.historicrugby.org.* 1880 mansard-roofed boarding house, 5 rooms plus 1 suite & 2 cottages, private baths, full breakfasts, antiques, pets in 1 cottage, tea/coffee, fireplace, verandah. $ to $$

Further Information

Historic Rugby, Inc., *P.O. Box 8, Rugby, TN 37733 (423) 628-2441/ 2430, (888) 214-3400, e-mail: rugbytn@highland.net, www.historicrugby.org.*

Directions

From Knoxville, I-75 north to exit 141, TN 63 west to US 27, US 27 south to TN 52 (Elgin), TN 52 west to Rugby.

Other Charming Tennessee Towns

Bell Buckle
Elizabethton
Franklin
LaGrange
Pittman Center
Rogersville

Chapter 43

TEXAS

BASTROP
Population 5,340

Established in 1832, **Bastrop** was here before Texas even became a republic. Built on the banks of the Colorado River and boasting over 130 buildings on the National Register of Historic Places, Bastrop is a peaceful, gracious old town. People who live here report a certain "magical quality" to it. It's the kind of place where a town tour begins with the arrival of a horse-drawn carriage at the bed and breakfast. And yet Bastrop is relatively uncommercialized—unusual for such an historic and attractive (and cosmopolitan) little Texas community, especially one within easy driving distance of Austin and Houston.

The late 19th-century **Main Street**, one of the quaintest and most genuine in Texas, is home to specialty stores, antique shops, restaurants, and other businesses. An especially interesting establishment here is **Lock Drugs**, a 19th-century doctor's office and drug store that still serves sodas and other treats in an old-fashioned ice cream parlor.

Many of Bastrop's historic structures lie in and around the downtown area. They include the **Bastrop Christian Church** (ca 1895), **Old Bastrop County Jail** (ca 1891), and **Courthouse** (ca 1883). The 1889 **Bastrop Opera House** offers year-round dinner-theater productions as well as other special activities.

The streets in and around downtown also contain an imposing collection of antebellum and late 19th-century homes and churches. One, a restored 1850 home, houses the **Bastrop County Historical Society Museum**. The museum's collection includes frontier tools, pictures, furnishings, documents, and other local artifacts.

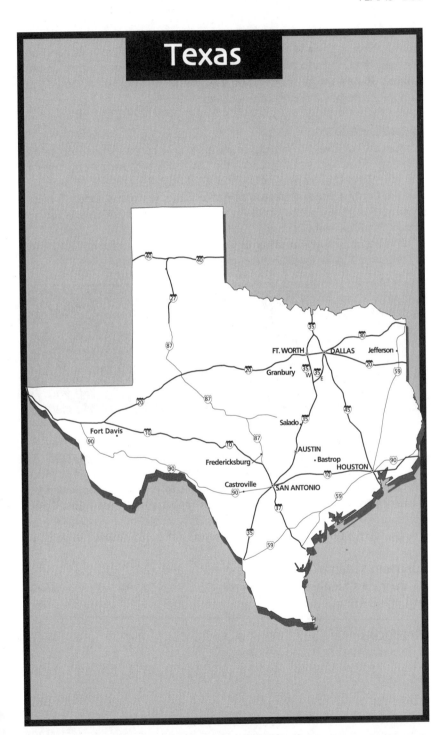

The Chamber of Commerce maintains information for self-guided driving, walking, bicycling, and Medallion Homes tours. With two lovely city parks on its banks, the **Colorado River** is accessible for fishing, canoeing, and tubing. **Bastrop State Park** (see below) offers fishing, swimming, nature study, and hiking. Bastrop has three fine golf courses.

Special Features

Just east of town, in **Bastrop State Park**, is an especially beautiful stand of loblolly pines. The trees are called the *Lost Pines* because they occur over 100 miles from their normal range in East Texas.

The **Central Texas Museum of Automotive History** is about 12 miles south of town. The museum displays some 85 beautiful vintage cars, including Model T's, a Duesenberg, and a 1911 Napier.

The Bastrop area offers a number of beautiful drives, including TX **71** east to Smithville. Inquire locally concerning scenic county roads.

• The "Bastrop Advertiser" is the oldest weekly newspaper in Texas (est. 1853).
• Bastrop was named after a Dutch nobleman, Felipe Enrique Neri, Baron de Bastrop, an important figure in Texas's settlement days. Unknown to the people of the day, Bastrop was an impostor, wanted in Holland for embezzlement.

▶ HISTORIC LODGING ◀

CABINS ON THE COLORADO, *601 Chestnut, (512) 321-7002,(512) 321-6359, fax (512) 321-7002, e-mail: jhoover7@austin.rr.com.* Four small 19th-century homes on 3-acre tract on Colorado River next to historic bridge, private baths, breakfast credit, Yacht Club restaurant & Green Chai Café, period furnishings, porches/decks, swings & rocking chairs, massage therapist, gift shops, clothing store, downtown location, wild flowers. $$ to $$$

Further Information

Bastrop Chamber of Commerce, *927 Main St., Bastrop, TX 78602 (512) 321-2419.*

Directions

From Austin, TX 71 east to Bastrop.

CASTROVILLE
Population 2,159

Settled in 1844 by immigrants from the French-German provinces of Alsace and Lorraine, **Castroville** was by the 1850s a picturesque little Alsatian village. *The Little Alsace of Texas* looks a little more like Texas these days, but the Alsatian flavor is still very much in evidence: Nearly 100 stone buildings from the original Alsatian village remain, Alsatian (a Germanic dialect) is spoken by some of the older townspeople, local kitchens and menus feature Alsatian dishes, and Alsatian folk music is preserved by the **Alsatian Dancers of Texas**.

There was a time when Castroville was one of Texas's largest cities, but in the 1880s the railroad bypassed the town, allowing the picturesque architectural heritage to survive. The historic district, encircled in part by one of those lazy Texas rivers, the **Medina**, contains 97 structures. Most were constructed of limestone and cypress timbers and finished with white plaster. Many go as far back as the 1840s and 1850s. The majority, one-story cottages with the asymmetric rooflines of their Alsatian ancestors, are private residences or homes to businesses, including some of Castroville's dozen or so antique and craft shops. The entire old part of town is a National Historic District.

Among the most imposing of the multi-story buildings are the **Carle House and Store** (1865), the porticoed **Tarde Hotel** (1852; now a private residence), and the unusually beautiful Gothic-style **St. Louis Catholic Church** (1870). The largest structure is the galleried **Moye Center**, now a retreat center but built originally (1873) as a convent and motherhouse.

Castroville's most famous building is the **Landmark Inn**, begun in 1849 and established as an inn in 1854. Now a part of the **Landmark Inn State Historical Park**, the inn still offers overnight accommodations (see below). Other structures in the historical park include a residence, stone grist mill, and arched stone waterway, all dating from the 1850s.

Castroville's newest acquisition is also its oldest possession. The **Steinbach House**, originally built in France between 1618 and 1648, was disassembled and rebuilt in Castroville between 1998 and 2002. Much of the work was done by volunteer craftsmen from Alsace. The half-timber and brick-and-mortar "fachwerk" house, furnished in period on the second floor, will serve as a visitors' center.

A guide for a walking tour of the historic district is distributed by the Chamber of Commerce. Guided tours are also available, as are tours of homes conducted by the Castroville Garden Club (by appointment).

Special Features
The Olympic-size pool in the **Castroville Regional Park** (also an RV park) is the perfect place to conclude a summer's day of sightseeing.

One of the country's most charming cities, **San Antonio**, is 20 miles to the east of Castroville. Top sights in San Antonio include the **Paseo del Rio**, several historic missions, the **Alamo**, and the **Institute of Texan Cultures**.

- Castroville is famous for its Alsatian sausage and pastries.
- Only Stephen F. Austin brought more settlers to Texas than the founder of Castroville, Henri Castro.
- Castroville was the first Texas town to be established west of San Antonio.

▶ HISTORIC INN ◀

LANDMARK INN, *402 Florence St., (830) 931-2133, fax (830) 538-3858. e-mail: lmishp@stionet.com, www.tpwd.state.tx.us/park/landmark/.* Inn with beginnings in 1849, National Register, 10 rooms, some private baths, expanded Cont. breakfasts, period furnishings, old rockers on second-floor gallery, patio, gardens, views. $

▶ HISTORIC RESTAURANT ◀

THE ALSATIAN, *1403 Angelo St., (830) 931-3260.* In quaint 1880s cottage setting; Alsatian cooking—e.g., Chicken Proviade, Trout on a Jalapeno Butter Sauce, Jagerschnitzel. $$

Further Information

Castroville Chamber of Commerce, *802 London St., P.O. Box 572, Castroville, TX 78009 (830) 538-3142.*

Directions

From San Antonio, US 90 west to Castroville.

FORT DAVIS
Population 1,200

Fort Davis is truly a town of the Old West, the Old West of history as well as of the movies. Throughout much of the 19th century wagon trains, the Pony Express, and stagecoaches passed through the area on their way west on the old San Antonio-El Paso road. Fort Davis (1854 to 1891) was one of several forts built to guard the road. Almost by Hollywood script, Apaches and Comanches attacked travelers on the road, and troops rode out of the fort to pursue the raiders. Infantrymen from the fort also escorted mail and freight trains and patrolled the region's vast spaces. And all of this took place in the foothills of the Davis Mountains, a made-to-order Western backdrop.

The town of Fort Davis grew up alongside the fort during the latter part of the century. In addition to serving the fort, the town was a center for ranchers and a kind of resort for Texans wishing to escape the heat and humidity of the coastal summers. The elevation, low humidity, and cool climate also attracted people suffering from tuberculosis.

It would be an exaggeration to say that the town's life style hasn't changed in 100 years, but there are those who claim that it hasn't changed much in 50 years. Crime is virtually non-existent, and the water remains clear and the air fresh. Nobody uses street names, and everybody knows everyone else. There are small old adobe houses, a tiny town square, and limestone and adobe buildings, public and commercial, from the late 19th and early 20th centuries. The gift shops and art galleries weren't here 50 years ago, but the old soda fountain was.

Three buildings of special note are churches: the 1904 **First Presbyterian Church**, the 1898 **St. Joseph's Catholic Church**, and the 1884 **Methodist Church**, the oldest Protestant church building between San Antonio and El Paso. The **Union Mercantile**, on the east end of the square, is the town's oldest building (1873).

According to the National Park Service, the old fort, now **Fort Davis National Historic Site**, is "considered the best surviving example of a frontier Indian Wars post in the Southwest." Many of the more than 50 original structures of the fort have been restored; some have been furnished in period and opened as museums. The site includes a visitor center, picnic grove, and nature trail system. During the summer months volunteers, when available, present demonstrations and conduct tours of refurnished buildings.

The **Overland Trail Museum** (1883), owned and operated by the **Fort Davis Historical Society**, features a large collection of county photos and a restored frontier kitchen and barber shop (open during the summer on Tuesdays, Fridays, and Saturdays and the rest of the year by appointment). The **Chihuahuan Desert Visitor Center**, just south of town, has gardens and walking trails that introduce the visitor to native flowers, cacti, and trees.

Special Features

The Scenic Loop is a 75-mile road that ascends into the **Davis Mountains**. At one point it reaches the highest elevation in the Texas highway system (6,791 feet). Along the way are the **Davis Mountains State Park**, the **McDonald Observatory** (see below), the **Barrel Springs Stage Stop**, the **Point of Rocks** picnic area, and other scenic and historic points. Most of the land fronting the Scenic Loop is private property, usually working ranches, and travelers are advised not to trespass. Flash floods are possible, as are native animals and cattle on the road.

The **McDonald Observatory**, 17 miles north of town (and on the Scenic Loop), features the second-largest telescope in the world. Check at the visitor center for information on tours of the dome, solar viewing, "star parties," and other public programs.

> Fort Davis was one of the first posts in the West where black troops, called "Buffalo Soldiers," served (1867 to 1885).

▶ HISTORIC HOTEL ◀

HOTEL LIMPIA, *P.O. Box 1838 (on the square), (800) 662-5517, (432) 426-3237, fax (432) 426-3983, e-mail: frontdesk@hotellimpia.com, www.hotellimpia.com.* Restored 1912 pink limestone hotel, 19 rooms & 12 suites, 3 turn-of-century guest houses, private baths, TV, dining room, bar, antiques, some pets, parlors, 12-ft ceilings with ornamental tin, glassed-in verandah, balconies, rocking chairs (hotel's "trademark"), gift shop, nature store. $$ to $$$

Further Information

Fort Davis Chamber of Commerce, *P.O. Box 378, Fort Davis, TX 79734 (915) 426-3015, www.fortdavis.com.*

Directions

From El Paso, I-10 east to exit 206, TX 17 south to Fort Davis.

FREDERICKSBURG
Population 7,900

Fredericksburg's considerable charm doesn't fit neatly into any category. The very wide straight streets and their limestone and frame houses, some with Victorian gingerbread trim, don't belong to a German town. Yet the biergartens and the large array of lovely 19th-century stone buildings hardly describe a typical Texas town. Fredericksburg is unique, and belongs on the itinerary of anyone touring Texas.

By all means the most unique, yet enchanting of Fredericksburg's 80-plus historic sites is the old **Nimitz Hotel** (1852)—now the **Admiral Nimitz Museum State Historical Center**. Looking very much like an old steamboat getting ready to plough across the Texas Hill Country, the former hotel was built and managed by the grandparents of Fleet Admiral Chester Nimitz, U.S. five-star admiral and hero of the Pacific in W.W.II. The Nimitz Museum tells the story of the old hotel's early period and documents the contributions of Fredericksburg's favorite son.

Close by is the **National Museum of the Pacific War**, a complex that includes a gallery with 23,000 square feet of interactive exhibits. Behind the hotel is the restful **Japanese Garden of Peace**, a gift from the people of Japan. The **Pacific Combat Zone** is located one block east of the main complex. The 4-acre complex features a recreated Pacific Island battle scene, the hangar deck of a WWII aircraft carrier, and the only PT boat left that saw action during the war.

The **Vereins Kirche Museum** is a reconstruction (1935) of an octagonal building erected in 1847 and torn down in 1896. The original building played a number of roles, including those of school, church, and fort, during the latter half of the 19th century. The landmark building is owned and operated by the **Gillespie County Historical Society**.

A good glimpse of an earlier Fredericksburg is provided by the 3.5-acre **Pioneer Museum Complex**. The complex includes the stone **Kammlah House** (1849), which served as a home and store through the 1920s. The building bears a National Historic Trust Site emblem. Eight furnished rooms, a wine cellar, and stone-covered yard (*hof*) are available for viewing. Among other structures in the complex is the limestone **Fassel-Roeder House**, a one-room schoolhouse, an authentic Texas Hill Country log cabin, the **Weber Sunday House**, and the **Fredericksburg Volunteer Fire Department Museum**.

Dotting the back streets are smallish houses that were once *Sunday Houses*, weekend houses where farming and ranching families stayed when they were in town to buy supplies, sell produce, visit relatives– and attend church. In the era of the horse and buggy, simply getting to and from town took such a large chunk of the day that staying over was often necessary.

The tastes and smells in the town's biergartens are very much like those of the Old Country, but the lovely old limestone walls and the live oaks shielding the tables from the Texas sun are uniquely Fredericksburg. This is Texas German at its delightful best!

Special Features

Fort Martin Scott, two miles east of town, was the first U.S. Army frontier fort in Texas (established 1848). Now a state historic site, the original stone guardhouse has been restored and two officers' quarters reconstructed; other construction is planned.

This is Texas **peach country**. The Chamber of Commerce/Convention & Visitor Bureau distributes a map of roadside stands and pick-your-own orchards. Homemade peach ice cream, pies, and preserves may be purchased at many locations throughout the county.

Reminding that this is also wildflower country, the **Wildseed Farms Market Center** invites visitors to tour a working wildflower farm (complete with biergarten). Herb enthusiasts will enjoy the **Fredericksburg Herb Farm** (with tea room and day spa), and lovers of the grape should relish the tastings, tours, and picnic facilities available at a number of local vineyards and wineries.

> Visitors may walk into 1,500-square-foot butterfly enclosures at the Fredericksburg Butterfly Ranch. The ranch offers insights into the life cycle of native Texas butterflies.

▶ HISTORIC LODGINGS ◀

Note: There are over 330 bed & breakfast and guest house properties in Gillespie County. Many are non-hosted guest houses. Information on eight of the traditional bed & breakfasts, all inspected and approved by Historic & Hospitality Accommodations of Texas, may be obtained at (800) 494-4678 and www.fredericksburgtrad.com.

Many of the remaining properties are listed through the following reservation services:

Be My Guest, *110 N. Milam, (830) 997-7227, (800) 364-8555, www.bemyguestfredericksburgtexas.com*

First Class Bed And Breakfast Reservation Service, *909 E. Main, (830) 997-0443, (888) 991-6749, www.fredericksburg-lodging.com*

Fredericksburg Traditional Bed & Breakfasts, *(800) 494-HOST, www.fredericksburgtrad.com*

Gastehaus Schmidt Reservation Service, *231 W. Main, (830) 997-5612, (866) 427-8374, e-mail: www.fbglodging.com*

Hill Country Lodging, *215 W. Main, (830) 990-8455, (800) 745-3591, www.fredericksburgbedandbreakfast.com*

Main Street Bed & Breakfast Reservation Service, *337 E. Main, (830) 997-0153, (888) 559-8555, www.travelmainstreet.com*

Further Information

Fredericksburg Convention & Visitor Bureau, *302 E. Austin, Fredericksburg, TX 78624 (888) 997-3600, (830) 997-6523, fax (830) 997-8588, e-mail: visitorinfo@fbg.net, www.fredericksburg-texas.com.*

Directions

From San Antonio, I-10 north to US 87, US 87 north to Fredericksburg (approximately 69 miles).

GRANBURY
Population 7,281

Granbury is an historic 19th-century town, an antique and art center, a place for Ft. Worthians and Dallasites to go for dinner and a play or musical, a resort nestled along the shores of 30-mile-long **Lake Granbury**.

Granbury's town square was the first in Texas to be listed on the National Register of Historic Places. More recently, readers of *Texas Highways Magazine* voted the square "The Best Town Square in Texas." On the square is the Second Empire-style **Hood County Courthouse** (1891). A Seth Thomas town clock was installed when the courthouse, built of native limestone, was completed. Around the square are beautifully restored late 19th-century and turn-of-the-century commercial structures. One of the handsomest is the 1886 **Granbury Opera House**, a two-story Italianate theater that is still in regular use (see below). Also of note are the limestone **Old Hood County Jail** (1885), which houses the **Jail Museum** (with a hanging tower), and the 1893 **Nutt House** (a hotel since 1919). The buildings on the square are home to more than 50 antique and specialty shops, art galleries, boutiques, and restaurants.

On the streets off the square is a collection of fine Victorian homes, many of them of the Queen Anne style. Granbury's historic buildings may be seen by guided group tours and by self-guided tours.

Lake Granbury, lined with vacation homes and condominiums, offers a variety of water sports and the setting for some scenic golf. Sightseeing excursions and dinner cruises are available. Lest the visitor forget that this is Texas, Granbury also boasts the world's largest 18-hole miniature golf course.

The Granbury Opera House presents plays and musicals throughout the year. For those preferring old-time entertainment, Granbury also boasts a 1950s **drive-in theater**. The **Texas Amphitheater** in nearby **Glen Rose** stages a musical drama, *The Promise*, which portrays the life of Christ.

Special Features
Dinosaur Valley State Park, west of Glen Rose, features the best-preserved dinosaur tracks in the state. The park also has nature trails and a visitor center.

Granbury has a rich folklore. Among the legends is that the real John Wilkes Booth, President Lincoln's assassin, was never captured and that he once resided in the town under the name of John St. Helen. Another legend is that Jesse James is buried here rather than in Missouri.

Also west of Glen Rose, the **Fossil Rim Wildlife Center** offers a 9-mile drive through a 2,900-acre conservation area containing over 1,000 endangered and exotic animals.

Further Information

Granbury Convention & Visitors Bureau, *116 W. Bridge, Granbury, TX 76048 (800) 950-2212, fax (817) 573-5789, www.granburytx.com.*

Directions

From Ft. Worth, US 377 southwest 35 mi to Granbury, take Business District/Historic District exit across lake to town square.

JEFFERSON
Population 2,200

During its early years, **Jefferson** acquired one of the most beautiful collections of mid-19th century homes in Texas. Located on **Big Cypress Bayou**, the town was a major Texas river port, second only to Galveston in tonnage shipped. It was also the "Gateway to Texas" for settlers, a home to wealthy planters, and a Confederate ammunition and food supply center. Then came the *Great Decline*: In 1873, while removing a major log jam on the Red River below Shreveport, Louisiana, U.S. Corps of Engineers dredgers unwittingly lowered the water level on the Big Cypress so much that shipping to Jefferson was no longer feasible.

The **Excelsior House Hotel** (see listing below), one of Jefferson's top sights, has been in continuous operation since the 1850s. Include the hotel and its New Orleans-style courtyard in your tour whether or not you're staying there. Another Jefferson treasure is the *Atalanta*, a private railroad car built in 1888 for railroad tycoon, Jay Gould. There is no better way to apprehend the extravagance of late 19th-century millionaire life than to tour this car.

Jefferson's shady streets can be toured by foot, motorized trolley, horse-drawn carriage, and several other ways. Many of the historic homes may be seen by appointment, several by regularly scheduled tour. Among those in the latter category are the single-story neoclassic **Beard House** (1860), the four-columned Greek Revival **Freeman Plantation** (1850), and the lovely transitional **House of Seasons** (1872), identified by its unique cupola.

Jefferson boasts a number of impressive collections, some public and some private. The **Jefferson Historical Museum** displays many of the public ones: Civil War artifacts, old Bibles, pioneer doctors' instruments, ironstone, old Jefferson bottles, etc. Another public collection, the new **Texas Heritage Archives and Library**, might just as well be called the *Museum of the*

Republic of Texas, so extensive and valuable are its holdings from the 1836-1845 period.

Jefferson's newest private museum, **Scarlett O'Hardy's Gone With The Wind Museum**, features rare foreign movie posters, promotional novelties, costume reproductions, and countless other mementos of one of the country's most beloved epics.

Private collections of antiques and artifacts may be seen in Jefferson's some 49 arts and crafts and collectibles shops.

> The final resting place and artifacts from the Jefferson-bound steamboat, the "Mittie Stephens," were finally located in 1993. The boat took the lives of 64 people when it burned and sank on Caddo Lake in 1869.

▶ HISTORIC HOTEL ◀

EXCELSIOR HOUSE, *211 W. Austin St., (903) 665-2513, fax (903) 665-9389, e-mail: excelsior@jeffersontx.com, www.Jeffersontx.com/excelsiorhouse*. Hotel in continuous operation since the 1850s, four presidents among guests, 15 rooms, private baths, TV, full breakfasts (extra charge), elegant antiques, ballroom & formal dining room, New Orleans-style courtyard, garden. $$ to $$$

▶ HISTORIC RESTAURANT ◀

STILLWATER INN, *203 E. Broadway, (903) 665-8415*. In chef-owned 1893 home with period décor; gourmet cooking—e.g., Escargot Bourguignon, Rack of Lamb, Chocolate Mousse; upstairs lodging; gift shop. $$$

Further Information

Marion County Chamber of Commerce, *118 N. Vale, Jefferson, TX 75657 (903) 665-2672, (888) 467-3529, fax (903) 665-8233, www.jefferson-texas.com*.

Directions

From Shreveport (LA), I-20 west to US 59, north (16 miles) to Jefferson; from Dallas, I-20 east to US 59, north to Jefferson.

SALADO
Population 3,500

Sitting on the tree-shaded banks of spring-fed **Salado Creek** in central Texas is what may be Texas's most charming little town. Although blessed with a lovely setting and a long and genteel history, **Salado** (sa LAY doh) is so little known that it is sometimes called the "undiscovered jewel of Texas." Many people who regularly travel the nearby interstate have never heard of the village, and there are people living in towns just a few miles away who have never even visited here.

Salado Creek once nourished a stage stop and later a branch of the **Chisholm Trail**. But Salado came into being because of the generosity of plantation owner Colonel Sterling C. Robertson, who in 1859 gave the land for the town. Once born, the town's character was molded by respected **Salado College** (1860 to about 1885), whose students and educators brought to Salado a level of culture and prestige foreign to most other Texas frontier towns.

Following the usual scenario, the railroads bypassed Salado, and the town was destined to become a small, quiet village. The village has undergone a recent revitalization as many of the old homes and other buildings have been restored to house bed and breakfasts, some of the finest restaurants in central Texas, and a very inviting collection of art galleries, potteries, antique and craft shops, boutiques, and book shops. Many of the new homes closely resemble the old; the two mingle comfortably. The setting and character remain strictly rural.

Eighteen of the village's buildings are listed on the National Register. Tapes for a driving tour may be rented at the **Stagecoach Inn**. Several of the houses are open during an historic homes tour held every December.

One of the historic homes is the **Baines home**, a 1866 saltbox built by the great-grandfather of President Lyndon Baines Johnson. Two other interesting homes include the 1868 Greek Revival **Armstrong-Adams House**, once occupied by a series of doctors as well as student boarders, and the old rock **Barton House**, built in 1866 by a Dr. and Mrs. Barton who wished to educate their 10 children at Salado College.

Salado Creek was the first Natural Landmark in Texas. The town is so proud of the creek that a committee has been established to monitor the quality of the water. One of the best places to enjoy the beauty of the crystal-clear waters is at **Pace Park**, once an Indian campground. A bronze statue of **Sirena**, a beautiful Indian maiden who by legend was transformed into a mermaid by a magical fish, graces a bubbling spring of the creek.

Special Features

In the country south of town stand the 22-room plantation home (1852/1857) and stone slave quarters built by Col. Robertson. The house remains in the hands of the Robertson family. Occasional tours are available – check with the Chamber of Commerce for information.

> • The ruins of Salado College have been stabilized preliminary to reconstruction efforts.
> • Salado hosts the Texas Scottish Games and Gathering of the Clans every November.
> • Dr. Barton, builder of Barton House, is believed to have introduced watercress to Salado Creek. The plant flourishes there today.

▶ HISTORIC LODGING ◀

INN ON THE CREEK, *602 Center Circle, P O. Box 858, (877) 947-5554, (254) 947-5554, fax (254) 947-9198, e-mail: iotc@vvm.com, www.inncreek.com*. 19th-century homes & cottages fronting to creek, 14 rooms & 1 cottage, private baths, TV & phones, full breakfasts, restaurant (weekends by reservation), bar, antiques, some room service, porches overlooking creek. $$ to $$$$

Further Information

Salado Chamber of Commerce, *P.O. Box 849, Salado, TX 76571 (254) 947-5040.*

Directions

From Austin, I-35 north to exit 283 (Salado exit); from Waco, I-35 south to exit 285, cross under highway to Main Street.

Other Charming Texas Towns
Albany
Alpine
Canyon
Columbus
Comfort
Ft. Stockton
Johnson City
Marathon
Miami
San Augustine
Wimberley

Chapter 44

UTAH

BLUFF
Population about 290

Guarded by the towering **Navajo Twin Rocks**, **Bluff** lies in a canyon along the **San Juan River** in southeastern Utah. The town is one of those legendary little Western settlements that combine the vestiges of Victoriana with some of the most spectacular scenery in the country.

Bluff was settled by Mormons in 1880. At first the settlers were compelled to group their cabins in a defensive fort, but as the region became safer, the cabins were moved to individual lots. There they provided shelter while larger stone houses were erected. Bluff's growth was to be short-lived, however, for in 1893 the county seat moved to Monticello and the town was progressively abandoned. Of the original 30 or so buildings, only about 14 survived. Fortunately, most of the survivors are being preserved, and in many cases restored to their original appearance.

In the center of town, scattered remains of old buildings and a newly erected replica of the meetinghouse where the pioneers gathered make up **Bluff Fort**. Signs here are designed to give the visitor a sense of what the early days were like.

Explore the tiny historic district on foot, and then climb or ride up **Cemetery Hill**. The memorials here remind of harsh times, including a diphtheria epidemic in 1900-01. Also on the hill are the remains of a prehistoric Great House, Great Kiva, and ancient road system.

Special Features
The area around Bluff is unusually rich in prehistoric sites, parks, mesas, and canyons—in other words, spectacular scenery. Within short driving, if not

Utah

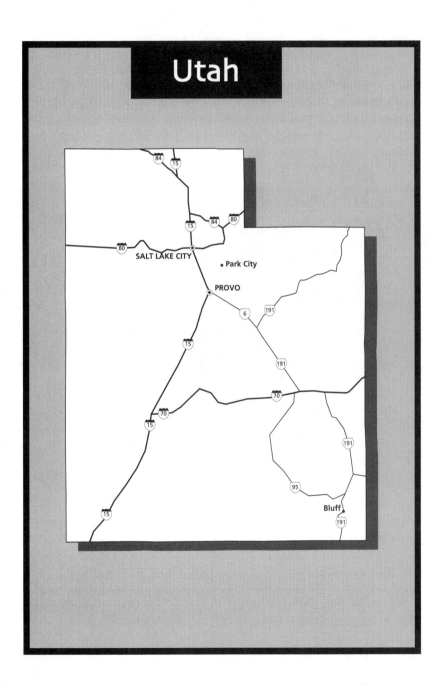

walking, distance are six or seven **Pueblo Anasazi** and **Navajo rock art panels** composed of various representational images and abstract motifs. There are also several **Pueblo Anasazi sites**. National parks, national monuments, and natural wonders abound in every direction. Many are within a 2-hour ride. A sample of some of the most popular would include **Monument Valley Navajo Tribal Park**, **Hovenweep National Monument**, **Natural Bridges National Monument**, **Arches National Park**, **Canyonlands National Park**, and **Mesa Verde National Park**.

Float trips down the San Juan River past ancient ruins and fascinating geological formations can be arranged for one day or many. Also, guides are available to help visitors explore local archaeological sites.

• Through a five-year effort by the Bluff City Historic Preservation Association and supporters, the historic 145-acre Curtis Jones Farm (along the San Juan River) has been preserved with a conservation easement.
• A unique black-on-red pottery was collected in 1936 at one of the local Pueblo Anasazi village sites. The pottery is now known to Southwest archaeologists as Bluff Black-on-red.
• At one time the Navajos crossed the river by means of a swinging bridge, still in place.

Further Information
Business Owners of Bluff, *P.O. Box 326, Bluff, UT 84512 (435) 672-2281, www.bluff-utah.org.*

Directions
From Moab (UT) US 191 south to Bluff (100 miles).

PARK CITY
Population 7,371

Named after its park-like setting, **Park City** is a unique and engaging mixture of the old and new. The old can be seen in the Victorian buildings and various mementos from the town's mining past. The new is seen in the condos, modern ski resorts, and variety of shops.

But the old and the new don't coexist, they blend. Many of the shops are housed in restored historic buildings, and transportation on historic **Main Street** is provided by an old-fashioned trolley. The blend is most beautiful in the winter, when people in colorful ski gear stroll through a wonderland of snow-covered Victorian buildings and inviting inns, restaurants, and pubs.

One of the few Utah towns not founded by Mormons, Park City boasted some 27 saloons at one point early in its history. The silver in the surrounding **Wasatch Mountains** helped turn 23 people into millionaires, including George Hearst, father of William Randolph Hearst. By the 1930s, however, it was clear that silver was becoming part of the town's past and the people began to look toward the snow for their future.

And what a future it turned out to be! Park City now has three major ski resorts that collectively boast 8,550 acres of "The Greatest Snow on Earth." And as host of one-third of the 2002 Winter Olympics, the town was crowned "The Alpine Heart of 2002." There are three shopping districts (including Main Street), around 20 art galleries, and a free bus system. There are also 113 restaurants, and the apres-ski and night life scenes are among the most highly rated in the country.

Park City has had 64 buildings placed on the National Register of Historic Places. Many are on Main Street. One of special interest to those wishing to know the town is the **Visitor Information Center & Museum**. Once the **City Hall**, the museum tells the story of Park City's mining past and transition to a major resort. In the basement is **Utah's Territorial Jail**, used longer than any other territorial jail in the West (until 1964).

Park City is both a summer and winter resort. The summer tourist will find six distinctive golf courses, hiking and horseback riding trails, and more than 100 miles of mountain-bike trails. A ski lift serves hikers and bikers. In addition to the ski resorts, winter sports fans will find opportunities and facilities for snowmobiling, cross-country skiing, and ice skating. Hot-air balloons color the skies in both summer and winter.

Special Features

Five Nordic ski jumps, a freestyle jump, a bobsled/luge track, and a snowboard half-pipe may be found at **Utah Olympic Park**, site of many of the events of the 2002 Winter Olympic Games. For the summer jumper there is a unique freestyle aerials splash pool, with four aerial ramps, and the 90-meter winter jump is equipped with high-tech materials for use in warm weather. Public bobsled rides are available in both summer and winter.

- Park City's ski resorts reported 1.2 million skier days during the 2001-02 Olympic season.
- More than 1,000 miles of tunnels, remnants of the mining area, lace through the surrounding mountains.

▶ HISTORIC LODGINGS ◀

1904 IMPERIAL HOTEL B&B INN, *221 Main St., P.O. Box 1628, (800) 669-8824, (435) 649-1904, e-mail: stay@1904imperial.com, www.1904imperial.com.* 1904 boarding house on National Register, 10 rooms, private baths, TV & phones, full breakfasts, antiques, "Western Victorian" décor, down comforters & pillows, front porch overlooking historic Main Street. $ to $$$ (summer) $$$ to $$$$ (winter)

THE OLD MINERS' LODGE, *615 Woodside Ave., P.O. Box 2639, (435) 645-8068, (800) 648-8068, fax (435) 645-8068, e-mail: stay@oldminerslodge.com, www.oldminerslodge.com.* 1889 boarding house in historic district, 9 rooms & 3 suites, private baths, full "hearty country" breakfasts, antiques, down pillows & comforters, afternoon refreshments, hot tub on upper deck, gazebo & porches. $ to $$$ (summer) $$$ to $$$$ (winter)

Further Information

Park City Chamber of Commerce/Convention & Visitors Bureau, *P.O. Box 1630, Park City, UT 84060 (800) 453-1360, www.parkcityinfo.com.*

Directions

From Salt Lake City, I-80 east to exit 145, UT 224 south to Park City (30 mi).

Other Charming Utah Towns
Garden City/Laketown
Midway
Springdale
Torrey

Chapter 45

VERMONT

GREENSBORO/CRAFTSBURY
Population 717/994

Greensboro and **Craftsbury** are up in the Northeast Kingdom of Vermont, a region that looks like what much of our country looked like – or should have looked like – 100 years ago. The setting is strictly rural. The roads, mostly dirt and often tree-lined, wind Currier & Ives style over rivers, through woods, and past farmsteads. Every turn in the road brings a new and delightful view. There is little traffic, leaving the driver free to watch for moose, blue herons, and wildflowers.

Greensboro and Craftsbury do not have many stores or other businesses. Both are little collections of white-painted homes, churches, and a general store or two. Villagers seeking anything more than bread, gasoline, and a few other necessities must make a 30- or 45-minute drive.

Craftsbury boasts two libraries and evening concerts on the large **Common** (lovely). The village is home to **Sterling College**, where academic studies are merged with hands-on research and application in sustainable agriculture, outdoor education, and wildlands ecology. There's a charming British woolen shop in **East Craftsbury**. Tucked at the southern end of **Caspian Lake**, Greensboro has an especially well-stocked old general store, **Willey's**.

The gently sloping countryside, the shaded back woods, the deep forests, the lakes and rivers are tailor-made for camping, hiking, biking, fishing, and water sports. There's an extensive trail network for cross-country skiing.

Special Features
Naturalists and others who prefer their countryside totally undeveloped will find true wilderness not far away in **Essex County**.

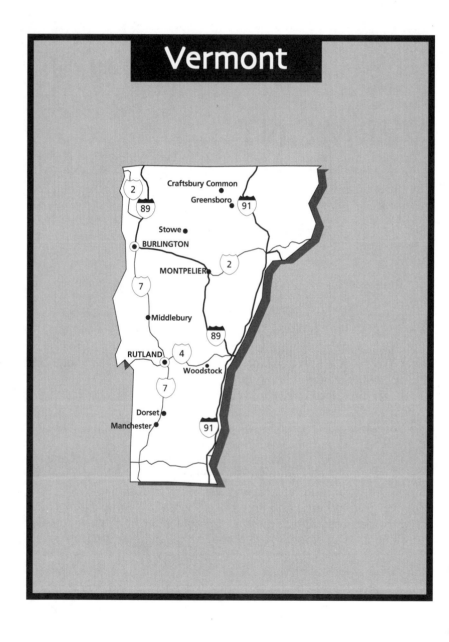

▶ HISTORIC INN ◀

INN ON THE COMMON, *N. Craftsbury Rd., Craftsbury Common (05827)*, *(800) 521-2233, (802) 586-9619, fax (802) 586-2249, e-mail: info@innonthecommon.com, www.innonthecommon.com.* Three meticulously restored Federal houses dating to 1795 & 1800, 16 rooms, private baths, full breakfasts, dining room, antiques, some pets, pool, English-style gardens, Wellness Barn, clay tennis court, views. $$$$ (incl. 5-course "gourmet" dinners)

Further Information

Northeast Kingdom Chamber of Commerce, *357 Western Ave., St. Johnsbury, VT 05819, (802) 748-3678, (800) 639-6379, fax (802) 748-0731, e-mail: execdir@vermontnekchamber.org, www.vermontnekchamber.com.*

Directions

From Springfield (MA), I-91 north to St. Johnsbury exit, US 2 west to W. Danville, VT 15 north to VT 16, VT 16 to Greensboro Bend, county road west to Greensboro and Craftsbury.

MANCHESTER/DORSET
Population 3622/550

Manchester and **Dorset** have 19th-century church steeples and houses, most of them white and *big*, many with green shutters, clustered about village greens and framed by hills and forests. The predominant colors are green and white, the particular proportions of each dependent on the season. Giant shade trees—including of course maples—and winding roads complete the foreground. The scene is perfect for gracious old inns, Colonial dining rooms, and crackling fireplaces.

Manchester Center is a colorful place designed for the shopper. **Manchester Village** and **Dorset**, on the other hand, are places of quiet and incomparable beauty. This is not a place where people typically go to seek work; it is a place to retreat from work. The interesting thing is that this has been true since the middle of the 19th century, at least. In the 1850s, as today, these villages were places of holiday or retirement. Indeed, the history of Manchester is virtually inseparable from the history of its centerpiece, the **Equinox**, Vermont's premier inn (listed below).

While benefiting from the past, Manchester and Dorset do not ignore the present and future: Their buildings are beautifully restored, Manchester's downtown thrives, Dorset's rural charm persists, and development rights for many of the nearby farms are held by land trusts. A lot of work, time, and love have gone to make this true.

Manchester is home to **Hildene** (1905), the 24-room Georgian Revival mansion built by Robert Todd Lincoln, the only son of Abraham and Mary Todd Lincoln to survive to maturity. The house's original furnishings and Lincoln family effects may be seen by daily tours (and candlelight tours during the Christmas season). The formal gardens have been restored. Of the estate's 412 acres, 200 have been set aside as "forever wild."

The **Southern Vermont Art Center** is housed in another Colonial Revival mansion, **Yester House** (1917), in Manchester. Paintings, sculptures, photographs and other works of art are exhibited in 11 of the house's 28 rooms. Classical and chamber music, jazz, and voice and instrumental solos and duets are performed in the adjacent **Louise Ryals Arkell Pavilion**. Also on the grounds are the Sculpture Garden and the lovely **Boswell Botany Trail**, managed by the **Manchester Garden Club**.

The **American Museum of Fly Fishing**, also in Manchester, boasts a collection of more than 1,000 rods and 400 reels. The collection includes fly rods used by Dwight D. Eisenhower, Daniel Webster, Ernest Hemingway, Winslow Homer, Bing Crosby, and other famous Americans.

The **Dorset Playhouse**, noted for good theater, offers a range of performances in both summer and winter. A resident professional group performs in the summer as the **Dorset Theatre Festival**. The **Dorset Players** present periodic shows during the winter.

Manchester is a gateway to several well-known Vermont ski areas. The region also offers groomed as well as ungroomed trails for cross-country skiing. Twenty-one groomed trails are on the grounds of Hildene (see above), along with a warming hut.

Special Features

From May through October a 5.2-mile winding toll road can be driven to the top of Mt. Equinox. Several states, and even Mount Royal in Montreal, can be seen from the top of the mountain on clear days. The **Monastery of the Carthusian Order** owns the mountain and encourages picnicking and hiking (designated areas).

- Among the summer residents in Manchester during the Civil War year of 1863 were Mary Todd Lincoln and her son Robert Todd.
- Mary Lincoln Beckwith, Abraham Lincoln's great granddaughter, was the last member of the Lincoln family to live at Hildene. Beckwith died in 1975.

▶ HISTORIC LODGINGS ◀

THE 1811 HOUSE, *Box 39 (Manchester Village), (800) 432-1811, fax (802) 362-2443, e-mail: house1811@adelphia.net, www.1811house.com.* 1770s Federal-style inn on National Register, 11 rooms & 2 suites, private baths, some TV, full breakfasts, British pub, English & American antiques, Oriental rugs, fireplaces, fine paintings, 7 acres of lawn & gardens, pond, views of mountains. $$$ to $$$$

THE EQUINOX, *P.O. Box 46 (Manchester Village), (800) 362-4747, e-mail: reservations@equinoxresort.com, www.equinoxresort.com.* 18th-century Vermont landmark (est. 1769), National Register, 136 rooms & 36 suites, private baths, TV & phones, dining rooms, bar, antiques, fitness spa, pools, tennis, golf course, Land Rover Driving School. $$$$

Further Information

Manchester and the Mountains Chamber of Commerce, *5046 Main St. (Suite 1), Manchester Center, VT 05255 (800) 362-4144, (802) 362-2100, www.manchestervermont.net;* also, **Dorset Chamber of Commerce,** *P.O. Box 121, Dorset, VT 05251 (802) 867-2450 (ZIP for Manchester Village is 05254.)*

Directions

From Boston, MA 2 west to I-91, I-91 north to exit 2 (Brattleboro, VT), follow signs to VT 30, VT 30 north and west to Manchester Center.

MIDDLEBURY
Population 8,183 (excluding students)

With a village green, shuttered Colonial houses, church steeples, museums, beautiful old inns, and a river with a waterfall, **Middlebury** is a resume of New England's charms. The countryside is pastoral. Visible to the east are the **Green Mountains**, to the west the **Adirondacks**. Other New England towns may also have this. What separates Middlebury is that its livelihood depends on a college campus rather than tourist promotion. College towns seem to offer a gentler way of life and a setting more appealing to retirees and others seeking quality in their lives.

Middlebury College is one of the oldest (1800) and most prestigious colleges in the United States. Its beautiful 1,200-acre main campus is dotted with Colonial buildings of gray limestone or white marble. Three of the oldest, **Painter Hall** (1816), **Old Chapel** (1836), and **Starr Hall** (1860) make up nostalgic **Old Stone Row**.

The **Middlebury College Center for the Arts** includes an award-winning concert hall, theater, and library. One of the center's five components, the **Middlebury College Museum of Art**, houses traveling exhibitions as well as a permanent collection. The latter is noted for its Cypriot pottery, 19th-century sculpture, and contemporary prints.

About the village green and along the tree-shaded streets are a number of lovely town landmarks. Of special note are the Federal-style **Painter House** and the much-photographed 1809 **Congregational Church**, with a many-faceted steeple designed to give a little in the wind. The **Community House**, an 1815 home, has hand-carved fireplaces and a spiral staircase. The house is in constant use for art and crafts classes and other community events.

One of the three locations of the **Frog Hollow Vermont State Craft Centers** is in Middlebury. A non-profit visual arts organization, the center displays the works of over 300 Vermont craftspeople in its galleries. The wood, fabric, painting, and other wares are for sale, but visitors are welcome to browse. The Middlebury site also has studios, demonstrations, and classes – and good views of **Otter Creek**.

Vermont arts and crafts may also be seen at the **Vermont Folklife Center**. In addition to displaying folk art, the center uses video tapes to illustrate the state's folk traditions.

The **Henry Sheldon Museum**, the first incorporated village museum in the country, contains one of Vermont's foremost collections of antiques and curios. Housed in an 1829 tavern, later a home, the museum's rooms display furniture, guns, newspapers, and countless other items. In the library are bound copies of everything published in Middlebury since 1801.

The **Historic Marble Works** makes shopping an historic experience. Here on the courtyards of 1890s buildings are restaurants and little shops. A footbridge with a lovely view of the waterfall leads to **Frog Hollow Mill**, an old three-story stone mill housing yet another shop and restaurant.

Middlebury College's **Snow Bowl** offers excellent alpine skiing (open to the public), and the area has a good selection of groomed cross-country trails. Snowshoeing is also very popular.

Special Features

The **Morgan Horse Farm**, the Home of the Morgans, is located just outside of town. A breeding farm since the 1800s, its mission is to preserve and promote the country's first breed of horses. The farm is operated by the University of Vermont (guided tours).

Peaceful rural landscapes abound in this part of Vermont. Get off of US 7 and roam the valley back roads. To aid in this, the Addison County Chamber of Commerce publishes a colorfully illustrated guide to four driving loops. The booklet lists (and pictures) inns, crafts shops, galleries, etc. as well as scenic and historic sites.

- The Pulp Mill Bridge (1806) is Vermont's only two-lane separated covered bridge still open to traffic.
- Otters can often be seen playing in Otter Creek, which flows through town.

▶ HISTORIC INN ◀

THE MIDDLEBURY INN, *P.O. Box 798, 14 Court House Sq., (800) 842-4666, e-mail: midinnvt@sover.net, www.middleburyinn.com.* 1827 inn now comprising 3 bldgs., on National Register, 72 rooms & 3 suites, private baths, TV & phones, Cont. breakfasts, highly recommended dining rooms, tavern, antiques, some pets, afternoon tea, porch, gardens, guest privileges to fitness center, walking distance to downtown & college. $$ to $$$$

Further Information

Addison County Chamber of Commerce, *2 Court St., Middlebury, VT 05753 (802) 388-7951, (800) 733-8376, fax (802) 388-8066, www.midvermont.com.*

Directions

From Burlington, US 7 south to Middlebury; from Rutland, US 7 north to Middlebury.

STOWE
Population 3,433

Stowe is a white-steepled, picture-book New England village nestled in the **Green Mountains** beneath **Mt. Mansfield**, Vermont's highest peak. One of the first ski resorts in the East, Stowe is second to none in the East in its number – and variety – of fine runs. What is less well known is that Stowe is also second to none in its number – and variety – of bed-and-breakfast inns. Although the village population is only about 450, the number of bed and breakfasts is somewhere between 30 and 40! B&B inns and guest houses vary from private home to stately inn, from rustic to Laura Ashley, from Tyrolean Austrian to Colonial American.

The beauty of Stowe Village is in part due to its age (200 years in 1994) and the charming old buildings, including a covered bridge, that come with age. It's also in part due to a very strict zoning code that governs even the size and shape of signs (neon not allowed). The village is popular as both a summer and winter resort. Because of Stowe's unique climate, flowers do especially well. Indeed, the gardens themselves merit a summer visit.

The **Stowe Recreation Path**, completed in 1989 and already a legend, weaves for 5.3 miles along and over **Mountain Road** (VT 108) and the tumbling **Little River**. Costing $680,000, the award-winning path is one of the country's most beautiful byways for non-motorists.

The lifts that got the first skiers up the Vermont mountains are on display at the new **Vermont Ski Museum**. Placing the emphasis on movement, the museum shows old ski movies and vintage ski footage on a giant plasma screen. The exhibits are housed in the **Old Town Hall** (1818, National Register).

Stowe is noted for the beautiful crafts and other items displayed in its shops. The **Helen Day Art Center** has changing art exhibits and maintains an active calendar of programs and classes. Among the evening options are summer performances of the **Stowe Theatre Guild** at Town Hall Theatre and beckoning tables in one of the village's cozy pubs.

The Stowe area offers about every outdoor recreation but sponging and deep-sea fishing. Included among the summer offerings are rollerblading, wildlife-watching on Mt. Mansfield, speeding down a 2,300-ft. alpine slide, trout fishing, and sightseeing from an enclosed gondola. In addition to fabulous downhill skiing, winter activities include snowshoeing, snowmobiling, ice skating, and thanks to the East's largest groomed-trail network, superb cross-country skiing.

Special Features

The **Stowe Flower Festival**, one of the many summer/fall events, offers sessions on everything from creating ponds and rock gardens to attracting birds and photographing flowers. Both guided and self-guided tours of local gardens are featured.

VT 108 north from Stowe through **Smugglers Notch** offers a particularly scenic drive during the summer months (closed winters). Along the way are waterfalls, hiking trails, and parking areas. Magnificent views can also be enjoyed from an auto toll road that climbs to the top of Mt. Mansfield.

Visitors may watch milking or purchase wool yarns or fresh vegetables at some of the area's **working farms**. Check locally for instructions, and always call the farm in advance.

There are over a dozen **covered bridges** in the Stowe vicinity. Check at the Stowe Visitor Center on Main Street for locations and routing.

During Prohibition liquor was smuggled from Canada through the mountain gorge that was named, subsequently and consequently, "Smugglers Notch."

▶ HISTORIC INN ◀

GREEN MOUNTAIN INN, *P.O. Box 60, Main St. (VT 100), (800) 253-7302, (802) 253-7301, fax (802) 253-5096, e-mail: info@gminn.com, www.greenmountaininn.com.* 1833 home converted to country inn in 19th century (with many additions since), 83 rooms, 17 suites, 5 village townhouses, private baths, TV & phones, Main Street Dining Room & Whip Bar & Grill, antiques & period furnishings, small pets (with some restrictions), afternoon refreshments, health club, game room, year-round outdoor pool, village location, packages. $$ to $$$$

Further Information

Stowe Area Association, *Main St., P.O. Box 1320, Stowe, VT 05672 (800) 247-8693, fax (802) 253-2159, www.gostowe.com.*

Directions

From Burlington, I-89 east to exit 10, VT 100 north to Stowe.

WOODSTOCK
Population 1,000 (village), 2,000 (town)

Back in the middle of the 19th century the American statesman from Vermont, Senator Jacob Collamer, put it very nicely: "The good people of Woodstock have less incentive than others to yearn for heaven." The sentiment could just as well have been expressed at the end of the 20th century. For a long tradition of architectural preservation combined with a century-old commitment to tourism rather than industrial development have kept safe an exceptionally fine collection of vintage New England buildings. When placed along the meandering **Ottauquechee River** in a narrow valley amongst the foothills of the **Green Mountains**, the buildings—along with their village green, of course—become one of Vermont's loveliest and most perfect townscapes.

Woodstock's many beautiful old homes bespeak early wealth. Settled in 1765, the village prospered as a county seat (for Windsor County) and as a center for industries ranging from lumber and woolen milling to animal husbandry and coopering and gin distilling to the manufacture of clocks and musical instruments. Later, as industries moved elsewhere, village leaders turned to tourism and in 1892 opened the famed Woodstock Inn. Tourists have been heading here ever since, and as evidenced by the introduction in 1934 of the country's first ski tow, in all seasons.

Constructed in the early 19th century, the stately homes and churches of the Historic District are generally of the Federal and, less often, Greek-Revival styles. One of the finest of the houses, the Federal **Dana House** (1807), is now maintained as a museum by the historical society (restricted schedule). On display are period furnishings (1740-1900) as well as antique toys and dolls, historic costumes, and local artifacts. The oldest of the several lovely churches are the **Congregational** (1807; remodeled 1880-1890) and the **Unitarian-Universalist** (1835).

There are also two unique bridges: **Middle Bridge**, an authentic covered bridge constructed in 1967-69, and the **Elm Street Bridge**, an iron bridge constructed in 1869-70 and reconstructed in 1979-81 to carry heavier traffic. The historic district is best toured with the aid of a nicely illustrated guidebook prepared by the Woodstock Historical Society (check at the Chamber of Commerce).

The **Billings Farm & Museum** (farm established 1871) includes a working dairy farm, restored 1890s farmhouse, heirloom vegetable garden, and agricultural museum. Housed in several connected barns, the museum employs an impressive range of exhibits to portray life on the farm during the late 19th century. The farm and museum are open to the public.

Across the road from the Billings Farm is the recently established **Marsh Billings Rockefeller National Historical Park**. Within the park's borders are 20 rolling miles of carriage roads and trails; the **Carriage Barn** (1895), which serves as the visitor center; and the **Marsh-Billings-Rockefeller Mansion** (1805-07), home to a notable collection of 19th-century American landscape paintings.

Twenty-four species of birds of prey, unreleasable because of injury, may be seen in outdoor flight habitats at the **Vermont Raptor Center**. The center, open to the public, also includes a display area with exhibits of snakes and other live animals, nature programs, and self-guided trails (guidebooks are available).

Woodstock's list of things to do and calendar of events rival those of much larger towns. Upscale shops, many located on historic **Central** and **Elm streets**, offer antiques, fine clothing, New England art and handicrafts, maple syrup, and Vermont cheeses. There are also auctions, crafts fairs, and flea markets. Although maybe best known for its golf and skiing, the Woodstock area offers an endless list of recreations—among them, horseback riding, back-road car touring, and sleigh riding. In addition, the Woodstock Inn & Resort maintains a fitness center with facilities for racquet sports, aerobics, croquet, aquatics, etc. For the evening, a diverse menu of musical and theatrical events is served up, sometimes inside and sometimes under the stars, by the Pentangle Council on Arts.

Special Features

A parade of horses and carriages, medieval merriment, the singing of the *Messiah*, and other festive events help to make **Woodstock's Wassail**

Celebration, held the second weekend in December, a warm and colorful time.

▶ HISTORIC RESTAURANT ◀

SIMON PIERCE, *Main St. (Quechee 05059), (802) 295-1470.* In restored mill; "creative" American cuisine with Irish accents—e.g., Sesame Seared Chicken, Horseradish Crusted Cod; award-winning wine list; glassblowers; potters; shop. $$$

Further Information

Woodstock Area Chamber of Commerce, *P.O. Box 486, Woodstock, VT 05091, (802) 457-3555, (888) 496-6378, fax (802) 457-1601, www.woodstockvt.com.*

Directions

From Boston, I-93 north to I 89 (south of Concord, NH), north to US 4 in Vermont (Exit 1), west to Woodstock.

Other Charming Vermont Towns

Grafton
Newfane
Weston

Chapter 46

VIRGINIA

ABINGDON
Population 7,003

Abingdon's two "A" words are Ambiance and Arts. Chartered in 1776, Abingdon is the oldest town of British ancestry west of the Blue Ridge Mountains. Bordering the brick sidewalks of the 20-square-block historic district are stately but warm old houses displaying Georgian, Adam, and other traditional architectural styles. Some of the finest now open their doors as bed-and-breakfast inns (see below). Perhaps the most imposing – and renowned – is the **Martha Washington Inn** (1832), originally a private residence but variously a women's college and Civil War hospital since. Now an elegant hotel, the Martha Washington has one of the most respected restaurants in this corner of the world (see below).

As for the arts, Abingdon bills itself as the "cultural center of southwest Virginia." And with excellent reason. For beginners, the town is home to the oldest professional resident theater in the United States, the **Barter Theatre**, State Theatre of Virginia. Earning its name from the Depression-era practice of bartering for tickets with home-grown produce, the theater's three stages present quality performances of classic and contemporary works. Actors appearing at the Barter have included Hume Cronyn, Gregory Peck, Patricia Neal, Ernest Borgnine, and Barry Corbin.

The visual arts are represented by an almost endless array of shops and galleries. The works represent a nice mix of the old and the new and range from contemporary paintings to centuries-old Appalachian crafts. Among the regional crafts are woodcarving, quilting, weaving, dried flowers, and corn shuckery.

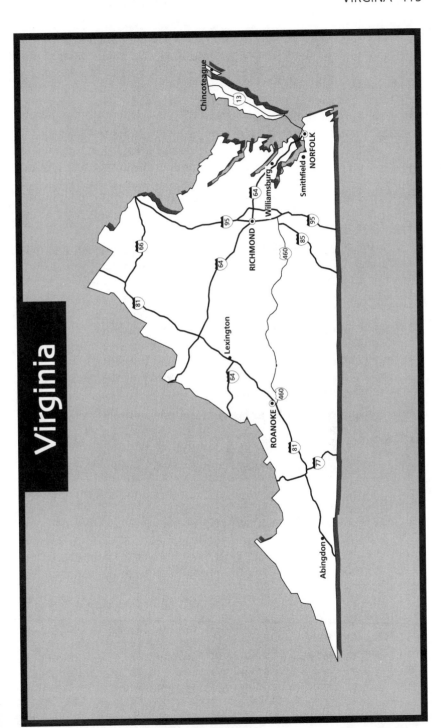

Rotating exhibits are held at the **William King Regional Arts Center**, a partner of the **Virginia Museum of Fine Arts**. The center houses studios and classrooms as well as galleries. Arts and crafts are also displayed in the **Cave House**, an 1858 Victorian landmark sitting on top of limestone grottos. The building, listed on the National Register, has three-story walnut stair railings and other features that complement the various displays. Yet another setting for the display of art is the **Arts Depot**, a restored 1870 freight station.

In a delightful setting just outside of town is **White's Mill**, the only water-powered commercial mill in southwest Virginia. Across from the mill is an old general store with long counters and a pot-bellied stove. The mill is listed on the National Register of Historic Places (guided tours).

Special Features

The **Virginia Creeper Trail**, a National Recreation Trail, originates just off **Main Street** and travels 34 miles to the summit of **Whitetop Mountain** near the Virginia/North Carolina border. Once a railroad, the pathway is popular with hikers, bikers, horseback riders, and cross-country skiers.

The 115,000-acre **Mount Rogers National Recreation Area** to the east of Abingdon boasts more than 300 miles of trails, including 60 miles of the great **Appalachian Trail**. Some of the trails form circuits. Included in the recreation area are the three highest mountains in Virginia.

One of the country's top tourist events, the **Virginia Highlands Festival**, is held the first two weeks in August.

> Abingdonians like to brag that their first visitor was Daniel Boone.

▶ HISTORIC INN ◀

MARTHA WASHINGTON INN, *150 W. Main St., (276) 628-3161, fax (276) 628-8885, www.marthawashngtoninn.com.* 1832 Federal mansion with history as women's college & Civil War hospital, 61 rooms, 9 suites, private baths, TV & phones, famed Victorian dining room, antiques, landscaped grounds. $$$$

▶ HISTORIC TAVERN ◀

THE TAVERN, *222 E. Main St., (276) 628-1118, www.abingdontavern.com.* In Abingdon's oldest Bldg. (1779); Eclectic International menu—e.g, Stuffed Filet Mignon, Chicken Saltimbocca. $$ to $$$

Further Information
Abingdon Convention & Visitors Bureau, *335 Cummings St., Abingdon, VA 24210 (276) 676-2282, (800) 435-3440, www.abingdon.com/tourism.*

Directions
From Roanoke, I-81 south to exits 19, 17, or 14 (Abingdon exits).

CHINCOTEAGUE
Population 4,317

Part of **Chincoteague's** charm comes from its location on an inviting island off Virginia's **Eastern Shore Peninsula**. Another part comes from its long association with wildlife, especially the abundant waterfowl and the famous Chincoteague ponies.

Chincoteague shares an island 7 miles long and 1 1/2 miles wide with marshes, pastures, and other open spaces. The village's history, going as far back as the 1670s, has largely centered on gathering food from the sea—oysters, clams, and fish. The village/island has developed as a resort in more recent times and offers excellent accommodations, restaurants, shops, and boutiques. The shops are known for their wildfowl carvings and their paintings and photographs of wildlife.

As the name suggests, the **Oyster and Maritime Museum** is designed to tell about the island's oyster and seafood industry. A diorama of the channel area, live exhibits of marine life, and implements used in oyster farming are among the items featured.

Chincoteague is also the gateway to **Chincoteague National Wildlife Refuge** and the **Assateague Island National Seashore**. Located at the southern end of Assateague Island, the wildlife refuge is home to over 316 species of birds and, among other animals, the **Chincoteague ponies**. According to legend (reinforced by Spanish archival evidence), the ponies descend from survivors of a wrecked Spanish galleon. Larger than real ponies but smaller than most horses, the animals won fame in Marguerite Henry's book, *Misty of Chincoteague*. Although allowed to roam wild, they are provided with regular veterinary care and plenty of good food. (Tours of the refuge are available. Pets are not allowed into the refuge, even in a car, so make arrangements with a pet-sitter in advance.)

The Assateague Island National Seashore occupies the only barrier island on Virginia's Eastern Shore that is open to the public. In addition to unspoiled woodlands, marshes, and sand dunes, the seashore offers more than 37 miles of beautiful, open beaches. The 145-foot tower of the **Assateague Lighthouse**, one of the few structures on the island, was built in 1857.

Along with the boating, swimming, fishing, and beachcombing that might be expected around coastal islands, Chincoteague and Assateague Islands offer bird-watching, biking along wilderness trails, crabbing, and shellfishing.

> • The sale of young ponies from the south (that is, Virginia) portion of the national seashore provides funds for the local firemen – and also the occasion for an annual carnival.
> • Unlike the rest of Virginia's Eastern Shore, Chincoteague Island maintained its association and commerce with the Union during the Civil War.

Further Information

Chincoteague Chamber of Commerce, *P.O. Box 258, Chincoteague, VA 23336 (757) 336-6161, www.chincoteaguechamber.com.*

Directions

From Norfolk, US 13 north (via Chesapeake Bay Bridge/Tunnel) to VA 175, VA 175 east to Chincoteague.

LEXINGTON
Population 7,568 (including students)

Home to the hallowed halls of **Washington and Lee University** and the **Virginia Military Institute (VMI)**, and once the home of Robert E. Lee and Stonewall Jackson, Lexington is among the South's most historic towns. Nestled in the glorious **Shenandoah Valley**, and boasting a solid collection of restored 19th-century buildings, Lexington is also one of the South's most beautiful towns.

The campuses of Washington and Lee and VMI are both National Historical Landmarks. Washington and Lee, founded in 1749, is a highly respected small (by choice) liberal arts college and law school. The college's most famous president was Robert E. Lee, who took over as head immediately after the Civil War (1865-1870). Probably the most visited building on campus is the **Lee Chapel** (1867), which contains the office (preserved) Lee used when he was the college's president. Also in the chapel are Edward V. Valentine's statue of Lee, Lee's burial place, and Charles W. Peale's famous portrait of George Washington. The 1842 **Lee-Jackson House** was a campus residence of both Stonewall Jackson and General Lee.

Adjacent VMI was the country's first state-supported military college (1839). The college's most famous professor was Stonewall Jackson, its most famous alumnus, George C. Marshall. The **VMI Museum** recalls the history of the college by focusing on the lives of its alums and faculty. Included in the exhibits are the bullet-pierced raincoat that Stonewall Jackson wore at Chancellorsville, 19th-century firearms and daguerreotypes, and uniforms and other items that provide a glimpse of cadet life.

The **George C. Marshall Museum and Library**, also on the VMI campus, features an electric map of World War II, Marshall's Nobel Peace Prize, the Academy Award Oscar won by the producer of the movie *Patton*, and other mementos of the great general's life.

Two sites associated with Stonewall Jackson are the antebellum **Stonewall Jackson Home**, a simple brick townhouse (1801) containing many of Jackson's personal possessions (guided tours available), and the **Stonewall Jackson Memorial Cemetery** (1797), location of Jackson's final resting place and also of Edward V. Valentine's 1891 statue honoring the general. The cemetery also contains the graves of Confederate veterans and two Virginia governors.

Lexington is known for its historic downtown and residential areas. The many lovely old Virginia homes date from the last two decades of the 18th century and from virtually every decade of the 19th, especially the 1840s. Among important non-residential structures are a group of offices, known as **Lawyers Row**, built in the 1880s, and the 1845 Greek Revival **Lexington Presbyterian Church**.

The town is designed for relaxed touring, on foot or maybe on a narrated carriage ride. The visitor center distributes brochures for two walking tours, one of 42 historic sites and one of downtown art galleries.

The two theaters of the **Lenfest Center for the Performing Arts**, on the Washington and Lee campus, stage a variety of plays, musicals, concerts, and recitals. In the summer, the unique outdoor **Theater at Lime Kiln** presents concerts and original stage productions.

Hikers will enjoy both the 2-mile walking trail through Lexington's beautiful **Woods Creek Park** and the 7-mile **Chessie Nature Trail**, which winds from Lexington to Buena Vista alongside the **Maury River**.

Special Features

Lexington is only minutes away from the **Blue Ridge Parkway**, the **Goshen Pass** (a 3-mile mountain gorge), and the famous **Natural Bridge**, a spectacular 215-foot-high limestone arch.

Horse shows and auctions are among the attractions of the nearby 400-acre **Virginia Horse Center**.

> • VMI's military heritage is colorfully displayed on most Fridays during the school year, when at 4:00 p.m. the cadets present a full military dress parade.
> • Thomas Jonathan "Stonewall" Jackson taught natural philosophy (physics) and military tactics at VMI for ten years prior to the Civil War.

▶ HISTORIC LODGINGS ◀

The **Historic Country Inns of Lexington**, *11 N. Main St., (540) 463-2044,* fax *(540) 463-7262, e-mail: mail@lexingtonhistoricinns.com, www.lexingtonhistoricinns.com.* **MAPLE HALL**, plantation home (ca 1850) on National Register and **ALEXANDER-WITHROW HOUSE & McCAMPBELL INN**, circa 1789 & 1809 homes in historic district; 31 rooms & 13 suites, private baths, TV, expanded Cont. breakfasts, dining room in Maple Hall (locally respected), antiques, some fireplaces, swimming pool, tennis. $$ to $$$$

▶ HISTORIC RESTAURANT ◀

THE WILLSON-WALKER HOUSE, *30 N. Main St., (540) 463-3020.* In circa 1820 Classical Revival home with period antiques; regional American cuisine—e.g., North Carolina Potato-Encrusted Trout, Virginia Piedmontese Ribeye, Upside-Down Apple Pie; outdoor dining on verandah. $$

Further Information

Lexington Visitor Center, *106 E. Washington St., Lexington, VA 24450 (540) 463-3777, fax (540) 463-1105, www.lexingtonvirginia.com*

Directions

From Roanoke, I-81 north to exit 188B, west 2 miles to Lexington

SMITHFIELD
Population 6,000

Given **Smithfield's** location near the historic **James River** in Virginia's Tidewater, it should come as no surprise to learn that the town and its county (Isle of Wight) lay claim to the oldest Protestant church, the oldest fort, and one of the oldest courthouses in the United States. But Smithfield is in a relatively quiet part of this venerable region—the Jamestown/Williamsburg/Yorktown Triangle, for example, lies by ferry far on the other side of the

James—and so the town is perfect for the visitor seeking to mix sightseeing and nostalgia with the slower pace of life of a small Southern town.

Isle of Wight County (or "Shire") was formed in 1634, but the river town of Smithfield wasn't chartered until a relatively "late" 1752. The event that eventually put the little town on the map—and a large map at that—was the establishment of a ham curing business in the late 18th century. Smithfield Hams have been famous ever since and have earned the town the title of "Ham Capital of the World."

Begin your stay in the Smithfield area with a stop at the restored **Old Courthouse of 1750**. The Visitors Center, located here, provides information on a walking tour (guided or self-guided) of the **Historic District** as well as on area attractions. The nicely displayed (and frequently changing) exhibits of the **Isle of Wight Museum** on Main Street highlight the county's past from prehistoric times to the present.

Just two miles south is Smithfield's most hallowed place, the restored **St. Luke's Church**, the country's oldest existing church of English foundation (ca 1632). The brick exterior is distinguished by unique buttresses and stepped gables. On the inside are a rare church organ (ca 1665) and 17th-century furnishings and silver. The structure's original traceried windows are especially lovely.

Fort Boykin, now **Fort Boykin Historic Park**, is the oldest fort on American soil (started 1623). Built in the shape of a seven-pointed star, the fort played a role in the Revolutionary War, the War of 1812, and the Civil War. The tree on the fort's parade ground is believed to the second largest black walnut in Virginia.

Like so many Virginia communities, Smithfield has its share of Civil War memories. Local soldiers destroyed a Union gunboat at the Battle of Smithfield (1864), St. Luke's Church was the site of a Confederate campground, and Fort Boykin helped anchor the Confederacy's defense structure. Smithfield was the only Tidewater town to remain in Confederate hands throughout the war.

Smithfield offers the shopper, especially the antiques shopper, a variety of interesting shops and galleries. Visitors are invited to enjoy fine art exhibits, observe working artists, and enroll in classes and workshops at the **Collage Arts Center.** The area, both town and country, is very bicycle-friendly (rentals available). The Pagan River, which Smithfield borders, and the river's tributaries are also very boat- and canoe-friendly (rentals available).

Special Features

The **Ragged Island Wildlife Management Area**, to the east of Smithfield and overlooking the James River, offers the nature hiker and bird watcher over 1,500 acres of native flora and fauna.

Just a few miles north of Smithfield is **Bacon's Castle** (ca 1665), believed to be the oldest house in Virginia (open to public). Given its age, the house has features that are usually seen only on the other side of the Atlantic.

- The salt-cured and pepper-coated Smithfield Ham can only be given the name Smithfield if cured within the town limits of Smithfield.
- Many of the region's most prominent settlers came from the Isle of Wight on England's southern coast; hence the name of the county.

▶ HISTORIC INN ◀

THE SMITHFIELD INN, *112 Main St., (757) 357-1752, e-mail: smithfieldinn@smithfieldfoods.com, www.smithfieldinn.com.* 1752 home with over 250 years of innkeeping experience, 4 rooms & 5 suites, private baths, TV & phones, full breakfasts, dining room with changing menu with "Southern slant," William Rand Tavern, antiques, some fireplaces, George Washington once a guest. $ to $$$

Further Information

Isle of Wight Tourism Bureau, *130 Main St., P.O. Box 37, Smithfield, VA 23431 (757) 357-5182, (800) 365-9339* (ZIP for Smithfield is 23430.)

Directions

From Richmond/Newport News/Hampton, I-64 to Mercury Blvd. & across James River Bridge, US 258 to Smithfield.

WILLIAMSBURG
Population 13,000

A model of restoration and reconstruction respected round the world, the capital of England's largest colony in America has been – and continues to be - retrieved from the 18th century. To understand and appreciate **Williamsburg**, it must be remembered that for many people the town was never a place of drudgery, of daily routine. Williamsburg was a place of government, of education, of intellectual discussion. It was also a place of balls, gambling, and other amusements for visiting members of Virginia's landed gentry. It was a lovely and pleasurable place, just as it is now.

The main artery of **Colonial Williamsburg** is **Duke of Gloucester Street**. Anchoring the western end of the street is the **College of William and Mary**, at the eastern end is the **Capitol**, and overlooking a mall not far from the street's midpoint is the **Governor's Palace**. On and about Duke of Gloucester Street are over 500 restored or reconstructed public buildings, homes, taverns, and stores. The buildings, scattered across 301 acres, are placed about large gardens and greens, giving the town a wonderful (and deliberate) sense of spaciousness.

Check in first at the Visitors Center for admission and other information. Additional information is available throughout the restoration from costumed Colonial interpreters. Do not try to do the town and its environs (see below) in a day—allow at least three days. Carriage rides add romance and relax tired feet.

Chartered in 1693, the **College of William and Mary** is the second oldest college in the country. Two of the campus's most interesting attractions are the restored **Wren Building**, the oldest college building in the country in continuous academic use, and the **Muscarelle Museum of Art**, known for the quality and variety of its changing exhibitions.

The **Governor's Palace** (1708-1720), restored and one of the town's (and nation's) landmarks, was home to seven British governors and Virginia's first two governors. The gardens are beautiful, especially in the spring. Among the rooms of the reconstructed **Capitol** (1705), another landmark, is the **Chamber of the General Court**, one of the country's most beautiful courtrooms.

Three other well-known structures are the **Bruton Parish Church** (1715), in continuous use since its construction, the restored **Magazine** (1715), and **Raleigh Tavern**, popular in the 18th century as well as today for its billiard room. The restored town contains a number of gracious, architecturally important homes.

Although the Historic Area is itself a vast living museum, Colonial Williamsburg is also home to two outstanding enclosed museums. The **Abby Aldrich Rockefeller Folk Art Center** features an incomparable collection of American folk art. The **DeWitt Wallace Gallery** displays English and American silver, glass, paintings, costumes, furniture, textiles, prints, ceramics, rare maps, and other treasures.

Artisans and tradespeople demonstrate 18th-century silversmithing, baking, basket weaving, blacksmithing, furniture making, wig making, bookbinding, gun making, and other skills. The products of their efforts are displayed and offered for sale in quaint restored shops.

The **Virginia Shakespeare Festival** stages productions during the summer months at the College of William and Mary. Visitors to Williamsburg may enjoy golfing, tennis, and swimming.

Special Features

The two other members of the **Historic Triangle**, **Jamestown** and **Yorktown**, are connected to Williamsburg by the Colonial Parkway. Jamestown, the original site of the country's English beginnings (1607), is administered by the **Colonial National Historical Park**. Here there are a visitor center, museum, remains of a 1639 church, and several other historical attractions.

Jamestown Settlement is a living history museum depicting life in Jamestown during the early settlement years. Included are the re-created palisaded fort and replicas of three ships that first brought settlers from England.

Yorktown Battlefield, also administered by the Colonial National Historical Park, is the site of the famous British defeat (self-guided auto tours begin here). The **Yorktown Victory Center**, a museum of the American Revolution, features several excellent indoor exhibits and, outdoors, a re-created Continental Army encampment and a 1780s farm.

Along the banks of the James River is a series of magnificent plantation homes, many graced by gardens and lovely antiques. Open to the public are **Berkeley**, **Edgewood**, **Evelynton**, and **Shirley** plantations.

Busch Gardens Williamsburg, one of the country's most beautiful theme parks, boasts nine European hamlets, each with its own food, entertainment, etc., and a variety of thrilling rides. Nearby **Water Country USA** is the mid-Atlantic's largest water play park.

> • The restoration and rebuilding of Williamsburg, spearheaded by Rev. W. A. R. Goodwin and John D. Rockefeller, Jr., began in the late 1920s.
> • Visitors to the Governor's Palace often are surprised by the communal nature of the royal privy.

▸ HISTORIC LODGINGS ◂

Colonial Williamsburg's Colonial Houses & Taverns offer lodgings in original 18-century houses and houses reconstructed on their original foundations. The houses accommodate from two to twelve people. Many have private gardens. Reservations may be made by calling (800) 447-8679.

▸ HISTORIC RESTAURANTS & TAVERNS ◂

Chowning's, Christiana Campbell's, King's Arms, & Shields taverns are housed in restored or reconstructed buildings in the Historic Area and offer authentic Colonial dishes and 18th-century furnishings. Colonial balladeers entertain diners in several. Call (757) 229-2141 or (800) 447-8679 for reservations (recommended) and information.

Further Information

The Williamsburg Area Convention & Visitors Bureau, *P.O. Box 3585, Williamsburg, VA 23187-3585 (800) 368-6511, www.visitwilliamsburg.com.*

Directions
From Richmond, I-64 east to Williamsburg exits.

Other Charming Virginia Towns
Bedford
Middleburg
Monterey
Strasburg
Warm Springs/Hot Springs
Waterford

Chapter 47

WASHINGTON

LA CONNER
Population 750

At first glance you might take **La Conner** for a New England fishing village, but one double take later and you'll know that the corner of the country you're in is the northwestern, not northeastern, one. For in the distance lie snow-covered peaks, and dotting the countryside are those tall—magnificently tall—spruces and firs and hemlocks that symbolize the Northwest. The yachtsmen and the browsers in the galleries and shops along First Street are far more likely to be Seattleites than Bostonians.

La Conner, known to old-timers as *Channel Town*, hugs a hillside along the Swinomish Channel at the mouth of the **Skagit River**. Originally a trading post founded after the Civil War, the town became a thriving port for produce from farms on the fertile Skagit Flats. The county courthouse and the railroad eventually ended up elsewhere, however, and these and other developments—or lack thereof—put an end to La Conner's growth. "Progress" stopped and many of the original buildings were spared the wrecking ball. It was only a matter of time—the late 1930s in La Conner's case—before the community was discovered by artists and a new life begun.

Now listed on the National Register, La Conner has an ambiance that remains unmistakably salt-water. The wharves, boat yards, and moorings bustle with activity. A favorite getaway for the city-weary, the village affords a variety of inviting shops, restaurants, lodgings, and as might be expected of a town with a long-standing reputation as an art colony, galleries.

Top sights include the colorful **Rainbow Bridge**, which connects the east and west sides of the channel, and three museums. The **Museum of Northwest Art** is known for its fine examples of the Northwest School of art,

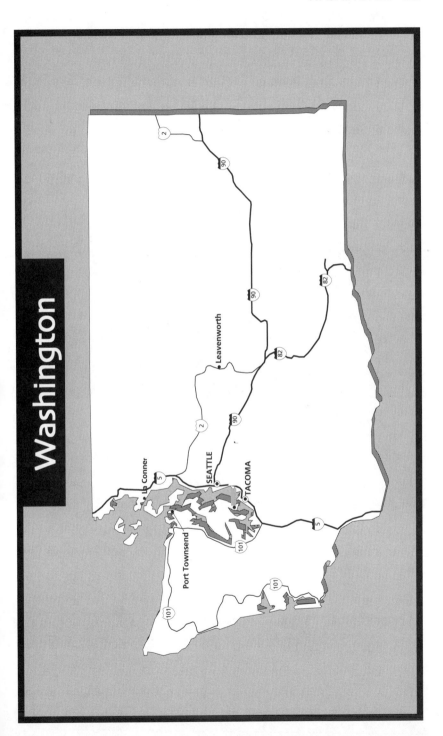

Washington

while the **Skagit County Historical Museum** displays artifacts from the Skagit Valley's pioneer period. The grounds of the historical museum offer wonderful views of La Conner and the landscape beyond. The third museum, the **La Conner Quilt Museum** ("A Quilt Museum for Quilters"), is located within the National Register **Gaches Mansion** (1891).

Special Features

The **Skagit Valley** is a leading producer of vegetables, vegetable seeds, and **flower bulbs**. Daffodils brighten the landscape during March, and during April tulips turn the fields into splashes of living color. Irises have their turn in May.

Views of the famed **San Juan Islands** are among the attractions of a 2 1/2-hour cruise through **Deception Pass**.

• Two of La Conner's more unusual events are February's La Conner Rotary Club Smelt Derby, when landing a fish takes only a jerk, and September's Orphan Car Show, which celebrates out-of-production makes of cars (e.g., Studebakers and Nashes).

• Grain grown on the Skagit Flats was once shipped to Seattle to feed the horses that pulled that city's streetcars.

▶ HISTORIC HOTEL ◀

HOTEL PLANTER, *715 First St., P.O. Box 702, (306) 466-4710, (800) 488-5409, fax (360) 466-1320, e-mail: hotelplanter@aol.com, www.hotelplanter.com.* Restored 1907 hotel on National Register, 12 rooms, private baths, TV & phones, handmade furniture, morning coffee & tea, courtyard, garden hot tub, downtown location. $ to $$$

Further Information

La Conner Chamber of Commerce, *P.O. Box 1610, La Conner, WA 98257 (360) 466-4778, (888) 642-9284.*

Directions

From Seattle, I-5 north to Conway/La Conner exit (Exit 221), west following directional signs through Conway and across Fir Island to Chilberg Road, west to La Conner.

LEAVENWORTH
Population 1,692

Lining the streets of **Leavenworth** are colorful Bavarian buildings with signs announcing "Andreas Keller," "Café Mozart," "Edelweiss Hotel," and dozens of other businesses. The architecture is authentic – some of it in fact was the work of a German designer. The cheerful baskets of flowers hanging from the old (and original) street lamps are distinctly Old World. The dishes in some of the restaurants are genuinely German, in taste as well as name. And although the snow-covered peaks in the background are not the Alps, they are indisputably alpine.

Leavenworth is a true American success story, albeit with a non-American flavor. With its once prosperous lumber and railroad industries gone, Leavenworth needed help. Then, in the 1960s several townspeople began to remodel their businesses using Bavarian styles, styles inspired by the lovely **Cascade Mountain** setting. The idea caught on, although not without controversy, and over the years the town was gradually Bavarianized and revitalized. Today even condominiums, drive-in banks, and motor inns display a Bavarian motif.

Many visitors to the *Bavarian Village of Leavenworth* enjoy the outdoors during the earlier hours of the day and then browse in the shops and relax in the restaurants and pubs during the later hours. The list of outdoor activities seems endless: downhill and cross-country skiing, whitewater or scenery-watching rafting down the **Wenatchee River**, wilderness and scenic canoe trips, guided downhill bicycle trips, rock climbing, fly fishing. For those wishing more passive pursuits there are helicopter tours of the Cascades and dog-sled tours. Neighboring farms and ranches offer old-fashioned sleigh rides, horse-drawn hayrides, horseback rides, and buggy rides.

The list of unique shops also appears endless: There are well over 100 of them. Their offerings describe every conceivable category of arts, crafts, gifts, clothing, foods, and furnishings. Some of the items are American, with emphasis on the Northwest; some are European – for example, Bavarian wax art, Bavarian clothing, and German steins.

Special Features
The **promenade** along the lovely Wenatchee River in **Waterfront Park** offers a cooling break from the shopping, eating, and beer sampling.

> The use of authentic Bavarian designs meant that city building codes governing rooflines, signage, and other features had to be changed.

East of town, along **US 2**, are some of the world's most important pear and apple orchards. Several of the orchards maintain seasonal fruit stands.

Further Information
Leavenworth Chamber of Commerce, *P.O. Box 327, Leavenworth, WA 98826 (509) 548-5807, www.leavenworth.org.*

Directions
From Seattle, I-405 north to WA 522, WA 522 east to US 2, US 2 east to Leavenworth.

PORT TOWNSEND
Population 8,500

Prosperous from its lumber trade with booming California, **Port Townsend** was just as important in the 1880s as the Port of Seattle, also on **Puget Sound**. Businesses flourished and mansions rose. But the train never came to Port Townsend, and that and several other fateful developments drove Seattle to greatness and froze Port Townsend in time. A hundred years later Port Townsend has the largest collection of Victorian buildings north of San Francisco. It is one of only four towns in the country designated a Victorian Seaport by the National Register of Historic Places.

Sailboats and other craft still move about the harbor of the old port town. The facades of the buildings on **Water Street**, Port Townsend's downtown, are authentically Victorian even if the specialty shops, galleries, and restaurants within are not. Many of the buildings in **Uptown**, on the bluff, are also original, and here too shops, galleries, and restaurants beckon. Elsewhere in the older parts of town are Victorian-era churches, cottages, and mansions. The Chamber of Commerce's historical tour map lists 72 sites. There is clearly much Victoriana to see, and the interested visitor is well-advised to take the self-guided Seagull Tour or one of the historical sidewalk tours.

Of special note downtown is the 1889 **Hastings Building**, the first building in town to sport a two-story court with skylight. On the bluff behind is the restored **Old Bell Tower** (1890). The **Jefferson County Courthouse** (1892), one of the two oldest courthouses in the state, is behind the bluff. The building's clock tower is a landmark, offshore as well as in town.

Port Townsend is probably best known for its many fine restored Victorian homes. So many of these are now bed and breakfasts that the town is sometimes nicknamed the *bed and breakfast capital of Washington.*

There are two houses of special historic interest that are open to the public but are not bed and breakfasts. One is the 1868 **Rothschild House**, a state heritage site on the National Register of Historic Places. Most of the house's furnishings, carpets, and wall papers are original. The second house is the **Commanding Officer's Quarters** at **Fort Worden State Park** (see below). This beautiful 1904 home has been carefully and authentically restored and refurnished.

Special Features

Fort Worden State Park adjoins the town on the north. Turn-of-the-century Fort Worden was built as part of a Puget Sound defense system. On the grounds are restored officers' houses, barracks (now available for conventions and conferences), parade grounds, and artillery bunkers.

The fort is also home to the **Centrum Foundation**, a non-profit organization that promotes the arts. Many varieties of Washington's state flower, the rhododendron, are on display in the **Centennial Rhododendron Garden**, also on the grounds.

- Uptown in Port Townsend was established so that Victorian women could shop somewhere other than the rowdy downtown waterfront area.
- The bell in St. Paul's Episcopal Church (1865) was donated by a ship's captain on condition that it be rung in foggy weather to warn vessels.

▶ HISTORIC RESTAURANT ◀

MANRESA CASTLE, *7th & Sheridan sts., (800) 732-1281*. In 1892 castle; fresh local seafood & regional cuisine—e.g., King Salmon Rosette, Curried Chicken Manresa; antiques. $$ to $$$

Further Information

Port Townsend Chamber of Commerce, *2437 E. Sims Way, Port Townsend, WA 98368 (360) 385-2722, www.olympus.net/ptchamber*

Directions

From Seattle, ferry from downtown to Bainbridge Island (Winslow), WA 305 to WA 3, north on WA 3 to WA 104, west on WA 104 across Hood Canal Bridge to WA 19, north on WA 19 to Port Townsend (approx. 1 3/4 hrs); from Tacoma, WA 16 north to WA 3, continue as from Seattle above.

Nearby **Jefferson County International Airport** is served by Port Townsend Airways flying from Sea-Tac International Airport.

Other Charming Washington Towns

Chelan
Gig Harbor
Ilwaco
Roslyn
Winthrop

Chapter 48

WEST VIRGINIA

BERKELEY SPRINGS
Population 735

Nestled in the hills of West Virginia, the village of **Berkeley Springs** has the distinction of being the country's first spa. George Washington used to come here to bathe in the warm mineral waters and to promenade and relax with friends. In fact, Washington—along with three signers of the Declaration of Independence, four signers of the Constitution, five Revolutionary generals, etc. – bought lots here when the town was platted in 1776. The place has been a resort ever since.

Today the name "Berkeley Springs" applies to a rather large area: the **springs**, the tiny **state park** that includes them, the tiny town that surrounds the park, the settled area around the town limits, and indeed, the entire eastern side of the mountains in Morgan County. The town is officially known as "Bath," but historically has been postmarked "Berkeley Springs" to avoid confusion with another Bath (in Virginia).

Within the state park, springs discharge about 2,000 gallons of clear, odorless mineral water per minute at a temperature of 74.3 degrees Fahrenheit. The park's two bathhouses allow the visitor a choice among a Roman bath in an individual sunken pool, a soak in a conventional tub, massage treatments, and in the summer, a plunge in a swimming pool. There are also several private spas. The **Roman Bath House** has been in service as a bathhouse since its construction around 1815. A museum on the second floor provides an excellent introduction to the park and its history. A row of unusual shops lines the street facing the park.

The town of Berkeley Springs (or Bath) has a number of quaint late 19th-century structures, some of them now bed and breakfasts. Markers identify

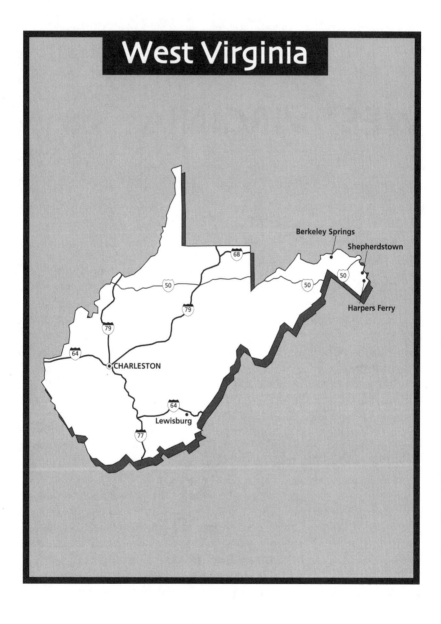

the village's first platted lots and their owners. The village and its setting are especially popular with artists.

Special Features

The overlook at **Prospect Peak**, five miles west of town on **WV 9**, offers a fabulous view. A couple of miles beyond is the quaint river-side hamlet of **Great Cacapon**.

> • The colors used throughout the state park—yellow, cream, and green—are original colors of the Federal period.
> • The large wooden hotels that visitors to the springs used to stay at have all disappeared, often through fire.

Further Information

Berkeley Springs-Morgan County Chamber of Commerce, *127 Fairfax St., Berkeley Springs, WV 25411 (304) 258-3738, Visitors Center (800) 447-8797, www.berkeleysprings.com.*

Directions

From Washington (DC), I-270 north to Frederick (MD), I-70 (by Hagerstown, MD) to exit 1B, US 522 south to Berkeley Springs.

HARPERS FERRY
Population about 308

Harpers Ferry is a photogenic little town situated in the **Blue Ridge Mountains** at the confluence of the Potomac and Shenandoah rivers. On a visit here in 1783 Thomas Jefferson described the view from the summit of (now) Jefferson Rock "worth a voyage across the Atlantic." Today a National Historical Park, Harpers Ferry's early to mid 19th-century architecture seems to compliment the scenery. Some of the town's streets look much as they did 140 years ago.

In the 1790s George Washington selected Harpers Ferry as a site for a national armory. Later, during the 1830s, both the **Chesapeake & Ohio Canal** and **Baltimore & Ohio Railroad** came through town. By the middle of the 19th century, Harpers Ferry had become an important arms-producing and transportation center with a population several times what it is today.

Then came John Brown's famous 1859 raid followed in a few months by the Civil War. The armory was burned in 1861 to keep it from falling into

Confederate hands. The rest of the town suffered, in spirit as well as structure, during the war years as control swung between the North and the South. A series of floods in the late 1800s pretty much put an end to any remaining hope that Harpers Ferry might revitalize. The little town and its buildings stood still and abandoned.

Many of the buildings have been restored by the National Park Service; others are undergoing, or will undergo, restoration. The best way to see Harpers Ferry is to park at the visitors center and take a shuttle bus to the "Lower Town." The center offers talks by park rangers, conducted tours, and information on self-guided tours.

Many of the town's (and park's) restored buildings have exhibits and media presentations. Of special interest are the **Stagecoach Inn** (1826-1834), which serves as the bookstore; the **Master Armorer's House** (1858), now an information center; and the **Harper House** (1775-1782), the oldest surviving structure in the park. The **Dry Goods Store** (1812) has been restored to look like an 1850s dry goods store. Also of interest is the **Confectionery** (1844-1857), once the home of one of Harper Ferry's most respected citizens. Two of the town's restored buildings house museums that recall the lives and suffering of the townspeople during the Civil War.

On **Camp Hill** are several buildings, constructed in the 1840s and 1850s, that once served as homes for armory officials. Although damaged in the Civil War, they were rebuilt after the war and used to establish **Storer College**, a school for freed blacks. Storer College operated between 1869 and 1955.

The **John Brown Wax Museum**, housed in a historic building, traces the career of the controversial Abolitionist with figures and scenes made life-like with electronic lighting, sound, and animation. Other points of interest in Harpers Ferry include **St. Peter's Catholic Church** (1830s, remodeled 1890s) and the **Appalachian Trail Conference Visitors Center**, which distributes information and items relating to the country's best-known footpath.

Harpers Ferry and its scenic surroundings support a rich variety of sports and other activities. White-water rafting, canoeing, kayaking, and tubing are popular on the area's rivers and streams. The restored **Chesapeake & Ohio Canal Towpath** offers great hiking and bicycling (bike rentals available). Hikers will find a number of other mapped trails as well, including the Appalachian Trail. Rumor has it that the small-mouth bass fishing doesn't get much better. The same goes for the antique hunting.

The remnants of 19th-century factories and waterways may be explored on **Virginius Island** on the **Shenandoah River**. The National Park Service maintains (and publishes a guide to) an island trail.

Special Features

The National Park Service's **Maryland Heights Trail** leads to Civil War batteries and fort ruins—and a series of magnificent views.

Five minutes to the west is historic **Charles Town**, laid out by George Washington's brother Charles. The tree-lined streets of the town are bordered by many lovely old homes, churches, and other buildings. Not far from Charles town is delightful little **Middleway**, also historic.

> • Members of the Lewis and Clark expedition carried arms made by Harper Ferry's armory.
> • A popular way to see Harpers Ferry is by an evening "ghost tour." Check locally for information.

Further Information
Jefferson County Convention & Visitors Bureau, *P.O. Box A, Harpers Ferry, WV 25425 (800) 848-8687.*

Directions
From Washington (DC), I-270 northwest to Frederick (MD), US 340 west to Harpers Ferry.

LEWISBURG
Population 3,980

It's rare for a town steeped in history and blessed with a scenic setting to show a natural continuity with time, to be more concerned with today's soccer game than with attempts to lure visitors with the contrived. But **Lewisburg** is that kind of town, the way towns used to be, at least according to the romantic. Some say the town is more 1940s than 1990s – the *real* '40s, that is.

Chartered in 1782, Lewisburg's 236-acre National Register Historic District has no fewer than 72 sites, including 50 antebellum homes and 11 buildings erected before the War of 1812. Antique and specialty shops now occupy many of these historic structures.

The first stop on a town tour should be the four-story **Carnegie Hall** (1902), which houses the visitors center. Funded by Andrew Carnegie and called "the other Carnegie Hall," the hall has 22 classrooms and studios, a 360-seat auditorium, and live performances by leading artists.

Two other tour musts are the **Old Stone Presbyterian Church** (1796), the oldest church west of the Alleghenies remaining in continuous use, and the Colonial 1820 **John A. North House**, now home to the museum of the **Greenbrier Historical Society**. (Schedule at least two and a half hours for a full walking tour of the town. Horse-and-carriage tours offer a less energetic option.)

Lewisburg's natural endowment is as rich as its history. Located in the gorgeous **Greenbrier River Valley**, Lewisburg sits amongst mountains and forests just three miles from the beautiful 126-mile unpolluted **Greenbrier River**. Evergreens, maples, rhododendrons, and other flora guarantee four seasons of color.

Special Features

Hikers and bikers will find the 76-mile-long **Greenbrier River Trail** (an old C&O Railroad bed) a custom-made paradise.

Smallmouth-bass fishing is reputed to be better in the Greenbrier River than in any other river in the country. Canoeing is also great.

The Monroe County Historical Society publishes a brochure, *The Springs Trail*, for a driving tour of the many historic springs and resorts of the Greenbrier Valley. Along the way are the 12-columned spring pavilion at **Blue Sulphur Springs**, once a magnificent resort, and the famous Greenbrier Resort at **White Sulphur Springs**. The latter has been a resort since Colonial times.

Names scratched by soldiers wounded in the Civil War Battle of Lewisburg can be seen in a section of old plaster in the Greenbrier County Library (1834).

▶ HISTORIC HOTEL ◀

THE GENERAL LEWIS, *301 E. Washington St., (304) 645-2600, (800) 628-4454, fax (304) 645-2601, e-mail: info@generallewisinn.com, www.generallewisinn.com*. East wing originally an 1834 house, 25 rooms, private baths, TV & phones, respected dining room, antiques throughout, worth a visit in own right. $$ to $$$

Further Information

Greenbrier County Convention & Visitors Bureau, *111 N. Jefferson St., Lewisburg, WV 24901 (800) 833-2068.*

Directions

From Charleston, I-64 south to exit 169, south to Lewisburg.

SHEPHERDSTOWN
Population 1,287

Shepherdstown is an historic little college town overlooking the **Potomac River**. West Virginia's oldest town (first settled around 1730), Shepherdstown is rich in 18th- and 19th-century commercial and residential buildings. It is also quite cosmopolitan, with sophisticated shops, restaurants, and entertainments. The town is nicely positioned for regional sightseeing – and the region offers much to see, including the **Antietam National Battlefield**, historic **Harpers Ferry** (see listing), and some gorgeous mountain scenery.

The **Historic Shepherdstown Museum**, housed in the **Entler Hotel** (1793/1809), displays items from the town's past. Among the exhibits are a restored formal parlor, hotel bedroom, and Victorian sitting room. On the grounds is the **Rumsey Steamboat Museum**, which houses a half-size working replica of the world's first steamboat, built and demonstrated at Shepherdstown by James Runsey in 1787. (Elsewhere in town an impressive monument to James Rumsey, built in 1917, overlooks the Potomac). Other historic structures include the **Public Library** (1800/1845), once a farmers' market, and the **Shepherd Grist Mill** (ca 1738), which boasts the oldest and largest (40 ft in diameter) cast-iron overshot waterwheel in the world (1891).

In July and August **Shepherd College's Contemporary American Theater Festival**, a professional repertory theater, presents new plays. The festival also offers a late-night improv cabaret. On-screen entertainment is provided at the restored **Old Opera House** (1909); foreign and contemporary American films are featured.

Shepherdstown's shops offer a variety of crafts, antiques, decorative accessories, books, and gifts. One of the bakeries specializes in European breads.

The restored **Chesapeake & Ohio Canal Towpath** is made to order for hikers and bikers (see also Harpers Ferry).

- Shepherdstown, then named Mecklenburg, was the starting point for a contingent of local volunteers who hiked with considerable speed to Boston to join George Washington's Continental Army. The march is remembered as the Bee Line March.
- It was at Shepherdstown Pack Horse Ford where General Lee's army recrossed the Potomac after withdrawing from Antietam.

Special Features

Antietam National Battlefield and Cemetery is four or so miles northeast of Shepherdstown. On September 17, 1862, more men were killed or wounded here than on any other day of the Civil War.

Further Information

Jefferson County Visitor & Convention Bureau, *P.O. Box A, Harpers Ferry, WV 25425 (800) 848-8687; also,* **Shepherdstown Visitors Center**, *P.O. Box 329, Shepherdstown, WV 25443 (304) 876-2786, www.ShepherdstownVisitorsCenter.com.*

Directions

From Baltimore, I-70 west to Frederick (MD), US 340 west to Harpers Ferry (WV), WV 230 (two miles past Harpers Ferry) to Shepherdstown; from Washington (DC), I-270 to Frederick (MD), proceed as from Baltimore above.

Other Charming West Virginia Towns

Charles Town
Elkins
Marlinton
Martinsburg
Sistersville
Union

Chapter 49

WISCONSIN

BAYFIELD
Population 686

The tiny fishing village of **Bayfield** lies on a natural harbor on the southern shore of **Lake Superior**. Commercial fishing, lumbering, brownstone quarrying, and tourism helped build the village, especially during the late 19th and very early 20th centuries. In the end tourism proved to be the only really reliable industry, however, and Bayfield stood still as Duluth and other cities took over. Left behind was a village containing, among other things, a delightful collection of Victorian houses.

Bayfield is today a popular summer resort for fishermen and deep-water sailors. Many of the old homes are listed on the National Register; some have been restored and opened as bed and breakfast inns.

A lush **Nature Trail** winds along a ravine and under the **Old Iron Bridge** (1912; pedestrians only). The trail begins across the street from the **Bayfield Library** (1903). Bayfield's streets can be explored by foot or bicycle. Many of the businesses stay open all winter.

Offshore are the 21 pristine islands of **Apostle Islands National Lakeshore**, guarded by six picturesque **lighthouses**. Information on the lighthouses and other features of the lakeshore can be obtained at the **Apostle Islands National Lakeshore Headquarters**, housed in the brownstone **Old Bayfield County Courthouse** (1894).

The beauty of the Apostle Islands and the lighthouses (all built before 1874) can be experienced by private or excursion boat. A lighthouse tour is one of several excursion options. Check with the Chamber of Commerce for schedules and other tour information.

Wisconsin

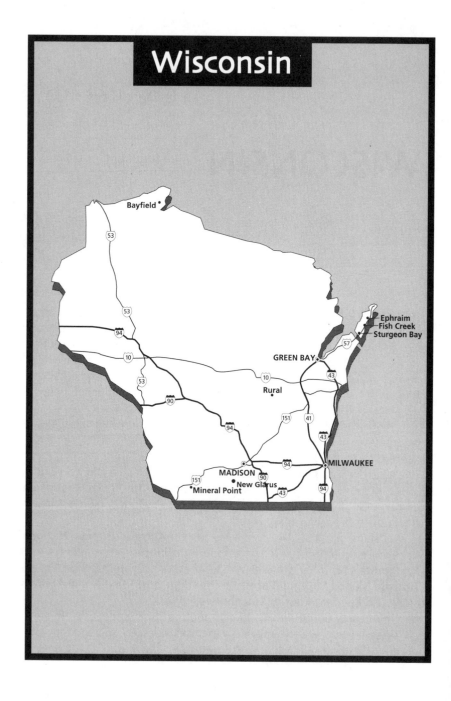

Bayfield

Ephraim
Fish Creek
Sturgeon Bay

GREEN BAY

Rural

MADISON

New Glarus

Mineral Point

MILWAUKEE

A 22nd island, **Madeline**, is big enough to support its own village (**La Pointe**) and other attractions. Access to Madeline Island (population 150) is made interesting by Bayfield's northern latitude. A ferry (20-minute ride) suffices for the warmer months. During the winter, however, the thickness of the ice makes it possible to drive your car to the island. Pine trees are set up on the ice to mark the way. During months when the ice is less thick, people are carried back and forth by a wind sled driven by a large propeller.

Special Features

Madeline Island is home to a historical museum, a state park with nature trails and sailboat charters, and a challenging 18-hole golf course. The historical museum, comprising four historic log buildings, preserves artifacts from the island's Indian, fur-trading, missionary, and later eras. Bus tours of the island are available from late June to early October.

Civil War songs, Broadway favorites, bluegrass, contemporary jazz, Swedish songs, and many other kinds of music fill the tent during the summer months at the **Lake Superior Big Top Chautauqua** three miles south of town.

Motorists, bicyclists, and hikers who wish to explore the local countryside will be treated to everything from purple drifts of lupine in the spring to bountiful orchards in the summer to riots of color in the fall. Honey, maple syrup, fresh-cut flowers, and preserves may be obtained along the way. Farmers and orchard keepers invite visitors to pick strawberries, raspberries, blueberries, blackberries, cherries, apples, and pears.

• Bayfield has its own delicacies: fish chowders, blueberry pancakes, fresh fruit pies, homegrown raspberries—and deep-fried whitefish livers! Depending on the age of the fish and skill of the cook, the flavor of the livers can vary from fishy and strong to delicately delicious.

• The first lighthouse authorized in these waters (1852) was mistakenly constructed on the wrong island.

Scuba divers will find sunken schooners, barges, and ore carriers preserved in the cold waters of Lake Superior. (Divers should register with the National Park Service.)

▶ HISTORIC INNS ◀

GREUNKE'S FIRST STREET INN, *17 Rittenhouse Ave., P.O. Box 768, (800) 245-3072, (715) 779-9840, e-mail: strom@ncis.net, www.greunkesinn.com.* 1865 boarding house with 12 rooms, some private baths, some TVs, respected dining room (featuring Lake Superior fish), antiques, some pets, down comforters. $ to $$$

OLD RITTENHOUSE INN, *301 Rittenhouse Ave., P.O. Box 584, (715) 779-5111, (800) 779-2129, fax (715) 779-5887, e-mail: gourmet@rittenhouseinn.com, www.rittenhouseinn.com.* Two late 19th- & early 20th-century Queen Anne mansions, 16 rooms & 2 suites, cottage, private baths (some whirlpools), expanded Cont. breakfasts, dining room, antiques, wood-burning fireplaces, lake views, wrap-around porch. $$ to $$$$

Further Information

Bayfield Chamber of Commerce, *P.O. Box 138, Bayfield, WI 54814 (715) 779-3335, (800) 447-4094.*

Directions

From Duluth (MN), US 53 south to WI 13, WI 13 east to Bayfield.

EPHRAIM/FISH CREEK
Population 200/200

Door County and its tiny harbor villages of **Ephraim** and **Fish Creek** are Wisconsin's answer to New England. Both villages have fine old white clapboard houses and inns and attract cyclists and other tourists with their upscale shops and magnificent fall foliage. Both also look out over blue water, shelter yachts in their harbors, and offer sailing cruises.

Maybe departing a little from some New England harbor towns, both back against scenic bluffs. And because they lie on the **Green Bay**, or west, side of the **Door Peninsula**, both depart dramatically from New England by enjoying sunsets over the water rather than sunrises. Indeed, some of the areas along the main road in Ephraim are kept undeveloped just to maintain the open views of the water and the spectacular sunsets.

Separated by five miles, Ephraim and Fish Creek are similar, but they're hardly twins. Ephraim is dry and Fish Creek is wet (this alone gives each a different character), Ephraim stretches along the water and Fish Creek is compact, Ephraim has more historic buildings and Fish Creek has more shops, galleries, and cultural events. Both are engaging.

Ephraim has several historic structures that are open to the public. The best known is the **Anderson Store**, a restored 1858 general store that displays merchandise from the early 20th century. Two other buildings are the 1869 **Pioneer School**, with desks and other artifacts of 1920s vintage, and the **Anderson Barn Museum** (ca 1880), which features historic exhibits and a permanent art collection.

Door County is famous for its strawberries, cherries, and apples – late May is the time to see the blooms. The county is also famous for its windsurfing and other water sports. Bicycle, sailboat, canoe, sea kayak, and cross-country ski rentals are available. So are sailboat and sea kayak lessons.

Special Features

Peninsula State Park, which lies between the two villages, offers breathtaking views of Green Bay from its limestone bluffs. The park is home to the charming **Eagle Bluff Lighthouse** (1868), also a museum; the **American Folklore Theater**, a professional theater company that does summer musicals; and the beautiful 18-hole **Peninsula Park Course**.

The oldest professional summer stock company in the country, the **Peninsula Players**, performs in the **Theater-in-a-Garden**, an open-to-air theater south of Fish Creek.

To do a "Door County Fish Boil," boil new potatoes and baby onions (optional) in a cauldron over an open fire until they're nearly done, add Lake Michigan whitefish or trout, and finally, stoke the fire with kerosene and boil unwanted "fishy" oils off the top. Serve with coleslaw and cherry pie.

▶ HISTORIC INN ◀

THE WHISTLING SWAN INN, *4192 Main St., P.O. Box 193 (Fish Creek), (920) 868-3442, fax (920) 868-1703, e-mail: jroberts@whistlingswan.com, www.whistlingswan.com.* Restored 1887 inn on National Register, Door Peninsula's oldest operating inn, 5 rooms & 2 suites, private baths, TV & phones, expanded Cont. breakfasts, antiques, lobby with fireplace & baby grand piano, refreshments, glass-enclosed verandah, gardens, views, boutique. $$ to $$$$

▶ HISTORIC RESTAURANT ◀

WILSON'S RESTAURANT & ICE CREAM PARLOR, *WI 42 (Ephraim), (920) 854-2041.* Est. 1906, famous ice cream, lighter fare. $

Further Information

Door County Chamber of Commerce, *P.O. Box 406, 1015 Green Bay Rd., Sturgeon Bay, WI 54235 (800) 527-3529, fax (920) 743-7873, www.doorcounty.com (ZIPS for Ephraim & Fish Creek are 54211 & 54212, respectively.)*

Directions

From Milwaukee, I-43 north to exit 185 (Green Bay), WI 57 north to Sturgeon Bay, WI 42 north to Fish Creek and Ephraim.

MINERAL POINT
Population 2,617

People from **Mineral Point** traveling in England have been known to remark on the similarity between parts of that country and the rolling, green countryside of their Wisconsin home. The pastoral beauty of southwestern Wisconsin does indeed recall the beauty of rural England, but there is more to the similarity than that.

Families from Cornwall (England) settled in Mineral Point following the discovery of lead early in the 19th century. Bringing with them the skills of the stonemason as well as the miner, the settlers built rock houses similar to those of their native Cornwall. Many of these houses survive, and continue even today to impart a certain English character to Mineral Point.

The hilly, winding streets of Mineral Point carry the similarity to parts of England even further. And so does the state historical society's **Pendarvis Complex**, a group of six restored Cornish miners' cottages built in the 1840s.

The architectural character and variety of many of Mineral Point's other buildings are much more American. The styles range from early log through Federal to Victorian and Italian Renaissance. Of special note are the limestone Italianate **Gundry House** (1867), now a museum owned and operated by the local historical society, and the **Mineral Point Theatre**, a vaudeville and performing arts house with full proscenium and balcony, built in 1914. The latter's magnificent 400-seat auditorium is still used for movie presentations, performances by a local theater group, and other events. A driving-tour brochure focusing on these and other important buildings in Mineral Point is distributed by the visitors bureau.

Mineral Point has been respected as an art center since the 1940s. Over 30 artists and artisans display their work in 15 (at last count) galleries, studios, and shops. Opportunity to observe work in progress is provided by artists in a wide variety of mediums. The town also boasts a large number of individual and group antique shops. The various studios and shops are scattered about town. Many are on **High Street** (the English name for a main street) and **Commerce Street**.

Special Features

North of Mineral Point is the **House on the Rock**, a contemporary 14-room house built on top of a tower of rock. The house is the original structure of a 200-acre complex featuring such attractions as a gas-lit Main Street, the world's largest carousel, a collection of animated music machines, a miniature circus, and a collection of 250 doll houses. Billed as Wisconsin's number-one tourist attraction, some visitors describe the exhibits as unique and fascinating, others as overwhelming, even dizzying.

North of the House on the Rock, near **Spring Green**, is Frank Lloyd Wright's famous home, **Taliesin East** (open to the public).

> • Early miners in Mineral Point dug out burrows resembling badger holes in the hillsides for shelter. Hence the Badger State, Wisconsin's nickname.
> • A Cornish pasty (PASS tee) usually consists of beef, potatoes, and onions sealed in a flaky crust. The Cornish dessert, Figgy Hobbin, consists of a pastry crust with raisins, nuts, and other sweets served with a caramel sauce. These and other Cornish items are available locally.

▶ HISTORIC RESTAURANT & LODGING ◀

MINERAL SPIRITS SALOON & CAFÉ, *20 Commerce St., (608) 987-3682*. In 1850s stone Cornish inn, recipient of award for best historic renovation in Wisconsin in 2000, daily pasta specials, vegetarian dishes, seafood & steak entrees, "The Art of Fish"—featuring a different fish experience nightly, local micro brews on tap served in chilled pints, brick-lined patio. $$

BREWERY CREEK INN, *23 Commerce St., (608) 987-3298, (fax) (608) 987-4388, e-mail: info@brewerycreek.com, www.brewerycreek.com*. In 1854 3-story limestone warehouse & 1845 stone home, 7 suites, private baths (whirlpools), TV & phones, expanded Cont. breakfasts, restaurant, microbrewery & pub with furnishings from England, antiques & reproductions, fireplaces, exposed stone walls. $$$ to $$$$

Further Information

Mineral Point Visitors Bureau, *225 High St., Mineral Point, WI 53565 (608) 987-3201, (888) 764-6894, www.mineralpoint.com*.

Directions

From Madison, US 151 west (via Dodgeville) to Mineral Point.

NEW GLARUS
Population 1,900

New Glarus, "America's Little Switzerland," nicely illustrates two reasons why Wisconsin's borders embrace such a large number of charming towns. First, the state is respected among preservationists for its strong commitment to protecting its past, and, sure enough, New Glarus has for decades committed itself to the preservation of its Swiss cultural heritage. Second, Wisconsin is blessed with some of the loveliest countryside in the Middle West, and indeed, New Glarus owes part of its charm to its setting in the rolling woods and pastureland of bucolic south-central Wisconsin.

New Glarus was established in 1845 by immigrants from Glarus, Switzerland. Unlike many towns in this book, the village's ethnic roots didn't gradually go underground and then resurface 100 or more years later; the people have always been conscious—and proud—of their Swiss roots. New Glarus is today a village with Swiss buildings surrounded by festive Swiss flags, canton shields, and gardens. And boxes and wine barrels full of flowers, especially geraniums. The town has been voted the most picturesque (and friendliest!) in Wisconsin in magazine polls.

The Victorian and other styles of most of New Glarus's homes remind that this is after all a wealthy Midwestern town, but many of the commercial and public buildings are of one or another Swiss design, contemporary as well as traditional. A good example is the **Chalet of the Golden Fleece Museum** (1937), built in the Bernese Mountain Chalet style. A recommended stop on any tour of the town, the museum has three floors packed with such unique antiques as a King Louis XVI jeweled watch, Etruscan earrings, a 1661 slate inlaid table, and a circa 1760 Swiss porcelain tile stove. Swiss woodcarvings, painted furniture, and samplers are among the many other items on display.

The **Swiss Historical Village Museum** is a grouping of 13 buildings situated on a beautifully landscaped hilltop. The central building is the **Hall of History**, with exhibits that trace the history of the Swiss immigration to New Glarus. Designed to portray 19th-century Midwestern life, other buildings in the museum include a replica of the town's first log church, a cheese factory, a firehouse, and a Swiss-style bee house. Live demonstrations of various crafts are sometimes offered.

Shops and restaurants offer Swiss food (fondue included), pastries, specialty sausages, cheeses, and European-style beers. Swiss bells, Swiss stoneware, Swiss alphorns, and, of course, Swiss chocolates also reside on shop shelves. An award-winning brewery and a winery that presses Wisconsin-grown grapes give even the economy a Swiss flavor. Swiss yodelers and accordion players are never far away, neither are speakers of Swiss German.

Special Features

One of the best ways to take in southern Wisconsin's delightful country-side is to bike the winding 23-mile **Sugar River State Trail** (bike rentals and shuttle service available). The trail's headquarters and northern entry point are in New Glarus. Two local golf courses offer additional outdoor recreation.

New Glarus's many **annual events** (e.g., Polkafest, Heidi Festival, Octoberfest, Volksfest, Wilhelm Tell Festival, New Glarus Winterfest) feature, among countless other entertainments, dancing, dramatic productions, and performances by the Maennerchor, a men's Swiss choral group.

> Visitors should keep an eye out for the whimsical painted cows that have been decorated by local artists. They tend to appear in some rather unexpected places.

▶ HISTORIC RESTAURANTS ◀

DEININGER'S RESTAURANT, *119 5th Ave., P.O. Box 789, (608) 527-2012, www.deiningers.com.* In charming 1896 home; Continental European cuisine—e.g., "Choucroute Garnie" Alsatian Sauerkraut Plate, Koningsberger Klopse, Breast of Turkey Schnitzel; daily specials; chef from Alsace (France): family-owned & operated; reservations recommended. $$

PUEMPEL'S OLD TAVERN, *18 6th Ave., (608) 527-2045.* Tavern est. in 1893, daily soup & sandwich specials, local sausage & cheese (incl. Limburger), original 1912 cherry-wood back bar, 1913 folk murals, beer garden. $ (lunch)

Further Information

New Glarus Visitor Information, *P.O. Box 713, New Glarus, WI 53574 (608) 527-2095, (800) 527-6838, www.swisstown.com.*

Directions

From Madison, US 18/151 west to Verona, WI 69 south to New Glarus.

RURAL
Population about 250

In tiny **Rural** the **Crystal River** twists and turns through back yards, front yards, sometimes both yards. Whenever and wherever you step outside, you're probably going to see this beautiful little river. During the warmer months you can even sit on your porch or in your gazebo and wave at the passing skiffs and canoes. And whenever you walk down the street – and walking is what people do – you're going to cross a bridge.

This idyllic place, now a National Historic District, is the only restored intact village in Wisconsin that was settled by immigrants from the British Isles. Many of the lovely homes date from the 1850s. Following a not uncommon scenario for charming towns, Rural was bypassed by the railroad and thereby condemned to be frozen in time.

The village measures no more than about two by four blocks. The commercial area is pretty much restricted to one genuinely old-fashioned general store and maybe one or two antique and craft shops. The rest of the village consists of homes, and all but a half dozen date from another era. The homes and intertwining river are exceptionally beautiful when the trees are in their October colors.

To the east of the village is the **Red Mill**, an old mill (1855) that today boasts the largest waterwheel in the state. Close by is a covered bridge authentically constructed in 1970 from original plans. The site also includes a gift shop and a quaint chapel popular for weddings.

Rural is just downstream from Wisconsin's renowned **Chain O'Lakes**, a chain of 22 scenic spring-fed lakes. The lakes can be toured by cruise boats or canoe—of course, if you go very far by canoe, you'll eventually find yourself winding back through Rural.

Special Features

The **Hutchinson House** in nearby **Waupaca** is an 1854 Greek Revival mansion overlooking a lake. The grand old house, now a museum, can be visited by appointment.

Miles of hiking and groomed ski trails can be pursued at **Hartman Creek State Park**, a few miles northwest of town. Among the park's attractions are sandy swimming beaches and facilities for winter camping.

Further Information

Gene & Lois Sorenson (Crystal River B&B), *1369 Rural Rd., Waupaca, WI 54981 (715) 258-5333*

Directions

From Milwaukee, US 41 north to Oshkosh, WI 21 west to Wautoma, WI 22 north to Rural.

STURGEON BAY
Population 9,176

Marking the 250-mile shoreline of Wisconsin's scenic **Door Peninsula** are cliffs, rocky coves, harbors, and little villages that are reminiscent of New England (see Ephraim and Fish Creek). In the peninsula's interior are some of Wisconsin's famous cherry and apple orchards. Straddling an isthmus half-way up the peninsula, 40 miles from its tip, **Sturgeon Bay** is ideally situated as a home base for touring this delightful area.

Decades of sawmills, stone quarries, an ice industry, shipbuilding, and most recently, tourism have brought prosperity to Sturgeon Bay and left a legacy of handsome buildings. There are over 100 buildings of historic or special architectural interest in the town; 42 are within two historic districts. Many were built during the last decade of the 19th century and first decade of the 20th. The styles range from those of the Victorian period to Craftsman and American Foursquare. The information center publishes a historic tour map for strollers, bikers, and drivers wishing a self-guided tour.

Sturgeon Bay has two good regional history museums. Among the displays of the **Door County Historical Museum** are a turn-of-the-century fire station with antique fire trucks, a replica of an early Door County home, and exhibits depicting the history of shipbuilding in Door County. The two-story **Maritime Museum** features boats from the early part of the 20th century as well as an actual 1907 Great Lakes pilothouse.

Helping to uphold Door County's traditional stress on the arts, the **Miller Art Museum** maintains a permanent collection of 20th-century Wisconsin art as well as a performing arts schedule. Another collection, that of the **William S. Fairfield Public Gallery**, features works of the renowned English sculptor and artist Henry Moore. Both galleries sponsor series of changing exhibits. Sturgeon Bay is also home to a number of art, craft, and antique shops.

Four-hour van tours of Door County depart regularly from Sturgeon Bay. Surrounded as it is by water and beautiful beaches, the Sturgeon Bay area offers a long list of water sports, including snorkeling, scuba diving and sailing. For those more interested in indoor pursuits, there are guided tours of a microbrewery and a winery.

Special Features

A magnificent view of **Door County** and **Green Bay** may be enjoyed from the observation platform at **Potawatomi State Park**, just northwest of town.

Laced as it is with interesting country roads, the Door Peninsula is ideal for impulsive, unhurried touring. A few spots, especially along WI 42, are showing signs of strip development, but for the most part the peninsula's pastoral and wooded beauty remains unscarred.

> The King of Spain and the late Shah of Iran owned yachts that were built in Sturgeon Bay.

▶ HISTORIC INNS ◀

INN AT CEDAR CROSSING, *336 Louisiana St., (920) 743-4200, fax (920) 743-4422, e-mail: innkeeper@innatcedarcrossing.com, www.innatcedarcrossing.com.* In 1884 brick vernacular bldg., National Register, 9 rooms, private baths (many with whirlpools), TV & phones, expanded Cont. breakfasts, Victorian-era dining room (highly rated), pub, antiques, many fireplaces, down-filled comforters, pressed-tin ceilings, refreshments, private porches, packages. $$ to $$$$

WHITE LACE INN, *16 N. 5th Ave., (920) 743-1105, (877) 948-5223, fax (920) 743-8180, e-mail: romance@whitelaceinn.com, www.WhiteLaceInn.com.* Four Victorian homes (ca 1880-1903) on National Register, 13 rooms & 5 suites, private baths with whirlpools, TV, full breakfasts, antiques, fireplaces, down comforters, refreshments, verandahs & balconies, garden. $ to $$$$ (seasonal)

Further Information

Door County Chamber of Commerce, *P.O. Box 406, 1015 Green Bay Rd., Sturgeon Bay, WI 54235 (800) 527-3529, www.doorcounty.com;* **Sturgeon Bay Area Information Center**, *P.O. Box 212, Sturgeon Bay, WI (920) 743-3924 (May-October).*

Directions

From Milwaukee, I-43 north to exit 185 (near Green Bay), WI 57 north to Sturgeon Bay.

Other Charming Wisconsin Towns

Alma
Cedarburg
Chippewa Falls
Hudson
Portage

Chapter 50

WYOMING

SARATOGA
Population 1,969

Few towns this side of the Hollywood screen can compete with **Saratoga's** *genuine* Western character and majestic Rocky Mountain setting. Away from the interstates and main tourist arteries, the town is large enough to be alive, yet small enough to be more concerned about gossip than crime. Stage-coaches used to stop in front of the old Hotel Wolf (see below). There are still people around who can tell personal stories – truthful ones - about the Old West.

Most people come here for the scenery and the outdoors, but Saratoga has sights of its own. Its natural hot springs (the town was named after its New York cousin and its springs) may be enjoyed in a year-round public pool area. There are also several good art galleries and interesting gift shops. The **Saratoga Museum**, located in the old **Union Pacific Railroad Depot** (1915), exhibits, among other things, railroad memorabilia, a country store, a pioneer home, and a land office. On the museum's grounds are a caboose, restored sheep wagon, and a new pavilion.

One of the town's most popular sights is the **Saratoga National Fish Hatchery** (five miles north). Dating back to 1915, the hatchery raises several kinds of trout, including rainbow and the endangered Greenback cutthroat trout, for stocking. Trout eggs are shipped to other hatcheries. For example, millions of lake trout eggs have been shipped to Great Lakes hatcheries.

Situated on the banks of the **North Platte River**, a blue-ribbon trout fishery, the town's motto reads *Where the Trout Leap in Main Street* (and before the advent of flood control, they did). Fishing is understandably the town's most popular activity, but baited by an especially beautiful golf course

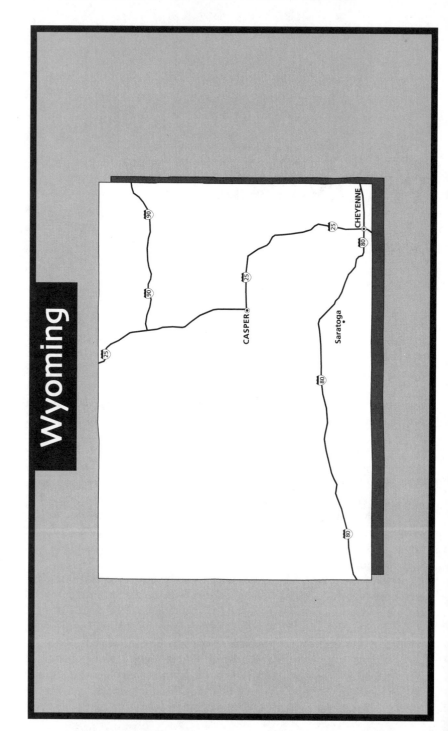

(open to public), golfing isn't far behind. Whitewater boating, float trips, cross-country skiing, and kayaking are also popular. The **Medicine Bow National Forest** offers a wealth of trails for hiking and backpacking.

One of the best ways to see this beautiful country is to take advantage of the knowledge and experience of an outfitter. Saratoga has many to choose from. Fishing float trips, horseback fishing trips, tours of historic mining towns, trail rides, and guided snowmobile rides are just a few of the adventures that can be safely undertaken with the aid of an outfitter.

Special Features

The **Grand Encampment Museum** in **Encampment**, 20 or so miles south of Saratoga, uses authentic buildings to recreate a Western community. Included among the buildings and collections are U.S. Forest Service memorabilia, a hat shop, the Palace Bakery, the Lake Creek Stage Station, and a homestead house. A two-story outhouse reminds visitors that the snows in this part of the world can drift well above ground level.

WY 130 between **Saratoga** and **Laramie** has been designated a **National Forest Scenic Byway** (closed winters). There are several spectacular loop tours in and around the Medicine Bow National Forest. Inquire locally for maps and instructions.

> • Hikers along major creeks in the neighboring mountains will encounter groups of old log cabins known locally as "tie hack camps." "Tie hacks" were men who produced ax-hewn railroad ties (during the period between 1868 and 1939).
> • Thomas Edison, a member of the Henry Draper Eclipse Expedition, got the idea for the electric light bulb in 1878 at Battle Lake (WY 70, south of Saratoga).

▶ HISTORIC HOTEL ◀

HOTEL WOLF, P.O. Box 1298, (307) 326-5525, e-mail: kcampbell@wolfhotel.com, www.wolfhotel.com. Restored 1893 hotel, National Register, 5 rooms & 4 suites, private baths, TV, dining room with Victorian setting, old-time saloon, original dressers & iron beds. $ to $$

Further Information

Saratoga-Platte Valley Chamber of Commerce, P.O. Box 1095, Saratoga, WY 82331 (307) 326-8855, e-mail: chamber@pmpc-eng.com, www.trib.com/spvcc/.

Directions

From Cheyenne, I-80 west (via Laramie) to exit 235, WY 130 south to Saratoga; alternatively, from Laramie, WY 230 through Snowy Range Scenic Byway.

Other Charming Wyoming Towns

Afton
Alpine
Cody
Jackson
Meeteetse

INDEX

Things Change!

Phone numbers, prices, addresses, quality of food, etc, all change. If you come across any new information, we'd appreciate hearing from you. No item is too small! Drop us an email note at: Jopenroad@aol.com, or write us at:

America's Most Charming Towns & Villages
Open Road Publishing, P.O. Box 284
Cold Spring Harbor, NY 11724

TRAVEL NOTES